SOURCES OF THE WEST

SOURCES OF THE WEST

READINGS IN WESTERN CIVILIZATION

SIXTH EDITION

VOLUME II
From 1600 to the Present

Mark A. Kishlansky, Editor
Harvard University

with the assistance of
Victor L. Stater
Louisiana State University

PEARSON
Longman

New York   San Francisco   Boston
London   Toronto   Sydney   Tokyo   Singapore   Madrid
Mexico City   Munich   Paris   Cape Town   Hong Kong   Montreal

Senior Acquisitions Editor: Janet Lanphier
Executive Marketing Manager: Sue Westmoreland
Production Manager: Donna DeBenedictis
Project Coordination, Text Design, and Electronic Page Makeup: Elm Street Publishing Services, Inc.
Cover Design Manager: John Callahan
Cover Designer: Kay Petronio
Cover Art: August Macke (1887–1914), German, *People by the Blue Pond,* 1913. Superstock, Inc.
Photo Researcher: Photosearch, Inc.
Senior Manufacturing Buyer: Alfred C. Dorsey
Printer and Binder: Hamilton Printing Co.
Cover Printer: Phoenix Color Corporation

For permission to use copyrighted material, grateful acknowledgment is made to the copyright holders on pp. 349–353, which are hereby made part of this copyright page.

Library of Congress Cataloging-in-Publication Data

Sources of the West: readings in Western civilization/Mark A. Kishlansky, editor;
    with the assistance of Victor L. Stater. — 6th ed.
        p. cm.
    Includes bibliographical references.
    ISBN 0-321-24341-2 (v.1)   ISBN 0-321-24342-0 (v.2)
    1. Civilization, Western—History—Sources. I. Kishlansky, Mark A.
II. Stater, Victor Louis, 1959–   .

CB245 .S578 2006
909'.09812—dc22   2004031108

Please visit us at http://www.ablongman.com

ISBN 0-321-24341-2 (Volume I)
ISBN 0-321-24342-0 (Volume II)

1 2 3 4 5 6 7 8 9 10—HT—08 07 06 05

CONTENTS

PREFACE

Sources of the West is a collection of documents designed to supplement textbooks and lectures in the teaching of Western Civilization. The use of primary materials is an essential component of the study of history. By hearing the voices of the past, students come to realize both the similarities and differences between their society and previous ones. In witnessing others ponder the same questions that rouse their own curiosity, students feel a connection between the past and the present. Moreover, by observing the ways in which such questions and experiences are worked out and described, they come to an understanding and respect for the integrity of other cultures. By confronting the materials of the past, students exercise an imagination that is at the heart of the teaching and learning of history.

Historical sources are the building blocks from which instructor and textbook writer have ultimately constructed their accounts and their explanations of Western historical development. It is essential that even beginning students learn that the past does not come to us prepackaged but is formed by historians who exercise their own imaginations on primary materials. Historical thinking involves examining the ideas of others, understanding past experiences on others' terms, and recognizing other points of view. This process makes everyone, student and instructor alike, a historian.

I have observed a number of principles in selecting the materials for this collection, which is designed for beginning-level college students. I believe strongly in the value of primary sources and feel that they should be made as accessible to contemporary students as possible. Thus I have preferred to use up-to-date translations of many texts despite the costliness of acquiring their rights. Many of the late-nineteenth-century translations that are commonly used in source books present texts that are syntactically too complex for modern students to comprehend easily. I have also chosen to present longer selections than is usual in books of this type. Unlike works that contain snippets of hundreds of documents, *Sources of the West* presents a sizable amount of a small number of sources. It therefore allows students to gain a deeper feeling for authors and texts and to concentrate their energies and resources. No selection is so long that it cannot be easily read at a sitting and none so short as to defy recall. Each selection raises a significant issue around which classroom discussion can take place or to which lectures can refer. Some may even stimulate students to seek out the complete original works.

Two other principles lie behind the selections I have made. The first is that a steady diet of even the greatest thinkers of the Western tradition is unpalatable without other varieties of social and cultural materials. For this reason I have tried to leaven the mass of intellectual history with materials that draw on social conditions or common experiences in past eras. These should not only aid students in making connections between past and present but also introduce them to the varieties of materials from which history is recreated. Second, I have been especially concerned to recover the voices or highlight the experiences of those who are not always adequately represented in surveys of Western Civilization. The explosion of work in social history, in the history of the family, and in the history of women have made possible the inclusion of materials here that were barely discovered a decade ago. While this effort can be clearly seen in the materials chosen for the modern sections, it is also apparent in the more traditional selections made from older documents.

By providing longer selections and by expanding the scope of the materials to be incorporated, I have necessarily been compelled to make some hard choices. There exists a superabundance of materials that demand inclusion in a collection such as this. I have chosen the principal texts that best illustrate the dominant themes of Western Civilization. Because Western Civilization is a basic course in the curriculum of most colleges and universities, it must carry the primary responsibility for introducing students to dominant historical events and personalities. But it is my conviction that it is the experience of using primary materials—more than the identity of the materials—that is vital. Thus I have tried to provide a balance among constitutional documents, political theory, philosophy, imaginative literature, and social description. In all cases I have made the pedagogical value of the specific texts the prime consideration, selecting for significance, readability, and variety.

The feature *How to Read a Document* is designed to introduce students to a disciplined approach of working with primary sources and to encourage them to use their imaginations in their historical studies. No brief introduction can pretend to be authoritative, and there are many other strategies and questions that can be adopted in training students to become critical readers. It is hoped that this introduction will remove some of the barriers that usually exist between student and source by walking them through a single exercise with a document in front of them. Any disciplined approach to source materials will sensitize students to the construction of historical documents, their content and meaning, and the ways in which they relate to modern experience. Individual instructors will easily be able to improve upon the example offered here.

NEW TO THIS EDITION

I have been gratified by the reception of the previous edition of *Sources of the West* and wish to take this opportunity to thank all of those users (both students and faculty members) for their comments and suggestions. The changes that I have made in this new edition reflect the recommendations of users for specific documents. I have tampered as little as possible with the bulk of the work so that those who have planned courses around these documents will not have their efforts disrupted. I have tried to enrich a variety of topics with new works. The inclusion of Polybius will provide more material on the structure of the Roman Empire than has previously been available in these selections. Michael Psellus's autobiographical account of his education will introduce students to the richness of Byzantine culture. The origin of European slave trading is here represented by the eyewitness account of Gomes de Zurara and introduces a subject of much contemporary interest and debate. The addition of Molière will allow students to encounter the way in which the European theater was the setting for a rich vein of social criticism while introducing them to an author whose works are frequently performed in repertory. Selections from the *Journals* of Captain James Cook continue the trend of expanding the horizons of Western Civilization into those parts of the world that Europeans encountered while capturing the sense of wonder as well as the fixed framework in which those encounters took place. The document selection that focuses on the Irish Potato famine enhances the social history component of *Sources of the West* while demonstrating to students how complex moral decisions were made without the benefit of hindsight. The excerpts from the 9/11 Commission Report bring *Sources of the West* up to the very present and introduce analysis of the issue of terrorism.

ACKNOWLEDGMENTS

In preparing this new edition of *Sources of the West,* I have been aided by innumerable suggestions from both adopters and users of the book. Letters from course heads and even some from students have helped me in choosing new documents for this edition. The result, I hope, will be a stronger, more balanced, and more up-to-date collection. I have had the opportunity to include a number of works in the modern period that now seem to have greater relevance than they did when the first edition was compiled. I would like to thank the following reviewers for their thoughtful critiques: Arthur H. Auten, *University of Hartford*; Lawrence Backlund, *Montgomery County Community College* (PA); Andrew Barnes, *Carnegie Mellon University;* Melvin E. Bender, *Central Baptist College* (AR); George C. Browder, *SUNY, Fredonia;* Ronald G. Brown, *Charles County Community College;* Karen Bruhn, *Arizona State University;* Clea Bunch, *University of Arkansas;* Robert Caputi, *Rochester Institute of Technology;* Barbara Evans Clements, *University of Akron;* Thomas H. L. Cornman, *Moody Bible Institute;* Mary Cygan, *University of Connecticut;* Alexander DeGrand, *North Carolina State University;* Carol A. Devlin, *Marquette University;* Gregory P. Elder, *Riverside Community College;* Eliga Gould, *University of New Hampshire;* John W. Langdon, *Le Moyne College;* Janine Lanza, *Appalachian State University;* Marshall Lee, *Pacific University;* Elizabeth A. Lehfeldt, *Cleveland State University;* Daniel

Meissner, *Marquette University;* Jesus Mendez, *Barry University;* Elise Moentmann, *University of Portland;* Sean Farrell Moran, *Oakland University;* David T. Murphy, *Anderson University;* Richard A. Oehling, *Assumption College;* Martha Rampton, *Pacific University;* Kevin C. Robbins, *Indiana University–Purdue University at Indianapolis;* Nancy Rupprecht, *Middle Tennessee State University;* Hugo Schwyzer, *Pasadena City College;* George H. Shriver, *Georgia Southern University;* Timothy Sistrunk, *Chicago State University;* Fran Sternberg, *University of Missouri;* William Stockton, *Johnson County Community College;* Norman Wilson, *Xavier University;* Sally Vaughn, *University of Houston.* Victor Stater was an indispensable assistant in reworking texts, consulting on new choices, and helping to edit the new documents over the course of editions.

MARK A. KISHLANSKY

HOW TO READ A DOCUMENT

Do you remember the first time you used a road map? After struggling to unfold it and find the right side up and the right way around, you were confronted by an astonishing amount of information. You could calculate the distance between places, from towns to cities, or cities to cities, even the distance between exits on the toll roads. You could observe relative population density and identify large and small places. You could even judge the quality of roads. Most likely, though, you opened that map to help you figure out how to get from one particular place to another, to find the best route for the trip you were making.

To let the map tell you that, you had to know how to ask the right questions. It all seems so obvious now: You put one finger on the place where you were and another on the place you wanted to get to, and then you found the best and most direct roads between them. But in order to do something this simple, you made a lot of assumptions about the map. First, you assumed that the map was directionally oriented—north at the top, east to the right, south and west opposite. Next, you assumed that the map was to scale—that the distance between places on the map was proportional to their distances in reality. Third, you assumed that intersections on the map represented intersections on the ground, that roads that appeared to cross on paper actually would cross when you reached them. These assumptions allowed you to draw conclusions about your route. Of course, if any of them were not true, you found out soon enough.

Learning to read a historical document is much like learning to read a map. It is important to ask the right questions and make the right assumptions. But unlike the real journey that the map makes possible, the journey that is made with an historical document is one of the imagination. It is not so easy to put your finger on the past. You will have to learn to test your assumptions and to sharpen your ability to ask questions before you can have any confidence that you are on the right road. As with anything else, mastery of these skills takes concentration and practice. You will have to discipline yourself to ask and answer questions about the document on three different levels. At first you will need to identify the basic components of the document itself: who wrote it, when, and for what purpose. Then you will want to understand its form and content. Finally you will want to know the ways in which it can be interpreted. At the beginning, you will be asking questions that you can answer directly; by the end you will be asking questions that will give full play to your imagination and your skills as a historian. Let's take an example.

Read this document slowly and carefully.

To the King's Most Excellent Majesty

1   *Humbly show unto our sovereign Lord the King, the Lords*
2   *Spiritual and Temporal, and Commons in Parliament assembled,*
3   *that whereas it is declared and enacted by a statute made in the*
4   *time of the reign of King Edward the First, commonly called "The*
5   *Statute of No Taxation Without Consent," that no tallage or aid*
6   *shall be laid or levied by the King or his heirs in this realm, without*
7   *the goodwill and assent of the Archbishops, Bishops, Earls,*
8   *Barons, Knights, Burgesses, and other the freeman of the*
9   *commonalty of this realm: and by authority of Parliament holden in*
10 *the five and twentieth year of the reign of King Edward the Third*
11 *[1352], it is declared and enacted, that from thenceforth no*
12 *person shall be compelled to make any loans to the King against his*
13 *will, because such loans were against reason and the franchise*
14 *of the land; and by other laws of this realm it is provided, that*
15 *none should be charged by any charge or imposition, called a*
16 *Benevolence. . . . Your subjects have inherited this freedom, that*
17 *they should not be compelled to contribute to any tax, tallage,*
18 *aid, or other charge not met by common consent in Parliament.*
19 *   Yet nevertheless, of late divers commissions directed to*
20 *sundry Commissioners in several counties with instructions have*
21 *issued, by means whereof your people have been in divers places*
22 *assembled, and required to lend certain sums of money unto your*
23 *Majesty, and many of them upon their refusal so to do have had*
24 *an oath administered unto them, not warrantable by the laws or*
25 *statutes of this realm, and have been constrained to become bound*
26 *to make appearance and give attendance before your Privy*
27 *Council, and in other places, and others of them have been therefore*
28 *imprisoned, confined, and sundry other ways molested and*
29 *disquieted; and divers other charges have been laid and leveled upon*
30 *your people in several counties, by Lords Lieutenants, Deputy*
31 *Lieutenants, Commissioners for Muster, Justices of Peace and*
32 *others, by command or direction from your Majesty or your Privy*
33 *Council, against the laws and free customs of this realm.*
34 *   And where also by the statute called "The Great Charter of*
35 *the Liberties of England," it is declared and enacted, that no free*
36 *man may be taken or imprisoned or be disseised [dispossessed]*
37 *of freeholds or liberties, or his free customs, or be outlawed or*
38 *exiled; or in any manner destroyed, but by the lawful judgment*

39 *of his peers, or by the law of the land:*

40 *   And in the eight and twentieth year of the reign of King*

41 *Edward the Third [1355] it was declared and enacted by authority*

42 *of Parliament, that no man of what estate or condition that he*

43 *be, should be put out of his lands or tenements, nor taken, nor*

44 *imprisoned, nor disinherited, nor put to death, without being*

45 *brought to answer by due process of law.*

46 *   Nevertheless, against the tenor of the said statutes and other*

47 *good laws and statutes of your realm to that end provided, divers*

48 *of your subjects have of late been imprisoned without any cause*

49 *showed, and when for their deliverance they were brought before*

50 *your justices, by your Majesty's writs of Habeas Corpus, there to*

51 *undergo and receive as the Court should order, and their keepers*

52 *commanded to certify the causes of their detainer, no cause was*

53 *certified, but that they were detained by your Majesty's special*

54 *command, signified by the Lords of your Privy Council, and yet*

55 *were returned back to several prisons, without being charged with*

56 *anything to which they might make answer according to the law.*

57 *   And whereas of late great companies of soldiers and mariners*

58 *have been dispersed into divers counties of the realm, and the*

59 *inhabitants against their wills have been compelled to receive*

60 *them into their houses, and there to suffer them to sojourn, against*

61 *the laws and customs of this realm, and to the great grievances*

62 *and vexation of the people:*

63 *   And whereas also by authority of Parliament, in the 25th year*

64 *of the reign of King Edward the Third [1352] it was declared and*

65 *enacted, that no man shall be forejudged of life or limb against*

66 *the form of the Great Charter, and the law of the land and by the*

67 *said Great Charter . . . no man ought to be adjudged to death, but*

68 *by the laws established in this your realm . . . : and whereas no*

69 *offender of what kind soever is exempted from the proceedings*

70 *to be used, and punishments to be inflicted by the laws and*

71 *statutes of this your realm: nevertheless of late divers commissions*

72 *under your Majesty's Great Seal have issued forth, by which*

73 *certain persons have been assigned and appointed Commissioners*

74 *with power and authority to proceed within the land, according*

75 *to the justice of martial law against such soldiers and mariners,*

76 *or other dissolute persons joining with them, as should commit*

77 *any murder, robbery, felony, mutiny, or other outrage or*

78 *misdemeanor whatsoever, and by such summary course and order*

79 *as is agreeable to martial law, and is used in armies in time of*

80 *war, to proceed to the trial and condemnation of such offenders,*

81 *and them to cause to be executed and put to death according to*

82 *the law martial:*

83   *By pretext whereof, some of your Majesty's subjects have been*
84   *by some of the said Commissioners put to death, when and where,*
85   *if by the laws and statutes of the land they had deserved death,*
86   *by the same laws and statutes also they might, and by no other*
87   *ought to, have been adjudged and executed:*
88   *And also sundry grievous offenders by color thereof, claim-*
89   *ing an exemption, have escaped the punishments due to them . . .*
90   *by reason that divers of your officers and ministers of justice have*
91   *unjustly refused, or forborne to proceed against such offenders*
92   *according to the same laws and statutes, upon pretense that the*
93   *said offenders were punishable only by martial law. . . .*
94   *They do therefore humbly pray for your Most Excellent*
95   *Majesty that no man hereafter be compelled to make or yield any*
96   *gift, loan, benevolence, tax, or such like charge, without common*
97   *consent by Act of Parliament; and that none be called to make*
98   *answer, or take such oath or to give attendence, or be confined,*
99   *or otherwise molested or disquieted concerning the same, or for*
100   *refusal thereof; and that no freeman, in any such manner as is*
101   *before-mentioned, be imprisoned or detained; and that your*
102   *Majesty will be pleased to remove the said soldiers and mariners,*
103   *and that your people may not be so burdened in time to come;*
104   *and that the foresaid commissions for proceeding by martial law,*
105   *may be revoked and annulled; and that hereafter no commissions*
106   *of like nature may issue forth to any person or persons whatsoever,*
107   *to be executed as aforesaid, lest by color of them any of your*
108   *Majesty's subjects be destroyed or put to death, contrary to the*
109   *laws and franchise of the land.*
110   *All which they most humbly pray of your Most Excellent*
111   *Majesty, as their rights and liberties according to the laws and*
112   *statutes of this realm: and that your Majesty would also vouchsafe*
113   *to declare that the awards, doings, and proceedings to the*
114   *prejudice of your people, in any of the premises shall not be drawn*
115   *hereafter into consequence or example: and that your Majesty*
116   *would be also graciously pleased, for the further comfort and*
117   *safety of your people, to declare your royal will and pleasure, that*
118   *in the things aforesaid all your officers and ministers shall serve*
119   *you according to the laws and statutes of this realm as they tender*
120   *the honor of your Majesty, and the prosperity of this kingdom.*

Now what sense can we make out of all of that? You have just read a historical document known as the Petition of Right. It was presented to King Charles I of England by his Parliament in 1628. In order to understand this document, you are going to need to find answers to a series of questions about it. Start at the beginning with a number of questions that might be designated "level-one" questions.

LEVEL ONE

The first set of questions that need to be addressed are those for which you should be able to find concrete answers. The answers to these questions will give you the basic information you need to begin the process of interpretation. Although "level-one" questions are seemingly straightforward, they contain important implications for deeper interpretation. If you do not consciously ask these questions, you will deprive yourself of some of the most important evidence there is for understanding documents. Train yourself to underline or highlight the information that will allow you to answer the following questions.

I. Who Wrote This Document?

In the first place, you need to know how this document came to be created. Written historical records were created by individuals in a specific historical setting for a particular purpose. Until you know who created the document you have read, you cannot know why it was created or what meanings its author intended to impart by creating it. Nor is it enough simply to learn the name of the author; it is equally important to learn about authors as people, what social background they came from, what position they held, to what group they belonged. Although you will learn the identity of the author from the headnotes, you will learn much about that person or group from the document. In the case of the Petition of Right, you know that the document was written by the Lords Spiritual and Temporal and the Commons assembled in Parliament (**line 2**). This document is the work of a political body rather than of an individual, and you probably know from your own experience that such a document must have been written by a committee and revised and amended by the rest of the body before it was completed. Such authorship, unlike the work of an identifiable individual, suggests a wide degree of support and probably more than one compromise between those who wanted a stronger statement and those who wanted a weaker one. You will need to learn as much as you can about the authors of a document to help you answer more complicated questions.

2. Who Is the Intended Audience?

Identifying the intended audience of a document will tell you much about its language, about the amount of knowledge that the writer is assuming, even sometimes about the best form for the document to take. The relationship between author and audience is one of the most basic elements of communication and one that will tell you much about the purpose of the document. Think of the difference between the audience for a novel and that for a diary, or for a law and for a secret treaty. In each case, knowing the intended audience determines your view of what to expect from the document. Knowing the audience allows you to begin to ask important questions, such as, "Should I believe what I am being told?" In the Petition of Right, you know that the intended audience was the king of England **(line 1)**. This knowledge helps you to establish the relationship between authors and audience, from which you can learn many things. In the Petition of Right, this relationship helps you understand the kind of language that is being used. You would expect Parliament to "most humbly pray" **(line 110)** when addressing the king. If you were reading a shopkeeper's bill to a customer or a mother's letter of advice to her daughter, you would be surprised by such language and alerted that something unusual was going on. The relationship between author and audience provides you with reasonable expectations, and it is well for you to ask if these are fulfilled. Is there language in the Petition of Right that is not appropriate to the relationship between a king and his parliament? Finally, you must remember that the writer may have intended to address more than one audience. Here you might wonder if the Petition of Right was not also intended to be read by government officials, lawyers, and even the educated public. How would such multiple audiences affect the nature of the document?

3. What Is the Story Line?

The final "level one" question has to do with the content of the document. You now know enough about it in a general way to pay attention to what it actually says. To learn the story line, you must take some notes while you are reading and underline or highlight important places in your text. The more often you ask yourself, "What is going on here?" the easier it will be to find out. No matter how obscure a document appears at first, deliberate attention to the story line will allow you to focus your reading. In this document, the story seems to be simple. Parliament has identified a number of violations of the laws of the realm. In their opinion, the king has attempted to raise taxes without parliamentary consent **(line 18)**; has imprisoned people without telling them the grounds for their imprisonment **(line 49)**; has quartered soldiers in the homes of citizens against their will **(line 60)**; and has allowed his agents to use the forms of martial law to try, convict, and punish unruly persons **(line 76)**. Parliament petitions the king to recognize that these are violations of the rights of citizens **(line 111)**, that they be halted at once, that they not be used as precedent for future actions **(line 95)**, and that those responsible be instructed to follow the laws of the realm more fully in the future **(line 119)**. While this is undoubtedly the "story" this document tells, you will soon see that while the story may be simple, its meaning may be very complicated. Notice how in trying to find the story line you were not concerned with the thick details of the document—those complicated facts and arguments that seemed so imposing when you first read it. It doesn't yet matter in which year in the reign of Edward III laws were passed **(line 41)**, what a writ of Habeas Corpus is **(line 50)**, or who the Lords of the Privy Council might have been **(line 54)**. At this point you want to know what this document is about, and unless understanding these thick details is absolutely essential to making any sense out of it at all, you are not going to be put off by them.

LEVEL TWO

If "level one" questions allow you to identify the nature of the document and its author, "level two" questions allow you to probe behind the essential facts. Now that you know who wrote the document, to whom it is addressed, and what it is about, you can begin to try to understand it. Since your goal is to learn what this document means, first in its historical context and then in your current context, you now want to study it from a more detached point of view, to be less accepting of "facts" and more critical in the questions you pose. At the first level, the document controlled you; at the second level, you will begin to control the document.

I. Why Was This Document Written?

Everything is written for a reason. You make notes to yourself to remember, you send cards to celebrate and sympathize, you correspond to convey or request information. The documents that historians traditionally study are more likely to have been written for public rather than private purposes, but not always. Understanding the purpose of a historical document is critical to analyzing the strategies that the author employs within it. A document intended to convince will employ logic; a document intended to entertain will employ fancy; a document attempting to motivate will employ emotional appeals. In order to find these strategies, you must know what purpose the document was intended to serve. The Petition of Right was intended to persuade. The case for the abuses of which Parliament was complaining is set out logically with clear examples. By the end of the petition, the case seems irrefutable, though, of course, there was undoubtedly another side to the story.

2. What Type of Document Is This?

The form of a document is vital to its purpose. You would expect a telephone book to be alphabetized, a poem to be in meter, and a work of philosophy to be in prose. The form or genre in which a document appears is always carefully chosen. Genre contains its own conventions, which fulfill the expectations of author and audience. A prose map of how one travels from Chicago to Boston might be as effective as a conventional map, but it would not allow for much of the incidental information that a conventional map contains and would be much harder to consult. A map in poetry would be mind-boggling! Here you have a petition, and even if you don't know much about the form of a seventeenth-century petition, you can learn more than enough about it from the presentation itself. This document is obviously very formal and written in legal language. It specifies certain laws **(lines 5, 34)** and then asserts that they have been violated **(line 46).** It takes the form of a request, "humbly praying," that the king "your most Excellent Majesty" **(line 110)** will grant the desires expressed in the petition. You can learn a variety of things from the petition form: the relationship between Parliament and king, the powers of the king, the role of a parliament, the way in which the legal or legislative process works.

3. What Are the Basic Assumptions Made in This Document?

All documents make assumptions that are bound up with their intended audience, with the form in which they are written, and with their purpose. Some of these assumptions are so integral to the document that they are left unsaid, others are so important to establish that they form a part of the central argumentation. The Petition of Right assumes that king and Parliament share a legal system and that both recognize certain precedents in it as valid. This is why statutes from past realms are quoted as authorities. If the Petition of Right had been written by the English Parliament to the French king, such assumptions would be invalid and the document would be incomprehensible. Similarly, the assumption that law is binding on both king and subjects—an assumption that might have been contested in the seventeenth century—runs through the entire petition. Of course, the authors continually frame this assumption in the language of "Your Majesty's law" so as to persuade the king that the violations are as much against the king as against his subjects. Finally, the form of the petition assumes that both king and Parliament desire to eliminate the grievances of the nation. The petition would make no sense if the king could reply, "They are taking your property, imprisoning you without cause, and hanging you arbitrarily? Good! Let's have more of this efficiency in government."

LEVEL THREE

So far, you have been asking questions of your document that you can learn directly from it. Sometimes it is more difficult to know who composed a document or who the intended audience was than it has been with the Petition of Right. Sometimes you have to guess at the purpose of the document. But essentially questions on level one and level two are questions with direct answers. Once you have learned to ask them, you will have a great deal of information about the historical document at your disposal. You will then be able to think historically—that is, to pose your own questions about the past and to use the material the document presents to seek for answers. In level three, you will exercise your critical imagination, probing the material and developing your own assessment of its value. "Level three" questions will not always have definite answers; in fact, they are the kind of questions that arouse disagreement and debate and that make for lively classroom discussion.

I. Can I Believe This Document?

To be successful, a document designed to persuade, to recount events, or to motivate people to action must be believable to its audience. For the critical historical reader, it is that very believability that must be examined. Every author has a point of view, and exposing the assumptions of the document is an essential task for the reader. You must treat all claims skeptically (even while admiring audacity, rhetorical tricks, and clever comparisons). One question you certainly want to ask is, "Is this a likely story?" Are you really persuaded that the king of England does not know the laws that the Petition of Right claims to be reasserting? Doesn't it seem that the authors want to have it both ways when they complain that martial law is too severe **(line 75)** but not severe enough **(line 93)**? Testing the credibility of a document means looking at it from the other side. How would the king of England respond to the Petition of Right, and what would his point of view be?

2. What Can I Learn About the Society That Produced This Document?

All documents unintentionally reveal things about their authors and about their era. It is the things that are embedded in the very language, structure, and assumptions of the document that can tell you the most about the historical period or event that you are studying. However angry the members of Parliament are about their grievances, they believe profoundly in monarchy. Look at the way they address their king **(lines 1, 94).** Notice how careful they are to blame everything on agents rather than on the monarch himself. You might think that this is just sweet-talking, that they know it is the king who is to blame, and they have him dead to rights with all the violations of law that they have documented. But, of course, if they really believed that the king was in the wrong, why petition him to reassert their rights? What expectation could they have that he would grant these rights or respect them? Notice also the hierarchical structure of English government—the "Lords Spiritual and Temporal," the earls and the barons, and so forth **(line 7).** You can learn many things about seventeenth-century English society by reading *into* this document rather than by simply reading it.

3. What Does This Document Mean to Me?

So what? What does the Petition of Right, written over 350 years ago, have to do with you? Other than for the practical purpose of passing your exams and getting your degree, why should you be concerned with historical documents?

What can you learn from them? Only you can answer those questions. But you won't be able to answer them until you have asked them. You should demand the meaning of each document you read: what it meant to the historical actors—authors, audience, and society—and what it means to your own society. In the case of the Petition of Right, the principles of freedom from arbitrary arrest, from the seizure of property, and the assurance of due process of law in criminal matters obviously have something to do with all of us. But not all documents will yield their meanings so easily.

Now that you have seen how to unfold the map of a historical document, you must get used to asking these questions by yourself. The temptation will be great to jump from level one to level three, to start in the middle, or to pose the questions in no sequence at all. After all, you probably have a ready-made answer to "What does this document mean to me?" But if you develop the discipline of asking all your questions in the proper order, you will soon find that you are able to gain command of a document on a single reading and that the complicated names and facts that ordinarily would confuse you will easily settle into a pattern around one or another of your questions. After a few weeks, reread these pages and ask yourself how careful you have been to maintain the discipline of posing historical questions. Think also about how much more comfortable you now feel about reading and discussing historical documents.

SOURCES OF THE WEST

Part IV

THE ANCIEN RÉGIME

(continued)

THE ENLIGHTENMENT

THE FRENCH REVOLUTION

The Wars of Religion

HENRY IV

THE EDICT OF NANTES

(1598)

Henry IV (1589–1610) was the Protestant king of Navarre who led the Huguenot cause during the French wars of religion. His grandmother was Marguerite de Navarre and his mother Jeanne d'Albret, both educated and remarkably talented women. Henry achieved the French throne through a series of accidents, the last of which was the assassination of Henry III in 1589. It was clear that no Protestant could ever command the allegiance of the mass of French people or peacefully rule in the Catholic capital of Paris. Henry converted to Catholicism, defeated his enemies, and ended the long years of religious warfare.

The Edict of Nantes was the compromise settlement that granted limited toleration for the Huguenots. It was a landmark in the history of religious toleration, though its main features were watered down under Louis XIII. The Edict was finally rescinded under Louis XIV in 1685.

Henry, by the grace of God king of France and of Navarre, to all to whom these presents come, greeting:

Among the infinite benefits which it has pleased God to heap upon us, the most signal and precious is his granting us the strength and ability to withstand the fearful disorders and troubles which prevailed on our advent in this kingdom. The realm was so torn by innumerable factions and sects that the most legitimate of all the parties was fewest in numbers. God has given us strength to stand out against this storm; we have finally surmounted the waves and made our port of safety—peace for our state. For which his be the glory all in all, and ours a free recognition of his grace in making use of our instrumentality in the good work. . . . We implore and await from the Divine Goodness the same protection and favor which he has ever granted to this kingdom from the beginning. . . .

We have, by this perpetual and irrevocable edict, established and proclaimed and do establish and proclaim:

First, that the recollection of everything done by one party or the other between March, 1585, and our accession to the crown, and during all the preceding period of troubles, remain obliterated and forgotten, as if no such things had ever happened.

We ordain that the Catholic Apostolic and Roman religion shall be restored and reestablished in all places and localities of this our kingdom and countries subject to our sway, where the exercise of the same has been interrupted, in order that it may be peaceably and freely exercised, without any trouble or hindrance; forbidding very expressly all persons, of whatsoever estate, quality, or condition, from troubling, molesting, or disturbing ecclesiastics in the celebration of divine service, in the enjoyment or collection of tithes, fruits, or revenues of their benefices, and all other rights and dues belonging to them; and that all those who during the troubles have taken possession of churches, houses, goods or revenues, belonging to the said ecclesiastics, shall surrender to them entire possession and peaceable enjoyment of such rights, liberties, and sureties as they had before they were deprived of them.

And in order to leave no occasion for troubles or differences between our subjects, we have permitted, and herewith permit, those of the said religion called Reformed to live and abide in all the cities and places of this our kingdom and countries of our sway, without being annoyed, molested, or compelled to do anything in the matter of religion contrary to their consciences . . . upon condition that they comport themselves in other respects according to that which is contained in this our present edict.

It is permitted to all lords, gentlemen, and other persons making profession of the said religion called Reformed, holding the right of high justice [or a certain feudal tenure], to exercise the said religion in their houses.

We also permit those of the said religion to make and continue the exercise of the same in all villages and places of our dominion where it was established by them and publicly enjoyed several and divers times in the year 1597, up to the end of the month of August, notwithstanding all decrees and judgements to the contrary.

We very expressly forbid to all those of the said religion its exercise, either in respect to ministry, regulation, discipline, or the public instruction of children, or otherwise, in this our kingdom and lands of our dominion, otherwise than in the places permitted and granted by the present edict.

It is forbidden as well to perform any function of the said religion in our court or retinue, or in our lands and territories beyond the mountains, or in our city of Paris, or within five leagues of the said city.

We also forbid all our subjects, of whatever quality and condition, from carrying off by force or persuasion, against the will of their parents, the children of the said religion, in order to cause them to be baptized or confirmed in the Catholic Apostolic and Roman Church; and the same is forbidden to those of the said religion called Reformed, upon penalty of being punished with especial severity.

Books concerning the said religion called Reformed may not be printed and publicly sold, except in cities and places where the public exercise of the said religion is permitted.

We ordain that there shall be no difference or distinction made in respect to the said religion, in receiving pupils to be instructed in universities, colleges, and schools; nor in receiving the sick and poor into hospitals, retreats and public charities.

Those of the said religion called Reformed shall be obliged to respect the laws of the Catholic Apostolic and Roman Church, recognized in this our kingdom, for the consummation of marriages contracted, or to be contracted, as regards the degrees of consanguinity and kinship.

QUESTIONS

1. Does Henry IV grant complete liberty of conscience in his edict? If not, how is freedom of religion restricted?

2. What is the position of the Catholic church under the edict?

3. *The Edict of Nantes* is often seen as a step toward religious toleration. How tolerant is it?

4. Although the edict helped restore order to France, many people argued that it created more problems than it solved. Can you think what some of these might have been?

5. The edict was a declaration made by the king alone, without the advice or assistance of any other governmental institution. What does it reveal about the power of the monarch? About the king's role in religious affairs?

---

73.   CARDINAL RICHELIEU

THE POLITICAL TESTAMENT

(1638)

Armand Jean du Plessis, Cardinal and Duke Richelieu (1585–1642), was the son of a minor official of the French court. He was trained for church service and made his mark as a delegate to the Estates-General of 1614. He was brought into the service of Louis XIII by the Queen Regent, Marie de Médicis, and eventually became the king's favorite and chief advisor. An able diplomat and a master politician, Richelieu played an important role in the consolidation of the royal state. His principal goal was to centralize administration and to harness the power of the nobility and localities. He was chiefly responsible for French foreign policy, including France's participation in the Thirty Years' War.

Written for the instruction of Louis XIII, Richelieu's *Political Testament* contains the cardinal's assessment of his own achievements. It was composed over the course of several years, with the last events mentioned dating from 1638. It was not published for another half century, and then only in a pirated Dutch edition.

When Your Majesty resolved to admit me both to your council and to an important place in your confidence for the direction of your affairs, I may say that the Huguenots shared the state with you; that the nobles conducted themselves as if they were not your subjects, and the most powerful governors of the provinces as if they were sovereign in their offices.

I may say that the bad example of all of these was so prejudicial to the welfare of this realm that even the best courts were affected by it, and endeavored, in certain cases, to diminish your legitimate authority as far as it was possible in order to carry their own powers beyond the limits of reason.

I may say that everyone measured his own merit by his audacity; that in place of esteeming the benefits which they received from Your Majesty at their proper worth, they all valued them only as they satisfied the demands of their imaginations; that the most scheming were held to be the wisest, and often found themselves the most prosperous.

In broadest outline, Sire, these have been the matters with which Your Majesty's reign has thus far been concerned. I would consider them most happily concluded if they were followed by an era of repose during which you could introduce into your realm a wealth of benefits of all types. In order to present the problem to you, it is necessary to look into the nature of the various classes in your realm and the state which it comprises, together with your own role, both as a private and a public person. In sum, what will be indicated is the need for a competent and faithful council, whose advice should be listened to and followed in governing the state. It is to the detailed explanation and urging of this that the remainder of my testament will be devoted.

While the nobility merits to be generously treated if it does well, it is necessary at the same time to be severe with it if it ever fails in what its status demands of it. I do not hesitate to say that those nobles who, degenerating from the virtuous conduct of their forebears, fail to serve the crown constantly and courageously with both their swords and their lives, as the laws of the state require, deserve the loss of the privileges of their birth and should be reduced to sharing the burdens of the common people. Since honor should be more dear to them than life itself, it would be much more of a punishment to them to be deprived of the former than the latter.

All students of politics agree that when the common people are too well off it is impossible to keep them peaceable. The explanation for this is that they are less well informed than the members of the other orders in the state, who are much more cultivated and enlightened, and so if not preoccupied with the search for the necessities of existence, find it difficult to remain within the limits imposed by both common sense and the law.

It would not be sound to relieve them of all taxation and similar charges, since in such a case they would lose the mark of their subjection and consequently the awareness of their station. Thus being free from paying tribute, they would consider themselves exempted from obedience. One should compare them with mules, which being accustomed to work, suffer more when long idle than when kept busy. But just as this work should be reasonable, with the burdens placed upon these animals proportionate to their strength, so it is likewise with the burdens placed upon the people. If they are not moderate, even when put to good public use, they are certainly unjust. I realize that when a king undertakes a program of public works it is correct to say that what the people gain from it is returned by paying the taille. In the same fashion it can be maintained that what a king takes from the people returns to them, and that they advance it to him only to draw upon it for the enjoyment of their leisure and their investments, which would be impossible if they did not contribute to the support of the state.

I also know that many princes have lost their countries and ruined their subjects by failing to maintain sufficient military forces for their protection, fearing to tax them too heavily. Some people have even fallen into slavery under their enemies because they have wanted too much liberty under their natural sovereign. There is, however, a certain level which one cannot exceed without injustice, common sense indicating in each instance the proportion which should prevail between the burden and the ability of those who sustain it. This consideration ought always to be religiously observed, although a prince cannot be esteemed good just because he taxes his subjects no more than necessary, nor considered evil because occasionally he takes more.

Also, just as when a man is wounded, his heart, weakened by the loss of blood, draws upon the reserves of the lower parts of the body only after the upper parts are exhausted, so in moments of great public need the king should, in so far as he is able, make use of the abundance of the rich before bleeding the poor heavily. This is the best advice Your Majesty can follow, and it is easy to put into practice since in the future you will draw the principal income for your state from the general tax farms, which are much closer to the interests of the rich than of the poor, since the latter, spending less, contribute less to the total.

The public interest ought to be the sole objective of the prince and his councillors, or, at the least, both are obliged to have it foremost in mind, and preferred to all private gain. It is impossible to overestimate the good which a prince and those serving him in government can do if they religiously follow this principle, and one can hardly imagine the evils which befall a state if private interest is preferred to the public good and actually gains the ascendency. True philosophy, as well as the precepts of both Christianity and sound politics, teach this truth so clearly that a prince's councillors can hardly too often remind him of so necessary a principle, nor the prince punish too severely those members of his council despicable enough not to practice it.

Princes ordinarily easily consent to the overall plans proposed for their states because in so doing they have nothing in mind save reason and justice, which they easily accept when they meet no obstacle which turns them off the path. When the occasion arises, however, of putting into practical action the wise programs they have adopted, they do not always show the same firmness. Distracting interests, pity and compassion, favoritism and importunities of all sorts obstruct their best intentions to a degree they often cannot overcome sufficiently to ignore private consideration, which ought never influence public affairs. It is in such matters that they should summon up all their strength against inclinations toward weakness, keeping before their eyes the fact that those whom God has destined to protect others should have no characteristics but those advantageous to the public interest, and to which they should adhere inflexibly.

Power being one of the things most necessary to the grandeur of kings and the success of their governments, those who have the principal management of states are particularly obliged to omit nothing which could contribute to making their masters fully and universally respected. As goodness is the object of love, so power is the cause of fear. It is certain that of all the forces capable of producing results in public affairs, fear, if based on both esteem and reverence, is the most effective, since it can drive everyone to do his duty. If this principle is of great efficacy with regard to internal affairs, it is of no less value externally, since both foreigners and subjects take the same view of redoubtable power and both refrain from offending a prince whom they recognize as being able to hurt them if he so wishes. I have said already that this power of which I speak should be based on esteem and respect. I hasten to add that this is so necessary that if it is based on anything else there is the grave danger that instead of producing a reasonable fear the result will be a hatred of princes, for whom the worst possible fate is to incur public disapprobation.

There are several kinds of power which can make princes respected and feared—it is a tree with various branches, all nourished by the same root. The prince ought to be powerful because of his good reputation, because of a reasonable number of soldiers kept continuously under arms, because of a sufficient revenue to meet his ordinary expenses, plus a special sum of money in his treasury to cover frequent but unexpected contingencies, and, finally, because of the possession of the hearts of his subjects, as we will clearly demonstrate.

A good reputation is especially necessary to a prince, for if we hold him in high regard he can accomplish more with his name alone than a less well esteemed ruler can with great armies at his command. It is imperative that he guard it above life itself, and it is better to risk fortune and grandeur than to allow the slightest blemish to fall upon it, since it is certain that the first lessening of his reputation, no matter how slight, is a step in the most dangerous of directions and can lead to his ruin.

Those who guide themselves by the rules and precepts contained in this testament will without doubt acquire names of no little weight in the minds of both their subjects and their foreign neighbors. This is particularly so if, being devoted to God, they are also devoted to themselves; that is, if they keep their word and are faithful to their promises. These are indispensable conditions to the maintenance of the reputation of a prince, for just as he who is destitute of them is esteemed by no one, so he who possess them is revered and trusted by all.

QUESTIONS

1. What problems did Richelieu face when he took power?

2. Richelieu is in a delicate position, because he is totally dependent upon the king's good will for his success. How is his weakness reflected in his testament?

3. Richelieu compares the common people with mules. Why? What does this analogy reflect about his view of society and social relations?

4. What, according to Richelieu, is the most important prop of a king's power?

5. Does the cardinal's advice resemble Machiavelli's program in any way? How do they differ?

74.   HANS VON GRIMMELSHAUSEN

SIMPLICISSIMUS

(1669)

Hans von Grimmelshausen (ca. 1622–76) was the son of a German innkeeper. Orphaned as a youth, he was carried away by soldiers during the Thirty Years' War. He was soon pressed into service as a musketeer in the imperial army. His literary skills, however, gained him a job as a secretary to a general and then as a clerk to a noble family. A charge of embezzlement brought his career full circle, for he ended his life as an innkeeper.

Grimmelshausen began his writings while still a soldier. He specialized in satires and in picaresque stories, of which *Simplicissimus* was the most famous.

The title is translated as "The Simplest of the Simple." Much of the early part of the work (which includes the section excerpted here) is thought to be autobiographical. No other work of the period so vividly depicts the horror of the Thirty Years' War.

Although it was not my intention to lead these riders to my dad's farm, truth demands that I leave to posterity the cruelties committed in this our German war, to prove these evils were done to our advantage. Who else would have told me there was a God in Heaven if the warriors had not destroyed my father's house and forced me, through my captivity, to meet other people, for till this moment I had imagined my dad, mum and the rest of our household to be the sole inhabitants of this earth as no other man nor human dwelling were known to me but the one where I daily went in and out. Soon I had to learn man's origin in this world. I was merely a human in shape and a Christian only in name, otherwise just an animal. Our gracious God looked upon my innocence with pity and wished to bring me both to his and my awareness, and although there were a thousand ways of doing this, he used the one by which my dad and mum were punished as an example to others for their careless education of me.

The first thing that the riders did was to stable their horses. After that each one started his own business which indicated nothing but ruin and destruction. While some started to slaughter, cook and fry, so that it looked as though they wished to prepare a gay feast, others stormed through the house from top to bottom as if the golden fleece of Colchis were hidden there. Others again took linen, clothing and other goods, making them into bundles as if they intended going to market; what they did not want was broken up and destroyed. Some stabbed their swords through hay and straw as if they had not enough pigs to stab. Some shook the feathers out of the beds and filled the ticks with ham and dried meat as if they could sleep more comfortably on these. Others smashed the ovens and windows as if to announce an eternal summer. They beat copper and pewter vessels into lumps and packed the mangled pieces away. Bedsteads, tables, chairs and benches were burned although many stacks of dried wood stood in the yard. Earthenware pots and pans were all broken, perhaps because our guests preferred roasted meats, or perhaps they intended to eat only one meal with us. Our maid had been treated in the stable in such a way that she could not leave it any more—a shameful thing to tell! They bound the farm-hand and laid him on the earth, put a clamp of wood in his mouth, and emptied a milking churn full of horrid dung water into his belly. This they called the Swedish drink, and they forced him to lead a party of soldiers to another place, where they looted men and cattle and brought them back to our yard. Among them were my dad, my mum and Ursula.

The soldiers now started to take the flints out of their pistols and in their stead screwed the thumbs of the peasants, and they tortured the poor wretches as if they were burning witches. They put one of the captive peasants into the baking-oven and put fire on him, although he had confessed nothing. Then they tied a rope round the head of another one, and twisted it with the help of a stick so tightly that blood gushed out through his mouth, nose and ears. In short everybody had his own invention to torture the peasants and each peasant suffered his own martyrdom. My dad alone appeared to me the most fortunate for he confessed with laughter what others were forced to say under pains and miserable lament, and such honour was done to him without doubt because he was the master of the house. They put him next to a fire, tied him so that he could move neither hands nor feet, and rubbed the soles of his feet with wet salt, which our old goat had to lick off. This tickled him so much that he almost wanted to burst with laughter, and it seemed to me so gentle and pleasant—for I had never seen nor heard my dad making such long-lasting laughter—that I half in companionship and half in ignorance joined heartily with him. In such merriment he confessed his guilt and revealed the hidden treasure, which was richer in gold, pearls and jewels than might have been expected of a peasant. What happened to the captive women, maids and daughters I do not know as the soldiers would not let me watch how they dealt with them. I only very well remember that I heard them miserably crying in corners here and there, and I believe my mum and Ursula had no better fate then the others.

In the midst of this misery I turned the spit and did not worry as I hardly understood what all this meant. In the afternoon I helped to water the horses and so found our maid in the stable looking amazingly dishevelled. I did not recognise her but she spoke to me with pitiful voice:

'Oh, run away, boy, or the soldiers will take you with them. Look out, escape! Can't you see how evil. . . .'

More she could not say.

So I made my way to a village but when I arrived found it in full flame; a troop of horsemen had just looted it and put it on fire. They had killed some of the peasants, driven away many and captured a few amongst whom was the vicar. Oh, God, how human life is full of pain and misery! Scarcely one misfortune has ended when we are overcome by another. The riders were ready to go and were leading the vicar on a rope. Some shouted: 'Shoot the rascal down!', and others demanded money from him. He raised his hands and asked for the sake of the Last Judgment for pardon and Christian charity.

But in vain. One of them rode toward him giving him a blow over the head so that he fell to the ground and recommended his soul to God. Nor had the other captive peasants any better fate.

The day following the burning of the village, as I was sitting in my hut saying my prayers and cooking carrots for sustenance, about forty to fifty musketeers surrounded me. These, although astonished at my unusual appearance, stormed through my hut seeking that which was not to be found; for I had nothing but books which they threw about as they were of no value to them. Finally, looking at me more carefully and seeing what a poor bird they had trapped, they realised that there was no good booty to be gained from me. My hard life amazed them and they had great pity for my tender youth, especially the officer who was in command. Indeed he honoured me and politely requested me to show him and his men the way out of the wood in which they had been lost for a long time. I did not refuse but led them by the nearest path toward the village where the vicar had been so badly treated, as I knew no other way. Before we left the wood we saw about ten peasants partly armed with blunderbusses and others occupied in burying something. The musketeers went up to them shouting: 'Halt! Halt!' The peasants answered with their guns but when they saw they were overpowered by the soldiers, they dispersed so that the tired musketeers could not follow them.

When I arrived back I discovered that my flintbox and all my belongings, including my whole store of miserable victuals, which I had grown all through the summer in my garden and saved up for the winter, had disappeared. Whither now, I thought. Need taught me to pray the more. I exercised all my poor wit to find out what to do and what not to do—but with my small experience I could not come to any real decision. The best was to recommend myself to God and put all my trust in him, otherwise I would have despaired and perished. My mind was still full of that which I had seen and heard that very day. I did not think so much about food and my own preservation as about the hatred between soldiers and peasants, and in my foolishness there seemed no other explanation than that there must undoubtedly be two kinds of men in the world, not one single stock derived from Adam, but as different as wild and tame animals, for they persecute each other so cruelly.

Once at the end of May when I again in my usual although forbidden way crept into a farmyard to fetch my food, I found myself in the kitchen, but soon realised that the folk were still awake (where dogs hung about I wisely never went). I kept the kitchen door leading into the courtyard wide open so that if danger came I should be able to run away, and there I remained quiet as a mouse, waiting until the people would go to bed. In the meantime I noticed a slit in the kitchen-hatch leading to the living room. There I stealthily crept to see whether the peasants would not soon go to sleep. But my hopes came to nothing, as they had just dressed themselves, and instead of a candle a sulphurous blue flame stood on a bench, near which they smeared grease on sticks, brooms, forks, stools and benches, and rode out on these through the windows. At this I was terribly amazed and felt great horror, but as I had been accustomed to still more horrible things and had all my life neither read nor heard of witches, I did not take it too seriously, mostly because everything happened so quietly.

After all had flown away, I went into the room and here I considered what I could take with me and where to look for it. With such thoughts I sat down astride on a bench but as soon as I did so, I flew with the bench out through the window, leaving behind knapsack and blunderbuss, which I had put down almost as a reward for witches' ointment. My sitting down, flying off and descent happened in one moment, for I arrived as it seemed to me instantly amongst a great mass of people; possibly because of fear I did not realise the length of my journey. These people were dancing a remarkable dance such as I had never seen in my life. They held hands and turned their backs inwards as one has seen the Three Graces painted, so that their faces turned outwards, forming many rings one within the other. The innermost ring consisted of seven or eight persons; the next one of double this number; the third more than both, and so on, so that in the outer circle were more than two hundred. And as always once circle danced to the left and the other to the right, I could not see how many rings they had formed nor what stood in the middle around which they danced. It looked strange and horrid as all bobbed their heads ludicrously, and just as strange was the music. Everyone, it appeared to me, sang as he danced which gave an amazing harmony. My bench which carried me there came to rest near the musicians who stood about outside the rings of the dancers. Some of the musicians had instead of flutes, bagpipes and shawms, nothing but adders, vipers and blindworms, on which they whistled merrily. Some had cats into whose behinds they blew and fingered on the tail, which sounded similar to bagpipes. Others bowed on the skulls of horses as on the best fiddles, and others played the harp upon cow skeletons like those which lie in the flayer's pit. One held a bitch under his arm whose tail he turned and fingered her teats. In between devils trumpeted through their noses that the whole forest echoed, and when the dance came to an end, the whole hellish crowd started to rage, shriek, rustle, roar, howl and storm as if they were all mad and senseless. And so one can imagine how I was struck by horror and fear.

In this turmoil a fellow approached me with a gigantic toad under his arm, easily as big as a kettledrum. Its guts had been pulled out through the arse and pushed into its mouth, which looked so revolting that I had to vomit.

'Look here, Simplicius,' he said, 'I know that you are a good lute player. Let's hear a fine tune!'

I was so terrified that I almost fell down on hearing the fellow call me by name; out of fear I became completely speechless and imagined I lay in a deep dream and prayed fervently in my heart that I might wake up. The fellow with the toad however, at whom I stared, pushed his nose forwards and backwards like a Calcutta cock, and at last he knocked me with it on the breast so that I nearly choked. At this I started to cry loudly to God and thereupon the whole host disappeared, and in a flash it was pitch dark and my heart felt so fearful that I fell to the ground, making the sign of the cross well nigh a hundred times.

QUESTIONS

1. What is the nature of war in the seventeenth century? Who appears to suffer most?

2. Why were soldiers so brutal toward the common people who crossed their paths?

3. *Simplicissimus* speculates that peasants and soldiers must have been different species; yet in fact most soldiers were of peasant stock themselves. What might this fact indicate about the peasantry and about the military?

4. How might Grimmelshausen's status as a village innkeeper have biased his views of peasants?

5. Grimmelshausen's description of a witches' coven is typical of many such accounts. What is it like? How does it demonstrate the taboos and dark fears of the age?

Subjects and Sovereigns

75.	JAMES I

TRUE LAW OF A FREE MONARCHY

(1598)

James VI of Scotland (1567–1625), who also reigned as James I of England from 1603 to 1625, was the product of the ill-fated love affair between Mary, Queen of Scots, and Henry, Lord Darnley. He was raised as a Presbyterian by the Protestant lords who declared that Mary had vacated the throne of Scotland. James fancied himself a theologian and scholar and wrote a number of works on both scholarly and popular issues, including an attack upon the use of tobacco. He became king of England at the death of Elizabeth I in 1603 and ruled there for over twenty years. He was considered generous to a fault, but his rough Scottish speech and manner came in for more than their fair share of criticism.

While still king of Scotland, James composed the *True Law of a Free Monarchy* for the instruction of his subjects. It is one of the clearest statements of both the powers and restrictions placed upon a divine right monarch.

THE TREW LAW OF FREE MONARCHIES: OR THE RECIPROCK AND MUTUALL DUTIE BETWIXT A FREE KING AND HIS NATURALL SUBJECTS

As there is not a thing so necessarie to be knowne by the people of any land, next the knowledge of their God, as the right knowledge of their alleageance, according to the forme of governement established among them, especially in a *Monarchie* (which forme of government, as resembling the Divinitie, approacheth nearest to perfection, as all the learned and wise men from the beginning have agreed upon; Unitie being the perfection of all things,) So hath the ignorance, and (which is worse) the seduced opinion of the multitude blinded by them, who thinke themselves able to teach and instruct the ignorants, procured the wracke and overthrow of sundry flourishing Common-wealths; and heaped heavy calamities, threatening utter destruction upon others. And the smiling successe, that unlawfull rebellions have oftentimes had against Princes in ages past (such hath bene the misery, and iniquitie of the time) hath by way of practise strengthened many in their errour: albeit there cannot be a more deceivable argument; then to judge by the justnesse of the cause by the event thereof; as hereafter shall be proved more at length. And among others, no Commonwealth, that ever hath bene since the beginning, hath had greater need of the trew knowledge of this ground, then this our so long disordered, and distracted Common-wealth hath: the misknowledge hereof being the onely spring, from whence have flowed so many endlesse calamities, miseries, and confusions, as is better felt by many, then the cause thereof well knowne, and deeply considered. The naturall zeale therefore, that I beare to this my native countrie, with the great pittie I have to see the so-long disturbance thereof for lack of the trew knowledge of this ground (as I have said before) hath compelled me at last to breake silence, to discharge my conscience to you my deare country men herein, that knowing the ground from whence these your many endlesse troubles have proceeded, as well as ye have already too-long tasted the bitter fruites thereof, ye may by knowledge, and eschewing of the cause escape, and divert the lamentable effects that ever necessarily follow thereupon. I have chosen then onely to set downe in this short Treatise, the trew grounds of the mutuall duty, and alleageance betwixt a free and absolute *Monarche,* and his people.

First then, I will set downe the trew grounds, whereupon I am to build, out of the Scriptures, since *Monarchie* is the trew paterne of Divinitie, as I have already said: next, from the fundamental Lawes of our owne Kingdome, which nearest must concerne us: thirdly, from the law of Nature, by divers similitudes drawne out of the same.

By the Law of Nature the King becomes a naturall Father to all his Lieges at his Coronation: And as the Father of his fatherly duty is bound to care for the nourishing, education, and vertuous government of his children; even so is the king bound to care for all his subjects. As all the toile and paine that the father can take for his children, will be thought light and well bestowed by him, so that the effect thereof redound to their profite and weale; so ought the Prince to doe towards his people. As the kindly father ought to foresee all inconvenients and dangers that may arise towards his children, and though with the hazard of his owne person presse to prevent the same; so ought the King towards his people. As the fathers wrath and correction upon any of his children that offendeth, ought to be by a fatherly chastisement seasoned with pitie, as long as

there is any hope of amendment in them; so ought the King towards any of his Lieges that offend in that measure. And shortly, as the Fathers chiefe joy ought to be in procuring his childrens welfare, rejoycing at their weale, sorrowing and pitying at their evil, to hazard for their safetie, travell for their rest, wake for their sleepe; and in a word, to thinke that his earthly felicitie and life standeth and liveth more in them, nor in himselfe; so ought a good Prince thinke of his people.

As to the other branch of this mutuall and reciprock band, is the duty and alleageance that the Lieges owe to their King: the ground whereof, I take out of the words of *Samuel,* dited by Gods Spirit, when God had given him commandement to heare the peoples voice in choosing and annointing them a King. And because that place of Scripture being well understood, is so pertinent for our purpose, I have insert herein the very words of the Text.

10. So *Samuel* tolde all the wordes of the Lord unto the people that asked a King of him.

11. And he said, this shall be the maner of the King that shall raigne over you: he will take your sonnes, and appoint them to his Charets, and to be his horsemen, and some shall runne before his Charet.

12. Also, hee will make them his captaines over thousands, and captaines over fifties, and to eare his ground, and to reape his harvest, and to make instruments of warre and the things that serve for his charets:

13. Hee will also take your daughters, and make them Apothicaries, and Cookes, and Bakers.

14. And hee will take your fields, and your vineyards, and your best Olive trees, and give them to his servants.

15. And he will take the tenth of your seed, and of your Vineyards, and give it to his Eunuches, and to his servants.

16. And he will take your men servants, and your maid-servants, and the chiefe of your young men, and your asses, and put them to his worke.

17. He will take the tenth of your sheepe: and ye shall be his servants.

18. And ye shall cry out at that day, because of your King, whom ye have chosen you: and the Lord God will not heare you at that day.

19. But the people would not heare the voice of *Samuel*, but did say: Nay, but there shalbe a King over us.

20. And we also will be all like other Nations, and our King shall judge us, and goe out before us, and fight our battels.

As likewise, although I have said, a good king will frame all his actions to be according to the Law; yet is hee not bound thereto but of his good will, and for good example-giving to his subjects: For as in the law of abstaining from eating of flesh in *Lenton*, the king will, for examples sake, make his owne house to observe the Law; yet no man will thinke he needs to take a licence to eate flesh. And although by our Lawes, the bearing and wearing of hag-buts, and pistolets be forbidden, yet no man can find any fault in the King, for causing his traine use them in any raide upon the Borderers, or other malefactours or rebellious subjects. So as I have alreadie said, a good King, although hee be above the Law, will subject and frame his actions thereto, for examples sake to his subjects, and of his owne free-will, but not as subject or bound thereto.

And the agreement of the Law of nature in this our ground with the Lawes and constitutions of God, and man, already alledged, will by two similitudes easily appeare. The King towards his people is rightly compared to a father of children, and to a head of a body composed of divers members: For as fathers, the good Princes, and Magistrates of the people of God acknowledged themselves to their subjects. And

Portrait of James I (1567–1625) by Van Somer.

for all other well ruled Common-wealths, the stile of *Pater patriae* was ever, and is commonly used to Kings. And the proper office of a King towards his Subjects, agrees very wel with the office of the head towards the body, and all members thereof: For from the head, being the seate of Judgement, proceedeth the care and foresight of guiding, and preventing all evill that may come to the body or any part thereof. The head cares for the body, so doeth the King for his people. As the discourse and direction flowes from the head, and the execution according thereunto belongs to the rest of the members, every one according to their office: so it is betwixt a wise Prince, and his people. As the judgement comming from the head may not onely imploy the members, every one in their owne office, as long as they are able for it; but likewise in case any of them be affected with any infirmitie must care and provide for their remedy, in-case it be curable, and if otherwise, gar cut them off for feare of infecting of the rest: even so is it betwixt the Prince, and his people. And as there is ever hope of curing any diseased member by the direction of the head, as long as it is whole; but by the contrary, if it be troubled, all the members are partakers of that paine, so is it betwixt the Prince and his people.

And now first for the fathers part (whose naturally love to his children I described in the first part of this my discourse, speaking of the duty that Kings owe to their Subjects) consider, I pray you what duty his children owe to him, & whether upon any pretext whatsoever, it will not be thought monstrous and unnaturall to his sons, to rise up against him, to control him at their appetite, and when they thinke good to sley him, or to cut him off, and adopt to themselves any other they please in his roome: Or can any pretence of wickednes or rigor on his part be a just excuse for his children to put hand into him? And although wee see by the course of nature, that love useth to descend more than to ascend, in case it were trew, that the father hated and wronged the children never so much, will any man, endued with the least sponke of reason, thinke it lawful for them to meet him with the line? Yea, suppose the father were furiously following his sonnes with a drawen sword, is it lawful for them to turne and strike againe, or make any resistance but by flight? I thinke surely, if there were no more but the example of bruit beasts & unreasonable creatures, it may serve well enough to qualifie and prove this my argument. We reade often the pietie that the Storkes have to their olde and decayed parents:

And generally wee know, that there are many sorts of beasts and fowles, that with violence and many bloody strokes will beat and banish their yong ones from them, how soone they perceive them to be able to fend themselves; but wee never read or heard of any resistance on their part, except among the vipers; which prooves such persons, as ought to be reasonable creatures, and yet unnaturally follow this example, to be endued with their viperous nature.

And it is here likewise to be noted, that the duty and alleageance, which the people sweareth to their prince, is not only bound to themselves, but likewise to their lawfull heires and posterity, the lineall succession of crowns being begun among the people of God, and happily continued in divers christian commonwealths: So as no objection either of heresie, or whatsoever private statute or law may free the people from their oathgiving to their king, and his succession, established by the old fundamentall lawes of the kingdom: For, as hee is their heritable over-lord, and so by birth, not by any right in the coronation, commeth to his crowne; it is a like unlawful (the crowne ever standing full) to displace him that succeedeth thereto, as to eject the former: For at the very moment of the expiring of the king reigning, the nearest and lawful heire entreth in his place: And so to refuse him, or intrude another, is not to holde out uncomming in, but to expell and put out their righteous King. And I trust at this time whole *France* acknowledgeth the superstitious rebellion of the liguers, who upon pretence of heresie, by force of armes held so long out, to the great desolation of their whole country, their native and righteous king from possessing of his owne crowne and naturall kingdome.

Not that by all this former discourse of mine, and Apologie for kings, I meane that whatsoever errors and intollerable abominations a sovereigne prince commit, hee ought to escape all punishment, as if thereby the world were only ordained for kings, & they without controlment to turne it upside down at their pleasure: but by the contrary, by remitting them to God (who is their onely ordinary Judge) I remit them to the sorest and sharpest schoolmaster that can be devised for them: for the further a king is preferred by God above all other ranks & degrees of men, and the higher that his seat is above theirs, the greater is his obligation to his maker. And therfore in case he forget himselfe (his unthankfulness being in the same measure of height) the sadder and sharper will his correction be; and according to the greatnes of the height he is in, the weight of his fall wil recompense the same: for the further that any person is obliged to God, his offence becomes and growes so much the greater, then it would be in any other. *Joves* thunderclaps light oftner and sorer upon the high & stately oakes, then on the low and supple willow trees: and the highest bench is sliddriest to sit upon. Neither is it ever heard that any king forgets himselfe towards God, or in his vocation; but God with the greatnesse of the plague revengeth the greatnes of his ingratitude: Neither thinke I by the force and argument of this my discourse so to perswade the people, that none will hereafter be raised up, and rebell against wicked Princes. But remitting to the justice and providence of God to stirre up such scourges as pleaseth him, for punishment of wicked kings (who made the very vermine and filthy dust of the earth to bridle the insolencie of proud *Pharaoh*) my onely purpose and intention in this treatise is to perswade, as farre as lieth in me, by these sure and infallible grounds, all such good Christian readers, as beare not onely the naked name of a Christian, but kith the fruites thereof in their daily forme of life, to keep their hearts and hands free from such monstrous and unnaturall rebellions, whensoever the wickednesse of a Prince shall procure the same at Gods hands: that, when it shall please God to cast such scourges of princes, and instruments of his fury in the fire, ye may stand up with cleane handes, and unspotted consciences, having prooved your selves in all your actions trew Christians toward God, and dutifull subjects towards your King, having remitted the judgement and punishment of all his wrongs to him, whom to onely of right it appertaineth.

But craving at God, and hoping that God shall continue his blessing with us, in not sending such fearefull desolation, I heartily wish our kings behaviour so to be, and continue among us, as our God in earth, and loving Father, endued with such properties as I described a King in the first part of this Treatise. And that ye´ (my deare countreymen, and charitable readers) may presse by all means to procure the prosperitie and welfare of your King; that as hee must on the one part thinke all his earthly felicitie and happinesse grounded upon your weale, caring more for himselfe for your sake then for his owne, thinking himselfe onely ordained for your weale; such holy and happy emulation may arise betwixt him and you, as his care for your quietnes, and your care for his honour and preservation, may in all your actions daily strive together, that the Land may thinke themselves blessed with such a King, and the king may thinke himselfe most happy in ruling over so loving and obedient subjects.

QUESTIONS

1. How is a king's power limited, according to James?

2. James's mother and predecessor on the Scottish throne, Queen Mary, was overthrown and driven into exile. How is this fact reflected in the king's political views?

3. Why is a strong monarchy the best form of government?

4.   What are the two main metaphors James employs in describing a king's power? How do they differ from modern political images such as the "ship of state"?

5.   Although James, of course, has an interest in arguing for a powerful monarchy, how would such a government be advantageous to a king's subjects?

76.   PHILIPPE DUPLESSIS-MORNAY

A DEFENSE OF LIBERTY AGAINST TYRANTS

(1579)

Philippe Duplessis-Mornay (1549–1623), a French nobleman of Huguenot extraction, entered the service of Henry of Navarre, the leading Huguenot prince, and became his chief advisor by 1573. Duplessis-Mornay took up arms during the Wars of Religion and was captured by Catholic forces. He avoided paying a ruinous fine by escaping in disguise and making his way back to the Huguenot lines. He continued in his role as advisor to the new king, Henry IV, but broke with him when Henry publicly converted to Catholicism. Duplessis-Mornay died in obscurity in 1623.

A Defense of Liberty was the most influential of Duplessis-Mornay's many writings. Although there remains some controversy over whether it was written alone or in collaboration, the *Defense* was the first Huguenot tract that attempted to justify resistance to lawful authority. It is a seminal work in the history of resistance theory.

First Question: Must Subjects Obey Princes Who Issue Orders Counter to the Law of God?

At first sight this question might appear to waste our time to no purpose because it seems to call the most evident axiom of Christianity into doubt as if it were still controversial, although it has been corroborated by so many testimonies of sacred Scripture, so many examples accumulated over the centuries, and the pyres of so many pious martyrs. What other reason, it might be asked, could explain the willingness of the pious to undergo such extraordinary suffering if not their conviction that God is to be obeyed simply and absolutely, kings, however, only so long as they do not issue orders counter to the law of God? How else are we to understand the apostolic precept to obey God rather than men? And since God's will alone is always just, whereas the will of anybody else can be unjust at any time, who could doubt that only the former is to be obeyed without exception, but the latter always with reservations?

There are, however, many princes nowadays who boast the name of Christ, yet dare to arrogate an immense power that most assuredly does not depend from God. There are also many adulators who worship them as gods on earth, and many others seized by fear, or else coerced by force, who either really believe that obedience is never to be denied to princes or at least wish to seem to believe it. The vice of our times indeed appears to be that nothing is so firm as that it could not be uprooted, nothing so certain that it could not be disputed, and nothing so sacred that it could not be violated. Therefore I am afraid that anyone carefully weighing the matter will consider this question to be not only far from useless, but even absolutely necessary, especially in our century. . . .

The question then is whether subjects are obliged to obey kings whose orders are in conflict with the law of God. Who of the two, in other words, is rather to be obeyed, God or the king? If an answer can be given for the king, whose power is deemed the greatest of all, the same answer will apply to other magistrates.

In short, we see that kings are invested with their kingdoms by God in almost the same manner in which vassals are invested with their fiefs by their superior lords, and that they are deprived of their benefices for the same reasons. Therefore we must on all counts conclude that the former are in an almost identical place as the latter and that all kings are vassals of God. Having said this, our question is easily finished. For if God occupies the place of a superior lord, and the king that of a vassal, who will not declare that one should rather obey the lord than the vassal? If God commands this, and the king the other, who will consider someone refusing to obey the king as a rebel? Who will not on the contrary condemn it as rebellion if he fails to obey God promptly or if he obeys the king instead? And finally, if the king calls us to this choice and God to that, who will not declare that we must desert the king in order to fight for God? Thus we are not only not obliged to obey a king who orders something against the law of God, but we even commit rebellion if we do obey him, in no other way than a landholder does who fights for a senior vassal against the king, or who prefers to obey the edict of the inferior rather than the superior, of the vicar rather than the prince, and of the minister rather than the king. . . .

Second Question: May Private Individuals Resist with Arms?

It only remains to deal with private persons. First of all, individuals as such are not bound by the covenant that is established between God and the people as a whole, that they should be God's people. For just as what is owed to a community is not owed to individuals, so individuals do not owe what the community owes. Furthermore they have none of the duties of office. The obligation to serve God depends upon the position to which one has been called. Private individuals, however, have no power, perform no magistracy, have no dominion and no power of punishment. God did not give the sword to private persons and therefore does not require them to use it. To private persons it is said: "Put thy sword into its scabbard"; to magistrates, however: "You do not bear the sword in vain." The former are guilty if they draw the sword, the latter are guilty of grave negligence unless they draw it when necessary.

But, you may ask, is there no covenant between God and the individuals at all, as there is between God and the community? No covenant with private persons as with magistrates? What could then be the purpose of circumcision and baptism? Why else is this sacred covenant mentioned over and over again in Scripture? Of course there is a covenant, but of a wholly different sort. For just as all the subjects of a just prince in general, of whatever rank they may be, are obliged to obey him, but only some of them have a special obligation, for example in the form of a magistracy, to take care that the others will be obedient, too, so all human beings in general are indeed obliged to serve God, but only some of them have taken on a greater burden along with their higher position so that, if they neglect their duty, they are responsible up to a point for the guilt of the rest. Kings, the community, and magistrates who have received the sword from the community must take care that the body of the church is governed according to the rite. Individuals, however, have no other function than to be members of that church. The former must pay heed that the temple of the lord is not polluted and does not collapse, but is safe from all internal corruption and external injury; the latter only that their body, which is the temple of God, is not impure, so that God's spirit can live in it. "Whosoever shall destroy God's temple, which you are," says Paul, "him shall God destroy." This is the reason why the former have been given a sword that can be fastened to their belts, whereas only the sword of the spirit has been entrusted to the latter, that is, the word of the lord with which Paul girds all Christians against the devil's attack.

When then shall private individuals do when the king urges impious rites upon them? If the nobles with authority from the entire people, or at least their own magistrates, oppose themselves to the king, they shall obey, follow, and assist the pious striving of the pious with all of their might as soldiers of God. If the nobles and magistrates applaud a raging king, however, or if at least they fail to resist him, the advice of Christ should be taken to heart: they should withdraw to another city. But if there is nowhere to escape to, they should rather forsake their lives than God, rather let themselves be crucified than, as the apostle says, crucify Christ once again. Do not, says our lord, fear those who can only kill the body, a lesson that has been taught to us by his own example as well as that of the apostles and innumerable pious martyrs.

Is no private person at all then permitted to resist with arms? But what about Moses, who led Israel out of Egypt against the will of Pharaoh? What about Ehud, who killed king Eglon of Moab and liberated Israel from the yoke of the Moabites after their rule had already lasted for eighteen years, when they might have seemed to acquire a right to the kingdom? And what about Jehu, who killed king Jehoram, for whom he himself had used to fight, who destroyed the line of Ahab and killed all the worshipers of Baal? Were they not private persons? As such you may of course consider them as private persons because they were not equipped with power in the normal way. But since we know them to have been called by extraordinary means, God himself, so to speak, evidently girding them with their swords, we may regard them not only as more than mere private persons, but also as placed above anyone equipped with power by ordinary means. The vocation of Moses is confirmed by an express word of God and by the most obvious signs. Ehud is explicitly said to have been incited by God to kill the tyrant and save Israel. And Jehu, anointed at the command of the prophet Elijah, was ordered to destroy the line of Ahab, although the leading people had greeted him as the king earlier on. The same can be shown for all others like them who can be adduced from Scripture.

But when God has spoken neither himself nor through prophets out of the ordinary, we must be especially sober and circumspect. If someone arrogates authority by reason of divine inspiration, he must find out whether he is not rather swelled up with arrogance, does not confuse God with himself, and creates his great spirits out of himself, lest he should conceive vanity and beget a lie. And the people, although they may be desiring to fight under the sign of Christ, must find out whether they are not perhaps fighting to their own great damage. I do not say that the same God who is sending us Pharaohs and Ahabs in this century does not occasionally also inspire liberators in an extraordinary way. His justice and his mercy have certainly never waned. But when external signs are lacking, we must at least recognize the inner ones by their effects, a mind devoid of all ambition, true and fervid zeal, good conscience, and knowledge, too, lest someone misled by error should serve false gods or being driven mad by ambition should serve himself rather than the true God.

Third Question: Is it Permitted to Resist a Prince Who Oppresses or Destroys the Commonwealth? To What Extent, by Whom, in What Fashion, and by What Right?

Kings Are Created by the People

We have previously shown that it is God who sets up kings, gives them their kingdoms, and chooses them. Now we add that it is the people who constitute kings, deliver them their kingdoms, and approve their election by vote. God wanted it to be like that so that, next to himself, the kings would receive all of their authority and power from the people. That is why they should devote all of their care, thought, and energy to the good of the people, but should not deem themselves to have been raised above the rest by some natural preeminence, as men are raised above sheep and cattle. They should rather remember that they have been born to exactly the same lot as all other human beings and that they have been raised from the earth to their rank by the votes of the people, as if by shoulders on which the burdens of the commonwealth may later for the greater part fall back again. . . .

In general, since no one is born as a king, can turn himself into a king, or is able to rule without a people, whereas the people can very well exist on their own before there are kings, all kings were obviously first created by the people. Although the sons and nephews of kings may seem to have turned their kingdoms into hereditary possessions by imitating their fathers' virtues, and although the power of free election seems to have vanished in certain regions, it thus remains the custom in all well-established kingdoms that children do not succeed to their fathers until they are constituted by the people, as if they had had no claims upon the throne at all. They are not born to their fathers as heirs of a family property, but are only considered kings as soon as those who represent the people's majesty have invested them with the kingdom through scepter and crown. Even in Christian kingdoms that are nowadays said to descend by hereditary succession there are obvious traces of this fact. In France, Spain, England, and other countries it thus is the custom that kings are inaugurated and put in possession of the kingdom, so to speak, by the estates of the realm, the peers, the patricians, and the magnates who represent the community of the people.

The Nature of Tyranny

So far we have described a king. Now we shall describe tyrants a little more accurately. We have said that a king is someone legitimately ruling over a kingdom conveyed to him by inheritance or election and properly committed to his care. It follows that a tyrant, is the direct opposite of a king, is someone who has either usurped power by force or fraud or who governs a kingdom that has been freely conveyed to him against human and divine law and persists in administering it in violation of the laws and pacts to which he has bound himself by oath. A single individual may of course fall into both kinds of tyranny at the same time. The former is commonly called a tyrant without title, the latter a tyrant by conduct. It can, however, also happen that someone governs justly over a kingdom that he has occupied by force, or governs unjustly over a kingdom legally conveyed to him. In that case, since kingship is a matter of right rather than of heredity, a function rather than a possession, someone administering his office badly is worthier of being called a tyrant than someone who has not entered his office in the proper way. . . .

Natural law, first of all, teaches us to preserve and protect our lives and liberty, without which life can hardly be lived, against all violence and injury. This is what nature has instilled in dogs against wolves, bulls against lions, doves against hawks, and chickens against kites. So much the more in man against man, if man becomes a wolf to man. Hence no doubt is permitted whether one should fight back, for nature herself is fighting here.

In addition there is the law of peoples, which distinguishes between countries, fixes limits and sets up borders that everybody is obliged to defend against foreign enemies. Hence it is just as permissible to resist Alexander if he mounts an enormous fleet in order to invade a people over which he has no rights and from which he has suffered no harm as it is to resist the pirate Diomedes if he raids the sea with but a single ship. Under such circumstances Alexander outdoes Diomedes, not by his greater right, but merely by his greater impunity. One may also resist Alexander's devastation of a region as though he were a vagabond stealing a cloak, and resist an enemy putting a city under siege as though he were a burglar breaking into a house.

Above all there is civil law, by which all human societies are constituted according to particular laws, so that each of them is governed by its own laws. Some societies are ruled by one man, others by several, and still others by all; some reject government by women, others accept it; some elect kings from a specific line, others do not; and so on. If anyone should try to break this law by force or fraud, all are obliged to resist him, because he violates society, to which everything is owed, and undermines the foundations of the fatherland, to which we are bound by nature, laws, and sacred oaths. If we neglect to resist him, we are truly traitors of our

fatherland, deserters of human society, and contemners of law. Since the laws of nature, of peoples, and civil law all command us to take up arms against tyrants of that kind, no reason at all can be offered to dissuade us from our obligation. No oath, no pact, no obligation of any kind, whether private or public, can intervene. Even a private individual is therefore permitted to resist usurpations by a tyrant of this sort. . . .

These considerations apply while the tyranny is still in the happening, as they say, that is, while the tyrant is still getting in motion, plotting, and tunneling. As soon, however, as he has gotten so much control over things that the people are conquered and swear an oath to him, that the commonwealth has been suppressed and transferred its power to him, and that the kingdom has regularly consented to a change in its laws, he has acquired the title that he was formerly lacking. He is then not only in factual but also in legal possession. Even though the people has only superficially agreed to accept his yoke, but has acted against the will of its heart, it is nevertheless right for it to obey and calmly to acquiesce in the will of God, who transfers kingdoms from one hand to another as he pleases. Otherwise there would be no kingdom at all whose jurisdiction could not be called into doubt. But this shall only apply if he who used to be a tyrant without title governs legitimately after he has acquired his title and does not continue to act as a tyrant by conduct. . . .

What the Law Permits to Be Done Against Tyrants by Conduct

We must be rather careful in examining the case of those who are tyrants by conduct, regardless of whether they acquired power by law or by force. First of all we must take into consideration that all princes are mere human beings. Their reason cannot be protected from passion any more than their souls can be separated from their bodies. It is therefore not the case that we should wish for none but perfect princes. We should rather regard ourselves lucky if we have been furnished middling ones. If a prince occasionally exceeds the proper measure, if he does not always follow reason, if he is a little lazy about the public good, a little negligent about providing justice, or not so keen on military defense, he is not really a tyrant at all times. Since a man does not govern other men as a god, as men do with oxen, but rather as a human being born to the same lot as they, it is not only presumptuous of a prince to mistreat human beings as though they were brutes, but also iniquitous of the people to look for a god in their prince, and a divinity in his fallible nature. If the prince, however, overturns the commonwealth on purpose, if he unabashedly demolishes the laws, if he cares not a bit about promises, conventions, justice, and piety, if he becomes an enemy to his people, and finally if he exercises all or the most important tyrannical skills that we have mentioned, then he can really be judged a tyrant, that is (although there was a time when that word had more pleasant connotations) an enemy of God and man.

QUESTIONS

1. Duplessis-Mornay was a Protestant living under the rule of a Roman Catholic. How might his status affect his political theory?

2. How might a monarch, like King James, argue against Duplessis-Mornay's theories?

3. How are the powers of a king limited?

4. Under what circumstances is resistance to a lawful ruler allowable? Who may offer resistance?

5. Absolute monarchs maintain that they received their authority from God. How does Duplessis-Mornay think monarchs get their power?

---

77.   SIR WILLIAM CLARKE

THE PUTNEY DEBATES

(1647)

This debate between the leaders of the New Model Army and a group of soldiers and civilians is one of the most remarkable in English history for the stark contrast in the positions of the antagonists; for the eloquence of the appeals to natural, civil, and divine law; and as expressions of the underlying themes of English political theory.

Among the main speakers, Henry Ireton (1611–51), son-in-law of Oliver Cromwell, was commissary-general of cavalry in the Army and one of its chief political strategists. From a modest landed background in Nottinghamshire, Ireton served under Parliament until his death in Ireland in 1653.

Thomas Rainsborough, whose immortal speech "the smallest hee in England" has always marked him out as a champion of the common man, was, in fact, the son of a wealthy naval officer. He was colonel of a regiment of infantry in the New Model Army.

John Wildman (1623–93) was only twenty-four when he came to Putney and is the most likely candidate for the authorship of the Agreement of the People that precipitated the debate. Wildman was to have a remarkable career over the course of the seventeenth century, sitting in Parliament under Charles II and holding the office of postmaster general.

The debates took place over a four-day period at the end of October 1647. They were recorded, in a shorthand cipher, by William Clarke, Secretary of the Army. Clarke's notes were hastily made, parts of important speeches are missing, and the cipher was not transcribed for over five years. Clarke's manuscript was not discovered until the end of the nineteenth century.

The Paper called the *Agreement* read:

The first article is, "That the people of England, being at this day very unequally distributed by Counties, Cities, and Burroughs, for the election of their Deputies in Parliament ought to be more indifferently proportioned, according to the number of the Inhabitants; the circumstances whereof, for number, place, and manner, are to be set down before the end of this present Parliament."

COMMISSARY IRETON. The exception that lies in itt is this. Itt is said: "The people of England" etc.... they are to bee distributed "according to the number of the inhabitants"; and this doth make mee thinke that the meaning is, that every man that is an inhabitant is to bee equally consider'd, and to have an equall voice in the election of the representors, those persons that are for the Generall Representative; and if that bee the meaning then I have somethinge to say against itt.

MR. PETTY, a soldier. Wee judge that all inhabitants that have nott lost their birthright should have an equall voice in Elections.

COL. RAINBOROW. I desir'd that those that had engaged in itt [should speak] for really I thinke that the poorest hee that is in England hath a life to live as the greatest hee; and therefore truly, Sir, I thinke itt's cleare, that every man that is to live under a Government ought first by his owne consent to putt himself under that Governement; and I doe thinke that the poorest man in England is nott att all bound in a stricte sence to that Governement that hee hath not had a voice to putt himself under; and I am confident that when I have heard the reasons against itt, something will bee said to answer those reasons, insoemuch that I should doubt whether he was an Englishman or noe that should doubt of these thinges.

COMMISSARY IRETON. That's [the meaning of] this ["according to the number of the inhabitants."]

Give mee leave to tell you, that if you make this the rule I thinke you must flie for refuge to an absolute naturall Right, and you must deny all Civill Right; and I am sure itt will come to that in the consequence. For my parte I thinke itt is noe right att all. I thinke that noe person hath a right to an interest or share in the disposing or determining of the affaires of the Kingedome, and in chusing those that shall determine what lawes wee shall bee rul'd by heere, noe person hath a right to this, that hath nott a permanent fixed interest in this Kingedome; and those persons together are properly the Represented of this Kingedome, and consequentlie are to make uppe the Representors of this Kingedome, who taken together doe comprehend whatsoever is of reall or permanent interest in the Kingedome. And I am sure I cannott tell what otherwise any man can say why a forraigner coming in amongst us—or as many as will coming in amongst us, or by force or otherwise setling themselves heere, or att least by our permission having a being heere—why they should nott as well lay claime to itt as any other. Wee talke of birthright. Truly [by] birthright there is thus much claime. Men may justly have by birthright, by their very being borne in England, that wee should nott seclude them out of England, that wee should nott refuse to give them aire, and place, and ground, and the freedome of the high wayes and other thinges, to live amongst us; nott [to] any man that is borne heere, though by his birth there come nothing att all to him that is parte of the permanent interest of this Kingedome. That I thinke is due to a man by birth. Butt that by a man's being borne heere hee shall have a share in that power that shall dispose of the lands heere, and of all thinges heere, I doe nott thinke itt a sufficient ground. I am sure if wee looke uppon that which is the utmost within man's view of what was originally the constitution of this Kingedome, [if wee] looke uppon that which is most radicall and fundamentall, and which if you take away there is noe man hath any land, any goods, [or] any civill interest, that is this: that those that chuse the Representors for the making of Lawes by which this State and Kingedome are to bee govern'd, are the persons who taken together doe comprehend the locall interest of this Kingedome; that is, the persons in whome all land lies, and those in Corporations in whome all trading lies. This is the most fundamentall Constitution of this Kingedome, which if

you doe nott allow you allow none att all. This Constitution hath limited and determined itt that onely those shall have voices in Elections. Itt is true as was said by a Gentleman neere mee, the meanest man in England ought to have [a voice in the election of the government he lives under]. . . . I say this, that those that have the meanest locall interest, that man that hath butt fourty shillinges a yeare, hee hath as great voice in the Election of a Knight for the shire as hee that hath ten thousand a yeare or more.

COL. RAINBOROW. Truly, Sir, I am of the same opinion I was; and am resolved to keepe itt till I know reason why I should nott. Therefore I say, that either itt must bee the law of God or the law of man that must prohibite the meanest man in the Kingdome to have this benefitt as well as the greatest. I doe nott finde any thinge in the law of God, that a Lord shall chuse 20 Burgesses, and a Gentleman butt two, or a poore man shall chuse none. I finde noe such thinge in the law of nature, nor in the law of nations. Butt I doe finde, that all Englishmen must bee subject to English lawes, and I doe verily believe, that there is noe man butt will say, that the foundation of all law lies in the people, and if [it lie] in the people, I am to seeke for this exemption. And truly I have thought something [else], in what a miserable distressed condition would many a man that hath fought for the Parliament in this quarrell bee? I will bee bound to say, that many a man whose zeale and affection to God and this Kingedome hath carried him forth in this cause hath soe spent his estate that in the way the State, the Army are going hee shall nott hold uppe his head; and when his estate is lost, and nott worth 40s. a yeare, a man shall nott have any interest; and there are many other wayes by which estates men have doe fall to decay, if that bee the rule which God in his providence does use. A man when hee hath an estate hath an interest in making lawes, when hee hath none, hee hath noe power in itt. Soe that a man cannott loose that which hee hath for the maintenance of his family, butt hee must loose that which God and nature hath given him.

Therefore I doe [think] and am still of the same opinion; that every man born in England cannot, ought nott, neither by the law of God nor the law of nature, to bee exempted from the choice of those who are to make lawes, for him to live under, and for him, for ought I know, to loose his life under. Therefore I thinke there can bee noe great sticke in this.

COMMISSARY GEN. IRETON. All the maine thinge that I speake for is because I would have an eye to propertie. I hope wee doe nott come to contend for victorie, butt lett every man consider with himself that hee doe nott goe that way to take away all propertie. For heere is the case of the most fundamentall parte of the Constitution of the Kingedome, which if you take away, you take away all by that. Heere are men of this and this qualitie are determined to bee the Electors of men to the Parliament, and they are all those who have any permanent interest in the Kingedome, and who taken together doe comprehend the whole interest of the Kingedome. I meane by permanent, locall, that is nott anywhere else. As for instance; hee that hath a freehold, and that freehold cannott bee removed out of the Kingedome; and soe there's a [freeman of a] Corporation, a place which hath the priviledge of a markett and trading, which if you should allow to all places equallie, I doe nott see how you could preserve any peace in the Kingedome, and that is the reason why in the Constitution wee have but some few markett townes. Now those people [that have freeholds] and those that are the freemen of Corporations, were look't upon by the former Constitution to comprehend the permanent interest of the Kingdom. For [firstly] hee that hath his livelihood by his trade, and by his freedome of trading in such a Corporation which hee cannott exercise in another, hee is tied to that place, his livelihood depends uppon itt. And secondly, that man hath an interest, hath a permanent interest there, uppon which hee may live, and live a freeman without dependance. These Constitutions this Kingedome hath look't att. Now I wish wee may all consider of what right

you will challenge, that all the people should have right to Elections. Is itt by the right of nature? If you will hold forth that as your ground, then I thinke you must deny all propertie too, and this is my reason. For thus: by the same right of nature, whatever itt bee that you pretend, by which you can say, "one man hath an equall right with another to the chusing of him that shall governe him"—by the same right of nature, hee hath an equal right in any goods hee sees: meate, drinke, cloathes, to take and use them for his sustenance. Hee hath a freedome to the land, [to take] the ground, to exercise itt, till itt; he hath the [same] freedome to any thinge that any one doth account himself to have any propriety in.

COL. RAINBOROW. To the thinge itt self propertie. I would faine know how itt comes to bee the propertie [of some men, and not of others]. As for estates, and those kinde of thinges, and other things that belonge to men, itt will bee granted that they are propertie; butt I deny that that is a propertie, to a Lord, to a Gentleman, to any man more then another in the Kingdome of England. Iff itt bee a propertie, itt is a propertie by a law; neither doe I thinke, that there is very little propertie in this thinge by the law of the land, because I thinke that the law of the land in that thinge is the most tyrannicall law under heaven, and I would faine know what wee have fought for, and this is the old law of England and that which inslaves the people of England that they should bee bound by lawes in which they have noe voice att all.

MR. PETTY. For this [argument] that itt destroyes all right [to property] that every Englishman that is an inhabitant of England should chuse and have a choice in the Representatives, I suppose itt is [on the contrary] the onely meanes to preserve all propertie. For I judge every man is naturally free; and I judge the reason why men when they were in soe great numbers [chose representatives was] that every man could nott give his voice; and therefore men agreed to come into some forme of Governement that they who were chosen might preserve propertie. I would faine know, if we were to begin a Governement, [whether you would say] 'you have nott 40s. a yeare, therefore you shall not have a voice.' Wheras before there was a Governement every man had such a choice, and afterwards for this very cause they did chuse Representatives, and putt themselves into formes of Governement that they may preserve propertie, and therefore itt is nott to destroy itt [to give every man a choice].

COL. RICH, a Cavalry officer.   I confesse [there is weight in] that objection that the Commissary Generall last insisted uppon; for you have five to one in the Kingedome that have noe permanent interest. Some men [have] ten, some twenty servants, some more, some lesse. If the Master and servant shall bee equall Electors, then clearlie those that have noe interest in the Kingedome will make itt their interest to chuse those that have noe interest. Itt may happen, that the majority may by law, nott in a confusion, destroy propertie; there may bee a law enacted, that there shall bee an equality of goods and estate. I thinke that either of the extreames may be urg'd to inconveniencie. That is, men that have noe interest as to Estate should have no interest as to Election.

COL. RAINBOROW.   I should nott have spoken againe. I thinke itt is a fine guilded pill, butt there is much danger and itt may seeme to some, that there is some kinde of remedy, I thinke that wee are better as wee are. That the poore shall chuse many, still the people are in the same case, are over voted still. And therfore truly, Sir, I should desire to goe close to the businesse; and the thinge that I am unsatisfied in is how itt comes about that there is such a propriety in some freeborne Englishmen, and nott [in] others.

COM. COWLING, an officer of the General Staff.   Whether the younger sonne have nott as much right to the Inheritance as the eldest?

COM. GEN. IRETON.   Will you decide itt by the light of nature?

COM. COWLING.   Why Election was only 40s a yeare, which was more then 40£ a yeare now,

the reason was [this], that the Commons of England were overpowr'd by the Lords, who had abundance of vassalls, butt that they might still make their lawes good against incroaching prerogatives, therefore they did exclude all slaves. Now the case is nott soe; all slaves have bought their freedomes. They are more free that in the common wealth are more beneficiall. There are men in the country ... there is a tanner in Stanes worth 3000£, and another in Reading worth 3 horseskins.

COM. GEN. IRETON.   In the beginning of your speech you seeme to acknowledge [that] by law, by civill Constitution, the propriety of having voices in Election was fixt in certaine persons. Soe then your exception of your arguement does nott prove that by civill constitution they have noe such propriety, butt your arguement does acknowledge [that] by civil [constitution they have such] propriety. You argue against this law, that this law is nott good.

MR. WILDMAN.   Unlesse I bee very much mistaken wee are very much deviated from the first Question. Instead of following the first proposition to inquire what is just, I conceive wee looke to prophesies, and looke to what may bee the event, and judge of the justnesse of a thinge by the consequence. I desire wee may recall [ourselves to the question] whether itt bee right or noe. I conceive all that hath bin said against itt will be reduc't to this and another reason; that itt is against a fundamental law, [and] that every person ought to have a permanent interest, because itt is nott fitt that those should chuse Parliaments that have noe lands to bee disposed of by Parliament.

COM GEN. IRETON.   If you will take itt by the way, itt is not fitt that the Representees should chuse the Representors, or the persons who shall make the law in the Kingedome, who have nott a permanent fix't interest in the Kingedome.

MR. WILDMAN.   Sir I doe soe take itt; and I conceive that that is brought in for the same reason, that forraigners might come to have a voice in our Elections as well as the native Inhabitants.

Com. Gen. Ireton. That is uppon supposition that these should bee all Inhabitants.

Mr. Wildman. Every person in England hath as cleere a right to Elect his Representative as the greatest person in England. I conceive that's the undeniable maxime of Governement: that all governement is in the free consent of the people. If [so], then upoon that account, there is noe person that is under a just Governement, or hath justly his owne, unlesse hee by his owne free consent bee putt under that Governement. This hee cannot bee unlesse hee bee consenting to itt, and therfore according to this maxime there is never a person in England [but ought to have a voice in elections]. And therfore I should humbly move, that if the Question bee stated—which would soonest bringe thinges to an issue—itt might rather bee this: whether any person can justly bee bound by law, who doth nott give his consent that such persons shall make lawes for him?

Com. Gen. Ireton. Lett the Question bee soe; whether a man can can bee bound to any law that hee doth nott consent to? And I shall tell you, that hee may and ought to bee [bound to a law] that hee doth nott give a consent to, nor doth nott chuse any [to consent to], and I will make itt cleare. If a forraigner come within this Kingedome, if that stranger will have libertie [to dwell here] who hath noe local interest heere—hee is a man itt's true, hath aire that by nature wee must nott expell our Coasts, give him noe being amongst us, nor kill him because hee comes uppon our land, comes uppe our streame, arrives att our shoare. Itt is a peece of hospitality, of humanity, to receive that man amongst us. Butt if that man bee received to a being amongst us I thinke that man may very well bee content to submitt himself to the law of the land: that is, the law that is made by those people that have a property, a fixt property, in the land.

Col. Rainborow. Sir I see, that itt is impossible to have liberty butt all propertie must be taken away. If itt be laid downe for a rule, and if you will say itt, itt must bee soe. Butt I would faine know what the souldier hath fought for all this while? Hee hath fought for all this while? Hee hath fought to inslave himself, to give power to men of riches, men of estates, to make him a perpetuall slave.

Com. Gen. Ireton I tell you what the souldier of the Kingedome hath fought for. First, the danger that wee stood in was, that one man's will must bee a law. The people of the Kingedome must have this right att least, that they should nott bee concluded [but] by the Representative of those that had the interest of the Kingedome. Some men fought in this, because they were imediately concern'd and engag'd in itt. Other men who had noe other interest in the Kingedome butt this, that they should have the benefitt of those lawes made by the Representative, yett [fought] that they should have the benefitt of this Representative. They thought itt was better to bee concluded by the common consent of those that were fix't men and setled men that had the interest of this Kingedome [in them], and from that way [said they] I shall know a law and have a certainty. Every man that was borne in itt that hath a freedome is a denizon, hee was capable of trading to gett money and to gett estates by, and therfore this man I thinke had a great deale of reason to build uppe such a foundation of interest to himself: that is, that the will of one man should not bee a law, butt that the law of this Kingedome should bee by a choice of persons to represent, and that choice to bee made by the generality of the Kingedome. Heere was a right that induced men to fight, and those men that had this interest, though this bee nott the utmost interest that other men have, yett they had some interest.

QUESTIONS

1. What is the radical view of equality expressed in the debate by people like Colonel Rainsborough, and how is this view justified?

2. What is the conservative response to the radical view?

3. Although the sides in the debate disagree about who should choose representatives in Parliament, they do share some political assumptions. What are they?

4. How do the views expressed in the debate differ from the political theories expounded by James I in his *True Law of a Free Monarchy*?

5. This debate was never officially published, and we know what was said only through Clarke's rough notes. How might this affect our understanding of what went on at Putney?

---

78.   **THOMAS HOBBES**

LEVIATHAN

(1651)

Thomas Hobbes (1588–1679), the son of a quarrelsome minister of the Church of England, was the greatest English philosopher of the seventeenth century. Raised by an uncle following his father's early death, Hobbes went to Oxford University in 1603. Unsatisfied with the medieval curriculum at Oxford, Hobbes was a lackluster student who preferred to design his own education by reading books independently. After his graduation, he began a career as a tutor in the household of the Earl of Devonshire. Hobbes spent most of the rest of his life closely associated with the heirs of the Devonshire title, who paid him an annual pension until his death. A major part of his duties as tutor was to guide his charges during their European tours. This allowed Hobbes entry into the increasingly international world of scholarship. He befriended Galileo and earned the enmity of the famous French philosopher Descartes when on a trip to Paris. The Civil Wars in England broke out and his patron chose the losing Royalist side. This resulted in a long Parisian exile, during which Hobbes began to formulate the ideas which later became a part of Leviathan. Following the

Restoration of Charles II, Hobbes returned to England where he spent much of his time refining his ideas and defending himself from the attacks of his enemies, who claimed that his work was anti-Christian and subversive.

Leviathan, published in 1651 while Hobbes was in exile, was the fruit of his experience as the subject of a kingdom torn apart by civil war. In later years his work was condemned as an apology for the military dictatorship of Oliver Cromwell, although in fact most of it was written well before Cromwell came to power. The selection reproduced here reflects Hobbes's vision of human nature.

Of the Naturall Condition *of Mankind, as* Concerning Their Felicity, *and* Misery

Nature hath made men so equall, in the faculties of body, and mind; as that though there bee found one man sometimes manifestly stronger in body, or of quicker mind than another; yet when all is reckoned together, the difference between man, and man, is not so considerable, as that one man can thereupon claim to himselfe any benefit, to which another may not pretend, as well as he. For as to the strength of body, the weakest has strength enough to kill the strongest, either by secret machination, or by confederacy with others, that are in the same danger with himselfe.

And as to the faculties of the mind, . . . I find yet a greater equality amongst men, than that of strength. For Prudence, is but Experience; which equall time, equally bestowes on all men, in those things they equally apply themselves unto. That which may perhaps make such equality incredible, is but a vain conceipt of ones owne wisdome, which almost all men think they have in a greater degree, than the Vulgar; that is, than all men but themselves, and a few others, whom by Fame, or for concurring with themselves, they approve. For such is the nature of men, that howsoever they may acknowledge many others to be more witty, or more eloquent, or more learned; Yet they will hardly believe there be many so wise as themselves: For they see their own wit at hand, and other mens at a distance. But this proveth rather that men are in that point equall, than unequall. For there is not ordinarily a greater signe of the equall distribution of any thing, than that every man is contented with his share.

From this equality of ability, ariseth equality of hope in the attaining of our Ends. And therefore if any two men desire the same thing, which neverthelesse they cannot both enjoy, they become enemies; and in the way to their End, (which is principally their owne conservation, and sometimes their delectation only,) endeavour to destroy, or subdue one an other. And from hence it comes to passe, that where an Invader hath no more to feare, than an other mans single power; if one plant, sow, build, or possesse a convenient Seat, others may probably be expected to come prepared with forces united, to dispossesse, and deprive him, not only of the fruit of his labour, but also of his life, or liberty. And the Invader again is in the like danger of another.

And from this diffidence of one another, there is no way for any man to secure himselfe, so reasonable, as Anticipation; that is, by force, or wiles, to master the persons of all men he can, so long, till he see no other power great enough to endanger him: And this is no more than his own conservation requireth, and is generally allowed. Also because there be some, that taking pleasure in contemplating their own power in the acts of conquest, which they pursue farther than their security requires; if others, that otherwise would be glad to be at ease within modest bounds, should not by invasion increase their power, they would not be able, long time, by standing only on their defence, to subsist. And by consequence, such augmentation of dominion over men, being necessary to a mans conservation, it ought to be allowed him.

Againe, men have no pleasure, (but on the contrary a great deale of griefe) in keeping company, where there is no power able to over-awe them all. For every man looketh that his companion should value him, at the same rate he sets upon himselfe: And upon all signes of contempt, or undervaluing, naturally endeavours, as far as he dares (which amongst them that have no common power to keep them in quiet, is far enough to make them destroy each other,) to extort a greater value from his contemners, by dommage; and from others, by the example.

So that in the nature of man, we find three principall causes of quarrell. First, Competition; Secondly, Diffidence; Thirdly, Glory.

The first, maketh men invade for Gain; the second, for Safety; and the third, for Reputation. The first use Violence, to make themselves Masters of other mens persons, wives, children, and cattell; the second, to defend them; the third, for trifles, as a word, a smile, a different opinion, and any other signe of undervalue, either direct in their Persons, or by reflexion in their Kindred, their Friends, their Nation, their Profession, or their Name.

Hereby it is manifest, that during the time men live without a common Power to keep them all in awe, they are in that condition which is called *Warre;* and such a warre, as is of every man, against every man. For *Warre,* consisteth not in Battell onely, or the act of fighting; but in a tract of time, wherein the Will to contend by Battell is sufficiently known: and therefore the notion of *Time,* is to be considered in the nature of Warre; as it is in the nature of Weather. For as the nature of Foule weather, lyeth not in a showre or two of rain; but in an inclination thereto of many dayes together: So the nature of War, consisteth not in actual fighting; but in the known disposition thereto, during all the time there is no assurance to the contrary. All other time is PEACE.

Whatsoever therefore is consequent to a time of Warre, where every man is Enemy to every man; the same is consequent to the time, wherein men live without other security, than what their own strength, and their own invention shall furnish them withall. In such condition, there is no place for Industry; because the fruit thereof is uncertain: and consequently no Culture of the Earth; no Navigation, nor use of the commodities that may be imported by Sea; no commodious Building; no Instruments of moving, and removing such things as require much force; no Knowledge of the face of the Earth; no account of Time; no Arts; no Letters; no Society; and which is worst of all, continuall feare, and danger of violent death; and the life of man, solitary, poore, nasty, brutish, and short.

It may seem strange to some man, that has not well weighed these things; that Nature should thus dissociate, and render men apt to invade, and destroy one another: and he may therefore, not trusting to this Inference, made from the Passions, desire perhaps to have the same confirmed by Experience. Let him therefore consider with himself, when taking a journey, he armes himselfe, and seeks to go well accompanied; when going to sleep, he locks his dores; when even in his house he locks his chests; and this when he knowes there bee Lawes, and publike Officers, armed, to revenge all injuries shall bee done him; what opinion he has of his fellow subjects, when he rides armed; of his fellow Citizens, when he locks his dores; and of his children, and servants, when he locks his chests. Does he not there as much accuse mankind by his actions, as I do by my words? But neither of us accuse mans nature in it. The Desires, and other Passions of man, are in themselves no Sin. No more are the Actions, that proceed from those Passions, till they know a Law that forbids them: which till Lawes be made they cannot know: nor can any Law be made, till they have agreed upon the Person that shall make it.

It may peradventure be thought, there was never such a time, nor condition of warre as this; and I believe it was never generally so, over all the world: but there are many places, where they live so now. For the savage people in many places of *America,* except the government of small Families, the concord whereof dependeth on naturall lust, have no government at all; and live at this day in that brutish manner, as I said before. Howsoever, it may be perceived what manner of life there would be, where there were no common Power to feare; by the manner of life, which men that have formerly lived under a peaceful government, use to degenerate into, in a civil Warre.

But though there had never been any time, wherein particular men were in a condition of warre one against another; yet in all times, Kings, and Persons of Soveraigne authority, because of their Independency, are in continual jealousies, and in the state and posture of Gladiators; having their weapons pointing, and their eyes fixed on one another; that is, their Forts, Garrisons, and Guns upon the Frontiers of their Kingdomes; and continuall Spyes upon their neighbours; which is a posture of War. But because they uphold thereby, the Industry of their Subjects; there does not follow from it, that misery, which accompanies the Liberty of particular men.

To this warre of every man against every man, this also is consequent; that nothing can be Unjust. The notions of Right and Wrong, Justice and Injustice have there no place. Where there is no common Power, there is no Law: where no Law, no Injustice. Force, and Fraud, are in warre, the two Cardinall vertues. Justice, and Injustice are none of the Faculties neither of the Body, nor Mind. If they were, they might be in a man that were alone in the world, as well as his Senses, and Passions. They are Qualities, that relate to men in Society, not in Solitude. It is consequent also to the same condition, that there be no Propriety, no Dominion, no *Mine* and *Thine* distinct; but onely that to be every mans, that he can get; and for so long, as he can keep it. And thus much for the ill condition, which man by meer Nature is actually placed in; though with a possibility to come out of it, consisting partly in the Passions, partly in his Reason.

The Passions that encline men to Peace, are Feare of Death; Desire of such things as are necessary to commodious living; and a Hope by their Industry to obtain them. And Reason suggesteth convenient Articles of Peace, upon which men may be drawn to agreement. These Articles, are they, which otherwise are called the Lawes of Nature.

QUESTIONS

1. Hobbes argues that "Nature hath made men . . . equall." What sort of equality is he talking about? How are people equal?

2. What is Hobbes's view of human nature? Is it a pessimistic or optimistic view? Why?

3. Why do people quarrel, according to Hobbes? What sort of society is the product of the "state of nature"?

4. How do you think Hobbes's experience of the English Civil Wars might have affected his point of view?

5. How do you think Hobbes's war of "every man against every man" could be stopped? What sort of government could break the natural human tendency towards war?

JOHN LOCKE

SECOND TREATISE OF GOVERNMENT

(1689)

John Locke (1632–1704) is one of the most influential political theorists in Western history. His *Two Treatises of Government* not only inspired the English tradition of parliamentary democracy, but influenced the French Enlightenment through the writing of Montesquieu and most famously became the foundation for the American Declaration of Independence and Constitution. Locke was educated at Oxford after which he became a physician. His early intellectual endeavors were devoted to science and he was elected to the Royal Society in 1668. In the employ of the earl of Shaftesbury, Locke wrote an *Essay Concerning Toleration* (1667) which argued for the peaceful coexistence of diverse religious groups in England. He wrote his most important philosophical work, *Essay Concerning Human Understanding* (1689) while recovering his health in France. Locke was actively engaged in domestic politics during the reign of Charles II and he wrote his *Two Treatises on Government* during the Exclusion Crisis (1679–81) to defend the principles that government originated in the consent of the governed and for their benefit alone. His account of an idyllic state of nature from which man emerged voluntarily to form companionable society was in sharp contrast to the brutal state of nature theorized by Hobbes. Locke was associated with the Whig party in England and he followed Lord Shaftesbury into self-imposed exile in Holland after the accession of James II returning only after the Revolution of 1688. He served briefly in the government of William III, mostly as a financial advisor, but ill health limited his public career. Locke died in 1704.

The *Second Treatise of Government* (1689) is one of the enduring works of political theory in the western tradition. Although it was written in 1681 as a polemical tract, Locke attempted to prove his ideas about the nature of government by returning first principles and stating them in simple, didactic terms. In this section on the Beginning of Political Society Locke demonstrates how a political nation came into existence and how it was ruled by the will of the majority.

§ 87. Man being born, as has been proved, with a title to perfect freedom, and uncontrolled enjoyment of all the rights and privileges of the law of nature, equally with any other man, or number of men in the world, hath by nature a power, not only to preserve his property, that is, his life, liberty, and estate, against the injuries and attempts of other men; but to judge of and punish the breaches of that law in others, as he is persuaded the offence deserves, even with death itself, in crimes where the heinousness of the fact, in his opinion, requires it. But because no political society can be, nor subsist, without having in itself the power to preserve the property, and, in order thereunto, punish the offences of all those of that society; there and there only is political society, where every one of the members hath quitted his natural power, resigned it up into the hands of the community in all cases that excludes him not from appealing for protection to the law established by it. And thus all private judgment of every particular member being excluded, the community comes to be umpire by settled standing rules, indifferent, and the same to all parties; and by men having authority from the community, for the execution of those rules, decides all the differences that may happen between any members of that society concerning any matter of right; and punishes those offences which any member hath committed against the society, with such penalties as the law has established, whereby it is easy to discern, who are, and who are not, in political society together. Those who are united into one body, and have a common established law and judicature to appeal to, with authority to decide controversies between them, and punish offenders, are in civil society one with another; but those who have no such common appeal, I mean on earth, are still in the state of nature, each being, where these is no other, judge for himself, and executioner; which is, as I have before showed, the perfect state of nature.

§ 88. And thus the commonwealth comes by a power to set down what punishment shall belong to the several transgressions which they think worthy of it, committed amongst the members of that society, (which is the power of making laws) as well as it has the power to punish any injury done unto any of its members, by any one that is not of it, (which is the power of war and peace,) and all this for the preservation of the property of all the members of that society, as far as is possible. But though every man who has entered into civil society, and is become a member of any commonwealth, has thereby quitted his power to punish offences against the law of nature, in prosecution of his own private judgment; yet with the judgment of offences, which he has given up to the legislative in all cases, where he can appeal to the magistrate, he has given a right to the commonwealth to

employ his force, for the execution of the judgments of the commonwealth, whenever he shall be called to it; which indeed are his own judgments, they being made by himself, or his representative. And herein we have the original of the legislative and executive power of civil society, which is to judge by standing laws, how far offences are to be punished, when committed within the commonwealth; and also to determine, by occasional judgments founded on the present circumstances of the fact, how far injuries from without are to be vindicated; and in both these to employ all the force of all the members, when there shall be need.

§ 89. Whenever therefore any number of men are so united into one society, as to quit every one his executive power of the law of nature, and to resign it to the public, there and there only is a political, or civil society. And this is done, wherever any number of men, in the state of nature, enter into society to make one people, one body politic, under one supreme government; or else when any one joins himself to, and incorporates with any government already made: for hereby he authorizes the society, or, which is all one, the legislative thereof, to make laws for him, as the public good of the society shall require; to the executive whereof, his own assistance (as to his own degrees) is due. And this puts men out of a state of nature into that of a commonwealth, by setting up a judge on earth, with authority to determine all the controversies, and redress the injuries that may happen to any member of the commonwealth: which judge is the legislative, or magistrate appointed by it. And wherever there are any number of men, however associated, that have no such decisive power to appeal to, there they are still in the state of nature.

§ 90. Hence it is evident, that absolute monarchy, which by some men is counted the only government in the world, is indeed inconsistent with civil society, and so can be no form of civil government at all; for the end of civil society being to avoid and remedy these inconveniencies of the state of nature, which necessarily follow from every man being judge in his own case, by setting up a known authority, to which every one of that society may appeal upon any injury received, or controversy that may arise, and which every one of the society ought to obey; wherever any persons are, who have not such an authority to appeal to for the decision of any difference between, there those persons are still in the state of nature; and so is every absolute prince, in respect of those who are under his dominion.

§ 91. For he being supposed to have all, both legislative and executive power in himself alone, there is no judge to be found, no appeal lies open to any one, who may fairly, and indifferently, and with authority decide, and from whose decision relief and redress may be expected of any injury or inconveniency that may be suffered from the prince, or by his order: so that such a man, however intitled, czar, or grand seignior, or how you please, is as much in the state of nature, with all under his dominion, as he is with the rest of mankind: for wherever any two men are, who have no standing rule, and common judge to appeal to on earth, for the determination of controversies of right betwixt them, there they are still in the state of nature, and under all the inconveniencies of it, with only this woful difference to the subject, or rather slave of an absolute prince; that whereas in the ordinary state of nature he has a liberty to judge of his right, and, according to the best of his power, to maintain it; now, whenever his property is invaded by the will and order of his monarch, he has not only no appeal, as those in society ought to have, but, as if he were degraded from the common state of rational creatures, is denied a liberty to judge of, or to defend his right; and so is exposed to all the misery and inconveniencies, that a man can fear from one, who being in the unrestrained state of nature, is yet corrupted with flattery, and armed with power.

§ 92. For he that thinks absolute power purifies men's blood, and corrects the baseness of human nature, need read but the history of this or any other age, to be convinced of the contrary. He that would have been so insolent and injurious in the woods of America, would not probably be much better in a throne; where perhaps learning and religion shall be found out to justify all that he shall do to his subjects, and the sword presently silence all those that dare question it: for what the protection of absolute monarchy is, what kind of fathers of their countries it makes princes to be, and to what a degree of happiness and security it carries civil society, where this sort of government is grown to perfection; he that will look into the late relation of Ceylon, may easily see.

§ 93. In absolute monarchies, indeed, as well as other governments of the world, the subjects have an appeal to the law, and judges to decide any controversies, and restrain any violence that may happen betwixt the subjects themselves, one amongst another. This every one thinks necessary, and believes he deserves to be thought a declared enemy to society and mankind, who should go about to take it away. But whether this be from a true love of mankind and society, and such a charity as we all owe one to another, there is reason to doubt: for this is no more than what every man, who loves his own power, profit, or greatness, may and naturally must do, keep those animals from hurting, or destroying one another, who labour and drudge only for his pleasure and advantage; and so are taken care of, not out of any love the master has for them, but love of himself, and the profit they bring him: for if it be asked, what security, what fence is there, in such a state, against the violence and oppression of this absolute ruler? the very question can scarce be borne. They are ready to tell you, that it deserves death only to ask after safety. Betwixt subject and subject, they will grant, there must be measures, laws, and judges, for their mutual peace and security: but as for the ruler he ought to be absolute, and is above all such circumstances; because he has power to do more hurt and wrong, it is right when he does it. To ask how you may be guarded from harm, injury, on that side where the strongest hand is to do it, is presently the voice of faction and rebellion: as if when men quitting the state of nature entered into society, they agreed that all of them but one should be under the restraint of laws, but that he should still retain all the liberty of the state of nature, increased with power, and made licentious by impunity. This is to think, that men are so foolish, that they take care to avoid what mischiefs may be done them by polecats, or foxes; but are content, nay think it safety, to be devoured by lions.

§ 94. But whatever flatterers may talk to amuse people's understandings, it hinders not men from feeling; and when they perceive, that any man, in what station soever, is out of the bounds of the civil society which they are of, and that they have no appeal on earth against any harm they may receive from him, they are apt to think themselves in the state of nature, in respect of him whom they find to be so: and to take care, as soon as they can, to have that safety and security in civil society, for which it was instituted, and for which only they entered into it. And therefore, though perhaps at first, (as shall be showed more at large hereafter in the following part of this discourse) some one good and excellent man having got a pre-eminency amongst the rest, had this deference paid to his goodness and virtue, as to a kind of natural authority, that the chief rule, with arbitration of their differences, by a tacit consent devolved into his hands, without any other caution, but

the assurance they had of his uprightness and wisdom; yet when time, giving authority, and (as some men would persuade us) sacredness to customs, which the negligent and unforeseen innocence of the first ages began, had brought in successors of another stamp; the people finding their own properties not secure under the government, as then it was, (whereas government has no other end but the preservation of property) could never be safe nor at rest, nor think themselves in civil society, till the legislature was placed in collective bodies of men, call them senate, parliament, or what you please. By which means every single person became subject, equally with other the meanest men, to those laws, which he himself, as part of the legislative, had established; nor could any one, by his own authority, avoid the force of the law, when once made; nor by any pretence of superiority plead exemption, thereby to license his won, or the miscarriages of any of his dependents. "No man in civil society can be exempted from the laws of it:" for if any man may do what he thinks fit, and there be no appeal on earth, for redress or security against any harm he shall do; I ask, whether he be not perfectly still in the state of nature, and so can be no part or member of that civil society: unless any one will say, the state of nature and civil society are one and the same thing, which I have never yet found any one so great a patron of anarchy as to affirm.

QUESTIONS

1. What is the relationship between civil society and property?

2. Where does the power of law making come from?

3. What is Locke's definition of a civil society?

4. Why does Locke believe that absolute monarchy is an illegitimate form of government?

80.   MOLIÈRE

THE WOULD-BE GENTLEMAN
(1670)

Jean Baptiste Poquelin (1622–73) was born into a wealthy family involved in trade. Though he studied law and first took up an office at court, his real love was the theater, where he acted, directed, and wrote under the pen name Molière. The theater was not yet considered a reputable occupation for a young man of good family—one of the reasons why Poquelin disguised his identity—and it was a difficult occupation in which to make one's way. There were already two theater companies resident in Paris during the reign of Louis XIV, and Molière began his career traveling from town to town putting on impromptu performances, mostly of satirical comedies that he composed. By the time he and his company returned to Paris in the 1660s, their skills had been honed and their material appeared fresh to a court always on the lookout for something new. Molière played before the king, and by 1665 his company received royal patronage and became preeminent in Paris. Molière's plays are mostly social satires, poking fun at the morals of the nobility and those who aspired to their rank. His satirical attacks on the clergy were less welcomed, but they were apiece with his detached and ironic view of the times in which he lived. His output was prodigious, and he helped usher in a golden age of French comedy.

Molière's plays have never gone out of fashion and remain popular to this day. *Le Bourgeois Gentilhomme* (1670), or *The Would-Be Gentleman,* is one of his greatest achievements. It deflates the ambitions of Monsieur Jourdain as he attempted to purchase the manners and habits of a gentleman.

ACT SECOND

Scene First

MONSIEUR JOURDAIN, THE MUSIC-MAKER, THE DANCING-MASTER

Monsieur Jourdain.

Well now, that's not bad; those fellows frisk about pretty well.

Music-Master.

When that dance is given with its music, the effect will be better still; and you will see something really chivalrous in the little ballet we have arranged for you.

Monsieur Jourdain.

And that will be very soon; the person for whom I am preparing all this is to dine with me to-day.

Dancing-Master.

All is ready for the occasion.

Music-Master.

But, monsieur, one occasion is not sufficient. A person like you, who is magnificent and has an inclination toward splendid things, should give a concert at your house every Wednesday or Thursday.

Monsieur Jourdain.

Do people of quality give concerts?

Music-Master.

Yes, Monsieur.

Monsieur Jourdain.

Then I shall give them. Will they be fine?

Music-Master.

Undoubtedly. You will need three voices: a treble, a counter-tenor, and a bass, accompanied by a bass-viol, a theorbo, a harpsichord for the continued bass, and a couple of treble-violins to play the air.

Monsieur Jourdain.

Yes, but you must have a trombone. A trombone is an instrument that pleases me; it is very harmonious.

Music-Master.

You must let us manage these things.

Monsieur Jourdain.

Well, don't forget to send me musicians who are to play while we are at dinner.

Music-Master.

You shall have all you wish.

Monsieur Jourdain.

Above all, the ballet must be fine.

Music-Master.

You shall be satisfied,—especially with the minuet.

Monsieur Jourdain.

Ah, ha! the minuet is my particular dance. I want you to see me dance it. Come, dancing-master.

Dancing-Master.

We want a hat, monsieur, if you please. (*Monsieur Jourdain takes the hat of his lacquey, and puts it on over his night-cap. Then the dancing-master takes his hands and makes him dance to the time of the minuet, which he sings.*) La, la, la; la, la, la; la, la, la la, la, la; la, la, la; la, la, la; la, la, la la, la, la; la, la, la, la, la, la, la; la, la, la. Keep time, if you please. La, la, la, la, la, Right leg, la, la, la. Don't move your shoulders so much. La, la, la; la, la, la; la, la, la la. Your arms look deformed. La, la, la, la, la. Raise your head. Turn out your toes. La, la, la. Straighten your body.

Monsieur Jourdain, *to music-master*

Hey! what do you think of that?

Music-Master.

It couldn't be better.

Monsieur Jourdain.

By the bye, teach me how to make a bow when I salute a marchioness; I shall have need of it before long.

Dancing-Master.

A bow to salute a marchioness?

Monsieur Jourdain.

Yes,—a marchioness, whose name is Dorimène.

Dancing-Master.

Give me your hand.

Monsieur Jourdain.

No, you do it, and let me see how; I shall remember.

Dancing-Master.

Well, if you wish to salute her with great respect, you must first bow at a distance, stepping backward; then you advance toward her, making three bows; at the third you bend low, to her knees.

Monsieur Jourdain.

Just do it. (*The dancing-master makes three bows.*) Good.

Scene Second

MONSIEUR JOURDAIN, MUSIC-MAKER, DANCING-MASTER, A LACQUEY

Lacquey.

Monsieur, your fencing-master is here.

Monsieur Jourdain.

Tell him to come in and give me my lesson. (*To the music-master and the dancing-master*) Stay; I want you to see me do it.

Scene Third

MONSIEUR JOURDAIN, MUSIC-MAKER, DANCING-MASTER, FENCING-MASTER, LACQUEY, *carrying two foils*

Fencing-Master, *after taking two foils from the lacquey, and giving one to Monsieur Jourdain.*

Come, monsieur, your salute. Body straight. Rest on the left hip a little. Legs not so wide apart. Feet on the same line. Wrist against the thigh. Point of blade at the shoulder. Arm not quite so stiff. Left hand at the height of the eye. Left shoulder well out. Head erect. Eye steady. Advance. Body firm. Touch me the blade in quarte and finish the same. One, two. Recover. Double, firm on the left foot. Backward. When you make a thrust, monsieur, the sword must start first; hold the body well back. Now: One, two. Touch me the blade in tierce and finish the same. Advance. Body firm. Advance. Start from there. One, two. Recover. Double. One, two. Back. On guard, monsieur, on guard! [*The fencing-master makes two or three lunges at him, calling out, On guard!*]

Monsieur Jourdain, *out of breath.*

There! what do you think of that?

Music-Master.

You do wonders.

Fencing-Master.

I have already told you that the whole secret of fencing lies in two things only,—to give, and not to receive; and, as I showed you the other day by demonstrative reason, it is impossible that you can receive if you know how to turn the sword of your opponent from the line of your own body; which depends solely on a little turn of the wrist outward or inward.

Monsieur Jourdain.

And in that way can a man who hasn't any courage be sure of killing his adversary without being killed himself?

Fencing-Master.

Quite sure; did you not see the demonstration?

Monsieur Jourdain.

Yes.

Fencing-Master.

From that you can judge of the distinguished position we hold in the State, and how the science of fencing stands high above all the other useless arts, like dancing, music, or—

Dancing-Master.

Stop, stop! Not so fast, Mr. Swordsman. Speak respectfully of dancing.

Music-Master.

Learn, if you please, to treat music properly.

Fencing-Master.

You are a pretty couple to compare your sciences with mine.

Music-Master.

Just look at his conceit!

Dancing-Master.

What a funny animal, with that plastron of his!

Fencing-Master.

My little dancing-master, I'll teach you to dance to another tune. And you, my little music-master, I'll make you sing small.

Dancing-Master.

And I'll teach you your own trade.

Monsieur Jourdain.

What fools you both are to quarrel with a man who knows quarte and tierce and can kill his enemy by demonstrative reason.

Dancing-Master.

I don't care a fig for his demonstrative reason, or his tierce or his quarte.

Monsieur Jourdain.

Gently, gently, I tell you.

Fencing-Master, *to dancing-master.*

What! you impertinent little fellow!

Monsieur Jourdain.

Hey! my fencing-master.

Dancing-Master, *to fencing-master.*

What! you great coach-horse!

Monsieur Jourdain.

Hey! my dancing-master.

Fencing-Master.

If I just fling myself at you—

Monsieur Jourdain.

Softly, softly.

Dancing-Master.

Let me just get my hand upon you—

Monsieur Jourdain.

There! there! gently.

Fencing-Master.

I'll give you such a thrashing.

Monsieur Jourdain.

Oh! pray—

Dancing-Master.

I'll rub you down in such a way!

Monsieur Jourdain.

I beg or you—

Music-Master.

We'll teach him to talk!

Monsieur Jourdain.

Good gracious! do stop—

Scene Fourth

PROFESSOR OF PHILOSOPHY, MONSIEUR JOURDAIN, MUSIC-MAKER, DANCING-MASTER, FENCING-MASTER, LACQUEY

Monsieur Jourdain.

Ha! philosopher, you've come just in time with your philosophy. Please make peace here among these people.

Professor of Philosophy.

What is it? What's the matter, gentlemen?

Monsieur Jourdain.

They are in a fury about which of their professions is the best; they are insulting each other and want to come to blows.

Professor of Philosophy.

Hey, what a thing that is! Why do you get so angry? Have you never read the learned treatise of Seneca against anger? There's nothing so low and shameful as that passion, which makes a man a brute beast. Reason ought to be master of all our actions.

Dancing-Master.

What! when that man comes here and says insulting things to both of us, and despises dancing which is my profession, and music which is monsieur's, are we to say nothing?

Professor of Philosophy.

A wise man is above insult; the grand response that should be made to all such outrage is patience and moderation.

Fencing-Master.

They both had the audacity to compare their professions with mine.

Professor of Philosophy.

Why need that stir your bile? Men ought not to contend over the vain glories and conditions of the world. The qualities which should distinguish us among our fellows are virtue and wisdom.

Dancing-Master.

I maintain to his face that dancing is a science to which too much honor cannot be paid.

Music-Master.

And I say that music is a science which the ages have revered.

Fencing-Master.

And I tell them, both of them, that the science of fencing is the finest and the most necessary that exists upon this earth,

Professor of Philosophy.

And pray what is philosophy? I think you are all three very impertinent to speak before me with such arrogance, and to impudently give the name of science to things which don't even deserve to be honored with the name of art,— mere pitiful trades, to be classed with wrestlers, fiddlers, mountebanks.

Fencing-Master.

Out of here, dog of a philosopher!

Music-Master.

Out of here, scoundrel of a pedant!

Dancing-Master.

Hence, arrant knave of a jackass!

Professor of Philosophy.

What! rabble that you are! [*The philosopher flings himself upon the others, who pommel him.*]

Monsieur Jourdain.

Oh, professor! philosopher!

Professor of Philosophy.

Infamous wretched, rascals!—

Monsieur Jourdain.

Philosopher!

Fencing-Master.

The brute beast—

Monsieur Jourdain.

Gentlemen!

Professor of Philosophy.

Impudent scoundrels!

Monsieur Jourdain.

Professor! philosopher!

Dancing-Master.

Booby of a pack-mule!—

Monsieur Jourdain.

Gentlemen!

Professor of Philosophy.

Arrant villains!—

Monsieur Jourdain.

Philosopher!

Music-Master.

To the devil with his insolence!—

Monsieur Jourdain.

Gentlemen!

Professor of Philosophy.

Knaves! beggars! traitors! imposters!

Monsieur Jourdain.

Philosopher! gentlemen! philosopher! gentlemen! philosopher!

[*Exeunt the professors fighting.*]

QUESTIONS

1. How does the music master treat Monsieur Jourdain?

2. Why are Monsieur Jourdain's questions to his masters different than their instruction to him?

3. How well does the philosopher follow his own advice?

4. What does Monsieur Jourdain think he needs to know to become a gentleman?

81.   DUC DE SAINT-SIMON

MEMOIRS

(1694–1723)

Louis de Rouvroy, Duke of Saint-Simon (1675–1755), led a privileged life at the very heart of the French absolute state. A godson of Louis XIV, Saint-Simon was brought up in Versailles in the shadow of the Sun King. Although he served briefly as an ambassador and as an officer in the French army, Saint-Simon never carved out a place for himself in either government service or court life. He tended to blame Louis XIV for his failures, but his record of achievement in the next reign was equally unimpressive. He died bitter and resentful in 1755.

Saint-Simon is remembered only for his voluminous *Memoirs,* from which much of our knowledge of the day-to-day life at the court of Versailles derives. He began keeping them when he was 19 and continued on into middle age; the *Memoirs* show his talent for observation, particularly of social detail, and his ear for the latest court gossip. His character sketches, such as the one of Louis XIV presented here, always unearth the darker side of the subject under study. There is always as much of Saint-Simon in his portrayals as there is of the people he is describing.

I shall pass over the stormy period of Louis XIV's minority. At twenty-three years of age he entered the great world as King, under the most favourable auspices. His ministers were the most skilful in all Europe; his generals the best; his Court was filled with illustrious and clever men, formed during the troubles which had followed the death of Louis XIII.

Louis XIV was made for a brilliant Court. In the midst of other men, his figure, his courage, his grace, his beauty, his grand mien, even the tone of his voice and the majestic and natural charm of all his person, distinguished him till his death as the King Bee, and showed that if he had only been born a simple private gentleman, he would equally have excelled in fêtes, pleasures, and gallantry, and would have had the greatest success in love. The intrigues and adventures which early in life he had been engaged in—when the Comtesse de Soissons lodged at the Tuileries, as superintendent of the Queen's household, and was the centre figure of the Court roup—had exercised an unfortunate influence upon him: he received those impressions with which he could never after successfully struggle. From this time, intellect, education, nobility of sentiment, and high principle, in others, became objects of suspicion to him, and soon of hatred. The more he advanced in years the more this sentiment was confirmed in him. He wished to reign by himself. His jealousy on this point unceasingly became weakness. He reigned, indeed, in little things; the great he could never reach: even in the former, too, he was often governed. The superior ability of his early ministers and his early generals soon wearied him. He liked nobody to be in any way superior to him. Thus he chose his ministers, not for their knowledge, but for their ignorance; not for their capacity, but for their want of it. He liked to form them, as he said; liked to teach them even the most trifling things. It was the same with his generals. He took credit to himself for instructing them; wished it to be thought that from his cabinet he commanded and directed all his armies. Naturally fond of trifles, he unceasingly occupied himself with the most petty details of his troops, his household, his mansions; would even instruct his cooks, who received, like novices, lessons they had known by heart for years. This vanity, this unmeasured and unreasonable love of admiration, was his ruin. His ministers, his generals, his mistresses, his courtiers, soon perceived his weakness. They praised him with emulation and spoiled him. Praises, or to say truth, flattery, pleased him to such an extent, that the coarsest was well received, the vilest even better relished. It was the sole means by which you could approach him. Those whom he liked owed his affection for them, to their untiring flatteries. This is what gave his ministers so much authority, and the opportunities they had for adulating him, of attributing everything to him, and of pretending to learn everything from him. Suppleness, meanness, an admiring, dependent, cringing manner—above all, an air of nothingness—were the sole means of pleasing him.

This poison spread. It spread, too, to an incredible extent, in a prince who, although of intellect beneath mediocrity, was not utterly without sense, and who had had some experience. Without voice or musical knowledge, he use to sing, in private, the passages of the opera prologues that were fullest of his praises! He was drowned in vanity; and so deeply, that at his public suppers—all the Court present, musicians also—he would hum these self-same praises between his teeth, when the music they were set to was played!

And yet, it must be admitted, he might have done better. Though his intellect, as I have said, was beneath mediocrity, it was capable of being formed. He loved glory, was fond of order and regularity; was by disposition prudent, moderate, discreet, master of his movements and his tongue. Will it be believed? He was also by disposition good and just! God had sufficiently gifted him to enable him to be a good King; perhaps even *a tolerably great King!* All the evil came to him from elsewhere. His early education was so neglected that nobody dared approach his apartment. He has often been heard to speak of those times with bitterness, and even to relate that, one evening he was found in the basin of the Palais Royale garden fountain, into which he had fallen! He was scarcely taught how to read or write, and remained so ignorant, that the most familiar historical and other facts were utterly unknown to him! He fell, accordingly, and sometimes even in public, into the grossest absurdities.

It was his vanity, his desire for glory, that led him, soon after the death of the King of Spain, to make that event the pretext for war; in spite of renunciations so recently made, so carefully stipulated, in the marriage contract. He marched into Flanders; his conquests there were rapid; the passage of the Rhine was admirable; the triple alliance of England, Sweden, and Holland only animated him. In the midst of winter he took Franche-Comté, by restoring which at the peace of Aix-la-Chapelle, he preserved his conquests in Flanders. All was flourishing then in the state. Riches everywhere. Colbert had placed the finances, the navy, commerce, manufactures, letters even, upon the highest point; and this age, like that of Augustus, produced in abundance illustrious men of all kinds—even those illustrious only in pleasures.

Thus, we see this monarch grand, rich, conquering, the arbiter of Europe; feared and admired as long as the ministers and captains existed who really deserved the name. When they were no more, the machine kept moving some time by impulsion, and from their influence. But soon afterwards we saw beneath the surface; faults and errors were multiplied, and decay came on with giant strides; without, however, opening the eyes of that despotic master, so anxious to do everything and direct everything himself, and who seemed to indemnify himself for disdain abroad by increasing fear and trembling at home.

So much for the reign of this vain-glorious monarch.

Let me touch now upon some other incidents in his career, and upon some points in his character.

He early showed a disinclination for Paris. The troubles that had taken place there during the minority made him regard the place as dangerous; he wished, too, to render himself venerable by hiding himself from the eyes of the multitude; all these considerations fixed him at St. Germains soon after the death of the Queen, his mother. It was to that place he began to attract the world by fêtes and gallantries, and by making it felt that he wished to be often seen.

His love for Madame de la Vallière, which was at first kept secret, occasioned frequent excursions to Versailles, then a little card castle, which had been built by Louis XIII—annoyed, and his suite still more so, at being frequently obliged to sleep in a wretched inn there, after he had been out hunting in the forest of Saint Leger. That monarch rarely slept at Versailles more than one night, and then from necessity; the King, his son, slept there, so that he might be more in private with his mistress, pleasures unknown to the hero and just man, worthy son of Saint Louis, who built the little château.

These excursions of Louis XIV by degrees gave birth to those immense buildings he erected at Versailles; and their convenience for a numerous court, so different from the apartments at St. Germains, led him to take up his abode there entirely shortly after the death of the Queen. He built an infinite number of apartments, which were asked for by those who wished to pay their court to him; whereas at St. Germains nearly everybody was obliged to lodge in the town, and the few who found accommodation at the château were strangely inconvenienced.

The frequent fêtes, the private promenades at Versailles, the journeys, were means on which the King seized in order to distinguish or mortify the courtiers, and thus render them more assiduous in pleasing him. He felt that of real favours he had not enough to bestow; in order to keep up the spirit of devotion, he therefore unceasingly invented all sorts of ideal ones, little preferences and petty distinctions, which answered his purpose as well.

He was exceedingly jealous of the attention paid him. Not only did he notice the presence of the most distinguished courtiers, but those of inferior degree also. He looked to the right and to the left, not only upon rising but upon going to bed, at his meals, in passing through his apartments, or his gardens of Versailles, where alone the courtiers were allowed to follow him; he saw and noticed everybody; not one escaped him, not even those who hoped to remain unnoticed. He marked well all absentees from the court, found out the reason of their absence, and never lost an opportunity of acting towards them as the occasion might seem to justify. With some of the courtiers (the most distinguished), it was a demerit not to make the court their ordinary abode; with others it was a fault to come but rarely; for those who never or scarcely ever came it was certain disgrace. When their names were in any way mentioned, "I do not know them," the King would reply haughtily. Those who presented themselves but seldom were thus characterised: "They are people I never see"; these decrees were irrevocable. He could not bear people who liked Paris.

Louis XIV took great pains to be well informed of all that passed everywhere; in the public places, in the private houses, in society and familiar intercourse. His spies and tell-tales were infinite. He had them of all species; many who were ignorant that their information reached him; others who knew it; others who wrote to him direct, sending their letters through channels he indicated; and all these letters were seen by him alone, and always before everything else; others who sometimes spoke to him secretly in his cabinet, entering by the back stairs. These unknown means ruined an infinite number of people of all classes, who never could discover the cause; often ruined them very unjustly; for the King, once prejudiced, never altered his opinion, or so rarely, that nothing was more rare. He had, too, another fault, very dangerous for others and often for himself, since it deprived him of good subjects. He had an excellent memory; in this way, that if he saw a man who, twenty years before, perhaps, had in some manner offended him, he did not forget the man, though he might forget the offence. This was enough, however, to exclude the person from all favour. The representations of a minister, of a general, of his confessor even, could not move the King. He would not yield.

The most cruel means by which the King was informed of what was passing—for many years before anybody knew it—was that of opening letters. The promptitude and dexterity with which they were opened passes understanding. He saw extracts from all the letters in which there were passages that the chiefs of the post-office, and then the minister who governed it, thought ought to go before him; entire letters, too, were sent to him, when their contents seemed to justify the sending. Thus the chiefs of the post, nay, the principal clerks were in a position to suppose what they pleased and against whom they pleased. A word of contempt against the King or the government, a joke, a detached phrase, was enough. It is incredible how many people, justly or unjustly, were more or less ruined, always without resource, without trial, and without knowing why. The secret was impenetrable; for nothing ever cost the King less than profound silence and dissimulation.

QUESTIONS

1. What qualities did Saint-Simon admire in Louis XIV?

2. To what does Saint-Simon attribute Louis's early successes?

3. Judging from Saint-Simon's description of courtly life, what did a courtier need to get along?

4. On balance, Saint-Simon believed Louis to have been a failure. Why?

5. What sort of a picture does Saint-Simon present of the workings of the absolutist state?

Science and Commerce

LETTER TO THE GRAND DUCHESS CHRISTINA
(1615)

Born in Florence and educated in Padua, Galileo Galilei (1564–1642) was one of the greatest of the seventeenth-century scientists. His early studies of motion led him to accept the basic theories of Copernicus, the Polish astronomer who postulated that the earth was a planet that revolved around the sun. Galileo perfected the first telescope, and with it he was able to identify the moons of Jupiter and describe the lunar surface. His work did much to confirm the theories of astronomers before him such as Copernicus and Kepler, whose work relied upon mathematical calculation. Galileo's telescope allowed for actual observation of the movements of heavenly bodies. His studies of motion were an important contribution to the development of a new scientific world view. At first Galileo was prohibited from publishing his findings, but in 1632 he received a license for the publication of *A Dialogue Between the Two Great Systems of the World,* a tract that took the form of a debate between an adherent of the old Aristotelian system and a convert to the new Copernican one. Galileo was subsequently arrested by the Inquisition, tried, condemned, and forced to recant his Copernican views. Galileo wrote this letter to the Grand Duchess Christina of Savoy, an important principality in northern Italy. The Savoyard court was well-known as a sponsor of learning and culture, and the Duchess was a generous patron, but a devout Roman Catholic. In this letter Galileo attempts to explain that his theories could be reconciled to Scripture.

I declare (and my sincerity will make itself manifest) not only that I mean to submit myself freely and renounce any errors into which I may fall in this discourse through ignorance of matters pertaining to religion, but that I do not desire in these matters to engage in disputes with anyone, even on points that are disputable. My goal is this alone; that if, among errors that may abound in these considerations of a subject remote from my profession, there is anything that may be serviceable to the holy Church in making a decision concerning the Copernican system, it may be taken and utilized as seems best to the superiors. And if not, let my book be torn and burnt, as I neither intend nor pretend to gain from it any fruit that is not pious and Catholic. And though many of the things I shall reprove have been heard by my own ears, I shall freely grant to those who have spoken them that they never said them, if that is what they wish, and I shall confess myself to have been mistaken. Hence let whatever I reply be addressed not to them, but to whoever may have held such opinions.

The reason produced for condemning the opinion that the earth moves and the sun stands still is that in many places in the Bible one may read that the sun moves and the earth stands still. Since the Bible cannot err, it follows as a necessary consequence that anyone takes an erroneous and heretical position who maintains that the sun is inherently motionless and the earth movable.

With regard to this argument, I think in the first place that it is very pious to say and prudent to affirm that the holy Bible can never speak untruth—whenever its true meaning is understood. But I believe nobody will deny that it is often very abstruse, and may say things which are quite different from what its bare words signify. Hence in expounding the Bible if one were always to confine oneself to the unadorned grammatical meaning, one might fall into error. Not only contradictions and propositions far from true might thus be made to appear in the Bible, but even grave heresies and follies. Thus it would be necessary to assign to God feet, hands, and eyes, as well as corporeal and human affections, such as anger, repentance, hatred, and sometimes even the forgetting of things past and ignorance of those to come. These propositions uttered by the Holy Ghost were set down in that manner by the sacred scribes in order to accommodate them to the capacities of the common people, who are rude and unlearned. For the sake of those who deserve to be separated from the herd, it is necessary that wise expositors should produce the true senses of such passages, together with the special reasons for which they were set down in these words. This doctrine is so widespread and so definite with all theologians that it would be superfluous to adduce evidence for it.

Hence I think that I may reasonably conclude that whenever the Bible has occasion to speak of any physical conclusion (especially those which are very abstruse and hard to understand), the rule has been observed of avoiding confusion in the minds of the common people which would render them contumacious toward the higher mysteries. Now the Bible, merely to condescend to popular capacity, has not hesitated to obscure some very important pronouncements, attributing to God himself some qualities extremely remote from (and even contrary to) His essence. Who then, would positively declare that this principle has been set aside, and the Bible has confined itself rigorously to the bare and restricted sense of its words, when speaking but casually of the earth, of water, of the sun, or of any other created thing? Especially in view of the fact that these things in no way concern the primary purpose of the sacred writings, which is the service of God and the salvation of souls— matters infinitely beyond the comprehension of the common people.

This being granted, I think that in discussions of physical problems we ought to begin not from the authority of scriptural passages, but from sense-experiences and necessary demonstrations; for the holy Bible and the phenomena of nature proceed alike from the divine Word, the former as the dictate of the Holy Ghost and the latter as the observant executrix of God's commands. It is necessary for the Bible, in order to be accommodated to the understanding of every man, to speak many things which appear to differ from the absolute truth so far as the bare meaning of the words is concerned. But Nature, on the other hand, is inexorable and immutable; she never transgresses the laws imposed upon her, or cares a whit whether her abstruse reasons and methods of operation are understandable to men. For that reason it appears that nothing physical which sense-experience sets before our eyes, or which necessary demonstrations prove to us, ought to be called in question (much less condemned) upon the testimony of biblical passages which may have some different meaning beneath their words. For the Bible is not chained in every expression to conditions as strict as those which govern all physical effects; nor is God any less excellently revealed in Nature's actions than in the sacred statements of the Bible. Perhaps this is what Tertullian meant by these words.

"We conclude that God is known first through Nature, and then again, more particularly, by doctrine; by Nature in His works, and by doctrine in His revealed word."

From this I do not mean to infer that we need not have an extraordinary esteem for the passages of holy Scripture. On the contrary, having arrived at any certainties in physics, we ought to utilize these as the most appropriate aids in the true exposition of the Bible and in the investigation of those meanings which are necessarily contained therein, for these must be concordant with demonstrated truths. I should judge that the authority of the Bible was designed to persuade men of those articles and propositions which, surpassing all human reasoning, could not be made credible by science, or by any other means than through the very mouth of the Holy Spirit.

Yet even in those propositions which are not matters of faith, this authority ought to be preferred over that of all human writings which are supported only by bare assertions or probable arguments, and not set forth in a demonstrative way. This I hold to be necessary and proper to the same extent that divine wisdom surpasses all human judgment and conjecture.

But I do not feel obliged to believe that that same God who has endowed us with senses, reason, and intellect has intended to forgo their use and by some other means to give us knowledge which we can attain by them. He would not require us to deny sense and reason in physical matters which are set before our eyes and minds by direct experience or necessary demonstrations. This must be especially true in those sciences of which but the faintest trace (and that consisting of conclusions) is to be found in the Bible. Of astronomy, for instance, so little is

Galileo Galilei (1564–1642).

found that none of the planets except Venus are so much as mentioned, and this only once or twice under the name of "Lucifer." If the sacred scribes had had any intention of teaching people certain arrangements and motions of the heavenly bodies, or had they wished us to derive such knowledge from the Bible, then in my opinion they would not have spoken of these matters so sparingly in comparison with the infinite number of admirable conclusions which are demonstrated in that science. Far from pretending to teach us the constitution and motions of the heavens and the stars, with their shapes, magnitudes, and distances, the authors of the Bible intentionally forbore to speak of these things, though all were quite well known to them. . . .

From these things it follows as a necessary consequence that, since the Holy Ghost did not intend to teach us whether heaven moves or stands still, whether its shape is spherical or like a discus or extended in a plane, nor whether the earth is located at its center or off to one side, then so much the less was it intended to settle for us any other conclusion of the same kind. And the motion or rest of the earth and the sun is so closely linked with the things just named, that without a determination of the one, neither side can be taken in the other matters. Now if the Holy Spirit has purposely neglected to teach us propositions of this sort as irrelevant to the highest goal (that is, to our salvation), how can anyone affirm that it is obligatory to take sides on them, and that one belief is required by faith, while the other side is erroneous? Can an opinion be heretical and yet have no concern with the salvation of souls? Can the Holy Ghost be asserted not to have intended teaching us something that does concern our salvation? I would say here something that was heard from an ecclesiastic of the most eminent degree: "That the intention of the Holy Ghost is to teach us how one goes to heaven, not how heaven goes."

But let us again consider the degree to which necessary demonstrations and sense experiences ought to be respected in physical conclusions, and the authority they have enjoyed at the hands of holy and learned theologians. From among a hundred attestations I have selected the following:

"We must also take heed, in handling the doctrine of Moses, that we altogether avoid saying positively and confidently anything which contradicts manifest experiences and the reasoning of philosophy or the other sciences. For since every truth is in agreement with all other truth, the truth of Holy Writ cannot be contrary to the solid reasons and experiences of human knowledge."

And in St. Augustine we read: "If anyone shall set the authority of Holy Writ against clear and manifest reason, he who does this knows not what he has undertaken; for he opposes to the truth not the meaning of the Bible, which is beyond his comprehension, but rather his own interpretation; not what is in the Bible, but what he has found in himself and imagines to be there."

This granted, and it being true that two truths cannot contradict one another, it is the function of wise expositors to seek out the true senses of scriptural texts. These will unquestionably accord with the physical conclusions which manifest sense and necessary demonstrations have previously made certain to us. Now the Bible, as has been remarked, admits in many places expositions that are remote from the signification of the words for reasons we have already given. Moreover, we are unable to affirm that all interpreters of the Bible speak by divine inspiration, for if that were so there would exist no differences between them about the sense of a given passage. Hence I should think it would be the part of prudence not to permit anyone to usurp scriptural texts and force them in some way to maintain any physical conclusion to be true, when at some future time the senses and demonstrative or necessary reasons may show the contrary. Who indeed will set bounds to human ingenuity? Who will assert that everything in the universe capable of being perceived is already discovered and known? Let us rather confess quite truly that "Those truths which we know are very few in comparison with those which we do not know."

We have it from the very mouth of the Holy Ghost that God delivered up the world to disputations, *so that man cannot find out the work that God hath done from the beginning even to the end.* In my opinion no one, in contradiction to that dictum, should close the road to free philosophizing about mundane and physical things, as if everything had already been discovered and revealed with certainty. Nor should it be considered rash not to be satisfied with those opinions which have become common. No one should be scorned in physical disputes for not holding to the opinions which happen to please other people best, especially concerning problems which have been debated among the greatest philosophers for thousands of years.

QUESTIONS

1. How is scientific argument carried on in Galileo's time? How does it differ from modern scientific debate?

2. How does Galileo answer those who condemned the new science because they claimed that it denied Scripture?

3. Why do people fall into erroneous beliefs about what goes on around them?

4. Galileo was one of the most distinguished practitioners of the scientific method. How is this revealed in the dialogue?

5. How do others react to the discoveries of scientists such as Galileo? Why?

83.   **RENÉ DESCARTES**

DISCOURSE ON METHOD
(1637)

René Descartes (1596–1650) was the son of a French provincial lawyer and judge. He was schooled by the Jesuits and attended university at Poitiers, where he took a degree in canon law. Although his father expected that Descartes would follow in his footsteps, his son decided, instead, to see the world. He enlisted in the military and fought in the Thirty Years' War in Germany. But mostly he continued his mathematical studies and contemplations. One night in an army camp he had a dream of devising a universal intellectual system. He moved to Holland in 1628 and spent most of the rest of his life there, writing and studying. Descartes became an international figure after the publication of his *Discourse on Method*. He died in 1650 while in residence at the Swedish court.

The system Descartes presents in the *Discourse on Method* combines the rigorous principles of reasoning found in mathematics with the central problems of moral philosophy. He propounds the view that all the universe is either matter or mind; this dualist idea tries to reconcile the new science and traditional authorities such as the Church.

Good sense is of all things in the world the most equitably distributed; for everyone thinks himself so amply provided with it, that even those most difficult to please in everything else do not commonly desire more of it than they already have. It is not likely that in this respect we are all of us deceived; it is rather to be taken as testifying that the power of judging well and of distinguishing between the true and the false, which, properly speaking, is what is called good sense, or reason, is by nature equal in all men; and that the diversity of our opinions is not due to some men being endowed with a larger share of reason than others, but solely to this, that our thoughts proceed along different paths, and that we are, therefore, not attending to the same things. For to be possessed of good mental powers is not of itself enough; what is all-important is that we employ them rightly. The greatest minds, capable as they are of the greatest virtues, are also capable of the greatest vices; and those who proceed very slowly may make much greater progress, provided they keep to the straight road, than those who, while they run, digress from it.

For myself, I have never supposed my mind to be in any way more perfect than that of the average man; on the contrary, I have often wished I could think as quickly, image as accurately and distinctly, or remember as fully and readily as some others. Beyond these I know of no other qualities making for the perfection of the mind; for as to reason, or sense, inasmuch as it is that alone which renders us men, and distinguishes us from the brutes, I am disposed to believe that it is complete in each one of us; and in this I am following the common opinion of those philosophers who say that differences of more and less hold in respect only of *accidents,* and not in respect of the *forms,* or natures, of the *individuals* of the same *species.*

Thus my present design is not to teach a method which everyone ought to follow for the right conduct of his reason, but only to show in what manner I have endeavored to conduct my own. Those who undertake to give precepts ought to regard themselves as wiser than those for whom they prescribe; and if they prove to be in the least degree lacking, they have to bear the blame. But in putting forward this piece of writing merely as a history, or, if you prefer so to regard it, as a fable, in which, among some examples worthy of imitation, there will also, perhaps, be found others we should be well advised not to follow, I hope that it will be of use to some without being harmful to anyone, and that all will welcome my plain-speaking. . . .

I came to believe that the four following rules would be found sufficient, always provided I took the firm and unswerving resolve never in a single instance to fail in observing them.

The first was to accept nothing as true which I did not evidently know to be such, that is to say, scrupulously to avoid precipitance and prejudice, and in the judgments I passed to include nothing additional to what had presented itself to my mind so clearly and so distinctly that I could have no occasion for doubting it.

The second, to divide each of the difficulties I examined into as many parts as may be required for its adequate solution.

The third, to arrange my thoughts in order, beginning with things the simplest and easiest to know, so that I may then ascend little by little, as it were step by step, to the knowledge of the more complex, and, in doing so, to assign an order of thought even to those objects which are not of themselves in any such order of precedence.

And the last, in all cases to make enumerations so complete, and reviews so general, that I should be assured of omitting nothing.

I then proceeded to consider, in a general manner, what is requisite to the truth and certainty of a proposition. Having found one—*I think, therefore I am*—which I knew to be true and certain, I thought that I ought also to know in what this certainty consists; and having noted that in this proposition nothing assures me of its truth save only that I see very clearly that in order to think it is necessary to be, I judged that I could take as being a general rule, that the things we apprehend very clearly and distinctly are true—bearing in mind, however, that there is some difficulty in rightly determining which are those we apprehend distinctly.

Reflecting in accordance with this rule on the fact that I doubted, and that consequently my being was not entirely perfect (seeing clearly, as I did, that it is a greater perfection to know than to doubt), I resolved to inquire whence I had learned to think of something more perfect than I myself was; and I saw clearly that it must proceed from some nature that was indeed more perfect. As to the thoughts I had of other things outside me, such as the heavens, the Earth, light, heat and a thousand others, I had not any such difficulty in knowing whence they came. Remarking nothing in them which seemed to render them superior to myself, I could believe that, if they were true, they were dependencies of my nature in so far as my nature had a certain perfection; and that if they were not true, I received them from nothing, that is to say, that they were in me in so far as I was in some respects lacking in perfection. But this latter suggestion could not be made in respect of the idea of a being more perfect than myself, since receiving the idea from nothing is a thing manifestly impossible. And since it is no less contradictory that the more perfect should result from, and depend on, the less perfect than that something should proceed from nothing, it is equally impossible I should receive it from myself. Thus we are committed to the conclusion that it has been placed in me by a nature which is veritably more perfect than I am, and which has indeed within itself all the perfections of which I have any idea, that is to say, in a single word, that is God. And since some perfections other than those I myself possess were known to me, I further concluded that I was not the only being in existence. There must of necessity exist some other more perfect being upon whom I was dependent, and from whom I had received all that I had. For if I alone had existed, independently of all else, in such wise that I had from myself all the perfection, however small in amount, through which I participated in the perfections of Divine Existence, I should have

been able, for the same reason, to have from myself the whole surplus of perfections which I know to be lacking to me, and so could of myself have been infinite, eternal, immutable, omniscient, all-powerful—in short, have been able to possess all the perfections that I could discern as being in God.

Consequently, in order to know the nature of God (in extension of the above reasonings in proof of His existence) so far as my own nature allows of my doing so, I had only to consider in respect of all the things of which I found in myself any idea, whether the possession of them was or was not a perfection; thereby I was at once assured that none of those which showed any imperfection was in Him, and that all the others were—just as I had learned that doubt, inconstancy, sadness and such like, could not be in Him, seeing that I myself should have been very glad to be free from them. In addition to these latter I had ideas of things which are sensible and corporeal. For although I might suppose that I was dreaming, and that all I saw or imaged was false, I yet could not deny that the ideas of them were indeed in my thought. But because I had already very clearly discerned in myself that the intelligent is distinct from the corporeal, and since I had also observed that all composition witnesses to dependence and that dependence is manifestly a defect, I therefore judged that it could not be a perfection in God to be composed of two natures, and that He was not so compounded. At the same time I likewise concluded that if there be in the world any bodies, or even any intelligences or other natures, which are not wholly perfect, their being must depend on His power in such a way that without Him they could not subsist for a single moment.

I then set myself to look for other truths, and having directed my attention to the object dealt with by geometers, which I took to be a continuous body, a space indefinitely extended in length, breadth, height and depth, which allowed of diverse shapes and sizes, and of their being moved or transposed in all sorts of ways (for all this the geometers take as being in the object of their studies), I perused some of their simples demonstrations; and while noting that the great certitude which by common consent is accorded to them is founded solely upon this that they are apprehended as evident, in conformity with the rule above stated, I likewise noted that there is nothing at all in them which assures me of the existence of their object. Taking, for instance, a triangle, while I saw that its three angles must be equal to two right angles, I did not on this account see anything which could assure me that anywhere in the world a triangle existed. On the other hand, on reverting to the examination of the idea of a Perfect Being, I found that existence is comprised in the idea precisely in the way in which it is comprised in the idea of a triangle that its three angles are equal to two right angles, or in that of a sphere that all its parts are equally distant from its center, and indeed even more evidently; and that in consequence it is at least as certain that God, who is this Perfect Being, is or exists, as any demonstration of geometry can possibly be.

The reason why many are persuaded that there is difficulty in knowing this truth, as also in knowing what their soul is, is that they never raise their minds above the things of sense, and that they are so accustomed to consider nothing except what they can image (a mode of thinking restricted to material things), that whatever is not imageable seems to them not intelligible. Even the philosophers in their schools do so, as is sufficiently manifest from their holding as a maxim that there is nothing in the understanding which was not previously in the senses, where, however, it is certain, the ideas of God and of the rational soul have never been. Those who employ their power of imagery to comprehend these ideas behave, as it seems to me, exactly as if in order to hear sounds or smell odors they sought to avail themselves of their eyes—unless, indeed, there is this difference,

that the sense of sight does not afford any less truth than do hearing and smell. In any case, neither our imagination nor our senses can ever assure us of anything whatsoever save so far as our understanding intervenes.

Finally, if there still be men who are not sufficiently persuaded of the existence of God and of their soul by the reasons which I have cited, I would have them know that all the other things which they think to be more assured, as that they have a body and that there are stars and an Earth, and such like things, are less certain. For though the moral assurance we have of these things is such that there is an appearance of extravagance in professing to doubt of their existence, yet none the less when it is a metaphysical certitude that is in question, no one, unless he is devoid of reason, can deny that we do have sufficient ground for not being entirely assured, namely, in the fact that, as we are aware, we can, when asleep, image ourselves as possessed of a different body and as seeing stars and another Earth, without there being any such things. For how do we know that the thoughts which come in dreams are more likely to be false than those we experience when awake? Are not the former no less vivid and detailed than the latter? The ablest minds may treat of this question at whatever length they please, but I do not believe that they will be able to find any reason sufficient to remove this doubt, unless and until they presuppose the existence of God. For, to begin with, even the maxim which a short time ago I adopted as a rule, viz., that the things we recognize very clearly and very distinctly are all true, is reliable only because God is or exists, because He is a Perfect Being, and because all that is in us comes from Him. Thereupon it follows that our ideas or notions, as being of real things, and as coming from God, must in so far as they are clear and distinct be to that extent true. So that, though quite often we have ideas which contain some falsity, this can only be in the case of those in which there is some confusion or obscurity, i.e., owing to their participation, in this respect, in nothingness; or, in other words, that in us they are thus confused because we are not wholly perfect. And it is evident that it is not less repugnant that the falsity or imperfection, in so far as it is such, should proceed from God, than that truth or perfection should proceed from nothing. If, however, we did not know that whatever in us is real and true comes from a Being perfect and infinite, our ideas, however clear and distinct, would yield us no ground of assurance that they had the perfection of being true.

QUESTIONS

1. How is Descartes's philosophy affected by the ideals of new science?

2. What are the four main principles of Descartes's method?

3. What does "I think, therefore I am" mean? How does Descartes prove the truth of this proposition?

4. How does Descartes know that God exists?

5. What sort of God does Descartes describe?

84.   THOMAS MUN

ENGLAND'S TREASURE BY FOREIGN TRADE

(1664)

Thomas Mun (1571–1641) was born into a successful London merchant family. Like many merchants of their day, the Mun family traded in high-value commodities such as spices, dyestuffs, and silks, which were purchased with gold and silver bullion from other traders in markets far removed from Britain. Mun's stepfather was a member of the powerful East India Company, as was one of his elder brothers. Mun appears to have traded for a time in the Mediterranean, but in 1615 he became a director of the East India Company. His first economic writings in the 1620s, when a severe depression in trade raised commodity prices, were a defense of overseas trade in general and of the East India Company in particular. Mun argued that the export of precious metals increased rather than decreased the nation's wealth. He continued to serve the East India Company until his death.

England's Treasure was probably written in 1630 but was not published until 1664. It repeated many of Mun's arguments on the balance of trade and the ways in which a nation slowly increased its wealth. Mun's work was influential for over a century after his death and served as a central reference point for Adam Smith, who regarded it as the classic statement of mercantilist doctrine. *Mercantilism,* the theory that a nation's prosperity depended upon the maintenance of a favorable balance of trade, dominated economic thought for decades. Not until Smith proposed the notion that free, not managed, trade created wealth did these ideas change significantly.

The Qualities which are required in a perfect Merchant of Forraign Trade.

The love and service of our Countrey consisteth not so much in the knowledge of those duties which are to be performed by others, as in the skilful practice of that which is done by our selves; and therefore (my Son) it is now fit that I say something of the Merchant, which I hope in due time shall be thy Vocation: Yet herein are my thoughts free from all Ambition, although I rank thee in a place of so high estimation; for the Merchant is worthily called *The Steward of the Kingdoms Stock,* by way of Commerce with other Nations; a work of no less *Reputation* than *Trust,* which ought to be performed with great skill and conscience, that so the private gain may ever accompany the publique good. And because the nobleness of this Profession may the better stir up thy desires and endeavours to obtain those abilities which may effect it worthily, I will briefly set down the excellent qualities which are required in a perfect Merchant.

1. He ought to be a good Penman, a good Arithmetician, and a good Accomptant, by that noble order of *Debtor* and *Creditor,* which is used onely amongst Merchants; also to be expert in the order and form of *Charter-parties, Bills of Lading, Invoyces, Contracts, Bills of Exchange,* and *Policies of Ensurance.*

2. He ought to know the Measures, Weights, and Monies of all forraign Countries, especially where we have Trade, & the Monies not onely by their several denominations, but also by their intrinsique values in weight & fineness, compared with the Standard of this Kingdom, without which he cannot well direct his affaires.

3. He ought to know the Customs, Tolls, Taxes, Impositions, Conducts and other charges upon all manner of Merchandize exported or imported to and from the said Forraign Countries.

4. He ought to know in what several commodities each Countrey abounds, and what be the wares which they want, and how and from whence they are furnished with the same.

5. He ought to understand, and to be a diligent observer of the rates of Exchanges by Bills, from one State to another, whereby he may the better direct his affairs, and remit over and receive home his Monies to the most advantage possible.

6. He ought to know what goods are prohibited to be exported or imported in the said forraign Countreys, lest otherwise he should incur great danger and loss in the ordering of his affairs.

7. He ought to know upon what rates and conditions to fraight his Ships, and ensure his adventures from one Countrey to another, and to be well acquainted with the laws, orders and customes of the Ensurance office both here and beyond the Seas, in the many accidents which may happen upon the damage or loss of Ships or goods, or both these.

8. He ought to have knowledge in the goodness and in the prices of all the several materials which are required for the building and repairing of Ships, and the divers workmanships of the same, as also for the Masts, Tackling, Cordage, Ordnance, Victuals, Munition, and Provisions of many kinds; together with the ordinary wages of *Commanders, Officers,* and *Mariners,* all which concern the Merchant as he is an Owner of Ships.

9. He ought (by the divers occasions which happen sometimes in the buying and selling of one commodity and sometimes in another) to have indifferent if not perfect knowledge in all manner of Merchandize or wares, which is to be as it were a man of all occupations and trades.

10. He ought by his voyaging on the Seas to become skilful in the Art of Navigation.

11. He ought, as he is a Traveller, and sometimes abiding in forraign Countreys, to attain to the speaking of divers Languages, and to be a diligent observer of the ordinary Revenues and expences of forraign Princes, together with their strength both by Sea and Land, their laws, customes, policies, manners, religions, arts, and the like; to be able to give account thereof in all occasions for the good of his Countrey.

12. Lastly, although there be no necessity that such a Merchant should be a great Scholar; yet is it (at least) required, that in his youth he learn the Latine tongue, which will the better enable him in all the rest of his endeavours.

The means to enrich this Kingdom, and to encrease our Treasure.

Although a Kingdom may be enriched by gifts received, or by purchase taken from some other Nations, yet these are things uncertain and of small consideration when they happen. The ordinary means therefore to increase our wealth and treasure is by *Forraign Trade,* wherein wee must ever observe this rule; to sell more to strangers yearly than wee consume of theirs in value. For suppose that when this Kingdom is plentifully served with the Cloth, Lead, Tinn, Iron, Fish and other native commodities, we doe yearly export the overplus to forraign Countreys to the value of twenty two hundred thousand pounds; by which means we are enabled beyond the Seas to buy and bring in forraign wares for our use and Consumptions, to the value of twenty hundred thousand pounds: By this order duly kept in our trading, we may rest assured that the Kingdom shall be enriched yearly two hundred

thousand pounds, which must be brought to us in so much Treasure; because that part of our stock which is not returned to us in wares must necessarily be brought home in treasure.

The Exportation of our Moneys in Trade of Merchandize is a means to encrease our Treasure.

This Position is so contrary to the common opinion, that it will require many and strong arguments to prove it before it can be accepted of the Multitude, who bitterly exclaim when they see any monies carried out of the Realm; affirming thereupon that wee have absolutely lost so much Treasure, and that this is an act directly against the long continued laws made and confirmed by the wisdom of this Kingdom in the High Court of Parliament, and that many places, nay *Spain* it self which is the Fountain of Mony, forbids the exportation thereof, some cases only excepted.

First, I will take that for granted which no man of judgement will deny, that we have no other means to get Treasure but by forraign trade, for Mines wee have none which do afford it, and how this mony is gotten in the managing of our said Trade I have already shewed, that it is done by making our commodities which are exported yearly to over ballance in value the forraign wares which we consume; so that it resteth only to shew how our moneys may be added to our commodities, and being jointly exported may so much the more encrease our Treasure.

Wee have already supposed our yearly consumptions of forraign wares to be for the value of twenty hundred thousand pounds, and our exportations to exceed that two hundred thousand pounds, which sum wee have thereupon affirmed is brought to us in treasure to ballance the accompt. But now if we add three hundred thousand pounds more in ready mony unto our former exportations in wares, what profit can we have (will some men say) although by this means we should bring in so much ready mony more than wee did before, seeing that wee have carried out the like value.

To this the answer is, that when wee have prepared our exportations of wares, and sent out as much of everything as wee can spare or vent abroad: It is not therefore said that then we should add our money thereunto to fetch in the more mony immediately, but rather first to enlarge our trade by enabling us to bring in more forraign wares, which being sent out again will in due time much encrease our Treasure.

For although in this manner wee do yearly multiply our importations to the maintenance of more Shipping and Mariners, improvement of His Majesties Customs and other benefits: yet our consumption of those forraign wares is no more than it was before; so that all the said encrease of commodities brought in by the means of our ready mony sent out as is afore written, doth in the end become an exportation unto us of a far greater value than our said moneys were.

The answer is (keeping our first ground) that if our consumption of forraign wares be no more yearly than is already supposed, and that our exportations be so mightily encreased by this manner of Trading with ready money, as is before declared: It is not then possible but that all the over ballance or difference should return either in mony or in such wares as we must export again, which, as is already plainly shewed will be still a greater means to encrease our Treasure.

For it is in the stock of the Kingdom as in the estates of private men, who having store of wares, does not therefore say that they will not venture out or trade with their money (for this were ridiculous) but do also turn that into wares, whereby they multiply their Mony, and so by a continual and orderly change of one into the other grow rich, and when they please turn all their estates into Treasure; for they that have Wares cannot want money.

Neither is it said that Mony is the Life of Trade, as if it could not subsist without the same;

for we know that there was great trading by way of commutation or barter when there was little mony stirring in the world. The *Italians* and some other Nations have such remedies against this want, that it can neither decay nor hinder their trade, for they transfer bills of debt, and have Banks both publick and private, wherein they do assign their credits from one to another daily for very great sums with ease and satisfaction by writings only, whilst in the mean time the Mass of Treasure which gave foundation to these credits is employed in Forraign Trade as a Merchandize, and by the said means they have little other use of money in those countreys more than for their ordinary expences. It is not therefore the keeping of our mony in the Kingdom, but the necessity and use of our wares in forraign Countries, and our want of their commodities that causeth the vent and consumption of all sides, which makes a quick and ample Trade. If wee were once poor, and now having gained some store of mony by trade with resolution to keep it still in the Realm; shall this cause other Nations to spend more of our commodities than formerly they have done, whereby we might say that our trade is Quickned and Enlarged? no verily, it will produce no such good effect: but rather according to the alteration of times by their true causes wee may expect the contrary; for all men do consent that plenty of mony in a Kingdom doth make the native commodities dearer, which as it is to the profit of some private men in their revenues, so is it directly against the benefit of the Publique in the quantity of the trade; for as plenty of mony makes wares dearer, so dear wares decline their use and consumption.

There is yet an objection or two as weak as all the rest: that is, if wee trade with our Mony wee shall issue out the less wares; as if a man should say, those Countreys which heretofore had occasion to consume our Cloth, Lead, Tin, Iron, Fish, and the like, shall now make use of our monies in the place of those necessaries, which were most absurd to affirm, or that the

Merchant had not rather carry out wares by which there is ever some gains expected, than to export mony which is still but the same without any encrease.

But on the contrary there are many Countreys which may yield us very profitable trade for our mony, which otherwise afford us no trade at all, because they have no use of our wares, as namely the *East Indies* for one in the first beginning thereof, although since by industry in our commerce with those Nations we have brought them into the use of much of our Lead, Cloth, Tin, and other things, which is a good addition to the former vent of our commodities.

Again, some men have alleged that those Countries which permit money to be carried out, do it because they have few or no wares to trade withall: but wee have great store of commodities, and therefore their action ought not to be our example.

To this the answer is briefly, that if we have such a quantity of wares as doth fully provide us of all things needful from beyond the seas: why should we then doubt that our monys sent out in trade, must not necessarily come back again in treasure; together with the great gains which it may procure in such manner as is before set down? And on the other side, if those Nations which send out their monies do it because they have but few wares of their own, how come they then to have so much Treasure as we ever see in those places which suffer it freely to be exported at all times and by whomsoever? I answer, *Even by trading with their Moneys;* for by what other means can they get it, having no Mines of Gold or Silver?

Thus may we plainly see, that when this weighty business is duly considered in his end, as all our humane actions ought well to be weighed, it is found much contrary to that which most men esteem thereof, because they search no further than the beginning of the work, which misinforms their judgments, and leads them into error: For if we only behold the actions of the husbandman in the seed-time when he casteth away much good corn into the ground, we will rather accompt him a mad man than a husbandman: but when we consider his labours in the harvest which is the end of his endeavours, we find the worth and plentiful encrease of his actions.

QUESTIONS

1. Even beyond the period when Mun wrote, trade was often considered to be a disreputable occupation. What is Mun's view of the importance of the merchant?

2. Mun gives a long list of the qualities of a good merchant. How are they different from what is required to succeed in business today?

3. How does a nation enrich itself?

4. The common economic argument of Mun's time was that exporting gold and silver coin to pay for imports was wrong. Mun disagrees. Why?

5. How does Mun's position as a merchant affect the presentation of his case?

85.   **ADAM SMITH**
_____

THE WEALTH OF NATIONS
(1776)

Adam Smith (1723–90) was the most important representative of the eigh-teenth-century Scottish enlightenment. Although his father was a cus-toms official, the younger Smith trained for a university career from an early age. Having entered Glasgow University in 1737 at a period when it was one of the leading European centers of learning, he studied moral philosophy and was judged so proficient in his subject that fifteen years later he was appointed to the chair of moral philosophy there. His interests turned to law and economics, and he began to formulate the principles that were to underlie his greatest work, *The Wealth of Nations.* Smith subsequently resigned his academic post to travel and lead a quiet life. He died in Edinburgh in 1790.

The Wealth of Nations is one of the classics of Western economic theory. In it, Smith postulates self-interest as the principal motivation of economic activity and demonstrates how a free marketplace enhances economic exchange among self-interested traders. Smith's views remain central to modern capital-ist organization and doctrine.

Of the Natural and Market Price of Commodities

There is in every society or neighbourhood an ordinary or average rate both of wages and profit in every different employment of labour and stock. This rate is naturally regulated, as I shall show hereafter, partly by the general circumstances of the society, their riches or poverty, their advancing, stationary, or declining condition; and partly by the particular nature of each employment.

There is likewise in every society or neigh-bourhood an ordinary or average rate of *rent,* which is regulated too, as I shall show hereafter, partly by the general circumstances of the soci-ety or neighborhood in which the land is situat-ed, and partly by the natural or improved fertili-ty of the land.

These ordinary or average rates may be called the natural rates of wages, profit, and rent, at the time and place in which they com-monly prevail.

When the price of any commodity is neither more nor less than what is sufficient to pay the rent of the land, the wages of the labour, and the profits of the stock employed in raising, prepar-ing, and bringing to market, according to their natural rates, the commodity is then sold for what may be called its natural price.

The commodity is then sold precisely for what it is worth, or for what it really costs the person who brings it to market; for though in common language what is called the prime cost of any com-modity does not comprehend the profit of the person who is to sell it again, yet if he sells it at a price which does not allow him the ordinary rate of profit in his neighbourhood, he is evidently a loser by the trade; since by employing his stock in some other way he might have made that profit. His profit, besides, is his revenue, the proper fund of his subsistence. As, while he is preparing and bringing the goods to market, he advances to his workmen their wages, or their subsistence; so he advances to himself, in the same manner, his own subsistence, which is generally suitable to the profit which he may reasonably expect from the sale of his goods. Unless they yield him this profit, therefore, they do not repay him what they may very properly be said to have really cost him.

Though the price, therefore, which leaves him this profit is not always the lowest at which a dealer may sometimes sell his goods, it is the lowest at which he is likely to sell them for any considerable time; at least where there is perfect liberty, or where he may change his trade as often as he pleases.

The actual price at which any commodity is commonly sold is called its market price. It may either be above, or below, or exactly the same with its natural price.

The market price of every particular commodity is regulated by the proportion between the quantity which is actually brought to market, and the demand of those who are willing to pay the natural price of the commodity, or the whole value of the rent, labour, and profit which must be paid in order to bring it thither. Such people may be called the effectual demanders, and their demand the effectual demand; since it may be sufficient to effectuate the bringing of the commodity to market. It is different from the absolute demand. A very poor man may be said in some sense to have a demand for a coach and six; he might like to have it; but his demand is not an effectual demand, as the commodity can never be brought to market in order to satisfy it.

When the quantity of any commodity which is brought to market falls short of the effectual demand, all those who are willing to pay the whole value of the rent, wages, and profit which must be paid in order to bring it thither, cannot be sup-

plied with the quantity which they want. Rather than want it altogether, some of them will be willing to give more. A competition will immediately begin among them, and the market price will rise more or less above the natural price, according as either the greatness of the deficiency, or the wealth and wanton luxury of the competitors, happen to animate more or less the eagerness of the competition. Among competitors of equal wealth and luxury the same deficiency will generally occasion a more or less eager competition, according as the acquisition of the commodity happens to be of more or less importance to them. Hence the exorbitant price of the necessaries of life during the blockade of a town or in a famine.

When the quantity brought to market exceeds the effectual demand, it cannot be all sold to those who are willing to pay the whole value of the rent, wages, and profit which must be paid in order to bring it thither. Some part must be sold to those who are willing to pay less, and the low price which they give for it must reduce the price of the whole. The market price will sink more or less below the natural price, according as the greatness of the excess increases more or less the competition of the sellers, or according as it happens to be more or less important to them to get immediately rid of the commodity. The same excess in the importation of perishable, will occasion a much greater competition than in that of durable commodities; in the importation of oranges, for example, than in that of old iron.

When the quantity brought to market is just sufficient to supply the effectual demand and no more, the market price naturally comes to be either exactly, or as nearly as can be judged of, the same with the natural price. The whole quantity upon land can be disposed of for this price, and cannot be disposed of for more. The competition of the different dealers obliges them all to accept of this price, but does not oblige them to accept of less.

The quantity of every commodity brought to market naturally suits itself to the effectual demand. It is the interest of all those who employ their land, labour, or stock in bringing any commodity to market, that the quantity never should exceed the effectual demand; and it is the interest of all other people that it never should fall short of that demand.

If at any time it exceeds the effectual demand, some of the component parts of its price must be paid below their natural rate. If it is rent, the interest of the landlords will immediately prompt them to withdraw a part of their land; and if it is wages or profit, the interest of the labourers in the one case, and of their employers in the other, will prompt them to withdraw a part of their labour or stock from this employment. The quantity brought to market will soon be no more than sufficient to supply the effectual demand. All the different parts of its price will rise to their natural rate, and the whole price to its natural price.

If, on the contrary, the quantity brought to market should at any time fall short of the effectual demand, some of the component parts of its price must rise above their natural rate. If it is rent, the interest of all other landlords will naturally prompt them to prepare more land for the raising of this commodity; if it is wages or profit, the interest of all other labourers and dealers will soon prompt them to employ more labour and stock in preparing and bringing it to market. The quantity brought thither will soon be sufficient to supply the effectual demand. All the different parts of its price will soon sink to their natural rate, and the whole price to its natural price.

But in some employments the same quantity of industry will in different years produce very different quantities of commodities; while in others it will produce always the same, or very nearly the same. The same number of labourers in husbandry will, in different years, produce very different quantities of corn, wine, oil, hops, &c. But the same number of spinners and weavers will every year produce the same or very nearly the same quantity of linen and woollen cloth. It is only the average produce of the one species of industry which can be suited in any respect to

the effectual demand; and as its actual produce is frequently much greater and frequently much less than its average produce, the quantity of the commodities brought to market will sometimes exceed a good deal, and sometimes fall short a good deal, of the effectual demand. Even though that demand therefore should continue always the same, their market price will be liable to great fluctuations, will sometimes fall a good deal below, and sometimes rise a good deal above their natural price. In the other species of industry, the produce of equal quantities of labour being always the same or very nearly the same, it can be more exactly suited to the effectual demand. While that demand continues the same, therefore, the market price of the commodities is likely to do so too, and to be either altogether, or as nearly as can be judged of, the same with the natural price. That the price of linen and woollen cloth is liable neither to such frequent nor to such great variations as the price of corn, every man's experience will inform him. The price of the one species of commodities varies only with the variations in the demand: that of the other varies, not only with the variations in the demand, but with the much greater and more frequent variations in the quantity of what is brought to market in order to supply that demand.

But though the market price of every particular commodity is in this manner continually gravitating, if one may say so, towards the natural price, yet sometimes particular accidents, sometimes natural causes, and sometimes particular regulations of policy, may, in many commodities, keep up the market price for a long time together a good deal above the natural price.

When by an increase in the effectual demand the market price of some particular commodity happens to rise a good deal above the natural price, those who employ their stocks in supplying that market are generally careful to conceal this change. If it was commonly known, their great profit would tempt so many new rivals to employ their stocks in the same way, that, the effectual demand being fully supplied, the market price would soon be reduced to the natural price, and perhaps for some time even below it. If the market is at a great distance from the residence of those who supply it, they may sometimes be able to keep the secret for several years together, and may so long enjoy their extraordinary profits without any new rivals. Secrets of this kind, however, it must be acknowledged, can seldom be long kept; and the extraordinary profit can last very little longer than they are kept.

A monopoly granted either to an individual or to a trading company has the same effect as a secret in trade or manufactures. The monopolists, by keeping the market constantly understocked, by never fully supplying the effectual demand, sell their commodities much above the natural price, and raise their emoluments, whether they consist in wages or profit, greatly above their natural rate.

The price of monopoly is upon every occasion the highest which can be got. The natural price, or the price of free competition, on the contrary, is the lowest which can be taken, not upon every occasion, indeed, but for any considerable time together. The one is upon every occasion the highest which can be squeezed out of the buyers, or which, it is supposed, they will consent to give: the other is the lowest which the sellers can commonly afford to take and at the same time continue their business.

The exclusive privileges of corporations, statutes of apprenticeship, and all those laws which restrain in particular employments the competition to a smaller number than might otherwise go into them, have the same tendency, though in a less degree. They are a sort of enlarged monopolies, and may frequently, for ages together, and in whole classes of employments, keep up the market price of particular commodities above the natural price, and maintain both the wages of the labour and the profits of the stock employed about them somewhat above their natural rate.

Such enhancements of the market price may last as long as the regulations of policy which give occasion to them.

The market price of any particular commodity, though it may continue long above, can seldom continue long below its natural price. Whatever part of it was paid below the natural rate, the persons whose interest it affected would immediately feel the loss, and would immediately withdraw either so much land, or so much labour, or so much stock, from being employed about it, that the quantity brought to market would soon be no more than sufficient to supply the effectual demand. Its market price, therefore, would soon rise to the natural price. This at least would be the case where there was perfect liberty.

QUESTIONS

1. What is the difference between what Smith defines as the natural price of an item and its market price?

2. How do supply and demand regulate the market?

3. How might merchants manipulate the price of commodities?

4. What is Smith's view of the regulation of markets? What, according to him, is the impact of such regulation?

5. Smith's work has often been pointed to as a masterful statement of the positive nature of free enterprise. What do you think free enterprise means for Smith?

Enlightened Monarchy

86.	CATHERINE THE GREAT

MEMOIRS

(ca. 1755)

Catherine II, the Great, who ruled from 1762 to 1796, was born in Germany in 1729 and married into the Russian royal family. Her marriage was a total disaster, since her husband neglected both his wife and his princely responsibilities. When he finally inherited the throne in 1762, he was so unpopular that Catherine led a coup against him and had herself proclaimed empress. Catherine was considered an "enlightened despot" who ruled with nearly absolute power, employing the latest philosophical and scientific thinking to improve the lives of her subjects. She is forever linked with Peter the Great (1682–1725) and the transformation of Russia into one of the great European powers.

While Catherine left many important political documents, including a new codification of Russian laws, she wrote a rather remarkable history of her early life as well. It is difficult to establish when her *Memoirs* were begun; they break off abruptly in the 1750s. The *Memoirs* reveal a private side of Catherine and are unusually graphic in their treatment of her childhood and youth.

I was born on April 21st, 1729 (forty-two years ago) at Stettin in Pomerania. I was told later that, a son having been more desired, my arrival as the first-born had given rise to some disappointment. My father, however, showed more satisfaction at the event than all the rest of the entourage. My mother almost died in bringing me into the world and it took her nineteen irksome weeks to recover.

My wet-nurse was the wife of a Prussian soldier; she was only nineteen, gay and pretty. I was placed in the care of a lady who was the widow of a certain Herr von Hohendorf and acted as companion to my mother.

I was told that the lady showed so little sense in her treatment of me that I developed an unaccountable obstinacy. She also showed little sense regarding my mother and was soon dismissed. She was very abrupt and fond of raising her voice; she succeeded so well in her method that I never did as I was told unless the order was repeated at least three times and very loudly.

My father, whom I saw very seldom, considered me to be an angel, my mother did not bother much about me. She had had, eighteen months after my birth, a son whom she passionately loved, whereas I was merely tolerated and often repulsed with violence and temper, not always with justice. I was aware of all this, but not always able to understand what I really felt about it.

At the age of seven I was suddenly seized with a violent cough. It was the custom that we should kneel every night and every morning to say our prayers. One night as I knelt and prayed I began to cough so violently that the strain caused me to fall on my left side, and I had such sharp pains in my chest that they almost took my breath away.

Finally, after much suffering, I was well enough to get up and it was discovered, as they started to put on my clothes, that I had in the meantime assumed the shape of the letter Z; my right shoulder was much higher than the left, the backbone running in a zigzag and the left side falling in. The women who attended me, also my mother's women, whom they consulted, decided to break the news to my father and my mother. The first step undertaken was to swear everybody to secrecy concerning my condition. My parents were distressed to see one of their children lame, the other cripple. Finally after consulting several experts in strict confidence, it was decided to summon a specialist in matters of dislocation.

They searched for one in vain; they were loath to ask the only man who knew anything about it, as he was the local hangman. For a long time they hesitated. Finally, under a pledge of great secrecy, he was called in. This man, after examining me, ordered that every morning at six, a girl should come to me on an empty stomach and rub my shoulder and backbone with her saliva. Then he proceeded to fabricate a sort of frame, which I never removed day or night except when changing my underclothes, and every other day he came to examine me in the morning. Besides this he made me wear a large black ribbon which went under the neck, crossed the right shoulder round the right arm, and was fastened at the back. I do not know whether it was because of all these remedies or that I was not meant to become a cripple, but after eighteen months I began to show signs of straightening out. I was ten or eleven when I was at last allowed to discard this more cumbersome framework.

At the age of seven all my dolls and other toys were taken away, and I was told that I was now a big girl and therefore it was no longer suitable that I should have them. I had never liked dolls, and found a way of making a plaything out of anything, my hands, a handkerchief, all served that purpose. The trend of my life went on as before and this deprivation of toys must have been a mere question of etiquette, as no one interfered with me in my games.

I began to grow taller and the extreme ugliness with which I was afflicted was beginning to disappear when I went to visit the future King of Sweden, my uncle, then Bishop of Lübeck.

I do not know if I was actually ugly as a child, but I know that I was so often told that I was and that because of this I should try to acquire wit and other merits that until the age of fourteen or fifteen I was convinced that I was a regular ugly duckling and tried much more to acquire these other virtues than rely upon my face. It is true that I have seen a portrait of myself painted when I was ten, excessively ugly—if it was a good likeness, then I was not being deceived.

The Grand Duke had shown some interest in me during my illness and continued to do so after I recovered. While he seemed to like me, I cannot say that I either liked or disliked him. I was taught to obey and it was my mother's business to see about my marriage, but to tell the truth I believe that the Crown of Russia attracted me more than his person. He was sixteen, quite good-looking before the pox, but small and infantile, talking of nothing but soldiers and toys. I listened politely and often yawned, but did not interrupt him and as he thought that he had to speak to me and referred only to the things which amused him, he enjoyed talking to me for long periods of time. Many people took this for affection, especially those who desired our marriage, but in fact we never used the language of tenderness. It was not for me to begin, for modesty and pride would have prevented me from doing so even if I had had any tender feelings for him; as for him, he had never even thought of it, which did not greatly incline me in his favour. Young girls may be as well brought up as you could wish, but they like sweet nonsense, especially from those whom they can hear it without blushing.

The next day, St. Peter's Day, when my betrothal was to be celebrated, the Empress's portrait framed in diamonds was brought to me early in the morning, and shortly afterwards the portrait of the Grand Duke, also encircled with diamonds. Soon after, he came to take me to the Empress who, wearing her crown and Imperial mantle, proceeded on her way under a canopy of massive silver, carried by eight major-generals and followed by the Grand Duke and myself. After me came my mother, the Princess of Homburg, and the other ladies according to their rank.

Towards St. Peter's Day the whole Court returned from Peterhof to town. I remember that on the eve of that feast I suddenly had the fancy to have all my ladies and maids sleeping in my room. For that purpose I had my mattress as well as theirs stretched out on the floor and that is how we spent the night, but before we went to sleep we had a prolonged discussion on the difference between the sexes.

I am certain that most of us were extremely innocent; for myself I can testify that though I was more than sixteen years old, I had no idea what this difference was; I went so far as to promise my women to question my mother the next morning about; they agreed that I should do so and we went to sleep. Next day I put the question to my mother and was severely scolded.

At last all the preparations for my wedding were almost completed and the day was fixed for August 21st of this year 1745. In vain did the doctors point out to the Empress that the delicate Grand Duke, who had only just recovered from a severe illness, had not yet reached puberty and that it would be wise to wait another few years.

The nearer my wedding-day approached, the more despondent did I become, and often found myself crying without quite knowing why; I tried to conceal my tears as much as I could, but my

women, who were constantly with me, could not help noticing my distress and tried to divert me. On the eve of the 21st we moved from the Summer to the Winter Palace. Until then I had lived in the stone building in the Summer Place which gives on to the Fontanka behind the pavilion of Peter I. In the evening my mother came to my rooms. We had a long and friendly talk, she exhorted me concerning my future duties, we cried a little together and parted very tenderly.

On the day of the ceremony I rose at 6 a.m. At eight the Empress ordered me to her apartments where I was to be dressed. I found a dressing-table prepared in her State bedroom and her Court ladies were already there. First came the hair-dressing and my valet was busy curling my forelock when the Empress came in. I rose to kiss her hand; as soon as she had embraced me, she began to scold my valet and forbade him to curl my fringe.

She wanted my hair to be flat in front because the jewels would not stay on my head if the forelock was curled. Having said this, she left the room. My man, who was obdurate, would not give up his curled forelock. He persuaded Countess Rumiantsev who herself affected curly hair and did not care for smooth dressing, to speak to the Empress in favour of the forelock. After the Countess had gone three or four journeys between the Empress and my valet, while I remained an impartial spectator of what was going on, the Empress sent word, not without anger, that he could do as he wished.

When my hair was dressed, the Empress came to place the Grand Ducal crown on my head and told me I could wear as many jewels as I wanted, both hers and mine. She left the room and the Court ladies continued dressing me in my mother's presence. My dress was of a silver moiré, embroidered in silver on all the hems, and of a terrible weight.

I would have been ready to like my new husband had he been capable of affection or willing to show any. But in the very first days of our marriage I came to a sad conclusion about him. I said to myself: 'If you allow yourself to love that man, you will be the unhappiest creature on this earth; with your temperament you will expect some response whereas this man scarcely looks at you, talks of nothing but dolls or such things, and pays more attention to any other woman than yourself; you are too proud to complain, therefore, attention, please, and keep on a leash any affection you might feel for this gentleman; you have yourself to think about, my dear girl.' This first scar made upon my impressionable heart remained with me for ever; never did this firm resolution leave my noddle, but I took good care not to tell anybody that I had

resolved never to love without restraint a man who would not return this love in full; such was my disposition that my heart would have belonged entirely and without reserve to a husband who loved only me and who would not have subjected me to taunts as this one did.

I have always considered jealousy, suspicion, mistrust, and all that follows them as the greatest misery, and maintained that it depended on the husband whether his wife loved him; if a woman has a kind heart and gentle disposition, a husband's courtesy and good nature would soon win her.

QUESTIONS

1. If Catherine's case may be taken as typical, what was childhood like for a member of a royal family in the eighteenth century?

2. Why did Catherine marry the heir to the Russian throne? What was her relationship with her husband like?

3. A memoir tells the story of an individual's life, but an author is always in a position to shape the story. How might Catherine have used her own memoir to justify her later coup against her husband?

4. Royal marriages were acts of state, not private affairs. Did Catherine appear to realize this when she married?

5. What sort of impression does Catherine's memoir make upon you? What sort of a person do you think the Empress was?

---

87.   **MARIA THERESA**

TESTAMENT

(1749–1750)

Maria Theresa (1717–80) was one of the most capable of all of the Habsburgs who ruled the Holy Roman Empire. After the death of Maria's only brother, her father, Emperor Charles VI, promulgated the Pragmatic Sanction, which allowed a woman to rule the empire (though not to take the title emperor). Maria Theresa came into this inheritance at the age of 23 and was immediately embroiled in warfare that aimed at dismembering her territories. She confounded the sages of Europe by rallying her people and repelling a Prussian invasion.

Her *Testament* details the reforms she initiated in her states. It is written mostly as an apologetic history, assessing praise and blame and casting her own actions in the best possible light, but it also shows flashes of her dynamic personality and shrewd political abilities.

Instructions drawn up out of motherly solicitude for the especial benefit of my posterity. I have thought well to divide these in sections according to their importance.

The first describes the situation of the Monarchy, both internal and international, as I found it when I began my reign.

The second, the abuses which gradually crept into the said Monarchy under my predecessors.

The third, the measures introduced during the nine difficult years of the recent war, and the reasons which induced me to take them.

The fourth, the changes effected after the conclusion of general peace in the internal constitution of the Ministries and the Provinces, in accordance with the system established for the preservation of the Monarchy.

The fifth, the benefit that will accrue to my posterity from this reorganization, this being the only means of consolidating the Monarchy and preserving it for my posterity.

The sixth, the necessity of maintaining the institutions so established, to avert ruin, and what maxims my successors must follow to achieve this end.

From the outset I decided and made it my principle, for my own inner guidance, to apply myself, with a pure mind and instant prayer to God, to put aside all secondary considerations, arrogance, ambition, or other passions, having on many occasions examined myself in respect of these things, and to undertake the business of government incumbent on me quietly and resolutely—a principle that has, indeed, been the one guidance which saved me, with God's help, in my great need, and made me follow the resolutions taken by me, making it ever my chief maxim in all I did and left undone to trust only in God, Whose almighty hand singled me out for this position without move or desire of my own and Who would therefore also make me worthy through my conduct, principles, and intentions to fulfill properly the tasks laid on me, and thus to call down and preserve His almighty protection for myself and those He has set under me, which truth I had held daily before my eyes and maturely considered that my duty was not to myself personally but only to the public.

After I had each time well tested my intentions by this principle, I afterwards undertook each enterprise with great determination and strong resolution, and was consequently tranquil in my spirit in the greatest extremity as though the issue did not affect me personally at all; and with the same tranquillity and pleasure, had Divine Providence so disposed, I would instantly have laid down the whole government and left it to the enemies who so beset me, had I believed that in so doing I would be doing my duty or promoting the best welfare of my lands, which two points have always been my chief maxims. And dearly as I love my family and children, so that I spare no effort, trouble, care, or labor for their sakes, yet I would always have put the general welfare of my dominions above them had I been convinced in my conscience that I should do this or that their welfare demanded it, seeing that I am the general and first mother of the said dominions.

I found myself in this situation, without money, without credit, without army, without experience and knowledge of my own and finally, also without any counsel, because each one of them at first wanted to wait and see what way things would develop.

In the first, difficult years of my reign it was quite impossible for me personally to investigate the conditions and resources of the Provinces, so that I was obliged to follow my Ministers' advice not to ask any more help from the Provinces, either in money or men, especially since the Ministers constantly pretended that any such demands would make my reign deeply detested at its very outset. Consequently, there was no money to mobilize the few regiments earmarked for use against Prussia. And when I found myself forced to ask for this purpose for some hundreds of thousands as loans or urgent grants in aid from private persons, I could not but see that the big men, and even the Ministers themselves, were plainly trying to spare their own pockets.

I have described the defects and abuses of the Constitution then in effect, and felt myself the more compelled to abolish it, because Divine Providence had shown me clearly that the measures essential for the preservation of the Monarchy could not be combined with these old institutions, nor put into effect while they existed.

Each one of my Ministers readily agreed that if the Crown and scepter were to be preserved, it was most necessary to keep a standing force of over 100,000 men, and consequently indispensable to bring a new system and order into the extreme confusion into which the finances had fallen.

To this end, I instructed the Ministers to put their views to me in writing, and to work out such a system as speedily as possible. When, however, no constructive idea emerged, my repeated reminders notwithstanding, and when I saw that the Ministers were more inclined to spread themselves in controversy and argument than genuinely to take the problem in hand—urgent

Maria Theresa and her family. Eleven of Maria Theresa's 16 children are posed with the empress and her husband, Francis of Lorraine. Standing next to his mother is the future emperor Joseph II.

as it was—that the work dragged on and on, and that no one was willing, or able, to attack the problem seriously, then, however, by the especial intervention and Providence of God, and to the salvation of these lands, I became acquainted with Count Haugwitz.

He was truly sent to me by Providence, for to break the deadlock I needed such a man, honorable, disinterested, without predispositions, and with neither ambition nor hangers-on, who supported what was good because he saw it to be good, of magnanimous disinterestedness and attachment to his Monarch, unprejudiced, with great capacity and industry and untiring diligence, not afraid to come into the open or to draw on himself the unjust hatred of interested parties.

Difficulties came with the three Inner Austrian Provinces. All the Austrian Provinces, but particularly these three, had managed their affairs in so irresponsible and unbusinesslike a fashion that the Court—that is, the Chancelleries of the day—had allowed them to accumulate a so-called domestic debt of twenty-four million, the interest on which amounted to 200,000 gulden. It was the financial weakness of these lands that involved them in this big debt, and was also the reason why the quotas allocated to them were regarded in advance as impossibly high, and in certain cases could really be regarded as such.

The Estates' persistent representations that the burdens were too heavy for them, which were not without their force, although the fault lay in their own unbusinesslike methods, naturally led me to make provision for a better and more equitable management of the local finances. And I must insist that it is generally true that the prime cause of the decay of my Hereditary Lands lies in the overgreat freedom the Estates had gradually usurped; for the Estates seldom behaved justly, their Presidents usually simply doing as their predecessors had done and furthering their private advantages, while refusing or rejecting any help that justice demanded should be given to the poor oppressed classes, and thus as a rule letting one Estate oppress another.

The final purpose of most of the so-called prerogatives of the Estates was simply to secure an arbitrary free hand for some of their members, who claimed an inordinate authority over the rest.

It was formerly the easier for all this to go on because the said overpowerful members of the Estates, who usually made common cause with the Ministers in charge of the Provinces, generally had in their hands the fortunes, both of the Crown and of the Estates themselves, and thus disposed of them according to their pleasure, for which very reason the Ministers here in Vienna gave every support to the prerogatives which brought them so much advantage.

And although the result was only detriment to the public interest, yet the Estates insisted on these prerogatives the more stubbornly because most of them failed to understand the position and easily allowed themselves to be hoodwinked by these their own representatives.

Neither do I myself wish, nor do I advise my successors, to encroach on the useful and legitimate privileges of the Estates, seeing that the welfare of my dominions is inexpressibly dear to me, and I cannot repeat often enough that if I had found their privileges so clear, or if they had conducted the administration more justly than I or the Crown, I should not merely not have hesitated to submit and abrogate my authority entirely to them, I should rather myself have diminished and renounced or limited it for my successors, because I should always have placed the welfare and prosperity of the Provinces before my own or that of my family and children.

But neither my own interest nor that of my successors, and least of all the public interest, can be sacrificed to illegitimate abuses which have taken root with the connivance of the Ministers; wherefore such alleged privileges as are founded on abuse and an evil tradition should not be confirmed without extreme caution and careful consideration, and I have often observed that Crown rights which have fallen into desuetude through the connivance of the Ministers are questioned with the object of tying the Monarch's hands in these respects also; this applies above all to the supervision of the Estates' domestic funds and the management of them, and also to the equalization and adjustment of taxation, which should be conscientiously undertaken in the interest of justice and of the general welfare.

In order to put all this on a firm and lasting foundation, I found myself forced to depart from the old, traditional Constitution, with the detrimental qualities which it had acquired, and to enact such new measures as could be harmonized with the new system.

QUESTIONS

1. How does Maria Theresa's *Testament* differ in style and content from Catherine the Great's *Memoirs?*

2. What problems did Maria Theresa face when she came to the throne?

3. Maria Theresa was one of the so-called enlightened despots of the eighteenth century. How do enlightenment and despotism manifest themselves in her *Testament?*

4. What stood in the way of reform in Maria Theresa's Austria?

5. Maria Theresa approaches her task with a set of political assumptions common among European rulers of the early modern period. What are these assumptions, and how are they reflected in her *Testament?*

88. VISCOUNT BOLINGBROKE

THE IDEA OF A PATRIOT KING

(1749)

Henry St. John, Viscount Bolingbroke (1678–1751), was the son of a prominent English gentleman. His social position and talents marked him for advancement in politics, and he entered Parliament before the age of twenty-five. Queen Anne appointed him secretary of war in 1706, in which capacity he became one of England's most important political figures. After a brief spell out of office, Bolingbroke returned as secretary of state in 1710. Bolingbroke opposed the Hanoverian succession and was dismissed from office and impeached by the government of George I. He fled to France in 1715 and devoted himself to pleasure and writing. He was as famous for his extravagant lifestyle as he was for his books. He was welcomed back to England in 1723 and became a foe of Sir Robert Walpole and the Whigs.

The Idea of a Patriot King, written in 1738 and published 11 years later, was addressed to George II's eldest son, Prince Frederick; but in fact its greatest influence was upon George III and his chief minister, the Earl of Bute. Bolingbroke argued against the rule of parties, urging the patriot king to put the national interest ahead of all others.

Now we are subject, by the constitution of human nature, and therefore by the will of the Author of this and every other nature, to two laws. One given immediately to all men by God, the same to all, and obligatory alike on all. The other given to man by man; and therefore not the same to all, nor obligatory alike on all: founded indeed on the same principles, but varied by different applications of them to times, to characters, and to a number which may be reckoned infinite, of other circumstances. By the first you see, that I mean the universal law of reason; and by the second the particular law, or constitution of laws, by which every distinct community has chosen to be governed.

The obligation of submission to both, is discoverable by so clear and so simple a use of our intellectual faculties, that it may be said properly enough to be *revealed to us by God;* and though *both* these laws cannot be said properly to be given by Him, yet our obligation to submit to the *civil* law is a principal paragraph in the *natural* law, which he has most manifestly given us. In truth we can no more doubt of the obligations of both these laws, than of the existence of the lawgiver. As supreme lord over all his works, his *general* providence regards immediately the *great commonwealth* of mankind; but then, as supreme Lord likewise, his authority gives a sanction to the *particular bodies* of law which are made under it. The law of *nature* is the law of *all* his subjects: the constitutions of *particular* governments are like the *bylaws* of cities, or the appropriated customs of provinces. It follows, therefore, that he who breaks the *laws of his country* resists the *ordinance of God,* that is, the law of his nature. God has instituted neither monarchy, nor aristocracy, nor democracy, nor mixed government: but though God has instituted no particular form of government among men, yet by the general laws of his kingdom, he exacts our obedience to the laws of those communities to which each of us is attached by birth, or to which we may be attached by a subsequent and lawful engagement.

From such plain, unrefined, and therefore I suppose true reasoning, the *just authority* of

kings, and the *due obedience* of *subjects,* may be deduced with the utmost certainty. And surely it is far better for kings themselves to have their authority thus founded on principles incontestible, and on fair deductions from them, than on the chimeras of madmen, or, what has been more common, the sophisms of knaves. A *human right,* that cannot be controverted, is preferable surely to a *pretended divine right,* which every man must believe implicitly, as few will do, or not believe at all.

But the principles we have laid down do not stop here. A divine right in kings is to be deduced evidently from them. A divine right to govern *well,* and conformably to the constitution at the head of which they are placed. A divine right to govern *ill,* is an absurdity: to assert it is blasphemy. A people may choose, or hereditary succession may raise, a *bad* prince to the throne; but a *good* king alone can derive his right to govern from *God.* The reason is plain: good government alone can be in the divine intention. God has made us to desire happiness; he has made our happiness dependent on society; and the happiness of society dependent on good or bad government. His intention therefore was, that government should be *good.*

This is essential to his wisdom; for wisdom consists surely in proportioning means to ends: therefore it cannot be said without absurd impiety, that he confers a right to oppose his intention.

The office of kings is then of *right divine,* and their persons are to be reputed *sacred.* As *men,* they have no such *right,* no such sacredness belonging to them: as *kings* they have both, unless they forfeit them. Reverence for government obliges to reverence governors, who, for the sake of it, are raised above the level of other men: but reverence for governors, independently of government, any further than reverence would be due to their virtues if they were private men, is preposterous, and repugnant to common sense. The spring from which this legal reverence, for so I may call it, arises, is *national,* not *personal.*

All this is as true of *elective,* as it is of *hereditary* monarchs; though the scriblers for tyranny, under the name of monarchy, would have us believe that there is something more august, and more sacred in one than the other. They are sacred *alike,* and this attribute is to be ascribed, or not ascribed to them, as they answer, or do not answer, the *Ends* of their institution. But there is another comparison to be made, in which a great and most important dissimilitude will be found between hereditary and elective monarchy. Nothing can be more absurd, in pure *speculation,* than an hereditary right in any mortal to govern other men: and yet, in *practice,* nothing can be more absurd than to have a king to choose at every vacancy of a throne. We draw at a *lottery* indeed in one case, where there are many chances to lose, and few to gain. But have we much more advantage of this kind in the other? I think not.

To conclude this head therefore, I think a *limited monarchy* the best of governments, so I think an *hereditary monarchy* the best of monarchies. I said a *limited monarchy;* for an *unlimited monarchy,* wherein arbitrary will, which is in truth no rule, is however the sole rule, or stands instead of all rule of government, is so great an absurdity, indefeasible right to *any part;* and really have such a right to *that part* which they have reserved to themselves. In fine, the *constitution* will be reverenced by him as the *law of God* and of *man;* the *force* of which binds the king as *much* as the meanest subject, and the *reason* of which binds him *much more.*

QUESTIONS

1. What is the duty of a subject to his government?

2. How does Bolingbroke modify the old idea of divine right monarchy?

3. What is the importance of liberty in a state, according to Bolingbroke?

4. What is a patriot king?

5. Bolingbroke wrote after long experience in the service of a constitutional monarchy, in which power was shared by the king and parliament, and was contested between political parties. How might this experience have affected the assumptions the author made about the workings of the constitution?

The Enlightenment

89.	**VOLTAIRE**

CANDIDE

(1759)

François-Marie Arouet, called Voltaire (1694–1778), was the son of a middle-class Parisian family. His wit sharpened by a Jesuit education, Voltaire abandoned the study of law and became a writer of plays and poetry, most with classical themes. He ran into trouble when he turned a critical eye on the French government and the Roman Catholic Church. After a short imprisonment in the Bastille for his opinions, he was forced into exile in England, where he came to admire the English Constitution. He returned to France, where his growing reputation as an enlightened thinker resulted in a wide correspondence with European monarchs and intellectuals. He was patronized by Catherine the Great of Russia and lived briefly at the Prussian court. Eventually settling in Switzerland with his mistress, he spent his later years writing works on religion, science, and culture.

Candide is Voltaire's most famous work, said to have been written over a weekend. It was enormously popular and went through 13 editions in its first year in print. The fictional story of the travels of a naive youth, *Candide* satirizes philosophical optimism and takes on religious bigotry and tyranny. It was condemned by both Catholic and Protestant religious authorities.

1. How Candide Was Brought Up in a Fine Castle, and How He Was Expelled Therefrom

In Westphalia, in the castle of My Lord the Baron of Thunder-ten-tronckh, there was a young man whom nature had endowed with the gentlest of characters. His face bespoke his soul. His judgment was rather sound and his mind of the simplest; this is the reason, I think, why he was named Candide. The old servants of the house suspected that he was the son of My Lord the Baron's sister and of a good and honorable gentleman of the neighborhood whom the lady never would marry because he could prove only seventy-one quarterings and the rest of his genealogical tree had been lost by the injuries of time.

My Lord the Baron was one of the most powerful lords in Westphalia, for his castle had a door and windows. His great hall was even adorned with a piece of tapestry. All the dogs of his stable yards formed a pack of hounds when necessary; his grooms were his huntsmen; the village vicar was his Grand Almoner. They all called him My Lord, and they laughed at the stories he told.

My Lady the Baroness, who weighed about three hundred and fifty pounds, attracted very great consideration by that fact, and did the honors of the house with a dignity that made her even more respectable. Her daughter Cunégonde, aged seventeen, was rosy-complexioned, fresh, plump, appetizing. The Baron's son appeared in all respects worthy of his father. The tutor Pangloss was the oracle of the house, and little Candide listened to his lessons with all the candor of his age and character.

Pangloss taught metaphysico-theologo-cosmolo-nigology. He proved admirably that there is no effect without a cause and that, in this best of all possible worlds, My Lord the Baron's castle was the finest of castles, and My Lady the best of all possible Baronesses.

"It is demonstrated," he said, "that things cannot be otherwise, for, everything being made for an end, everything is necessarily for the best end. Note that noses were made to wear spectacles, and so we have spectacles. Legs were visibly instituted to be breeched, and we have breeches. Stones were formed to be cut and to make into castles; so My Lord has a very handsome castle; the greatest baron in the province should be the best housed; and, pigs being made to be eaten, we eat pork all year round: consequently, those who have asserted that all is well have said a foolish thing; they should have said that all is for the best."

Candide listened attentively and believed innocently; for he thought Mademoiselle Cunégonde extremely beautiful, though he never made bold to tell her so. He concluded that after the happiness of being born Baron of Thunder-ten-tronckh, the second degree of happiness was to be Mademoiselle Cunégonde; the third, to see her every day; and the fourth, to listen to Doctor Pangloss, the greatest philosopher in the province and consequently in the whole world.

One day Cunégonde, walking near the castle in the little wood they called The Park, saw in the bushes Doctor Pangloss giving a lesson in experimental physics to her mother's chambermaid, a very pretty and very docile little brunette. Since Mademoiselle Cunégonde had much inclination for the science, she observed breathlessly the repeated experiments of which she was a witness; she clearly saw the Doctor's

sufficient reason, the effects and the causes, and returned home all agitated, all pensive, all filled with the desire to be learned, thinking that she might well be the sufficient reason of young Candide, who might equally well be hers.

She met Candide on the way back to the castle, and blushed; Candide blushed too; she said good morning to him in a faltering voice; and Candide spoke to her without knowing what he was saying. The next day, after dinner, as everyone was leaving the table, Cunégonde and Candide found themselves behind a screen; Cunégonde dropped her handkerchief, Candide picked it up, she innocently took his hand, the young man innocently kissed the young lady's hand with a very special vivacity, sensibility, and grace; their lips met, their eyes glowed, their knees trembled, their hands wandered. My Lord the Baron of Thunder-ten-tronckh passed near the screen and, seeing this cause and this effect, expelled Candide from the castle with great kicks in the behind; Cunégonde swooned; she was slapped in the face by My Lady the Baroness as soon as she had come to herself; and all was in consternation in the finest and most agreeable of all possible castles. . . .

29. How Candide Found Cunégonde and the Old Woman Again

While Candide, the Baron, Pangloss, Martin, and Cacambo were relating their adventures, reasoning on the contingent or noncontingent events of this universe, arguing about effects and causes, moral and physical evil, free will and necessity, and the consolations that may be experienced when one is in the galleys in Turkey, they landed on the shore of Propontis at the house of the prince of Transylvania. The first objects that met their eyes were Cunégonde and the old woman, who were spreading out towels on lines to dry.

The Baron paled at this sight. The tender lover Candide, on seeing his fair Cunégonde dark-skinned, eyes bloodshot, flat-bosomed, cheeks wrinkled, arms red and rough, recoiled three steps in horror, and then advanced out of good manners. She embraced Candide and her brother; they embraced the old woman; Candide ransomed them both.

There was a little farm in the neighborhood; the old woman proposed to Candide that he buy it while waiting for the entire group to enjoy a better destiny. Cunégonde did not know that she had grown ugly, no one had told her so; she reminded Candide of his promises in so positive a tone that the good Candide did not refuse her. So he notified the Baron that he was going to marry his sister.

"I shall never endure," said the Baron, "such baseness on her part and such insolence on yours; no one shall ever reproach me with that infamy; my sister's children would not be able to enter the chapters* of Germany. No, never shall my sister marry anyone but a baron of the Empire."

Cunégonde threw herself at his feet and bathed them with tears; he was inflexible.

"You maddest of madmen," said Candide, "I rescued you from the galleys, I paid your ransom, I paid your sister's too; she was washing dishes here, she is ugly, I am kind enough to make her my wife, and you still presume to oppose it; I would kill you again if I heeded my anger."

"You may kill me again," said the Baron, "but you shall not marry my sister while I am alive."

30. Conclusion

At the bottom of his heart, Candide had no desire to marry Cunégonde. But the Baron's extreme impertinence determined him to clinch the marriage, and Cunégonde urged him on so eagerly that he could not retract. He consulted Pangloss, Martin, and the faithful Cacambo. Pangloss composed a fine memoir by which he proved that the Baron had no rights over his sister, and that according to all the laws of the Empire she could make a left-handed marriage** with Candide. Martin's judgement

*Knightly assemblies.

**A morganatic marriage, giving no equality to the party of lower rank.

was to throw the Baron in the sea; Cacambo decided that he should be returned to the Levantine captain and put back in the galleys, after which he would be sent by the first ship to the Father General in Rome. The plan was considered very good; the old woman approved it; they said nothing about it to his sister; for a little money the thing was carried out, and they had the pleasure of trapping a Jesuit and punishing the pride of a German Baron.

It was quite natural to imagine that after so many disasters Candide, married to his mistress and living with the philosopher Pangloss, the philosopher Martin, the prudent Cacambo, and the old woman, moreover having brought back so many diamonds from the land of the ancient Incas, would lead the most pleasant life in the world. But he was so cheated that he had nothing left but his little farm; his wife, becoming uglier every day, became shrewish and intolerable; the old woman was an invalid and was even more bad-humored than Cunégonde. Cacambo, who worked in the garden and who went and sold vegetables at Constantinople, was worn out with work and cursed his destiny. Pangloss was in despair at not shining in some university in Germany. As for Martin, he was firmly persuaded that a man is equally badly off anywhere; he took things patiently.

In the neighborhood there was a very famous dervish who was considered the best philosopher in Turkey; they went to consult him; Pangloss was the spokesman and said to him: "Master, we have come to ask you to tell us why such a strange animal as man was ever created."

"What are you meddling in?" said the dervish. "Is that your business?"

"But, Reverend Father," said Candide, "there is a horrible amount of evil on earth."

"What does it matter," said the dervish, "whether there is evil or good? When His Highness sends a ship to Egypt, is he bothered about whether the mice in the ship are comfortable or not?"

"Then what should we do?" said Pangloss.

"Hold your tongue," said the dervish.

"I flattered myself," said Pangloss, "that you and I would reason a bit together about effects and causes, the best of all possible worlds, the origin of evil, the nature of the soul, and pre-established harmony." At these words the dervish shut the door in their faces.

During this conversation the news had gone round that in Constantinople they had just strangled two viziers of the Divan and the mufti and impaled several of their friends. This catastrophe caused a great stir everywhere for a few hours. Pangloss, Candide, and Martin, returning to the little farm, came upon a good old man enjoying the fresh air by his door under a bower of orange trees. Pangloss, whose curiosity was as great as his love of reasoning, asked him the name of the mufti who had just been strangled.

"I know nothing about it," replied the good man, "and I have never known the name of any mufti or any vizier. I am entirely ignorant of the adventure that you are telling me about; I presume that in general those who meddle with public affairs sometimes perish miserably, and that they deserve it; but I never inquire what is going on in Constantinople; I content myself with sending there for sale the fruits of the garden that I cultivate."

Having said these words, he had the strangers come into his house; his two daughters and his two sons presented them with several kinds of sherbets which they made themselves, Turkish cream flavored with candied citron peel, oranges, lemons, limes, pineapples, pistachios, and Mocha coffee that had not been mixed with the bad coffee from Batavia and the West Indies. After which the two daughters of this good Moslem perfumed the beards of Candide, Pangloss, and Martin.

"You must have a vast and magnificent estate?" said Candide to the Turk.

"I have only twenty acres," replied the Turk; "I cultivate them with my children; work keeps away three great evils: boredom, vice, and need."

As Candide went back to this farm, he reflected deeply on the Turk's remarks. He said to Pangloss and Martin: "That good old man seems to me to have made himself a life far preferable to that of the six Kings with whom we had the honor of having supper."

"Great eminence," said Pangloss, "is very dangerous, according to the report of all philosophers. For after all Eglon, King of the Moabites, was assassinated by Ehud; Absalom was hanged by his hair and pierced with three darts; King Nadab son of Jeroboam was killed by Baasha, King Elah by Zimri, Ahaziah by Jehu, Athaliah by Jehoiada; Kings Jehoiakim, Jeconiah, and Zedekiah became slaves. You know how Croesus perished, Astyages, Darius, Dionysius of Syracuse, Pyrrhus, Perseus, Hannibal, Jugurtha, Ariovistus, Caesar, Pompey, Nero, Otho, Vitellius, Domitian, Richard II of England, Edward II, Henry VI, Richard III, Mary Stuart, Charles I, the three Henrys of France, the Emperor Henry IV? You know . . . "

"I also know," said Candide, "that we must cultivate our garden."

"You are right," said Pangloss, "for when man was put in the Garden of Eden, he was put there *ut operaretur eum,* to work; which proves that man was not born for rest."

"Let us work without reasoning," said Martin, "it is the only way to make life endurable."

All the little society entered into this laudable plan; each one began to exercise his talents. The little piece of land produced much. True, Cunégonde was very ugly; but she became an excellent pastry cook; Paquette embroidered; the old woman took care of the linen. No one, not even Friar Giroflée, failed to perform some service, he was a very good carpenter, and even became an honorable man; and Pangloss sometimes said to Candide: "All events are linked together in the best of all possible worlds; for after all, if you had not been expelled from a fine castle with great kicks in the backside for love of Mademoiselle Cunégonde, if you had not been subjected to the Inquisition, if you had not traveled about America on foot, if you had not given the Baron a great blow with your sword, if you had not lost all your sheep from the good country of Eldorado, you would not be here eating candied citrons and pistachios."

"That is well said," replied Candide, "but we must cultivate our garden."

QUESTIONS

1. What seems to be Voltaire's opinion of the nobility?

2. Voltaire satirized the philosophy of his time with his description of Pangloss's opinions. What is the tutor's philosophy? How does he support what he says?

3. Characterize Voltaire's philosophy. Is he pessimistic or optimistic?

4. Why do you think *Candide* was such a popular book in its time? People of different classes read the story, and it appealed to them all. Why? Do you think that everyone came away with the same message?

5. How, in the end, do Candide and his friends resolve their questions about the meaning of life?

90. JEAN-JACQUES ROUSSEAU

THE SOCIAL CONTRACT

(1762)

Jean-Jacques Rousseau (1712–78) was born in Geneva and was raised by his unstable father. Alternately neglected and overprotected, Rousseau received little formal education and was eventually apprenticed to an engraver. He escaped from service and traveled throughout Europe before settling in Paris, where he began writing. He was taken up by the leaders of the salons, the fashionable meetings of French intellectuals, and gained wide popularity for his writings on educational and social issues. Living in constant motion, fearing both his friends and enemies, he finally settled down and married his longtime mistress.

The Social Contract was Rousseau's most significant political work. Despite his own experiences, he had an optimistic view of human nature. He believed that people were essentially good, and that government was formed by them to provide the greatest possible amount of personal freedom. His ideas were central to many of the reforms of the French Revolution.

The Social Contract

I suppose man arrived at a point where obstacles, which prejudice his preservation in the state of nature, outweigh, by their resistance, the force which each individual can employ to maintain himself in this condition. Then the primitive state can no longer exist; and mankind would perish did it not change its way of life.

Now, as men cannot engender new forces, but can only unite and direct those which exist, they have no other means of preservation than to form by aggregation a sum of forces which could prevail against resistance and to put them in play by a single motive and make them act in concert.

This sum of forces can be established only by the concurrence of many; but the strength and liberty of each man being the primary instruments of his preservation, how can he pledge them without injury to himself and without neglecting the care which he owes to himself? This difficulty as related to my subject may be stated as follows: "To find a form of association which shall defend and protect with the public force the person and property of each associate, and by means of which each, uniting with all, shall obey however only himself, and remain as free as before." Such is the fundamental problem of which the *Social Contract* gives the solution.

The clauses of this contract are so determined by the nature of the act, that the least modification would render them vain and of no effect; so that, although they may, perhaps, never have been formally enunciated, they are everywhere the same, everywhere tacitly admitted and recognized until, the social compact being violated, each enters again into his first rights and resumes his natural liberty, thereby losing the conventional liberty for which he renounced it.

Theses clauses, clearly understood, may be reduced to one: that is the total alienation of each associate with all his rights to the entire community, for, first, each giving himself entirely, the condition is the same for all, and the conditions being the same for all, no one has an interest in making it onerous for the others.

Further, the alienation being without reserve, the union is as complete as it can be, and no associate has anything to claim: for, if some rights remained to individuals, as there would be no common superior who could decide between them and the public, each, being in some points his own judge, would soon profess to be so in everything: the state of nature would exist, and the association would necessarily become tryannical and useless.

Finally, each giving himself to all, gives himself to none; and as there is not an associate over whom he does not acquire the same right as is ceded, an equivalent is gained for all that is lost, and more force to keep what he has.

If, then, we remove from the social contract all that is not of its essence, it will be reduced to the following terms: "Each of us gives in common his person and all his force under the supreme direction of the general will; and we receive each member as an indivisible part of the whole."

Immediately, instead of the individual person of each contracting party, this act of association produces a moral and collective body, composed of as many members as the assembly has votes, which receives from this same act its unity—its common being, its life and its will. This public personage, thus formed by the union of all the others, formerly took the name of the city, and now takes that of republic or body politic. This is called the *state* by its members when it is passive; the *sovereign* when it is active; and a *power* when comparing it to its equals. With regard to the associates, they take collectively the name *people,* and call themselves individually *citizens,* as participating in the sovereign authority, and *subjects,* as submitted to the laws of the state. But these terms are often confounded and are taken one for the other. It is enough to know how to distinguish them when they are employed with all precision.

Signs of a Good Government

When it is asked positively which is the best government, a question is asked which is unanswerable as it is indeterminate; or, if you will, it has as many good answers as there are combinations possible in the absolute and relative positions of peoples.

But if it be asked by what sign it may be known whether a given people is well or ill governed, it would be another thing, and the question of fact could be answered.

However, it is not answered because each wishes to answer it in his own way. Subjects vaunt public tranquility; citizens, individual liberty; one prefers the safety of property, and the other that of the person; one thinks that the best government is the most severe, the other maintains that it is the most gentle; this one wishes that crimes be punished, and that one that they be prevented; one finds it delightful to be feared by his neighbors, another prefers to be unknown to them; one is content when money circulates, another requires that the people have bread. Even were an agreement reached upon these

Jean-Jacques Rousseau.

and similar points, would an advance be made? Moral qualities lacking exact measurements—if an agreement were reached as to the sign, how could it be reached as to the estimate to be put upon them?

As for me, I am always astonished that so simple a sign fails to be recognized, or that such bad faith prevails that it is not acknowledged. What is the *object* of political association? The preservation and prosperity of its members. And what is the surest sign that they are preserved and prospered? It is their number and population. Do not look elsewhere for this much disputed sign. Other things being equal, the government under which—without outside means, without naturalization, without colonies—the citizens increase and multiply most, is invariably the best. That under which a people diminishes and perishes is the worst. Statisticians, it is now your affair; count, measure, compare.

The General Will is Indestructible

As long as men united together look upon themselves as a single body, they have but one will relating to the common preservation and general welfare. Then all the energies of the state are vigorous and simple; its maxims are clear and luminous; there are no mixed contradictory interests; the common prosperity shows itself everywhere, and requires only good sense to be appreciated. Peace, union, and equality are enemies of political subtleties. Upright, honest men are difficult to deceive, because of their simplicity; decoys and pretexts do not impose upon them, they are not cunning enough to be dupes. When we see among the happiest people in the world troops of peasants regulating the affairs of state under an oak, and conducting themselves wisely, can we help despising the refinements of other nations, who make themselves illustrious and miserable with so much art and mystery?

A state thus governed has need of few laws; and, in proportion as it becomes necessary to promulgate new ones this necessity will be universally recognized. The first to propose them will say only what all have already felt, and it requires neither intrigues nor eloquence to cause to become laws what each has already resolved upon, as soon as he can be sure that others will do likewise.

But when the social knot begins to relax, and the state to weaken, when individual interests commence to be felt, and small societies to influence the great, the common interest changes and finds opponents: unanimity no longer rules in the suffrages; the general will is no longer the will of all; contradictions and debates arise, and the best counsel does not prevail without dispute.

Finally, when the state, near its fall, exists only by a vain and illusory form; when the social tie is broken in all hearts; when the vilest interests flaunt boldly in the sacred name of the public welfare, then the general will becomes silent; all being guided by secret motives think no more like citizens than if the state had never existed. Iniquitous decrees are passed falsely under the name of the law, which have for object individual interests only.

Does it follow that the general will is annihilated or corrupted? No; it is always constant, inalterable, and pure; but it is subordinated to others which overbalance it. Each in detaching his interest from the common interest, sees that he cannot separate it entirely; but his part of the public misfortune seems nothing to him compared to the exclusive good which he thinks he has appropriated to himself. This particular good excepted, he desires the general well-being for his own interest as strongly as any other. Even in selling his vote for money he has not extinguished in himself the general will—he eludes it. The fault which he commits is in evading the question and answering something which has not been asked him; instead of saying by his vote, "It is advantageous to the state," he says, "It is advantageous to such a man or party that such or such counsel prevail." The law of public order in assemblies is not so much to maintain the general will there, as to see that it is always interrogated and always answers.

I should have here many reflections to make upon the simple right to vote upon each act of sovereignty, a right which nothing can take from citizens, and upon the right to think, to propose, to divide, to discuss, which the government has always taken great care to allow only to its members; but this important matter will require a separate treatise, and I cannot consider it fully here.

QUESTIONS

1. What is the fundamental problem the social contract is meant to solve?

2. What are the signs of good government?

3. How do Rousseau's assumptions about how a society is organized differ from the assumptions of earlier theorists like Machiavelli or Richelieu?

4. Rousseau has much to say about the general will. What is it, and how do we know what it is?

5. Rousseau's view of human nature colors his political views. How does his general optimism affect his work? What assumptions does he make about human nature?

91.   MONTESQUIEU

SPIRIT OF THE LAWS
(1748)

Charles-Louis, Baron de Montesquieu (1689–1755), was one of the most important political philosophers of the Enlightenment. He received a legal education and at the age of twenty-seven became an officer in the French law courts. His provincial post was an important one, but he was attracted by life in the capital and soon moved to Paris. Once there, he threw himself into Parisian social and intellectual life. He won considerable fame as a wit, publishing several works of satire. Influenced by English models, he embarked upon a course of study on the nature of government and politics that resulted in his most important work, *Spirit of the Laws*. Although his work brought him great fame outside France, Montesquieu remained a modest, good-humored man. He died quietly in Paris in 1755.

Spirit of the Laws was one of the most celebrated books of its time. Montesquieu spent 14 years writing it, and he produced a careful analysis of the origins of government and politics. The book had great impact throughout the West; among its contributions was the principle of separation of powers, now enshrined in the U.S. Constitution.

Of the Nature of the Three Different Governments

There are three species of government; *republican, monarchical,* and *despotic.* In order to discover their nature, it is sufficient to recollect the common notion, which supposes three definitions or rather three facts, that the *republican government is that in which the body or only a part of the people is possessed of the supreme power: monarchy that in which a single person governs but by fixed and established laws: a despotic government, that in which a single person directs every thing by his own will and caprice.*

This is what I call the nature of each government; we must examine now which are those laws that follow this nature directly, and consequently are the first fundamental laws.

Of the Republican Government and the Laws Relative to Democracy

When the body of the people in a republic are possessed of the supreme power, this is called a *democracy.*

In a democracy the people are in some respect the sovereign, and in others the subject.

There can be no sovereign but by suffrages, which are their own will; and the sovereign's will is the sovereign himself. The laws therefore which establish the right of suffrage, are fundamental to this government. In fact, it is as important to regulate in a republic, in what manner, by whom, to whom, and concerning what, suffrages are to be given, as it is in a monarchy to know who is the prince and after what manner he ought to govern.

It is an essential point to fix the number of citizens that are to form the public assemblies; otherwise it might be uncertain whether the whole body or only a part of the people have voted.

The people in whom the supreme power resides, ought to do of themselves whatever conveniently they can; and what they cannot well

do, they must commit to the management of ministers.

The ministers are not properly theirs, unless they have the nomination of them: it is therefore a fundamental maxim in this government, that the people should choose their ministers, that is, their magistrates.

The people are extremely well qualified for choosing those whom they are to entrust with part of their authority. They can tell when a person has been often in battle, and has had particular success; they are therefore very capable of electing a general. They can tell when a judge is assiduous in his office, when he gives general satisfaction, and has never been charged with bribery. These are all facts of which they can have better information in a public forum, than a monarch in his palace. But are they able to manage an affair, to find out and make a proper use of places, occasions, moments? No, this is beyond their capacity.

The law which determines the manner of giving the suffrages is likewise fundamental in a democracy. It is a question of some importance, whether the suffrages ought to be public or secret. Cicero observes, that the laws which rendered them secret towards the close of the republic, were the cause of its decline. But as this is differently practiced in different republics, I shall offer here my thoughts concerning this subject.

The people's suffrages ought doubtless to be public; and this should be considered as a fundamental law of democracy. The lower sort of people ought to be directed by those of higher rank, and restrained within bounds by the gravity of certain personages. Hence by rendering the suffrages secret in the Roman republic all was lost; it was no longer possible to direct a populace that sought its own destruction.

It is likewise a fundamental law in democracies, that the people should have the sole power to enact laws. And yet there are a thousand occasions on which it is necessary the senate should have a power of decreeing; nay it is frequently proper to make some trial of a law before it is established. The constitution of Rome and Athens were extremely wise. The decrees of the senate had the force of laws for the space of a year, and did not become perpetual till they were ratified by the consent of the people.

Of the Relation of Laws to the Nature of Monarchical Government

The intermediate, subordinate, and dependent powers, constitute the nature of monarchical government, that is, of that in which a single person governs by fundamental laws. I said, *intermediate, subordinate,* and *dependent powers.* In fact, in monarchies the prince is the source of all power political and civil. These fundamental laws necessarily suppose the intermediate channels through which the power flows: for if there be only the momentary and capricious will of a single person to govern the state, nothing can be fixed, and, of course there can be no fundamental law.

The most natural, intermediate and subordinate power is that of the nobility. This in some measure seems to be essential to a monarchy, whose fundamental maxim is, *no monarch, no nobility; no nobility, no monarch;* but there may be a despotic prince.

There are men who have endeavoured in some countries in Europe to abolish all the jurisdiction of the nobility; not perceiving that they were driving at the very thing that was done by the parliament of *England.* Abolish the privileges of the lords, of the clergy, and of the cities in a monarchy, and you will soon have a popular state, or else an arbitrary government.

Though the ecclesiastic power is so dangerous in a republic, yet it is extremely proper in a monarchy, especially of the absolute kind. What would become of *Spain* and *Portugal* since the subversion of their laws, were it not for this only barrier against the torrent of arbitrary power? A barrier that is always useful when there is no other: for as a despotic government is productive of the most frightful calamities to human nature, the very evil that restrains it, is beneficial to the subject.

Of the Condition or State of Women in Different Governments

In monarchies women are subject to very little restraint, because as the distinction of ranks calls them to court, they repair thither in order to assume that spirit of liberty, which is the only one there tolerated. The aspiring courtier avails himself of their charms and passions, in order to advance his fortune; and as their weakness admits not of pride, but of vanity: luxury constantly attends them.

In despotic governments women do not introduce, but are themselves an object of luxury. They must be here in a state of the most rigorous servitude. Every one follows the spirit of the government, and adopts in his own family the customs he sees elsewhere established. As the laws are very severe and executed on the spot, they are afraid lest the liberty of women should involve them in dangers. Their quarrels, indiscretions, repugnancies, jealousies, piques, and that art, in fine, which little souls have of interesting great ones, would be attended there with fatal consequences.

In republics women are free by the laws, and constrained by manners; luxury is banished from thence, and with it corruption and vice.

Of the Corruption of the Principle of Democracy

The principle of democracy is corrupted, not only when the spirit of equality is extinct, but likewise when they fall into a spirit of extreme equality, and when every citizen wants to be upon a level with those he has chosen to command him. Then the people, incapable of bearing the very power they have entrusted, want to do every thing of themselves, to debate for the senate, to execute for the magistrate, and to strip the judges.

When this is the case, virtue can no longer subsist in the republic. The people want to exercise the functions of the magistrates; who cease to be revered. The deliberations of the senate are slighted; all respect is then laid aside for the senators, and consequently for old age. If respect ceases for old age, it will cease also for parents; deference to husbands will be likewise thrown off, and submission to masters. This licentiousness will soon captivate the mind; and the restraint of command be as fatiguing as that of obedience. Wives, children, slaves, will shake off all subjection. No longer will there be any such thing as manners, order, or virtue.

Democracy hath therefore two excesses to avoid, the spirit of inequality which leads to aristocracy or monarchy; and the spirit of extreme equality, which leads to despotic power, as the latter is completed by conquest.

Of the Corruption of the Principle of Monarchy

As democracies are destroyed when the people despoil the senate, magistrates and judges of their functions; so monarchies are corrupted when the prince insensibly deprives societies of their prerogatives, or cities of their privileges. In the first case the multitude usurp a despotic power; in the second it is usurped by a single person.

Monarchy is destroyed, when a prince thinks he shows a greater exertion of power in changing than in conforming to the order of things; when he deprives some of his subjects of their hereditary employments to bestow them arbitrarily upon others, and when he is fonder of being guided by his fancy than by his judgment.

Monarchy is destroyed when the prince directing every thing entirely to himself, calls that state to his capital, the capital to his court, and the court to his own person.

Monarchy is destroyed in fine, when the prince mistakes his authority, his situation, and the love of his people; and when he is not fully persuaded that a monarch ought to think himself secure, as a despotic prince ought to think himself in danger.

The principle of monarchy is corrupted, when the first dignities are marks of the first servitude, when the great men are stripped of popular respect, and rendered the low tools of arbitrary power.

It is still more corrupted, when honor is set up in contradiction to honors, and when men are capable of being loaded at the very same time with infamy and dignities.

QUESTIONS

1. What are the three types of government?

2. Montesquieu attaches a great deal of importance to the vote in a republic but argues against secrecy of the ballot. Why?

3. Where does power reside in a monarchy?

4. What prevents a king from becoming a tyrant in a monarchical state?

5. How does the status of women vary under the three different forms of government?

6. Both monarchy and democracy, according to Montesquieu, are subject to decay. What are the special pitfalls each faces?

92.   **CAPTAIN JAMES COOK**

JOURNALS

(1769)

James Cook (1728–79) was born in Yorkshire, educated in a local school, and apprenticed to a shipowner who prepared him for sea travel. He joined the Royal Navy, where his skill in navigation and cartography led to an early command of a royal scientific excursion to the South Seas. Cook made three long journeys to the Pacific, charting New Zealand and the coast of Australia and discovering chains of islands including Hawaii. He was killed by local inhabitants there in 1779. Cook maintained meticulous records of his voyages including a narrative account of his first voyage that was later published. His journals have been not only the source of much knowledge about early encounters with the South Sea islanders but also a treasure trove of information about European assumptions in dealing with native peoples.

Cook's first voyage was made in 1768 as part of a venture sponsored by the Royal Society to measure the distance between the earth and the sun by taking readings from different parts of the globe during an appearance of the planet Venus in the night sky. To this purpose Cook was sent to Tahiti (then known as King George's Islands), which had been discovered previously by HMS Dolphin and where the natives were believed to be friendly. The following selection details the first meeting between Captain Cook and the Tahitians.

We had no sooner come to an Anchor in Royal Bay as before Mentioned than a great number of the natives in their Canoes came off to the Ship and brought with them Cocoa-nuts &c* and these they seem'd to set a great Value upon. Amongst those that came off to the Ship was an elderly Man whose name is *Owhaa*, him the Gentlemen that had been here before in the Dolphin knew and had often spoke of him as one that had been of service to them, this man (together with some others) I took on board, and made much of him thinking that he might on some occasion be of use to us. As our stay at this place was not likly to be very Short, I thought it very necessary that some order

Should be Observed in Trafficing with the Natives: that such Merchantdize as we had on board for that purpose might continue to bear a proper value, and not leave it to every ones own particular fancy which could not fail to bring on confution and quarels between us and the Natives, and would infallible lesen the Value of such Articles as we had to Traffic with: in order to prevent this the following Rules were orderd to be observed, viz.

RULES to be observe'd by every person in or belonging to His Majestys Bark the Endevour for the better establishing a regular and uniform Trade for Provisions &c* with the Inhabitants of Georges Island.

1ˢᵗ *To endevour by every fair means to cultivate a friendship with the Natives and to treat them with all imaginable humanity.*

2ᵈ *A proper person or persons will be appointed to trade with the Natives for all manner of Provisions, Fruit, and other productions of the earth; and no officer or Seaman, or other person belonging to the Ship, excepting such as are so appointed, shall Trade or offer to Trade for any sort of Provisions, Fruit, or other productions of the earth unless they have my leave so to do.*

3ᵈ *Every person employ'd a Shore on any duty what soever is strictly to attend to the same, and if by neglect he looseth any of his Arms or woorking tools, or suffers them to be stole, the full Value thereof will be charge'd against his pay according to the Custom of the Navy in such cases, and he shall recive such farther punishment as the nature of the offence may deserve.*

4ᵗʰ *The same penalty will be inflicted on every person who is found to imbezzle, trade or offer to trade with any part of the Ships Stores of what nature soever.*

5ᵗʰ *No Sort of Iron, or any thing that is made of Iron, or any sort of Cloth or other usefull or necessary articles are to be given in exchange for any thing but provisions.*

J. C.

As soon as the Ship was properly secure'd I went on Shore accompanied by Mr Banks and the other gentlemen, with a party of Men under arms, we took along with us Owhaa who conducted us to the place where the Dolphin water'd, and made signs to us as well as we could understand that we might occupy that ground but it happen'd not to be fit for our purpose. No one of the Natives made the least oppossission at our landing but came to us with all imaginable marks of friendship and submission. We afterwards made a circuit through the Woods, and then came on board. We did not find the Inhabitants to be numerous and therefore at first imagined that several of them had fled from their habitations upon our arrival in the Bay but Mr Gore & some others who had been here before observ'd that a very great revolution must have happen'd—not near the number of inhabitants a great number of houses raiz'd, har[d]ly a vestage of some to be seen particularly what was call'd the Queens and not so much as a Hog or Fowl was to be seen—no very agreeable discovery to us whose Ideas of plenty upon our arrival at this Island (from the report of the Dolphin) was carried to the very highest pitch.

FRIDAY Apl. 14*th.* This morning we had a great many Canoes about the Ship, the Most of them came from the westward but brought nothing with them but a few Cocoa-nuts &c*. Two that appear'd to be Chiefs we had on board together with several others for it was a hard matter to keep them out of the Ship as they clime like Munkeys, but it was still harder to keep them from Stealing but every thing that came within their reach, in this they are prodiges expert. I made each of the two Chiefs a present of a Hatchet things that they seem'd mostly to Value. As soon as we had partly got clear of these people, I took two Boats and went to the Westward all the Gentlemen being along with me, my design was to see if there was not a more comm[o]dious Harbour and to try the disposission of the Natives having along with us the two Chiefs above mentioned: the first place we landed at was in Great Canoe Harbour (so call'd by Cap' Wallis) here the Natives Flock'd about us in great Numbers and in as friendly a Manner as we could wish, only that they shew'd a great inclination to pick our pockets. We were conducted to a Chief who for distinction sake we call'd *Hercules*, after staying a Short time with him and distributing a few presents about us, we proceeded further and came to a Chief who I shall call *Lycurgus*, this Man entertain'd us with Broil'd fish Bread fruit Cocoa-nuts &c* with great hospitality, and all the time took great care to tell us to take care of our pockets, as a great number of people had crowded about us. Notwithstanding the care we took Dʳ Solander and Dʳ Munkhouse had each of them their pockets pick'd the one of his spy glass and the other of his snuff Box, as soon as Lycurgus was made acquainted with the theift he disperse'd the people in a Moment and the method he made use of was to lay hold of the first thing that came in his way and throw it at them and happy was he or she that could get first out of his way; he seem'd very much concern'd for what had happend and by way of recompence offer'd us but every thing that was in his House, but we refuse'd to except of any thing and made signs to him that we only wanted the things again. He had already sent people out after them and it was not long before they were return'd. We found the Natives very Numerous where ever we came and from what we could judge seem'd very peaceably inclin'd. About 6 oClock in the evening we return'd on board very well satisfied with our little excursion.

SATURDAY 15*th*. Winds at East during the day, in the night a light breeze off the land, and as I apprehend it be usual here for the Trade wind to blow during great part of the Day from the Eastern board and to have it Calm or light breezes from the land that is Southerly during the night with fair weather, I shall only mention the wind and weather when they deviate from this rule.

This morning several of the Chiefs we had seen yesterday came on board and brought with them Hogs, Bread fruit &c* for these we gave them Hatchets, Linnen and such things as they Valued. Having not met with yesterday a more convenient situation for every purpose we wanted than the place where we now are, I therefore without delay resolved to pitch upon some spot upon the NE point of the Bay properly situated for observing the Transit of Venus and at the same time under the command of the Ships Guns, and there to throw up a small fort for our defence, accordingly I went a Shore with a party

of men accompanie'd by Mʳ Banks Dʳ Solander and Mʳ Green. We took along with us one of Mʳ Banks Tents, and after we had fix'd upon a place fit for our purpose we set up the Tent and Mark'd out the ground we intended to occupy. By this time a great number of the Natives had got collected together about us, seemingly only to look on as not one of them had any weapon either offensive or defensive. I would suffer none to come within the lines I had marked out excepting one who appear'd to be a Chief and old Owhaa, to these two men we endeavour'd to explain as well as we could that we wanted that ground to sleep upon such a number of nights and than we should go a way. Whether they understood us or no is uncertain but no one appear'd the least displeased at what we was about. Indeed the ground we had fix'd upon was of no use to them being part of the Sandy beach upon the shore of the Bay and not near to any of their habitations. It being too late in the Day to do any thing more a party with a Petty officer was left to guard the Tent while we with a nother party took a walk into the woods and with us most of the natives. We had but just cross'd the River when Mʳ Banks shott three Ducks at one shott which surprise'd them so much that the most of them fell down as tho they had be shott likewise. I was in hopes this would have had some good effect but the event did not prove it, for we had not been gone long from the Tent before the natives again began to gather about it and one of them more daring than the rest push'd one of the Centinals down, snatched the Musquet out of his hand and made a push at him and then made off and with him all the rest, emmidiatly upon this the officer order'd the party to fire and the Man who took the Musquet was shott dead before he had got far from the Tent but the Musquet was carried quite off; when this happen'd I and Mʳ Banks with the other party were about half a Mile off returning out of the woods, upon hearing the fireing of musquets and the natives leaving us at the same time we susspected that some thing was the Matter and hasten'd our march, but before we arrive'd the whole was over and every one of the Natives fled except old Owhaa who stuck by us the whole time, and I beleive from the first either knew or had some suspicion that the People would attempt something at the Tent as he was very much agai[n]st our going into the woods out of sight of this Tent. However he might have other reasons for Mr Hicks being a shore the Day before the natives would not permit him to go into the woods, this made me resolve to go to see whether they mea[n]t to proscribe bounds to us or no. Old Owhaa as I have said before was the only one of the Natives that stay'd by us and by his means we prevail'd on about 20 of them to come to the Tent and their sit down with us and endeavour'd by every means in our power to convence them that the man was kill'd for taking away the Musquet and that we still would be friends with them. At sunset they left us seemingly satisfied and we struck our Tent and went on board.

FRIDAY 21*st.* Got the Copper Oven aShore and fix'd it in the Bank of the breast works.

Yesterday as Mr Green and Dr Munkhouse were taking a Walk they happen'd to meet with the Body of the Man we had Shot, as the Natives by signs made them fully understand, the manner in which the body was enterr'd being a little extraordinary I went to day with some others to see it. Close by the House wherein he resided when living was built a small Shade, but whether for the purpose or no I cannot say for it was in all respects like some of the Shades or houses they live in. This Shade was about 14 or 16 feet long, 10 or 12 broad and of a proportional height, one end was wholy open the other end [and] the two sides were partly inclosed with a kind of wicker'd work. In this shade lay the Corps upon a Bier or frame of wood with a Matted bottom like a Cot frame use'd at sea, and supported by 4 posts about 5 feet from the Ground, the Body was cover'd with a Mat and over that a white Cloth, along side of the Body

lay a wooden Club, one of their weapons of warr. The head of the Corps lay next the close end of the Shad[e], and at this end lay 2 Cocoanut Shells such as they some times use to carry water in. At the other end of the Shade was a bunch of Green leaves with some dry'd twigs tied all together and stuck in the ground and a stone lying by them about as big as a Cocoa-nut, near to these lay a young Plantain tree, such as they use as Emblems of Peace, and by it lay a stone Axe; at the open end of the Shade was hung in several Strings a great number of Palm nuts. Without the Shad[e] was Stuck upright in the ground the Stem of a Plantain tree about 5 feet high on the Top of which stud a Cocoa-nut shell full of fresh water, and on the side of the Post hung a small Bag wherein were a few peices of Bread fruit roasted ready for eating, some of the peices were fresh and others stale. The Natives did not seem to like that we should go near the Body and stud at a little distance themselves while we examine'd these matters and appear'd to be please'd when we came away. It certainly was no very agreeable place for it Stunk intollerably and yet it was not above 10 yards from the Huts wherein several of the Living resided. The first day we landed we saw the Skeleton of a human being laying in this manner under a Shade that was just big enough to cover it, and some days after that when some of the gentlemen went with a design to examine it more narrowly it was gone.

It was at this time thought that this manner of enterring their Dead was not common to all ranks of people as this was the first we had seen except the Skeleton just mentioned, but various were the opinions concerning the Provisions &c* laid about the dead; upon the whole it should seem that these people not only beleive in a Supream being but on a futerue state also, and that this must be meant either as an offering to some Deitie, or for the use of the dead in the other world, but this last is not very probable as there appear'd to be no Priest craft in the thing, for what ever provisions were put there, it appear'd very plain to us that there it remain untill it consum'd away of it self. It is most likely that we shall see more of this before we leave the Island, but if it is a Religious ceremoney we may not be able to understand it, for the Misteries of most Religious are very dark and not easily understud even by those who profess them.

QUESTIONS

1. Why did Captain Cook establish rules for dealing with the natives?

2. How did the Tahitians treat Captain Cook when he first landed?

3. How was the pickpocketing incident handled? What did it show about the assumptions of the Tahitians?

4. What did Captain Cook find remarkable about the burial customs of the Tahitians?

93.   JOSEPH CRASSONS DE MEDEUIL

NOTES ON THE FRENCH SLAVE TRADE

(1784–1785)

The west African slave trade began with the first Portuguese excursions into Africa and continued for centuries. Few Europeans settled in Africa, therefore the trade was organized through African tribes, which took slaves from among their rivals and held them until European slave traders arrived to exchange arms and manufactured goods for black Africans. All of the European nations participated in the slave trade, although outside of Portugal there were few blacks enslaved in Europe. Rather, the trade was used to provide plantation workers for the New World. The slave trade reached its height in the eighteenth century, when the demand for slaves in North American and the West Indies was greatest. After that, both the natural increase of the transplanted slaves and the political movements for abolition of the slave trade depressed demand.

The following account was written by a French sea captain who spent time on the East African coast and who believed that the slave trade could be made more efficient through better organization and the application of rigorous mercantile principles.

Almost the whole of the East Coast of Africa is unknown to us. The detailed maps of Mr. D'Apris [Jean Baptist Nicolas Denis d'Après de Mannevillette] are not accurate. The mapping of the coast line seems to have been done in a haphazard manner and [a] number of islands and reefs known to certain navigatiors are not marked on these maps.

We only have approximate knowledge of the coast from the Cape of Good Hope to Cape Corrientes. Even in this stretch several bays are still unknown to us, in particular the Bay of Lourenço Marques. This bay merits the most careful attention.

From Cape Corrientes to Cape Natal the coast looks most inviting and attractive. It is presumably thickly populated if one can judge by the number of fires visible along it.

The coast, from Cape Corrientes to Cape Delgado and in particular as far as the Angoxa Islands, is very sparsely inhabited and little known. The Portuguese have always made a mystery of this section. We are assured that they have trading posts on all the rivers, including the Quilimani, stretching fifty miles inland.

The stretch between Mozambique and Ibo is fairly thickly populated. It is there we go in search of our blacks. We trade for them at Kerimba, Ibo and Mozambique, small islands detached from the coast and inaccurately marked on the map.

From Cape Delgado to Kilwa the coast is inhabited only by Moors and Arabs who take from it a prodigious number of blacks (*in margin:* inferior to those of Kilwa but which they bring there to sell to us), particularly from the river Mongallo, a little-known river which flows through fertile and thickly populated country stretching a long way inland.

This stretch of country is entirely unknown to us, the approach to it is very difficult and we rarely go there.

From Kilwa to Mafia, a large and lovely island which is at the moment engaged in making itself independent of the King of Kilwa, the sea, according to the map, appears to be without haz-ards and easily navigable. But there is a mass of islands which occupies a space of more that ten leagues and notably the island of Songo Songo, which is thickly populated. Here M. Crassons bargained for blacks and food supplies in 1754. This island is six leagues from the mainland. The channel is from twelve to fifteen cubits deep.

The Islands of Zanzibar are well known. It was among them that the vessel *St. Pierre*, carrying a rich cargo of *piastres*, and commanded by M. Maurice [M. Morice of the preceding passage] was lost. The vessel had been equipped in Mauritius. (*Marginal note:* There is [in Zanzibar] a fortress which belongs to the Imam of Muscat, to whom the Moors and Arabs of Mombasa, Pate and Barawa pay dues. The whole of the remaining part of this coast as far as the entrance to the Red Sea itself ought to be better known to us.) He escaped to Kilwa with the remains of his fortune. This man was a surgeon and he rendered such valuable services that the King of Kilwa treated him with friendliness and wanted to settle him in his domains. For the sum of 4,000 *piastres* he ceded to him the northern portion of Kilwa in which is situated the ancient Portuguese citadel. It is very favourably situated as it commands the northern channel which has a depth of fifteen to twenty-two cubits. Death put an end to M. Moric's progress. He was mourned for and is still spoken of with tenderness and veneration. The original of this deed of sale was sent to Mauritius. The counterpart is in the possession of the son of the former minister Bwana Muhammad by name, leader of the religion of Kilwa and whose father was our friend.

A Communication Presented to M. de Curt, Royal Commissioner, to Make to Monseigneur le Marechal de Castries, Minister of the Navy

Kilwa

Let it be known that the Seigneur Joseph Crassons de Medeuil, a captain in the merchant navy, who has served in the wars of 1758 and 1778, sometimes as a pilot and sometimes as an auxiliary officer in His Majesty's ships, and who has recently come from India, feels it his duty to report to His Excellency the Marshal on what he has seen and done during his voyages along the East Coast of Africa in his ship *La Créolle*, and particularly in the port of Kilwa situated in latitude nine degrees and a few minutes south. He went thither on two occasions to trade for blacks and found this island friendly disposed towards establishing this type of trade in a manner likely to commend itself to the Ministry, which appears to wish to engage in it, since it has had time to study and to take note of the size and safety of this port for the accommodation of a very great number of ships and even of fighting fleets. In view of the type of slaves obtainable in this area and the qualities of the piece of land adjacent to this great bay, which has been released by the king whom they call sultan, and also in view of the fact that the great majority of the natives are disposed to be friendly to us, ardently desiring as they do to be able to enjoy and share in the protection of France and to make an effective treaty of alliance with us, a letter was composed in a general assembly held for this purpose, addressed to the king, asking for his protection and for a guarantee against all foreign invasion, particularly against the Arabs and the Portuguese who are the two neighbours most likely to give them trouble; in the said address made to His Majesty they offer to hand over a part of the island on its North Coast in which is situated the fort formerly belonging to the Portuguese and from which they were driven out by the present king's [of Kilwa] father, with immediate possession of the same piece of land which was formerly purchased by M. Maurice, a Frenchman who died in the said place, with permission to build there a fortress, to plant our flag, to have sole exclusive right to the trade in negroes and in all other such materials and products as may suit us; that in the said fortress we may have as many soldiers as we find necessary and establish everywhere on the coast and in the interior the trading centres required for purposes of cultivation. They even offer to main-

tain 200 men and in order to do so to divide with the officer who is given command of the fort the six *piastres* which they levy on each captive. The above document, with which I have been entrusted, I put into the hands of the governor on my arrival in Pondichéry.

Furthermore

While we were busy with the King or Sultan of Kilwa drawing up the above-mentioned document, an armed corvette arrived at the said place carrying the son of the Imam of Muscat, who is a pretender to the Government of the town and to the succession of the Estates of his father, who died about three or four years ago, but this son was despoiled of his inheritance by another brother, whose faction is the more powerful; in consequence the former fled from Muscat to come and collect supporters on this coast from Zanzibar, Pate, Mombasa, Barawa, as far as the island of Socotra, which is almost entirely inhabited by Moors and Arabs who are in sympathy with his cause; and he being anxious to be able to take possession again of Muscat and seeing the zeal of the Sultan of Kilwa in invoking the protection of France, has joined him and made a special request on his behalf, offering and promising full satisfaction of France's commercial needs on the seas and in the ports of Arabia and the Persian Gulf and a fort and a counting house at Muscat under the [French] flag. Further he undertakes to pay and reimburse all expenses which might arise in this connexion and he is eager to come to France in person to ask for these things. He even wished to buy my ship but found it too small as he was purposing at that time to attack the fortress of Zanzibar (whose commander had been appointed by his brother) and was levying troops in Kilwa; for his enterprise I had offered him everything at my disposal, two twenty-four inch cannon, twenty guns, powder, bullets and money. He did not see fit to accept these, assuring me that he would make himself master by the force of persuasion alone and of the respect that these people generally have for their chiefs. As he had always treated me with the greatest deference and with all the marks of open friendship we parted with a desire to meet again. In consequence I promised to come in person to submit his request to the attention of the Ministry, and on his part he gave me a passport signed by himself and bearing his seal with which I can present myself at any of the Arab ports belonging to his faction with a very strong recommendation that I should be served, protected and welcomed as he would be himself, whose envoy I am. This is the sole motive of my journey to Paris, having sought in this negotiation only to procure for the king and the nation such things as might be useful, to extend the glory and importance of his protection; to extend our trade and our sea routes which are too restricted in this area and in which we could develop our trade and influence very profitably.

Concerning the Port of Kilwa

This Port is well placed particularly for doing damage in time of war to English warships on their way to India as it is situated at the Northern exit of the Mozambique Channel.

The Port is vast and safe and can hold a prodigious number of ships. The timber there is of good quality and appearance and is easily worked and plentiful. Water might be a little less plentiful because the inhabitants have only the number of wells necessary to them on the island. But it must be possible to find water in the neighbouring rivers of which there are five in as much as a ship of 200 tons could go up some of them to a distance of more than ten leagues, the sea is fifteen feet deep and I have been inland with my *pirogue* for more than eleven leagues. I found two delightful springs and there must be others, seeing that the river ends up in two charming mountains; in the two passes there is enough water for the largest-vessels, it being at its shallowest fourteen fathoms deep. The coun-

try is superb and pleasing once one has extricated oneself from the forests of half submerged trees called Mangroves. Judging from the ruins of stone-built houses, which can be seen not only on the island of Kilwa but also on the southern side of the pass, it appears that this was once a very important town and that it must have had a big trade; at Kilwa one can see the whole of a big mosque built in stone whose arches are very well constructed. Within the last three years a pagoda which stood at the southern extremity, and which was very curious looking, fell. Finally, this country produces millet, indigo, superb cotton, silkier even than the cotton produced on the Ile de Bourbon, sugar cane, gums in abundance, brown cowries of the second sort which are currency at Jiddah and in Dahomey, besides elephant ivory which is very common, as are elephants, and lastly negroes—superb specimens if they are selected with care. This selection we cannot make ourselves, being at the discretion of the traders, who are now aware of our needs and who know that it is absolutely essential for us to sail at a given season in order to round the Cape of Good Hope. In addition to competition amongst ourselves the expeditions have been properly thought out and always left to chance, and so it happens that three or four ships find themselves in the same place and crowd each other out. This would not happen if there were a properly organized body and the expeditions were planned to fit in with the seasons and the quantity of cargo and the means of using up surplus also planned, since it is not the business of seamen to concern themselves with correspondence and administration. To my knowledge, the trading that has been done in this port for the last three years, without counting traders not personally known to me is as follows:

La Pintade	Capt	600 blacks	
La Victoire	" La Touche	224 "	1st voyage
Les bons amis	" Beguet	336 "	
La Samaritaine	" Herpin	254 "	
La Créolle	" Crassons	176	

La Victoire	" La Touche				
	3rd voyage	230	690	"	In his three voyages
[omitted]	" Berton		233	"	
La Grande Victoire	" Michel		289	"	
La Thémis	" Bertau		450	"	
La Grande Victaire	" Michel		289	"	
La Créolle	" Crassons		211	"	
La Thimis 2nd voyage	" Bertau		480	"	
La Grande Victorie	" Rouillard		250	"	
			4,193	"	

A total, to my knowledge, of 4,193, and certainly there must have been more in three years.

It is clear that if this number of captives, i.e. 4,193, who were traded for at least in this period of three years, cost forty *piastres* each, this represents a sum of 167,720 *piastres,* raised for the most part from the Ile de France and from Bourbon, or from France direct. It is therefore important not only to safeguard this trade but also to find a way of spending rather fewer *piastres,* which would be quite possible if one considers that the *piastres* which we give them for their captives do not remain long in their hands and that they almost immediately give them to the Moors and Arabs who provide them with their needs which are rice, millet, lambs, tunics, shirts, carpets, needles, swords, shoes, and silk materials for dresses and linings. The Arabs obtain most of these things from Surat, and why should we not get them direct from there ourselves? We should make the profit they make, and we should employ men and ships and we should keep a good number of out *piastres* which would remain in the Ile de France and in Bourbon; more certainly still, if privately owned ships from Europe or these islands could not go to the coast of Mozambique and if ships belonging to a private company sent out from Europe could participate in this trade only by means of *piastres* taken to Kilwa, it can be estimated how much we have paid into the hands of the Portuguese at Mozambique, Kerimba and . . . [omitted: Ibo] where they make us pay fifty or sixty *piastres* each for them. This does not include presents and tiresome vexations. What need is there to give our money to the Portuguese, when we have the means to operate among ourselves and when we can use our own industry and keep our money? I have heard for a long time talk of establishing a settlement or trading post in Madagascar. Truly, seeing the number of idle hands we have and the great number of poor and needy and foundlings in our almshouses it is surprising that we have not yet considered this plan, at least as far as that part of the island which we have most visited over a long period is concerned, and also, in certain ports which are particularly well situated, trading posts could be established without straining the resources of the State.

QUESTIONS

1. Do you think that the natives of Kilwa were ardent for a treaty with France?

2. Why did the Sultan of Kilwa reject the French offer of arms?

3. What is Captain Crassons de Medeuil's analysis of the French slave trade?

4. What was the author's purpose in making these observations about Africa?

94.   THOMAS JEFFERSON

THE DECLARATION OF INDEPENDENCE

(1776)

Thomas Jefferson (1743–1826) was born into one of Virginia's most prominent families. With wide-ranging interests—from architecture, to education, to politics—he spent most of his early life on his plantation studying the wisdom of the past. Jefferson had an abiding interest in politics and first served in the Virginia colonial assembly. In 1775 he was named a delegate to the Second Continental Congress, where he quickly distinguished himself as a speaker and writer. During the American Revolution he served as governor of Virginia, was the first secretary of state in the Washington government, was vice-president, and in 1801 was elected president of the United States. After his retirement from public life, he founded the University of Virginia in 1819. He is today regarded as one of the greatest of all American thinkers.

Jefferson wrote the Declaration of Independence at the request of the Continental Congress. This document was at once a succinct statement of liberal principles and a brilliant piece of political propaganda. The Declaration is one of the central documents in the history of democratic government.

In Congress, July 4, 1776.

The unanimous Declaration of the Thirteen United States of America.

When in the Course of human events, it becomes necessary for one people to dissolve the political bands which have connected them with another, and to assume among the Powers of the earth, the separate and equal station to which the Laws of Nature and of Nature's God entitle them, a decent respect to the opinions of mankind requires that they should declare the causes which impel them to the separation.

We hold these truths to be self-evident, that all men are created equal, that they are endowed by their Creator with certain unalienable Rights, that among these are Life, Liberty and the pursuit of Happiness. That to secure these rights, Governments are instituted among Men, deriving their just powers from the consent of the governed, That whenever any Form of Government becomes destructive of these ends, it is the Right of the People to alter or to abolish it, and to institute new Government, laying its foundation on such principles and organizing its powers in such form, as to them shall seem most likely to effect their Safety and Happiness. Prudence, indeed, will dictate that Governments long established should not be changed for light and transient causes; and accordingly all experience hath shown, that mankind are more disposed to suffer, while evils are sufferable, than to right themselves by abolishing the forms to which they are accustomed. But when a long train of abuses and usurpations, pursuing invariably the same Object, evinces a design to reduce them under absolute Despotism, it is their right, it is their duty, to throw off such Government, and to provide new Guards for their future security. Such has been the patient sufferance of these Colonies; and such is now the necessity which constrains them to alter their former Systems of Government. The history of the present King of Great Britain is a history of repeated injuries and usurpations, all having in direct object the establishment of an absolute Tyranny of these States. To prove this, let Facts be submitted to a candid world.

He has refused his Assent to Laws, the most wholesome and necessary for the public good.

He has forbidden his Governors to pass Laws of immediate and pressing importance, unless suspended in their operation till his Assent should be obtained; and when so suspended, he has utterly neglected to attend to them.

He has refused to pass other Laws for the accommodation of large districts of people, unless those people would relinquish the right of Representation in the Legislature, a right inestimable to them and formidable to tyrants only.

He has called together legislative bodies at places unusual, uncomfortable, and distant from the depository of their Public Records, for the sole purpose of fatiguing them into compliance with his measures.

He has dissolved Representative Houses repeatedly, for opposing with manly firmness his invasions on the rights of the people.

He has refused for a long time, after such dissolutions to cause others to be elected; whereby the Legislative Powers, incapable of Annihilation, have returned to the People at large for their exercise; the State remaining in the mean time exposed to all the dangers of invasion from without, and convulsions within.

He has endeavoured to prevent the population of these States; for that purpose obstructing the Laws for Naturalization of Foreigners; refusing to pass others to encourage their migration hither, and raising the conditions of new Appropriations of Lands.

He has obstructed the Administration of Justice, by refusing his Assent to Laws for establishing Judiciary Powers.

He has made Judges dependent on his Will alone, for the tenure of their offices, and the amount and payment of their salaries.

He has erected a multitude of New Offices, and sent hither swarms of Officers to harass our People, and eat out their substance.

He has kept among us, in times of peace, Standing Armies without the Consent of our legislature.

He has affected to render the Military independent of and superior to the Civil Power.

He has combined with others to subject us to a jurisdiction foreign to our constitution, and unacknowledged by our laws; giving his Assent to their Acts of pretended Legislation:

For quartering large bodies of armed troops among us:

For protecting them, by a mock Trial, from Punishment for any Murders which they should commit on the Inhabitants of these States:

For cutting off our Trade with all parts of the world:

For imposing taxes on us without our Consent:

For depriving us in many cases, of the benefits of Trial by Jury:

For transporting us beyond Seas to be tried for pretended offences:

For abolishing the free System of English Laws in a neighboring Province, establishing therein an Arbitrary government, and enlarging its Boundaries so as to render it at once an example and fit instrument for introducing the same absolute rule into these Colonies:

For taking away our Charters, abolishing our most valuable Laws, and altering fundamentally the Forms of our Governments:

For suspending our own Legislatures, and declaring themselves invested with Power to legislate for us in all cases whatsoever.

He has abdicated Government here, by declaring us out of his Protection and waging War against us.

He has plundered our seas, ravaged our Coasts, burnt our towns, and destroyed the lives of our people.

He is at this time transporting large armies of foreign mercenaries to compleat the works of death, desolation and tyranny, already begun with circumstances of Cruelty, and perfidy scarcely paralleled in the most barbarous ages, and totally unworthy the Head of a civilized nation.

He has constrained our fellow Citizens taken Captive on the high Seas to bear Arms against their Country, to become the executioners of their friends and Brethren, or to fall themselves by their Hands.

He has excited domestic insurrections amongst us, and has endeavoured to bring on the inhabitants of our frontiers, the merciless Indian Savages, whose known rule of warfare, is an undistinguished destruction of all ages, sexes and conditions.

In every stage of these Oppressions we have Petitioned for Redress in the most humble terms: Our repeated Petitions have been answered only by repeated injury. A Prince, whose character is thus marked by every act which may define a Tyrant, is unfit to be the ruler of a free People.

Nor have we been wanting in attention to our British brethren. We have warned them from time to time of attempts by their legislature to extend an unwarrantable jurisdiction over us. We have reminded them of the circumstances of our emigration and settlement here. We have appealed to their native justice and magnanimity and we have conjured them by the ties of our common kindred to disavow these usurpations, which, would inevitably interrupt our connections and correspondence. They too have been deaf to the voice of justice and of consanguinity. We must, therefore, acquiesce in the necessity which denounces our Separation, and hold them, as we hold the rest of mankind, Enemies in War, in Peace Friends.

We, therefore, the Representatives of the United States of America, in General Congress, Assembled, appealing to the Supreme Judge of the world for the rectitude of our intentions, do, in the Name, and by Authority of the good People of these Colonies, solemnly publish and declare, that these United Colonies are, and of Right ought to be Free and Independent States; that they are Absolved from all allegiance to the British Crown, and that all political connection between them and the State of Great Britain, is and ought to be totally dissolved; and that as Free and Independent States, they have full power to levy War, conclude Peace, contract Alliances, establish Commerce, and to do all other Acts and Things which Independent States may of right do. And for the support of the Declaration, with a firm reliance on the Protection of Divine Providence, we mutually pledge to each other our Lives, our Fortunes and our sacred Honor.

QUESTIONS

1. *The Declaration of Independence* is a statement of political principles. What are they?

2. The *Declaration* was meant to be a piece of political propaganda as well as political philosophy. How is this reflected in the document?

3. Why does Jefferson single out George III as the principal villain in his story?

4. Jefferson's argument was very persuasive for many people, but there were also those who remained unconvinced. Can you construct an argument against his case?

5. The *Declaration*'s ultimate goal is the achievement of the public welfare. This was also the aim of enlightened despots such as Maria Theresa. Would Jefferson and Maria Theresa agree about what the "public good" was? How would their means to this common end differ?

95.   CESARE BECCARIA

ON CRIMES AND PUNISHMENTS
(1764)

Cesare Beccaria (1738–94) came from an aristocratic family in northern Italy. He received the standard legal education of the day and became a doctor of laws in 1758. In Milan at the time resided a group of enlightened intellectuals who called themselves the "academy of fists"; they were social reformers who were dedicated to overthrowing bigotry and narrow-mindedness. Beccaria's work on legal reform grew out of their inspiration and his commitment to an improved legal system. His proposals made him famous throughout Europe, and he was appointed to high office in Milan, where he served for the rest of his life.

On Crimes and Punishments had an enormous impact on European law. The first systematic treatment of crime and punishment to be published, it opened debate on such controversial issues as the use of torture to extract confessions and the use of capital punishment to deter offenders. Law codes were reformed in light of Beccaria's principles and entire schools of legal and social reform, especially the English Utilitarians, took their inspiration from it.

If we glance at the pages of history, we will find that laws, which surely are, or ought to be, compacts of free men, have been, for the most part, a mere tool of the passions of some, or have arisen from an accidental and temporary need. Never have they been dictated by a dispassionate student of human nature who might, by bringing the actions of a multitude of men into focus, consider them from this single point of view; the *greatest happiness shared by the greatest number.* Happy are those few nations that have not waited for the slow succession of coincidence and human vicissitude to force some little turn for the better after the limit of evil has been reached, but have facilitated the intermediate progress by means of good laws.

Imprisonment

An error no less common that it is contrary to the purpose of association—which is assurance of personal security—is that of allowing a magistrate charged with administering the laws to be free to imprison a citizen at his own pleasure, to deprive an enemy of liberty on frivolous pretexts, and to leave a friend unpunished notwithstanding the clearest evidences of his guilt. Detention in prison is a punishment which, unlike every other, must of necessity precede conviction for crime, but this distinctive character does not remove the other which is essential—namely, that only the law determines the cases in which a man is to suffer punishment. It pertains to the law, therefore, to indicate what evidences of crime justify detention of the accused, his subjection to investigation and punishment. A man's notoriety, his flight, his nonjudicial confession, the confession of an accomplice, threats and the constant enmity of the injured person, the manifest fact of the crime, and similar evidences, are proofs sufficient to justify imprisonment of a citizen. But these proofs must be determined by the law, not by judges, whose decrees are always contrary to political liberty when they are not particular applications of a general maxim included in the public code. When punishments have become more moderate, when squalor and hunger have been removed from prisons, when pity and mercy have forced a way through barred doors, overmastering the inexorable and obdurate ministers of justice, then may the laws be content with slighter evidences as grounds for imprisonment.

A man accused of a crime, who has been imprisoned and acquitted, ought not to be branded with infamy. How many Romans accused of very great crimes, and then found innocent, were revered by the populace and honored with public offices! For what reason, then, is the fate of an innocent person so apt to be different in our time? It seems to be because, in the present system of criminal law, the idea of power and arrogance prevails over that of justice, because accused and convicted are thrown indiscriminately into the same cell, because imprisonment is rather the torment than the confinement of the accused, and because the internal power that protects the laws and the external power that defends the throne and nation are separated when they ought to be united. By means of the common sanction of the laws, the former [internal power] would be combined with judicial authority, without, however, passing directly under its sway; the glory that attends the pomp and ceremony of a military corps would remove infamy, which, like all popular sentiments, is more attached to the manner than to the thing itself, as is proved by the fact that military prisons are, according to the common opinion, less disgraceful than the civil. Still discernible in our people, in their customs and laws, which always lag several ages behind the actual enlightened thought of a nation—still discernible are the barbaric impressions and savage notions of those people of the North who hunted down our forefathers.

The Death Penalty

This useless prodigality of torments, which has never made men better, has promoted me to examine whether death is really useful and just in a well-organized government.

What manner of right can men attribute to themselves to slaughter their fellow beings? Certainly not that from which sovereignty and the laws derive. These are nothing but the sum of the least portions of the private liberty of each person; they represent the general will, which is the aggregate of particular wills. Was there ever a man who can have wished to leave to other men the choice of killing him? Is it conceivable that the least sacrifice of each person's liberty should include sacrifice of the greatest of all goods, life? And if that were the case, how could such a principle be reconciled with the other, that man is not entitled to take his own life? He must be, if he can surrender that right to others or to society as a whole.

The punishment of death, therefore, is not a right, for I have demonstrated that it cannot be such; but it is the war of a nation against a citizen whose destruction it judges to be necessary or useful. If, then, I can show that death is neither useful nor necessary I shall have gained the cause of humanity.

There are only two possible motives for believing that the death of a citizen is necessary. The first: when it is evident that even if deprived of liberty he still has connections and power such as endanger the security of the nation—when, that is, his existence can produce a dangerous revolution in the established form of government. The death of a citizen thus becomes necessary when a nation is recovering or losing its liberty or, in time of anarchy, when disorders themselves take the place of laws. But while the laws reign tranquilly, in a form of government enjoying the consent of the entire nation, well defended externally and internally by force, and by opinion, which is perhaps even more efficacious than force, where executive power is lodged with the true sovereign alone, where riches purchase pleasures and not authority. I see no necessity for destroying a citizen, except if his death were the only real way of restraining others from committing crimes; this is the second motive for believing that the death penalty may be just and necessary.

It is not the intensity of punishment that has the greatest effect on the human spirit, but its duration, for our sensibility is more easily and more permanently affected by slight but repeated impressions than by a powerful but momentary action. The sway of habit is universal over every sentient being; as man speaks and walks and satisfies his needs by its aid, so the ideas of morality come to be stamped upon the mind only by long and repeated impressions. It is not the terrible yet momentary spectacle of the death of a wretch, but the long and painful example of a man deprived of liberty, who, having become a beast of burden, recompenses with his labors the society he has offended, which is the strongest curb against crimes. That efficacious idea—efficacious, because very often repeated to ourselves—"I myself shall be reduced to so long and miserable a condition if I commit a similar misdeed" is far more potent than the idea of death, which men envision always at an obsure distance.

The death penalty becomes for the majority a spectacle and for some others an object of compassion mixed with disdain; these two sentiments rather than the salutary fear which the laws pretend to inspire occupy the spirits of the spectators. But in moderate and prolonged punishments the dominant sentiment is the latter, because it is the only one. The limit which the legislator ought to fix on the rigor of punishments would seem to be determined by the sentiment of compassion itself, when it begins to prevail over every other in the hearts of those who are the witnesses of punishment, inflicted for their sake rather than for the criminal's.

For a punishment to be just it should consist of only such gradations of intensity as suffice to deter men from committing crimes. Now, the person does not exist who, reflecting upon it, could choose for himself total and perpetual loss of personal liberty, no matter how advantageous a crime might seem to be. Thus the inten-

sity of the punishment of a life sentence of servitude, in place of the death penalty, has in it what suffices to deter any determined spirit. It has, let me add, even more. Many men are able to look calmly and with firmness upon death—some from fanaticism, some from vanity, which almost always accompanies man even beyond the tomb, some from a final and desperate attempt either to live no longer or to escape their misery. But neither fanaticism nor vanity can subsist among fetters or chains, under the rod, under the yoke, in a cage of iron, where the desperate wretch does not end his woes but merely begins them. Our spirit resists violence and extreme but momentary pains more easily than it does time and incessant weariness, for it can, so to speak, collect itself for a moment to repel the first, but the vigor of its elasticity does not suffice to resist the long and repeated action of the second.

If one were to cite against me the example of all the ages and of almost all the nations that have applied the death penalty to certain crimes, my reply would be that the example reduced itself to nothing in the face of truth, against which there is no prescription; that the history of men leaves us with the impression of a vast sea of errors, among which, at great intervals, some rare and hardly intelligible truths appear to float on the surface. Human sacrifices were once common to almost all nations, yet who will dare to defend them? That only a few societies, and for a short time only, have abstained from applying the death penalty, stands in my favor rather than against me, for that conforms with the usual lot of great truths; which are about as long-lasting as a lightning flash in comparison with the long dark night that envelops mankind. The happy time has not yet arrived in which truth shall be the portion of the greatest number, as error has heretofore been. And from this universal law those truths only have been exempted which Infinite Wisdom has chosen to distinguish from others by revealing them.

QUESTIONS

1. What should be the basic underlying principle of a law, according to Beccaria?

2. Beccaria condemns the contemporary form of sentencing individuals. What is wrong with it, and how would he change it?

3. What is Beccaria's opinion of the death penalty?

4. *On Crimes and Punishments* argues that capital punishment is not a deterrent. Why? What is a better deterrent?

5. *On Crimes and Punishments* is a work of the Enlightenment. Think about some of the other documents of the same period: What general characteristics do they seem to share?

96.   MARQUIS DE CONDORCET

THE PROGRESS OF THE HUMAN MIND
(1793)

Marie-Jean-Antoine de Caritat, Marquis de Condorcet (1743–94), was the eldest son of an old French noble family. Trained as a mathematician, he wrote a number of technical treatises early in his career and contributed to the great French encyclopedia. Condorcet was a member of a small circle of French philosophers and scientists who popularized the Enlightenment. Although he held a government post as inspector general of the Royal Mint, Condorcet was an enthusiastic supporter of the French Revolution and became secretary of the revolutionary Legislative Assembly. Interested in educational reform, he drafted a plan for the founding of free public schools. He also supported the creation of the Republic but opposed the execution of Louis XVI. Condorcet's moderate stand compromised him with the radical Jacobins, and he was arrested and became a fugitive in 1793. He was eventually caught after a dramatic chase and died in prison.

Condorcet wrote *The Progress of the Human Mind* while he was in hiding. He believed that although humans begin as savages, humanity is steadily progressing toward a state of perfection. Enlightened education is critically important to this progress, while monarchy and religion stand in its way. This work is one of the most important contemporary statements of Enlightenment belief.

The Future Progress of the Human Mind

If man can, with almost complete assurance, predict phenomena when he knows their laws, and if, even when he does not, he can still, with great expectation of success, forecast the future on the basis of his experience of the past, why, then, should it be regarded as a fantastic undertaking to sketch, with some pretence to truth, the future destiny of man on the basis of his history? The sole foundation for belief in the natural sciences is this idea, that the general laws directing the phenomena of the universe, known or unknown, are necessary and constant. Why should this principle be any less true for the development of the intellectual and moral faculties of man than for the other operations of nature? Since beliefs founded on past experience of like conditions provide the only rule of conduct for the wisest of men, why should the philosopher be forbidden to base his conjectures on these same foundations, so long as he does not attribute to them a certainty superior to that warranted by the number, the constancy, and the accuracy of his observations?

Our hopes for the future condition of the human race can be subsumed under three important heads: the abolition of inequality between nations, the progress of equality within each nation, and the true perfection of mankind. Will all nations one day attain that state of civilization which the most enlightened, the freest and the least burdened by prejudices, such as the French and the Anglo-Americans, have attained already? Will the vast gulf that separates these peoples from the slavery of nations under the rule of monarchs, from the barbarism of African tribes, from the ignorance of savages, little by little disappear?

If we glance at the state of the world today we see first of all that in Europe the principles of the French constitution are already those of all enlightened men. We see them too widely propagated, too seriously professed, for priests and

despots to prevent their gradual penetration even into the hovels of their slaves; there they will soon awaken in these slaves the remnants of their common sense and inspire them with that smouldering indignation which not even constant humiliation and fear can smother in the soul of the oppressed.

The time will therefore come when the sun will shine only on free men who know no other master but their reason; when tyrants and slaves, priests and their stupid or hypocritical instruments will exist only in works of history and on the stage; and when we shall think of them only to pity their victims and their dupes; to maintain ourselves in a state of vigilance by thinking on their excesses; and to learn how to recognize and so to destroy, by force of reason, the first seeds of tyranny and superstition, should they ever dare to reappear amongst us.

In looking at the history of societies we shall have had occasion to observe that there is often a great difference between the rights that the law allows its citizens and the rights that they actually enjoy, and, again, between the equality established by political codes and that which in fact exists amongst individuals; and we shall have noticed that these differences were one of the principal causes of the destruction of freedom in the Ancient republics, of the storms that troubled them, and of the weakness that delivered them over to foreign tyrants.

These differences have three main causes: inequality in wealth; inequality in status between the man whose means of subsistence are hereditary and the man whose means are dependent on the length of his life, or, rather, on that part of his life in which he is capable of work; and, finally, inequality in education.

We therefore need to show that these three sorts of real inequality must constantly diminish without however disappearing altogether: for they are the result of natural and necessary causes which it would be foolish and dangerous to wish to eradicate; and one could not even attempt to bring about the entire disappearance of their effects without introducing even more fecund sources of inequality, without striking more direct and more fatal blows at the rights of man.

With all this progress in industry and welfare which establishes a happier proportion between men's talents and their needs, each successive generation will have larger possessions, either as a result of this progress or through the preservation of the products of industry; and so, as a consequence of the physical constitution of the human race, the number of people will increase.

There is another kind of progress within the sciences that is no less important; and that is the perfection of scientific language which is at present so vague and obscure. This improvement could be responsible for making the sciences genuinely popular, even in their first rudiments. Genius can triumph over the inexactitude of language as over other obstacles and can recognize the truth through the strange mask that hides or disguises it. But how can someone with only a limited amount of leisure to devote to his education master and retain even the simplest truths if they are distorted by an imprecise language? The fewer the ideas that he is able to acquire and combine, the more necessary is it that they should be precise and exact. He has no fund of knowledge stored up in his mind which he can draw upon to protect himself from error, and his understanding, not being strengthened and refined by long practice, cannot catch such feeble rays of light as manage to penetrate the obscurities, the ambiguities of an imperfect and perverted language.

Once people are enlightened they will know that they have the right to dispose of their own life and wealth as they choose; they will gradually learn to regard war as the most dreadful of scourges, the most terrible of crimes. The first wars to disappear will be those into which usurpers have forced their subjects in defence of their pretended hereditary rights.

Nations will learn that they cannot conquer other nations without losing their own liberty; that permanent confederations are their only means of preserving their independence; and that they should seek not power but security. Gradually mercantile prejudices will fade away: and a false sense of commercial interest will lose the fearful power it once had of drenching the earth in blood and of ruining nations under pretext of enriching them. When at last the nations come to agree on the principles of politics and morality, when in their own better interests they invite foreigners to share equally in all the benefits men enjoy either through the bounty of nature or by their own industry, then all the causes that produce and perpetuate national animosities and poison national relations will disappear one by one; and nothing will remain to encourage or even to arouse the fury of war.

QUESTIONS

1. How does Condorcet try to predict the future of mankind?

2. What stands in the way of progress? How will these obstacles be overcome?

3. In Condorcet's future world, will there be inequality among individuals?

4. What role does education play in Condorcet's vision?

5. How realistic do you think Condorcet was when he wrote his book?

The French Revolution

97.   ABBÉ DE SIEYÈS

WHAT IS THE THIRD ESTATE?

(1789)

Emmanuel-Joseph Sieyès (1748–1836) came from a middle-class family in provincial France. Son of a notary, he studied at the Sorbonne, and sought a career in the Church, where his talents caused him to rise rapidly in the Catholic hierarchy. Nevertheless, he found that his modest origins hampered his career. Sieyès saw in the French Revolution an opportunity to end the noble privilege that had blighted his own prospects. He championed the interests of the commoners—the third estate—and achieved considerable fame and political influence as a result. He was elected to the National Assembly and voted for the execution of the king. Sieyès's political effectiveness dwindled, however, because of his quarrelsome personality. He did remain at the center of the turbulent events of the 1790s and was instrumental in planning the coup that brought Napoleon Bonaparte to power in 1799. Ironically, Napoleon rewarded him with a title of nobility, and thereafter Sieyès faded into the background. Exiled from France for 15 years after Napoleon's fall, Sieyès did not return to Paris until he was near the end of his days.

What Is the Third Estate?, a pamphlet published in January 1789, posed one of the central questions of the Revolution. In it, Sieyès argued that only the underprivileged majority of the nation had the right to reform the French constitution. Government did not belong to the king—it was the prerogative of the people.

The plan of this pamphlet is very simple. We have three questions to ask:

1st. What is the third estate? Everything.

2nd. What has it been heretofore in the political order? Nothing.

3rd. What does it demand? To become something therein.

We shall see if the answers are correct. Then we shall examine the measures that have been tried and those which must be taken in order that the third estate may in fact become *something*. Thus we shall state:

4th. What the ministers have *attempted,* and what the privileged classes themselves *propose* in it favor.

5th. What *ought* to have been done.

6th. Finally, what *remains* to be done in order that the third estate may take its rightful place.

The Third Estate Is a Complete Nation

What are the essentials of national existence and prosperity? *Private* enterprise and *public* functions.

Private enterprise may be divided into four classes: 1st. Since earth and water furnish the raw material for man's needs, the first class will comprise all families engaged in agricultural pursuits. 2nd. Between the original sale of materials and their consumption or use, further workmanship, more or less manifold, adds to these materials a second value, more or less compounded. Human industry thus succeeds in perfecting the benefits of nature and in increasing the gross produce twofold, tenfold, one hundredfold in value. Such is the work of the second class. 3rd. Between production and consumption, as well as among the different degrees of production, a group of intermediate agents, useful to producers as well as to consumers, comes into being; these are the dealers and merchants. . . . 4th. In addition to these three classes of industrious and useful citizens concerned with goods for consumption and use, a society needs many private undertakings and endeavors which are *directly* useful or agreeable to the *individual.* The fourth class includes from the most distinguished scientific and liberal professions to the least esteemed domestic services. Such are the labors which sustain society. Who performs them? The third estate.

Public functions likewise under present circumstances may be classified under four well known headings: the Sword, the Robe, the Church, and the Administration. It is unnecessary to discuss them in detail in order to demonstrate that the third estate everywhere constitutes nineteen-twentieths of them, except that it is burdened with all that is really arduous, with all the tasks that the privileged order refuses to perform. Only the lucrative and honorary positions are held by members of the privileged order. . . . nevertheless they have dared lay the order of the third estate under an interdict. They have said to it: "Whatever be your services, whatever your talents, you shall go thus far and no farther. It is not fitting that you be honored.". . .

It suffices here to have revealed that the alleged utility of a privileged order to public service is only a chimera; that without it, all that is arduous in such service is performed by the third estate; that without it, the higher positions would be infinitely better filled; that they naturally ought to be the lot of and reward for talents and recognized services; and that if the privileged classes have succeeded in usurping all the lucrative and honorary positions, it is both an odious injustice to the majority of citizens and a treason to the commonwealth.

Who, then, would dare to say that the third estate has not within itself all that is necessary to constitute a complete nation? It is the strong and robust man whose one arm remains enchained, If the privileged order were abolished, the nation would not be something less but something more. Thus, what is the third estate? Everything; but an everything shackled and oppressed. What would it be without the privileged order? Everything; but an everything free and flourishing. Nothing can progress without it; everything would proceed infinitely better without the others. It is not sufficient to have demonstrated that the privileged classes, far from being useful to the nation, can only enfeeble and injure it; it is necessary, moreover, to prove that the nobility does not belong to the social organization at all; that, indeed, it may be a *burden* upon the nation, but that it would not know how to constitute a part thereof.

The third estate, then, comprises everything appertaining to the nation; and whatever is not the third estate may not be regarded as being of the nation. What is the third estate? Everything!

What Has the Third Estate Been Heretofore? Nothing

We shall examine neither the state of servitude in which the people has suffered so long, nor that of constraint and humiliation in which it is still confined. Its civil status has changed; it must change still more; it is indeed impossible that the nation as a whole, or that even any order in particular, may become free if the third estate is not. Freedom is not the consequence of privileges, but of the rights appertaining to all. The third estate must be understood to mean the mass of the citizens belonging to the common order. Legalized privilege in any form deviates from the common order, constitutes an exception to the common law, and, consequently, does not appertain to the third estate at all. We repeat, a common law and a common representation are what constitute *one nation*. It is only too true that one is *nothing* in France when one has only the protection of the common law; if one does not possess some privilege, one must resign oneself to enduring contempt, injury, and vexations of every sort. . . .

But here we have to consider the order of the third estate less in its civil status than in its relation with the constitution. Let us examine its position in the Estates General.

Who have been its so-called representatives? The ennobled or those privileged for a period of years. These false deputies have not even been always freely elected by the people. Sometimes in the Estates General, and almost always in the provincial Estates, the representation of the people has been regarded as a perquisite of certain posts of offices. Add to this appalling truth that, in one manner or another, all branches of the executive power also have fallen to the caste which furnishes the Church, the Robe, and the Sword. A sort of spirit of brotherhood causes the nobles to prefer themselves . . . to the rest of the nation. Usurpation is complete; in truth, they reign.

. . . [I]t is a great error to believe that France is subject to a monarchical régime.

. . . It is the court, and not the monarch, that has reigned. It is the court that makes and unmakes, appoints and discharges ministers, creates and dispenses positions, etc. And what is the court if not the head of this immense aristocracy which overruns all parts of France; which through its members attains all and everywhere does whatever is essential in all parts of the commonwealth?. . .

Let us sum up: the third estate has not heretofore had real representatives in the Estates General. Thus its political rights are null.

What Does the Third Estate Demand? To Become Something

. . . The true petitions of this order may be appreciated only through the authentic claims directed to the government by the large municipalities of the kingdom. What is indicated therein? That the people wishes to be *something*, and, in truth, the very least that is possible. It wishes to have real representatives in the Estates General, that is to say, deputies *drawn from its order*, who are competent to be interpreters of its will and defenders of its interests. But what will it avail it to be present at the Estates General if the predominating interest there is contrary to its own! Its presence would only consecrate the oppression of which it would be the eternal victim. Thus, it is indeed certain that it cannot come to vote at the Estates General unless it is to have in that body *an influence at least equal to that of the privileged classes;* and it demands a number of representatives equal to that of the first two orders together. Finally, this equality of representation would become completely illusory if every chamber voted separately. The third estate demands, then, that votes be taken *by head and not by order.* This is the essence of those claims so alarming to the privileged classes, because they believed that thereby the reform of abuses would become inevitable. The real intention of the third estate is to have an influence in the Estates General equal to that of the privileged classes. I repeat, can it ask less? And is it not clear that if its influence therein is less than equality, it cannot be expected to emerge from its political nullity and become *something*?

But what is indeed unfortunate is that the three articles constituting the demand of the third estate are insufficient to give it this equality of influence which it cannot, in reality, do without. In vain will it obtain an equal number of representatives drawn from its order; the influence of the privileged classes will establish itself and dominate even in the sanctuary of the third estate. . . .

Besides the influence of the aristocracy . . . there is the influence of property. This is natural. I do not proscribe it at all; but one must agree that it is still all to the advantage of the privileged classes. . . . The more one considers this matter, the more obvious the insufficiency of the three demands of the third estate becomes. But finally, such as they are, they have been vigorously attacked. Let us examine the pretexts for this hostility.

[Sieyès then proceeds to this examination by analyzing the three demands under these headings: 1. That the representation of the third estate be chosen only among citizens who really belong to the third estate; 2. That its deputies be equal in number to those of the two privileged orders; 3. That the Estates General vote not by order, but by head. In discussing the third demand he makes the following comment.]

I have only one observation to make. Obviously there are abuses in France; these abuses are profitable to someone; they are scarcely advantageous to the third estate—indeed, they are injurious to it in particular. Now I ask if, in this state of affairs, it is possible to destroy any abuse so long as those who profit therefrom control the *veto*? All justice would be powerless; it would be necessary to rely entirely on the sheer generosity of the privileged classes. Would that be your idea of what constitutes the social order?

What Ought to Have Been Done— Basic Principles

In every free nation—and every nation ought to be free—there is only one way to terminate differences which arise over the constitution. Recourse must be had not to the notables, but to the nation itself. If we lack a constitution we must make one; the nation alone has that right. If we have a constitution, as some persist in maintaining, and if, according thereto, the national assembly is divided, as they claim, into three deputations of three orders of citizens, one cannot, at all events, avoid seeing that one of these orders possesses so strong a claim that further progress cannot be made without giving it consideration. But who has the right to settle such disputes?

1st, Where shall we find the nation? Where it is; in the 40,000 parishes which comprise all the territory, all the inhabitants, and all the tributaries of the commonwealth; there, without a doubt, is the nation. A territorial division should have been indicated to facilitate the means of resolving itself into *arrondissements* of from twenty to thirty parishes for the first deputies. According to a similar plan, the *arrondissements* would have formed provinces, and these would have sent real, special representatives to the capital, with special power to decide on the constitution of the Estates General.

But, you will say, if the majority of citizens had named special representatives, what would have become of the distinction of the three orders? What would have become of privileges? They would have become what they deserve to be. . . .

As we see it, the privileged classes have good reasons for confounding ideas and principles in this matter. Today they will support with intrepidity the contrary of what they advocated six months ago. Then there was only one cry in France: we had no constitution at all and we were demanding the formation of one.

Today not only do we have a constitution, but, if one believes the privileged classes, it comprises two excellent and unassailable provisions. The first [of these] is the division of citizens by order; the second is equality of influence for each and every order in the formation of the national will. Already we have sufficiently proved that even if all these things composed our constitution, the nation could always alter them.

The nature of this *equality* of influence on the national will, which would be attributed to each order, remains to be examined more particularly. We shall see that no idea could be more absurd, and that no nation can show anything similiar in its constitution. . . .

If, then, the French constitution supposedly provides that 200,000 or 300,000 individuals out of 26,000,000 citizens constitute two-thirds of the common will, what to reply if not to affirm that two and two make five?

Individual wills are the sole elements of the general will. The majority may not be deprived of the right to concur in it, nor may ten wills be decreed worth only one against ten others that are worth thirty. These are contradictions in terms, veritable absurdities.

It is useless to talk reason if, for a single instant, this first principle, that the general will is the opinion of the majority and not of the minority, is abandoned. By the same token, it may be decided that the will of one alone will be called the majority, and there is no longer need for either Estates General or national will, etc. . . . for if one will can equal ten, why should it not be worth one hundred, one million, twenty-six millions?

What Remains to Be Done. Development of Some Principles

The time is past when the three orders, thinking only of defending themselves from ministerial despotism, were ready to unite against the common enemy. . . .

The third estate awaits, to no purpose, the meeting of all classes, the restitution of its political rights, and the plenitude of its civil rights; the fear of seeing abuses reformed alarms the first two orders far more than the desire for liberty inspires them. Between liberty and some odious privileges, they have chosen the latter. Their soul is identified with the favors of servitude. Today they dread this Estates General which but lately they invoked so ardently. All is well with them; they no longer complain, except of the spirit of innovation. They no longer lack anything; fear has given them a constitution.

The third estate must perceive in the trend of opinions and circumstances that it can hope for nothing except from its own enlightenment and courage. Reason and justice are in its favor; . . . there is no longer time to work for the conciliation of parties. What accord can be anticipated between the energy of the oppressed and the rage of the oppressors?

They have dared pronounce the word secession. They have menaced the King and the people. Well! Good God! How fortunate for the nation if this so desirable secession might be made permanently! How easy it would be to dispense with the privileged classes! How difficult to induce them to be citizens!

It is certain, then, that only nonprivileged members are capable of being electors and deputies to the national assembly. The wishes of the third estate will always be good for the majority of citizens, those of the privileged classes would always be bad. . . . The third estate, therefore, is sufficient for whatever one may expect from a national assembly; it alone, then, is capable of procuring all the advantages that may reasonably be expected from the Estates General.

QUESTIONS

1. Sieyès wrote to persuade readers of the justice of his cause. How effective is his work? What must such a work accomplish to succeed?

2. What is the position of the third estate under the old régime?

3. What is the part of the privileged classes in France, according to Sieyès?

4. How does Sieyès propose to enfranchise the third estate?

5. If Sieyès's argument for reform were accepted, what would the new French constitution be like?

98.

THE DECLARATION OF THE RIGHTS OF MAN

(1789)

OLYMPE DE GOUGES

THE DECLARATION OF THE RIGHTS OF WOMAN

(1791)

The Declaration of the Rights of Man was one of the earliest and most important political documents of the French Revolution. The National Assembly, having just overthrown the ancien régime, decided to secure the Revolution with a declaration of principle. The *Declaration* was heavily influenced by transatlantic examples. The English Bill of Rights was one model, but more important were the statements of rights in the American state constitutions. These were quickly translated into French and had considerable influence upon the members of the Assembly. *The Declaration of the Rights of Man* is a brief but powerful statement of the central themes of the revolution: Liberty, Equality, and Fraternity.

The political and intellectual ferment of the Revolution also gave rise to a new assertiveness by some French women. Olympe de Gouges, the daughter of a provincial butcher, was one who felt that the declaration of 1789 did not go far enough. In 1791, dissatisfied with the unequal position women continued to hold in spite of the Revolution, she wrote *The Declaration of the Rights of Woman*. Addressing herself to the queen rather than to Louis XVI or the National Assembly, de Gouges demanded political and social rights for women.

THE DECLARATION OF THE RIGHTS OF MAN AND OF THE CITIZEN

The representatives of the French people, organized as a National Assembly, believing that the ignorance, neglect, or contempt of the rights of man are the sole cause of public calamities and of the corruption of governments, have determined to set forth in a solemn declaration the natural, inalienable, and sacred rights of man, in order that this declaration, being constantly before all the members of the social body, shall remind them continually of their rights and duties; in order that the acts of the legislative power, as well as those of the executive power, may be compared at any moment with the objects and purposes of all political institutions and may thus be more respected; and, lastly, in order that the grievances of the citizens, based hereafter upon simple and incontestable principles, shall tend to the maintenance of the constitution and redound to the happiness of all. Therefore the National Assembly recognizes and proclaims, in the presence and under the auspices of the Supreme Being, the following rights of man and of the citizen:

1.   Men are born and remain free and equal in rights. Social distinctions may be founded only upon the general good.

2.   The aim of all political association is the preservation of the natural and imprescriptible rights of man. These rights are liberty, property, security, and resistance to oppression.

3.   The principle of all sovereignty resides essentially in the nation. No body nor individual may exercise any authority which does not proceed directly from the nation.

4.   Liberty consists in the freedom to do everything which injures no one else; hence the exercise of the natural rights of each man has no limits except those which assure to the other members of the society the enjoyment of the same rights. These limits can only be determined by law.

5.   Law can only prohibit such actions as are hurtful to society. Nothing may be prevented which is not forbidden by law, and no one may be forced to do anything not provided for by law.

6.   Law is the expression of the general will. Every citizen has a right to participate personally, or through his representative, in its formation. It must be the same for all, whether it protects or punishes. All citizens, being equal in the eyes of the law, are equally eligible to all dignities and to all public positions and occupations, according to their abilities, and without distinction except that of their virtues and talents.

7.   No person shall be accused, arrested, or imprisoned except in the cases and according to the forms prescribed by law. Any one soliciting, transmitting, executing, or causing to be executed, any arbitrary order, shall be punished. But any citizen summoned or arrested in virtue of the law shall submit without delay, as resistance constitutes an offense.

8. The law shall provide for such punishments only as are strictly and obviously necessary, and no one shall suffer punishment except it be legally inflicted in virtue of a law passed and promulgated before the commission of the offense.

9. As all persons are held innocent until they shall have been declared guilty, if arrest shall be deemed indispensable, all harshness not essential to the securing of the prisoner's person shall be severely repressed by law.

10.   No one shall be disquieted on account of his opinions, including his religious views, provided their manifestation does not disturb the public order established by law.

11.   The free communication of ideas and opinions is one of the most precious of the rights of man. Every citizen may, accordingly, speak, write, and print with freedom, but shall be responsible for such abuses of this freedom as shall be defined by law.

12.   The security of the rights of man and of the citizen requires public military forces. These forces are, therefore, established for the good of all and not for the personal advantage of those to whom they shall be intrusted.

13. A common contribution is essential for the maintenance of the public forces and for the cost of administration. This should be equitably distributed among all the citizens in proportion to their means.

14. All the citizens have a right to decide, either personally or by their representatives, as to the necessity of the public contribution; to grant this freely; to know to what uses it is put; and to fix the proportion, the mode of assessment and of collection and the duration of the taxes.

15. Society has the right to require of every public agent an account of his administration.

16. A society in which the observance of the law is not assured, nor the separation of powers defined, has no constitution at all.

17. Since property is an inviolable and sacred right, no one shall be deprived thereof except where public necessity, legally determined, shall clearly demand it, and then only on condition that the owner shall have been previously and equitably indemnified.

THE DECLARATION OF THE RIGHTS OF WOMAN

Man, are you capable of being just? It is a woman who poses the question; you will not deprive her of that right at least. Tell me, what gives you sovereign empire to oppress my sex? Your strength? Your talents? Observe the Creator in his wisdom; survey in all her grandeur that nature with whom you seem to want to be in harmony, and give me, if you dare, an example of this tyrannical empire. Go back to animals, consult the elements, study plants, finally glance at all the modifications of organic matter, and surrender to the evidence when I offer you the means; search, probe, and distinguish, if you can, the sexes in the administration of nature. Everywhere you will find them mingled; everywhere they cooperate in harmonious togetherness in this immortal masterpiece.

Man alone has raised his exceptional circumstances to a principle. Bizarre, blind, bloated with science and degenerated—in a century of enlightenment and wisdom—into the crassest ignorance, he wants to command as a despot a sex which is in full possession of its intellectual faculties; he pretends to enjoy the Revolution and to claim his rights to equality in order to say nothing more about it.

Declaration of the Rights of Woman and the Female Citizen

For the National Assembly to decree in its last sessions, or in those of the next legislature:

Preamble

Mothers, daughters, sisters [and] representatives of the nation demand to be constituted into a national assembly. Believing that ignorance, omission, or scorn for the rights of woman are the only causes of public misfortunes and of the corruption of governments, [the women] have resolved to set forth in a solemn declaration the natural, inalienable, and sacred rights of woman in order that this declaration, constantly exposed before all the members of the society, will ceaselessly remind them of their rights and duties; in order that the authoritative acts of women and the authoritative acts of men may be at any moment compared with and respectful of the purpose of all political institutions; and in order that citizens' demands, henceforth based on simple and incontestable principles, will always support the constitution, good morals, and the happiness of all.

Consequently, the sex that is as superior in beauty as it is in courage during the sufferings of maternity recognizes and declares in the presence and under the auspices of the Supreme Being, the following Rights of Woman and of Female Citizens.

Article I

Woman is born free and lives equal to man in her rights. Social distinctions can be based only on the common utility.

Article II

The purpose of any political association is the conservation of the natural and imprescriptible rights of woman and man; these rights are liberty, property, security, and especially resistance to oppression.

Article III

The principle of all sovereignty rests essentially with the nation, which is nothing but the union of woman and man; no body and no individual can exercise any authority which does not come expressly from it [the nation].

Article IV

Liberty and justice consist of restoring all that belongs to others; thus, the only limits on the exercise of the natural rights of woman are perpetual male tyranny; these limits are to be reformed by the laws of nature and reason.

Article V

Laws of nature and reason proscribe all acts harmful to society; everything which is not prohibited by these wise and divine laws cannot be prevented, and no one can be constrained to do what they do not command.

Article VI

The law must be the expression of the general will; all female and male citizens must contribute either personally or through their representatives to its formation; it must be the same for all: male and female citizens, being equal in the eyes of the law, must be equally admitted to all honors, positions, and public employment according to their capacity and without other distinctions besides those of their virtues and talents.

Article VII

No woman is an exception; she is accused, arrested, and detained in cases determined by law. Women, like men, obey this rigorous law.

Article VIII

The law must establish only those penalties that are strictly and obviously necessary, and no one can be punished except by virtue of a law established and promulgated prior to the crime and legally applicable to women.

Article IX

Once any woman is declared guilty, complete rigor is [to be] exercised by the law.

Article X

No one is to be disquieted for his very basic opinions; woman has the right to mount the scaffold; she must equally have the right to mount the rostrum, provided that her demonstrations do not disturb the legally established public order.

Article XI

The free communication of thoughts and opinions is one of the most precious rights of woman, since that liberty assures the recognition of children by their fathers. Any female citizen thus may say freely, I am the mother of a child which belongs to you, without being forced by a barbarous prejudice to hide the truth; [an exception may be made] to respond to the abuse of this liberty in cases determined by the law.

Article XII

The guarantee of the rights of woman and the female citizen implies a major benefit; this guarantee must be instituted for the advantage of all, and not for the particular benefit of those to whom it is entrusted.

Article XIII

For the support of the public force and the expenses of administration, the contributions of woman and man are equal; she shares all the duties [*corvées*] and all the painful tasks; therefore, she must have the same share in the distribution of positions, employment, offices, honors and jobs [*industrie*].

Article XIV

Female and male citizens have the right to verify, either by themselves or through their representatives, the necessity of the public contribution. This can only apply to women if they are granted an equal share, not only of wealth, but also of public administration, and in the determination of the proportion, the base, the collection, and the duration of the tax.

Article XV

The collectivity of women, joined for tax purposes to the aggregate of men, has the right to demand an accounting of his administration from any public agent.

Article XVI

No society has a constitution without the guarantee of rights and the separation of powers; the constitution is null if the majority of individuals comprising the nation have not cooperated in drafting it.

Article XVII

Property belongs to both sexes whether united or separate; for each it is an inviolable and sacred right; no one can be deprived of it, since it is the true patrimony of nature, unless the legally determined public need obviously dictates it, and then only with a just and prior indemnity.

Postscript

Woman, wake up; the tocsin of reason is being heard throughout the whole universe; discover your rights. The powerful empire of nature is no longer surrounded by prejudice, fanaticism, superstition, and lies. The flame of truth has dispersed all the clouds of folly and usurpation. Enslaved man has multiplied his strength and needs recourse to yours to break his chains. Having become free, he has become unjust to his companion. Oh, women! When will you cease to be blind? What advantage have you received from the Revolution? A more pronounced scorn, a more marked disdain. In the centuries of corruption you ruled only over the weakness of men. The reclamation of your patrimony, based on the wise decrees of nature—what have you to dread from such a fine undertaking? . . .

QUESTIONS

1. Where does sovereignty lie according to the National Assembly?

2. What rights do citizens have under *The Declaration of the Rights of Man*?

3. What is the status of personal property in the Assembly's view?

4. How is *The Declaration of the Rights of Man* similar to the position expressed by other eighteenth-century political thinkers, such as Jefferson and Rousseau?

5. Compare the *Rights of Man* with the *Rights of Woman*. How are they different? How are they alike?

6. What have women achieved in the Revolution, according to de Gouges?

---

99.   EDMUND BURKE

REFLECTIONS ON THE REVOLUTION IN FRANCE
(1790)

Edmund Burke (1729–97) came from the Anglo-Irish gentry. He received a legal education but was always more interested in politics and political theory than the practice of law. Burke entered the House of Commons in 1765, where he remained for almost 30 years. In the 1770s, Burke favored conciliation with the American colonies and argued for a less oppressive government in Ireland. Despite these liberal views, however, he is generally characterized as a conservative political thinker. The French Revolution deeply alarmed him, and he spent much of the rest of his life warning of its dangers.

Reflections is the most important expression of Burke's opposition to revolution. He wrote in defense of tradition and hierarchy in society. Burke believed that the institutions of his day owed much to the wisdom of past generations and that to overthrow them in favor of a new theory or speculation was as dangerous as it was foolish. Burke's conservative arguments against radical change have become vital to conservative thought everywhere.

You might, if you pleased, have profited of our example, and have given to your recovered freedom a correspondent dignity. Your privileges, though discontinued, were not lost to memory. Your constitution, it is true, whilst you were out of possession, suffered waste and dilapidation; but you possessed in some parts the walls, and in all the foundations of a noble and venerable castle. You might have repaired those walls; you might have built on those old foundations. Your constitution was suspended before it was perfected; but you had the elements of a constitution very nearly as good as could be wished.

You had all these advantages in your ancient states; but you chose to act as if you had never been moulded into civil society, and had everything to begin anew. You began ill, because you began by despising every thing that belonged to you. You set up your trade without a capital. If the last generations of your country appeared without much lustre in your eyes, you might have passed them by, and derived your claims from a more early race of ancestors. Under a pious predilection to those ancestors, your imaginations would have realized in them a standard of virtue and wisdom, beyond the vulgar practice of the hour: and you would have risen with the example to whose imitation you aspired. Respecting your forefathers, you would have been taught to respect yourselves. You would not have chosen to consider the French as a people of yesterday, as a nation of low-born servile wretches until the emancipating year of 1789. In order to furnish, at the expense of your honour, an excuse to your apologists here for several enormities of yours, you would not have been content to be represented as a gang of Maroon slaves, suddenly broke loose from the house of bondage, and therefore to be pardoned for your abuse of the liberty to which you were not accustomed and ill fitted.

By following wise examples you would have given new examples of wisdom to the world. You would have rendered the cause of liberty venerable in the eyes of every worthy mind in every nation. You would have shamed despotism from the earth, by showing that freedom was not only reconcilable, but as, when well disciplined it is, auxiliary to law. You would have had an unoppressive but a productive revenue. You would have had a flourishing commerce to feed it. You would have had a free constitution; a potent monarchy; a disciplined army; a reformed and venerated clergy; a mitigated but spirited nobility, to lead your virtue, not to overlay it; you would have had a liberal order of commons, to emulate and to recruit that nobility; you would have had a protected, satisfied, laborious, and obedient people, taught to seek and to recognize the happiness that is to be found by virtue in all conditions; in which consists the true moral equality of mankind, and not in that monstrous fiction, which, by inspiring false ideas and vain expectations into men

destined to travel in the obscure walk of laborious life, serves only to aggravate and embitter that real inequality, which it never can remove; and which the order of civil life establishes as much for the benefit of those whom it must leave in an humble state, as those whom it is able to exalt to a condition more splendid, but not more happy. You had a smooth and easy career of felicity and glory laid open to you, beyond any thing recorded in the history of the world; but you have shewn that difficulty is good for man.

Compute your gains: see what is got by those extravagant and presumptuous speculations which have taught your leaders to despise all their predecessors, and all their contemporaries, and even to despise themselves, until the moment in which they became truly despicable. By following those false lights, France has brought undisguised calamities at a higher price than any nation has purchased the most unequivocal blessings! France has bought poverty by crime! France has not sacrificed her virtue to her interest; but she has abandoned her interest, that she might prostitute her virtue. All other nations have begun the fabric of a new government, or the reformation of an old, by establishing originally, or by enforcing with greater exactness some rites or other of religion. All other people have laid the foundations of civil freedom in severe manners, and a system of a more austere and masculine morality. France, when she let loose the reins of regal authority, doubled the licence, of a ferocious dissoluteness in manners, and of an insolent irreligion in opinions and practices; and has extended through all ranks of life, as if she were communicating some privilege, or laying open some secluded benefit, all the unhappy corruptions that usually were the disease of wealth and power. This is one of the new principles of equality in France.

This was unnatural. The rest is in order. They have found their punishment in their success. Laws overturned; tribunals subverted; industry without vigour; commerce expiring; the revenue unpaid, yet the people impoverished; a church pillaged, and a state not relieved; civil and military anarchy made the constitution of the kingdom; every thing human and divine sacrificed to the idol of public credit, and national bankruptcy the consequence; and to crown all, the paper securities of new, precarious, tottering power, the discredited paper securities of impoverished fraud, and beggared rapine, held out as a currency for the support of an empire, in lieu of the two great recognized species that represent the lasting conventional credit of mankind, which disappeared and hid themselves in the earth from whence they came, when the principle of property, whose creatures and representatives they are, was systematically subverted.

Were all these dreadful things necessary? Were they the inevitable results of the desperate struggle of determined patriots, compelled to wade through blood and tumult, to the quiet shore of a tranquil and prosperous liberty? No! nothing like it. The fresh ruins of France, which shock our feelings wherever we can turn our eyes, are not the devastation of civil war; they are the sad but instructive monuments of rash and ignorant counsel in time of profound peace. They are the display of inconsiderate and presumptuous, because unresisted and irresistible authority. The persons who have thus squandered away the precious treasure of their crimes, the persons who have made this prodigal and wild waste of public evils (the last stake reserved for the ultimate ransom of the state) have met in their progress with little, or rather with no opposition at all.

When men of rank sacrifice all ideas of dignity to an ambition without a distinct object, and work with low instruments and for low ends, the whole composition becomes low and base. Does not something like this now appear in France? Does it not produce something ignoble and inglorious? A kind of meanness in all the prevalent policy? A tendency in all that is done to lower along with individuals all the dignity and importance of the state? Other revolutions have been conducted by persons, who whilst they attempted or effected changes in the commonwealth, sanctified their ambition by advancing the dignity of the people whose peace they troubled. They had long views. They aimed at the rule, not at the destruction of their country. They were men of great civil, and great military talents, and if not for the terror, the ornament of their age.

It is said, that twenty-four millions ought to prevail over two hundred thousand. True; if the constitution of a kingdom be a problem of arithmetic. This sort of discourse does well enough with the lamp-post for its second: to men who *may* reason calmly, it is ridiculous. The will of the many, and their interest, must very often differ; and great will be the difference when they make an evil choice. A government of five hundred country attornies and obscure curates is not good for twenty-four millions of men, though it were chosen by eight and forty millions; nor is it the better for being guided by a dozen of persons of quality, who have betrayed their trust in order to obtain that power.

In France you are now in the crisis of a revolution, and in the transit from one form of government to another—you cannot see that character of men exactly in the same situation in which we see it in this country. With us it is militant; with you it is triumphant; and you know how it can act when its power is commensurate to its will. The worst of these politics of revolution is this; they temper and harden the breast, in order to prepare it for the desperate strokes which are sometimes used in extreme occasions. But as these occasions may never arrive, the mind receives a gratuitous taint; and the moral sentiments suffer not a little, when no political purpose is served by the depravation. This sort of people are so taken up with their theories about the rights of man, that they have totally forgot his nature. Without opening one new avenue to the understanding, they have succeeded in stopping up those that lead to the heart.

QUESTIONS

1. What, according to Burke, did the French do when they overthrew their monarchy? What was their attitude toward the past?

2. What is Burke's view of equality in society?

3. What has been the result of the Revolution, according to Burke? Why has it failed?

4. How do you think Burke, as an Englishman, was influenced by his own nation's constitution?

5. Burke argues that representative democracy is not the best way to run a state. What is wrong with it?

Part V

THE AGE OF REFORM

(continued)

Industrialization in Britain

100.   **ARTHUR YOUNG**

POLITICAL ARITHMETIC

(1774)

Arthur Young (1741–1820) originally intended to pursue a career as a merchant but eventually became a farmer. Although he was never a financial success, Young was a tireless promoter of the use of new scientific and technological methods in farming. He edited an agricultural journal and wrote constantly on the subject. His writings did much to convert British farmers to more efficient techniques; eventually he was appointed to the newly established Board of Agriculture. Young traveled throughout Europe studying agricultural methods and comparing European techniques with English ones.

Political Arithmetic, one of Young's most important works, deals with both economics and politics. Concentrating on agriculture and trade, subjects on which he was an acknowledged expert, Young propounded his views on the connections among a free citizen, a free market, and free trade. His arguments for efficiency and productivity conflicted with the views of those who saw other dimensions to economic activity. His opponent in this selection was Dr. Richard Price (1723–91), a well-known social and political reformer.

Liberty

The advance which the agriculture of this country has made, is owing primarily to the excellency of our constitution—to that general liberty which is diffused among all ranks of the people, and which ensures the legal possessions of every man from the hand of violence and power: This is the original and animating soul that enlivens the husbandry of *Britain.* But it is not owing to this alone that we have attained to an high degree of excellence; other causes also have operated, and very powerful ones, for freedom alone will not do, as we see by *Scotland,* where the constitution is the same, but agriculture abundantly different. This we see also in *Ireland.* Our farmers, and all the people employed by them, enjoy that general freedom and security

which is the birthright, I will not say of *Britons,* but of all mankind. The operations of a correct and spirited agriculture require considerable expence; the returns of which are some years before they come in; such a business, above most others, requires every favour that legislation can shew: A great degree of security of possession is necessary in such a case, not only from the effects of arbitrary power, but also from all oppressions that the nobility, gentry, and wealthy landlords can throw upon their tenants. An *English* farmer, with a lease, is as independent of his landlord, as the landlord is of the farmer; and if he has no lease, we may be sure he is favoured in the rent proportionably to such circumstance. This general liberty, which our farmers enjoy in common with the rest of their fellow-subjects, it must be evident, to all attentive observers, cannot fail of being of the highest consequence to the promotion of good husbandry. It is impossible to enter into a full explanation of all the advantages they receive under this general head; which, in fact, is of all others the greatest encouragement, not only to agriculture, but equally so to arts, manufactures, commerce, and, in a word, every species of industry in the state.

Size of Farms

A statesman, in his ideas of improving the agriculture of his country, ought to give a perfect freedom to landlords and tenants, the one in letting their estates in whatever sized farms they please, and the other in hiring them. But there are writers that will give very different advice, who will assert, that instead of giving such entire liberty, both landlords and tenants ought to be restrained in the circumstance of rendering farms great—since it is supposed that great farms are pernicious to population, and raise the prices of provisions too high. Now as listening to such ideas would in any legislature be a most mischievous circumstance, it is necessary to offer a few general reasons to shew the necessity of giving perfect liberty in this respect.

A considerable farmer, with a greater proportioned wealth than the smaller occupier, is able to work greater improvements in his business, and experience tells us, that this is constantly the case; he can build, hedge, ditch, plant, plough, harrow, drain, manure, hoe, weed, and, in a word, execute every operation of his business, better and more effectually than a little farmer: In the same manner as a wealthy manufacturer always works greater improvements in a fabric than a poor one. He also employs better cattle, and uses better implements; he purchases more manures, and adopts more improvements; all very important objects in making the soil yield its utmost produce. The raising greater crops of every sort, so far increases the solid public wealth of the kingdom; himself, his landlord, and the

nation are the richer for the size of his farm; his wealth is raised by those improvements which are most of them wrought by an increase of labour; he employs more hands in proportion than the little tenant, consequently he promotes population more powerfully; for in every branch of industry *employment is the soul of population*. Thus he employs more people and he creates more wealth, which again sets more hands to work, and in the whole of his course does more effectual service to his country. The gentlemen who maintain a contrary opinion must virtually assert that good husbandry is pernicious, bad husbandry beneficial; a position which I leave them to meditate on.

Dr. *Price* has the following observation:— "Let a tract of ground be supposed in the hands of a multitude of little proprietors and tenants who maintain themselves and families by the produce of the ground they occupy, by sheep kept on a common, by poultry, hogs, &c. and who therefore have little occasion to purchase any of the means of subsistence. If this land gets into the hands of a few great farmers, the consequence must be, that the little farmers will be converted into a body of men who earn their subsistence by working for others, and who will be under a necessity of going to market for all they want: And subsistence in this way being difficult, families of children will become burthens, marriage will be avoided, and population will decline. At the same time perhaps there will be more labour because there will be more compulsion to it. More bread will be consumed, and therefore more corn grown; because there will be less ability of going to the price of other food. Parishes likewise will be more loaded, because the number of poor will be greater. And towns and manufactures will increase, because more will be driven to them in quest of places and employments. This is the way in which the engrossing of farms naturally operates: And this is the way in which for many years it has been actually operating in this kingdom."

It is a very barren disquisition to enquire into the different means of promoting population, without we previously shew that the increase of people will be of any use comparable to the evils that will attend it. The Doctor sets out with the idea that the minute sub-division of landed property is favourable to population: It may be so. But what would a nation of cottagers do for their defence? They would become the prey of the first invader: they are to have neither manufactures nor commerce; for, says he, a flourishing commerce whilst it flatters may be destroying. What does this mean but proscribing it? For we must take men's sentiments in their tendency, and not admit the ideal measure and degree of trade and luxury which they will allow, as if it was in human power to say to wealth, So far shalt thou go, and no farther. This nation of cottagers therefore must pay all taxes, which we may suppose sufficiently productive to support the magnificence of a shepherd king—no army—no fleet—no wars— What has such a situation to do with the state of the modern world! If the author says it is extravagant to carry his idea so far, I reply, such a supposition shews the necessity of limits—shews that we must have something else in a modern state than the cultivators of seven jugers. If this is admitted, how far is the exception to go? Who is to lay down the line of division, and say, Here propriety ends—there excess begins? In a word, the great fact proved by this argument is, that you must give up a degree of population in favour of more important objects—that is, you must admit commerce and wealth—This must be admitted—I desire no other concession: your whole system at once tumbles about your ears. My politics of classing national wealth before population, needs no exception—it sets population at defiance—Yours of giving populousness the first rank, necessitates you to call in a superior to your assistance—and like all superior powers called to the support of the weaker, it destroys their independence.

But to proceed: the Doctor says, when the land is got into few hands, the little farmers must become labourers: Certainly; and in that state are just as useful to the nation as in their former. But, says he, subsistence then being difficult,

Arthur Young, Esq., served as secretary to the Board of Agriculture in the 1700s.

they will not marry: So marriage, in a given state, thrives in proportion to the ability of maintaining families. In the back country of *America,* where every child is 50 acres to the father, and the wife 100—where there is no society beyond the cottage, and where a woman is necessary almost to the existence of a man—I admit this. In a modern *European* state, I deny it: I appeal to every man's observation for telling him that celibacy is more common among the wealthy than the poor—and that the classes least able to support a family, marry more readily than the rich. At the same time, says the Doctor, there will be more labour: then I reply, there is every thing we want, for labour is the valuable effect of population. In a great farm there is but one idle person, in a small one there is the same. Sure, therefore, the supernumerary farmers are a mere burthen to the state; an idea applicable to every one who stands in the place of a labourer without performing his office, but consumes those products that ought to go to market.

There is one argument I have heard in conversation against large farms, which appears more specious than any to be found against them in Dr. *Price.* It is said, that large farms are in fact machines in agriculture, which enable the cultivators of the soil to do that with few hands which before they did with many; resembling a stockingloom, for instance, which enables the master manufacturer to turn off half his hands, and yet make more stockings than ever. A lively argument, but false in almost every particular; indeed the resemblance holds no farther than the capacity of performing in some operations much more with ten men in one farm, than with the same number divided among the five farms; of which there can be no doubt: But I appeal to all persons conversant in husbandry, if this holds true through one-tenth of the labour of a farm; witness ploughing, harrowing, sowing, digging, mowing, reaping, threshing, hedging, ditching, and an hundred other articles in which one man, separately taken, performs the full tenth of ten men collected. The saving of labour is but in few articles, such as carting hay or corn; carting dung or marl; keeping sheep, &c.

But take the comparison in another light. Who dungs most? Who brings most manure from towns? Who digs most chalk, clay or marl? Who cultivates most turnips? Which hoes them best? Which plants most peas, beans, potatoes, &c. in rows for hand-hoeing? Who digs most drains? Who digs the largest and deepest ditches? Which gives the soil the most numerous, deep and effective ploughings? Which brought into culture the most waste land? Who in all this, and many things more, expends most labour in proportion to their acres, the great or the little farmers? That any man who pretends to know wheat from barley should assert so preposterous an idea as the *poorer* occupier to be the *best* cultivator, is not a little astonishing. Nothing appears to me so reasonable as the contrary; and when I compared the population of 250 different-sized farms, the fact turned out as every one might suppose.

As to the change of the consumption from meat to bread, it is perfectly harmless—for I know no good in one being consumed more than in another, as long as meat is dear enough to induce the farmers to keep proper stocks of cattle for manure. But it is a little extraordinary if the consumption of meat declines so much, that the price should continue so high. Farther, towns and manufactures will increase—This is a great misfortune in the Doctor's political creed—but I would recommend him, if he will hold national wealth in contempt, to consider manufactures in that most beautiful idea of Mr. *Hume's*—*a storehouse of labour for the public:* those hands which are employed in these fabrics yield a surplus always at the service of government—but what navies, what armies are recruited from farmers? The people employed in raising food must be tied to the soil, and so we every where see them. The fewer employed (consistently with good husbandry) the better; for then the less product is intercepted before it reaches the markets, and you may have so many the more for manufacturers, sailors and soldiers.

QUESTIONS

1.   How does government affect the agricultural economy?

2.   Young argues that farmers should be free to farm as much land as they choose. What is the argument in favor of small farms? How does Young reply to it?

3. Dr. Price maintains that a growing population is at the heart of national well-being; Young argues that national wealth is more important. What is the difference?

4. Young has been criticized for ignoring the needs of the poor. Would you agree?

5. The author reveals a number of assumptions about what makes a nation important and powerful. What are these? Do they apply today?

101.   SAMUEL SMILES

SELF-HELP

(1859)

Samuel Smiles (1812–1904) was born in Scotland, one of 11 children. His father died when he was a child, and Smiles was forced to learn firsthand the value of hard work and independence. Although he was trained as a doctor, he gave up his medical practice for journalism when he moved to England. Ultimately, Smiles came to edit the *Leeds Times,* a newspaper that championed radical reform. He believed in the benefits of science and progress and stood squarely behind such liberal values as free trade and private enterprise; most of all, he was an advocate of self-reliance. He wrote several books, all promoting the Victorian values he most cherished: *Character* (1871), *Thrift* (1875), and *Duty* (1880).

Smiles's most successful book was *Self-Help.* The examples of successful English manufacturers, such as Josiah Wedgwood, captured the interest of government leaders and the imagination of the urban middle classes. *Self-Help* was translated not only into the major European languages, but also into Turkish, Arabic, and Japanese, and was a worldwide best-seller.

Josiah Wedgwood was one of those indefatigable men who from time to time spring from the ranks of the common people, and by their energetic character not only practically educate the working population in habits of industry, but by the example of diligence and perseverance which they set before them, largely influence the public activity in all directions, and contribute in a great degree to form the national character. He was, like Artwright, the youngest of a family of thirteen children. His grandfather and granduncle were both potters, as was also his father, who died when he was a mere boy, leaving him a patrimony of twenty pounds. He had learned to read and write at the village school; but on the death of his father he was taken from it and set to work as a "thrower" in a small pottery carried on by his elder brother. There he began life, his working life, to use his own words, "at the lowest round of the ladder," when only eleven years old. He was shortly after seized by an attack of virulent smallpox, from the effects of which he suffered during the rest of his life, for it was followed by a disease in the right knee, which recurred at frequent intervals, and was only got rid of by the amputation of the limb many years later. Mr. Gladstone, in his eloquent eulogy on Wedgwood recently delivered at Burslem, well observed that the disease from which he suffered was not improbably the occasion of his subsequent excellence. "It prevented him from growing up to be the active, vigorous English workman, possessed of all his limbs, and knowing right well the use of them; but it put him upon considering whether, as he could not be that, he might not be something else, and something greater. It sent his mind inward; it drove him to meditate upon the laws and secrets of his art. The result was, that he arrived at a perception and a grasp of them which might, perhaps, have been envied, certainly have been owned, by an Athenian potter."

When he had completed his apprenticeship with his brother, Josiah joined partnership with another workman, and carried on a small business in making knife-hafts, boxes, and sundry articles for domestic use. Another partnership followed, when he proceeded to make melon table-plates, green pickle leaves, candlesticks, snuff-boxes, and such like articles; but he made comparatively little progress until he began business on his own account at Burslem in the year 1759. There he diligently pursued his calling,

introducing new articles to the trade, and gradually extending his business. What he chiefly aimed at was to manufacture cream-colored ware of a better quality than was then produced in Staffordshire as regarded shape, color, glaze and durability. To understand the subject thoroughly, he devoted his leisure to the study of chemistry; and he made numerous experiments on fluxes, glazes, and various sorts of clay. Being a close inquirer and accurate observer, he noticed that a certain earth containing silica, which was black before calcination, became white after exposure to the heat of a furnace. This fact, observed and pondered on, led to the idea of mixing silica with the red powder of the potteries, and to the discovery that the mixture becomes white when calcined. He had but to cover this material with a vitrification of transparent glaze to obtain one of the most important products of fictile art—that which, under the name of English earthenware, was to attain the greatest commercial value and become of the most extensive utility.

Wedgwood was for some time much troubled by his furnaces, though nothing like to the same extent that Palissy was; and he overcame his difficulties in the same way—by repeated experiments and unfaltering perseverance. His first attempts at making porcelain for table use were a succession of disastrous failures—the labors of months being often destroyed in a day. It was only after a long series of trials, in the course of which he lost time, money and labor, that he arrived at the proper sort of glaze to be used; but he would not be denied, and at last he conquered success through patience. The improvement of pottery became his passion, and was never lost sight of for a moment. Even when he had mastered his difficulties, and become a prosperous man—manufacturing white stone ware and cream-colored ware in large quantities for home and foreign use—he went forward perfecting his manufactures, until, his example extending in all directions, the action of the entire district was stimulated, and a great branch of British industry was eventually established on firm foundations. He aimed throughout at the highest excellence, declaring his determination "to give over manufacturing any article, whatsoever it might be, rather than to degrade it."

Wedgwood was cordially helped by many persons of rank and influence; for, working in the truest spirit, he readily commanded the help and encouragement of other true workers. He made for Queen Charlotte the first royal table-service of English manufacture, of the kind afterward called "queen's-ware," and was appointed Royal Potter: a title which he prized more than if he had been made a baron. Valuable sets of porcelain were intrusted to him for imitation, in which he succeeded to admiration. Sir William Hamilton lent him specimens of ancient art from Herculaneum, of which he produced accurate and beautiful copies. The Duchess of Portland outbid him for the Barberini Vase when that article was offered for sale. He bid as high as seventeen hundred guineas for it: her grace secured it for eighteen hundred; but when she learned Wedgwood's object she at once generously lent him the vase to copy. He produced fifty copies at a cost of about £2,500, and his expenses were not covered by their sale; but he gained his object, which was to show that whatever had been done, that English skill and energy could and would accomplish.

Wedgwood called to his aid the crucible of the chemist, the knowledge of the antiquary, and the skill of the artist. He found out Flaxman when a youth, and while he liberally nurtured his genius, drew from him a large number of beautiful designs for his pottery and porcelain; converting them by his manufacture into objects of taste and excellence, and thus making them instrumental in the diffusion of classical art among the people. By careful experiment and study he was even enabled to rediscover the art of painting on porcelain or earthenware vases and similar articles—an art practiced by the ancient Etruscans, but which had been lost since the time of Pliny. He distinguished himself by his own contributions to science; and his name is still identified with the pyrometer which he invented. He was an indefatigable supporter of all measures of public utility; and the construction of the Trent and Mersey Canal, which completed the navigable communication between the eastern and western sides of the island, was mainly due to his public-spirited exertions, allied to the engineering skill of Brindley. The road accommodation of the district being of an execrable character, he planned and executed a turnpike-road through the potteries, ten miles in length. The reputation he achieved was such that his works at Burslem, and subsequently those at Etruria, which he founded and built, became a point of attraction to distinguished visitors from all parts of Europe.

The result of Wedgwood's labors was, that the manufacture of pottery, which he found in the very lowest condition, became one of the staples of England; and instead of importing what we needed for home use from abroad, we became large exporters to other countries, supplying them with earthenware even in the face of enormous prohibitory duties on articles of British produce. Wedgwood gave evidence as to his manufactures before Parliament in 1785, only some thirty years after he had begun his operations; from which it appeared, that instead of providing only casual employment to a small number of inefficient and badly remunerated workmen, about 20,000 persons then derived their bread directly from the manufacture of earthenware, without taking into account the increased numbers to which it gave employment in coal-mines, and in the carrying trade by land and sea, and the stimulus which it gave to employment in many ways in various parts of the country. Yet, important as had been the advances made in his time, Mr. Wedgwood was of opinion that the manufacture was but in its infancy, and that the improvements which he had effected were of but small amount compared with those to which the art was capable of attaining, through the continued industry and growing intelligence of the manufacturers, and the natural facilities and political advantages enjoyed by Great Britain; an opinion which has been fully borne out by the progress which has since been effected in this important branch of industry. In 1852 not fewer than 84,000,000 pieces of pottery were exported from England to other countries, besides what were made for home use. But it is not merely the quantity and value of the produce that is entitled to consideration, but the improvement of the condition of the population by whom this great branch of industry is conducted.

When Wedgwood began his labors, the Staffordshire district was only in a half-civilized state. The people were poor, uncultivated, and few in number. When Wedgwood's manufacture was firmly established, there was found employment at good wages for three times the number of population; while their moral advancement had kept pace with their material improvement.

Men such as these are fairly entitled to take rank as the Industrial Heroes of the civilized world. Their patient self-reliance amid trials and difficulties, their courage and perseverance in the pursuit of worthy objects, are not less heroic of their kind than the bravery and devotion of the soldier and the sailor, whose duty and pride it is heroically to defend what these valiant leaders of industry have so heroically achieved.

QUESTIONS

1. What qualities does Smiles admire most in a person?

2. Josiah Wedgwood became one of the most successful manufacturers of his time. What were the principal factors behind his rise?

3. Smiles's account of Wedgwood's success reveals something about early Victorian views about formal education and practical experience. Which was more important?

4. What was Wedgwood's contribution to the British economy?

5. From whose point of view is *Self-Help* written? How might Smiles's account have been different if he had been writing from the perspective of one of Wedgwood's employees or a member of the titled aristocracy?

INQUIRY INTO THE CONDITION
OF THE POOR

(1842)

Sir Edwin Chadwick (1800–90) was one of the most active of all nineteenth-century social reformers in Britain. Born in the industrial north, he saw the effects of the new industrialization on both people and the environment. He made public health issues his own specialty and advocated a wide range of health reforms. He worked first as an investigator for the Royal Commission that examined the effectiveness of the Poor Laws, and later rose to become its secretary. His work led to the creation of a Board of Health and to one of the first Public Health Acts in European history. Local authorities were required to improve sewerage, roads, and housing and to appoint local medical examiners.

Chadwick compiled his *Inquiry into the Condition of the Poor* for the use of the British government. He documented the unsafe and unhealthy conditions of Britain's working poor and pressed for parliamentary reform. It was this report and his constant agitation that led to the Public Health Act (1848).

The evils arising from the bad ventilation of places of work will probably be most distinctly brought to view, by the consideration of the evidence as to its effects on one particular class of workpeople.

The frequency of cases of early deaths, and orphanage, and widowhood amongst one class of labourers, the journeymen tailors, led me to make some inquiries as to the causes affecting them; and I submit the following evidence for peculiar consideration, as an illustration of the operation of one predominant cause; bad ventilation or overcrowding, and the consequences on the moral habits, the loss of healthful existence and happiness to the labourer, the loss of profit to the employer, and of produce to the community, and the loss in expenditure for the relief of the destitution, which original cause (the bad ventilation) we have high scientific

authority for stating to be easily and economically controllable.

Mr. Thomas Brownlow, tailor, aged 52:

"It is stated that you have been a journeyman tailor, and now work for yourself. At what description of places have you worked?—I have always worked at the largest places in London; one part of my time I worked at Messrs. Allen's, of Old Bond-street where I worked eight years; at another part of my time I worked at Messrs. Stultze's, in Clifford-street, where I worked four years. At Messrs. Allen's they had then from 80 to 100 men at work; at Messrs. Stultze's they had, when I worked there, about 250 men.

"Will you describe the places of work, and the effects manifested in the health of the workmen?—The place in which we used to work at Messrs. Allen's was a room where 80 men worked together. It was a room about 16 or 18 yards long, and 7 or 8 yards wide, lighted with skylights; the men were close together, nearly knee to knee. In summer time the heat of the men and the heat of the irons made the room 20 or 30 degrees higher than the heat outside; the heat was then most suffocating, especially after the candles were lighted. I have known young men, tailors from the country, faint away in the shop from the excessive heat and closeness; persons, working-men, coming into the shop to see some of the men, used to complain of the heat, and also of the smell as intolerable; the smell occasioned by the heat of the irons and the various breaths of the men really was at times intolerable. The men sat as loosely as they possibly could, and the perspiration ran from them from the heat and the closeness. It is of frequent occurrence in such workshops that light suits of clothes are spoiled from the perspiration of the hand, and the dust and flue which arises darkening the work. I have seen £40 or £50 worth of work spoiled in the course of the summer season from this cause.

"In what condition are these work-places in winter?—They are more unhealthy in winter, as the heat from the candles and the closeness is much greater. Any cold currents of air which come in give annoyance to those who are sitting near the draught. There is continued squabbling as to the windows being opened; those who are near the windows, and who do not feel the heat so much as the men near the stoves, objecting to their being opened. The oldest, who had been inured to the heat, did not like the cold, and generally prevailed in keeping out the cold or the fresh air. Such has been the state of the atmosphere, that in the very coldest nights large thick tallow candles (quarter of a pound candles) have melted and fallen over from the heat.

"What was the effect of this state of the work-places upon the habits of the workmen?—It had a very depressing effect on the energies; that was the general complaint of those who came into it.

Many could not stay out the hours, and went away earlier. Those who were not accustomed to the places generally lost appetite. The natural effect of the depression was, that we had recourse to drink as a stimulant. We went into the shop at six o'clock in the morning; but at seven o'clock, when orders for the breakfast were called for, gin was brought in, and the common allowance was half-a-quartern. The younger hands did not begin with gin.

"Was gin the first thing taken before any solid food was taken?—Yes, and the breakfast was very light; those who took gin generally took only half-a-pint of tea and half a twopenny loaf as breakfast.

"When again was liquor brought in?—At eleven o'clock.

"What was taken then?—Some took beer, some took gin again. In a general way, they took a pint of porter at eleven o'clock. It was seldom the men took more than the half-quatern of gin.

"When again was liquor brought in?—At three o'clock, when some took beer and some gin, just the same as in the morning. At five o'clock the beer and gin came in again, and was usually taken in the same quantities. At seven o'clock the shop was closed.

"After work was there any drinking?—Yes; nearly all the young men went to the public-house, and some of the others.

"What were the wages they received?—Sixpence per hour, which, at the full work, made 6s. a-day, or 36s. a-week.

"Did they make any reserves from this amount of wages?—No; very few had anything for themselves at the end of the week.

"How much of the habit of drinking was produced by the state of the work-place?—I should say the greater part of it; because when men work by themselves, or only two or three together, in cooler and less close places, there is scarcely any drinking between times. Nearly all this drinking proceeds from the large shops, where the men are crowded together in close rooms: it is the same in the shops in the country, as well as those in the town. In a rural place, the tailor, where he works by himself, or with only two or three together, takes very little of the fermented liquor or spirits which the men feel themselves under a sort of necessity for doing in towns. The closer the ventilation of the place of work, the worse are the habits of the men working in them.

"You referred to the practice of one large shop where you worked some time since; was that the general practice, and has there been no alteration?—It was and is now the general practice. Of late, since coffee has become cheaper, somewhat more of coffee and less of beer has been brought in; but there is as much gin now brought in between times, and sometimes more.

"What would be the effect of an alteration of the place of work—a ventilation which would give them a better atmosphere?—It would, without doubt, have an immediately beneficial effect on the habits. It might not cure those who have got into the habit of drinking; but the men would certainly drink less, and the younger ones would not be led into the habit so forcibly as they are.

"What is the general effect of this state of things upon the health of the men exposed to them?—Great numbers of them die of consumption.'A decline' is the general disease of which they die. By their own rules, a man at 50 years of age is superannuated, and is thought not to be fit to do a full day's work.

"What was the average of the ages of men at work at such shops as those you have worked at?—Thirty-two, or thereabouts.

"In such shops were there many superannuated men, or men above 50 years of age?—Very few. Amongst the tailors employed in the shops, I should say there were not 10 men in the hundred above 50 years of age.

"When they die, what becomes of their widows and children, as they seldom make any reserve of wages?—No provision is made for the families; nothing is heard of them, and, if they cannot provide for themselves, they must go upon the parish.

"Are these habits created by the closeness of the rooms, attended by carelessness as to their mode of living elsewhere?—I think not as to their lodgings. The English and Scotch tailors are more careful as to their places of lodging, and prefer sleeping in an open place. The men, however, who take their pint of porter and their pipe of tobacco in a public-house after their hours of work, take it at a place which is sometimes as crowded as a shop. Here the single men will stay until bedtime.

"Are gin and beer the only stimulants which you conceive are taken in consequence of the want of ventilation and the state of the place of work when crowded?—No: snuff is very much taken as a stimulant; the men think snuff has a beneficial effect on the eyes. After going into these close shops from the open air, the first sensation experienced is frequently a sensation of drowsiness, then a sort of itching or uneasiness at the eye, then a dimness of the sight. Some men of the strongest sight will complain of this dimness; all eyes are affected much in a similar manner. Snuff is much used as a stimulant to awaken them up; smoking in the shops is not approved of, though it is much attempted; and the journeymen tailors of the large shops are in general great smokers at the public-houses.

"Do the tailors from villages take snuff or smoke as well as drink so much as the tailors in the large shops in the towns?—They neither take so much snuff nor tobacco, nor so much of any of the stimulants, as are taken by the workmen in the crowded shops of the towns.

"Do their eyes fail them as soon?—No, certainly not.

"With the tailors, is it the eye that fails first?—Yes; after long hours of work the first thing complained of by the tailors is that the eyes fail; the sight becomes dim, and a sort of mist comes between them and their work.

"Judging from your own practical experience, how long do you conceive that a man would work in a well-ventilated or uncrowded room, as compared with a close, crowded, ill-ventilated room?—I think it would make a difference of two hours in the day to a man. He would, for example, be able, in an uncrowded or well-ventilated room, to do his twelve hours' work in the twelve hours; whereas in the close-crowded room he would not do more than ten hours' work in the twelve."

The following is the account given by a miner himself of the lodging-places:

William Eddy, one of the miners, states:

"I went to work in Greenside four years. Our lodging-rooms were such as not to be fit for a swine to live in. In one house there was 16 bedsteads in the room up stairs, and 50 occupied these beds at the same time. We could not always get all in together, but we got in when we could. Often three at a time in the bed, and one at the foot. I have several times had to get out of bed, and sit up all night to make room for my little brothers, who were there as washers. There was not a single flag or board on the lower floor, and there were pools of water 12 inches deep. You might have taken a coal-rake and raked off the dirt and potatoe peelings six inches deep. At one time we had not a single coal. After I had been there two years, rules were laid down, and two men were appointed by the master to clean the house up stairs twice a week. The lower apartment was to be cleaned twice a day. Then the shop floor was boarded, and two tables were placed in the shop. After that two more shops were fitted up, but the increase of workmen more than kept up with the increased accommodation. The breathing at night when all were in bed was dreadful. The workmen received more harm from the sleeping-places than from the work. There was one pane of glass which we could open, but it was close to a bed-head.

"The mines at Greenside were well ventilated, and in that respect there was nothing to complain of.

"In the winter time the icicles came through the roof, and within 12 inches of the people sleeping in bed. During a thaw, water dropped plentifully into the beds. In the upper beds the person sleeping next to the wall cannot raise his head or change his shirt."

Joseph Eddy, another workman, states:

"I consider the lodging-shops more injurious to the health of the miners than their work itself. So many sleeping in the same room, so many breaths, so much stour arising from their working-clothes, so much perspiration from the men themselves, it is impossible to be comfortable. Two miners occupy one bed, sometimes three. The beds are shaken once a week on the Monday morning, when the miners come. Some miners make their beds every night. The rooms are in general very dirty, being never washed, and very seldom swept, not over once a month. There is no ventilation, so that the air is very close at night."

The evidence already given will, to some extent, have furnished answers to the question—how far the physical evils by which the health, and strength, and morals of the labouring classes are depressed may be removed, or can reasonably be expected to be removed by private and voluntary exertions. I now submit for consideration the facts which serve to show how far the aid of the legislature, and of administrative arrangements are requisite for the attainment of the objects in question.

It will have been perceived, that the first great remedies, external arrangements, *i.e.,* efficient drainage, sewerage and cleansing of towns, come within the acknowledged province of the legislature. Public opinion has of late required legislative interference for the regulation of some points of the internal economy of certain places of work, and the appointment of special agents to protect young children engaged in certain classes of manufactures from mental deterioration from the privation of the advantages of education, and from permanent bodily deterioration from an excess of labour beyond their strength. Claims are now before Parliament for an extension of the like remedies to other classes of children and to young persons, who are deemed to be in the same need of protection. The legislature has interfered to put an end to one description of employment which was deemed afflicting and degrading, *i.e.,* that of climbing-boys for sweeping chimneys, and to force a better means of performing by machinery the same work. It will be seen that it has been the policy of the legislature to interfere for the public protection by regulating the structure of private dwellings to prevent the extension of fires; and the common law has also interposed to protect the public health by preventing overcrowding in private tenements. The legislature has recently interfered to direct the poorer description of tenements in the metropolis to be properly cleansed. On considering the evidence before given with relation to the effects of different classes of buildings, the suggestion immediately arises as to the extent to which it is practicable to protect the health of the labouring classes by measures for the amendment of existing buildings, and for the regulation of new buildings in towns in the great proportion of cases where neither private benevolence nor enlightened views can be expected to prevail extensively.

It will have been perceived how much of the existing evils originate from the defects of the external arrangements for drainage, and for cleansing, and for obtaining supplies of water. Until these are completed, therefore, the force of the evils arising from the construction of the houses could scarcely be ascertained.

QUESTIONS

1. How did the condition of the poor affect the rest of nineteenth-century British society?

2. What were the main problems faced by workers in the tailoring trade?

3. Miners were given lodging by their employers when they were on the job. What were these places like?

4. How did workers cope with the conditions in industry?

5. Many people argued that Parliament had no right to interfere in the areas of working conditions and public health. How does Chadwick respond to that charge?

6. Chadwick's aim was to convince Parliament of the need for legislative reform of working conditions. Is his case persuasive? How might he have manipulated the outcome to achieve his goal?

103.   **FRIEDRICH ENGELS**

THE CONDITION OF THE
WORKING CLASS IN ENGLAND
(1845)

Friedrich Engels (1820–95) was a historian, philosopher, and lifelong collaborator of Karl Marx. His father was a German industrialist, with whom he had a tempestuous relationship: the more his father pushed him into business, the stronger became Engel's inclination toward socialism. As a youth he joined a number of German socialist organizations even while serving his apprenticeship in industry. For a time he joined the Prussian army. Moving to Berlin in the 1840s, Engels attended university lectures and imbibed the heady atmosphere of political radicalism. There he met Marx and the two became close friends. In 1842 Engels moved to England, where his father owned an interest in a cotton mill. There he worked as a businessman by day and a sociological inquirer by night. He entered the homes of working people, questioned them about the conditions of their employment, and observed their diet and their health.

From these studies came *The Condition of the Working Class in England,* a scathing attack upon English industrial capitalism. Engels describes the lives of the poor workers in pitiless detail, exposing the horror of the conditions in which they worked. His observations did not differ much from those of the English parliamentary commission that had been officially charged with the task, but his conclusions were starkly different. He believed that no possible reform could be undertaken that would successfully improve the lives of poor workers. The only solution was the overthrow of the capitalist system.

That a class which lives under the conditions already sketched and is so ill-provided with the most necessary means of subsistence, cannot be healthy and can reach no advanced age, is self-evident. Let us review the circumstances once more with especial reference to the health of the workers. The centralisation of population in great cities exercises of itself an unfavourable influence; the atmosphere of London can never be so pure, so rich in oxygen, as the air of the country; two and a half-million pairs of lungs, two hundred and fifty thousand fires, crowded upon an area three to four miles square, consume an enormous amount of oxygen, which is replaced with difficulty, because the method of building cities in itself impedes ventilation. The carbonic acid gas, engendered by respiration and fire, remains in the streets by reason of its specific gravity, and the chief air current passes over the roofs of the city. The lungs of the inhabitants fail to receive the due supply of oxygen, and the consequence is mental and physical lassitude and low vitality. For this reason, the dwellers in cities are far less exposed to acute, and especially to inflammatory, affections than rural populations, who live in a free, normal atmosphere; but they suffer the more from chronic afflictions. And if life in large cities is, in itself, injurious to health, how great must be the harmful influence of an abnormal atmosphere in the working-people's quarters, where, as we have seen, everything combines to poison the air. In the country, it may, perhaps, be comparatively innoxious to keep a dung-heap adjoining one's dwelling, because the air has free ingress from all sides; but in the midst of a large town, among closely built lanes and courts that shut out all movement of the atmosphere, the case is different. All putrefying vegetable and animal substances give off gases decidedly injurious to health, and if these gases have no free way of escape, they inevitably poison the atmosphere. The filth and stagnant pools of the working-people's quarters in the great cities have, therefore, the worst effect upon the public health, because they produce precisely those gases which engender disease; so, too, the exhalations from contaminated streams. But this is by no means all. The manner in which the great multitude of the poor is treated by society to-day is revolting. They are drawn into the large cities where they breathe a poorer atmosphere than in the country; they are relegated to districts which, by reason of the method of construction, are worse ventilated than any others; they are deprived of all means of cleanliness, of water itself, since pipes are laid only when paid for, and the rivers so polluted that they are useless for such purposes, they are obliged to throw all offal and garbage, all dirty water, often all disgusting drainage and excrement into the streets, being without other means of disposing of them; they are thus compelled to infect the region of their own dwellings. Nor is this enough. All conceivable evils are heaped upon the heads of the poor. If the population of great cities is too dense in general, it is they in particular who are packed into the least space. As though the vitiated atmosphere of the streets were not enough,

they are penned in dozens into single rooms, so that the air which they breathe at night is enough in itself to stifle them. They are given damp dwellings, cellar dens that are not waterproof from below, or garrets that leak from above. Their houses are so built that the clammy air cannot escape. They are supplied bad, tattered, or rotten clothing, adulterated and indigestible food. They are exposed to the most exciting changes of mental condition, the most violent vibrations between hope and fear; they are hunted like game, and not permitted to attain peace of mind and quiet enjoyment of life. They are deprived of all enjoyments except that of sexual indulgence and drunkenness, are worked every day to the point of complete exhaustion of their mental and physical energies, and are thus constantly spurred on to the maddest excess in the only two enjoyments at their command. And if they surmount all this, they fall victims to want of work in a crisis when all the little is taken from them that had hitherto been vouchsafed them.

How is it possible, under such conditions, for the lower class to be healthy and long lived? What else can be expected than an excessive mortality, an unbroken series of epidemics, a progressive deterioration in the physique of the working population? Let us see how the facts stand.

That the dwellings of the workers in the worst portions of the cities, together with the other conditions of life of this class, engender numerous diseases, is attested on all sides. The article already quoted from the *Artisan* asserts with perfect truth, that lung diseases must be the inevitable consequence of such conditions, and that, indeed, cases of this kind are disproportionately frequent in this class. That the bad air of London, and especially of the working people's districts, is in the highest degree favourable to the development of consumption, the hectic appearance of great numbers of persons sufficiently indicates. If one roams the streets a little in the early morning, when the multitudes are on their way to their work, one is amazed at the number of persons who look wholly or half-consumptive. Even in Manchester the people have not the same appearance; these pale, lank, narrow-chested, hollow-eyed ghosts, whom one passes at every step, these languid, flabby faces, incapable of the slightest energetic expression, I have seen in such startling numbers only in London, though consumption carries off a horde of victims annually in the factory towns of the North. In competition with consumption stands typhus, to say nothing of scarlet fever, a disease which brings most frightful devastation into the ranks of the working-class. Typhus, that universally diffused affliction, is attributed by the official report on the sanitary condition of the working-class, directly to the bad state of the dwellings in the matters of ventilation, drainage, and cleanliness. This report, compiled, it must not be forgotten, by the leading physicians of England from the testimony of other physicians, asserts that a single ill-ventilated court, a single blind alley without drainage, is enough to engender fever, and usually does engender it, especially if the inhabitants are greatly crowded. This fever has the same character almost everywhere, and develops in nearly every case into specific typhus. It is to be found in the working-people's quarters of all great towns and cities, and in single ill-built, ill-kept streets of smaller places, though it naturally seeks out single victims in better districts also. In London it has now prevailed for a considerable time; its extraordinary violence in the year 1837 gave rise to the report already referred to.

When one remembers under what conditions the working-people live, when one thinks how crowded their dwellings are, how every nook and corner swarms with human beings, how sick and well sleep in the same room, in the same bed, the only wonder is that a contagious disease like this fever does not spread yet farther. And when one reflects how little medical assistance the sick have at command, how many are without any medical advice whatsoever, and

ignorant of the most ordinary precautionary measures, the mortality seems actually small. Dr. Alison, who has made a careful study of this disease, attributes it directly to the want and the wretched condition of the poor, as in the report already quoted. He asserts that privations and the insufficient satisfaction of vital needs are what prepare the frame for contagion and make the epidemic widespread and terrible. He proves that a period of privation, a commercial crisis or a bad harvest, has each time produced the typhus epidemic in Ireland as in Scotland, and that the fury of the plague has fallen almost exclusively on the working-class. It is a noteworthy fact, that according to his testimony, the majority of persons who perish by typhus are fathers of families, precisely the persons who can least be spared by those dependent upon them; and several Irish physicians whom he quotes bear the same testimony.

Another category of diseases arises directly from the food rather than the dwellings of the workers. The food of the labourer, indigestible enough in itself, is utterly unfit for young children, and he has neither means nor time to get his children more suitable food. Moreover, the custom of giving children spirits, and even opium is very general; and these two influences, with the rest of the conditions of life prejudicial to bodily development, give rise to the most diverse affections of the digestive organs, leaving life-long traces behind them. Nearly all workers have stomachs more or less weak, and are yet forced to adhere to the diet which is the root of the evil. How should they know what is to blame for it? And if they knew, how could they obtain a more suitable regimen so long as they cannot adopt a different way of living and are not better educated?

The employment of the wife dissolves the family utterly and of necessity, and this dissolution, in our present society, which is based upon the family, brings the most demoralizing consequences for parents as well as children. A mother who has no time to trouble herself about her child, to perform the most ordinary loving services for it during its first year, who scarcely indeed sees it, can be no real mother to the child, must inevitably grow indifferent to it, treat it unlovingly like a stranger. The children who grow up under such conditions are utterly ruined for later family life, can never feel at home in the family which they themselves found, because they have always been accustomed to isolation, and they contribute therefore to the already general undermining of the family in the working-class. A similar dissolution of the family is brought about by the employment of the children. When they get on far enough to earn more than they cost their parents from week to week, they begin to pay the parents a fixed sum for board and lodging, and keep the rest for themselves. This often happens from the fourteenth or fifteenth year. In a word, the children emancipate themselves, and regard the paternal dwelling as a lodging-house, which they often exchange for another, as suits them.

In many cases the family is not wholly dissolved by the employment of the wife, but turned upside down. The wife supports the family, the husband sits at home, tends the children, sweeps the room and cooks. This case happens very frequently; in Manchester alone, many hundred such men could be cited, condemned to domestic occupations. It is easy to imagine the wrath aroused among the working-men by this reversal of all relations within the family, while the other social conditions remain unchanged. There lies before me a letter from an English working-man, Robert Pounder, Baron's Buildings, Woodhouse, Moorside, in Leeds (the bourgeoisie may hunt him up there; I give the exact address for the purpose), written by him to Oastler:

He relates how another working-man, being on tramp, came to St. Helens, in Lancashire, and there looked up an old friend. He found him in a miserable, damp cellar, scarcely furnished; and when my poor friend went in, there sat poor Jack near the fire, and what did he, think you? Why he sat and mended his wife's stockings with the bodkin; and as soon as he saw his old friend at the door-post, he tried to hide them. But Joe, that is my friend's name, had seen it, and said: "Jack, what the devil art thou doing? Where is the missus? Why, is that thy work?" and poor Jack was ashamed, and said: "No, I know this is not my work but my poor missus is i' th' factory; she has to leave at half-past five and works till eight at night, and then she is so knocked up that she cannot do aught when she gets home, so I have to do everything for her what I can, for I have no work, nor had any for more nor three years, and I shall never have any more work while I live;" and then he wept a big tear. Jack again said: "There is work enough for women folks and childer hereabouts, but none for men; thou mayest sooner find a hundred pound on the road than work for men—but I should never have believed that either thou or any one else would have seen me mending my wife's stockings, for it is bad work. But she can hardly stand on her feet; I am afraid she will be laid up, and then I don't know what is to become of us, for it's a good bit that she has been the man in the house and I the woman; it is bad work, Joe;" and he cried bitterly, and said, "It has not been always so." "No," said Joe; "but when thou hadn't no work, how hast thou not shifted?" "I'll tell thee, Joe, as well as I can, but it was bad enough; thou knowest when I got married I had work plenty, and thou knows I was not lazy." "No, that thou wert not." "And we had a good furnished house, and Mary need not go to work. I could work for the two of us; but now the world is upside down. Mary has to work and I have to stop at home, mind the childer, sweep and wash, bake and mend; and, when the poor woman comes home at night, she is knocked up. Thou knows, Joe, it's hard for one that was used different." "Yes, boy, it is hard." And then Jack began to cry again, and he wished he had never married, and that he had never been born; but he had never thought, when he wed Mary, that it would come to this. "I have often cried over it," said Jack. Now when Joe heard this, he told me that he had cursed and damned the factories, and the masters, and the Government, with all the curses that he had learned while he was in the factory from a child.

Can any one imagine a more insane state of things than that described in this letter? And yet this condition, which unsexes the man and takes from the woman all womanliness without being able to bestow upon the man true womanliness, or the woman true manliness—this condition which degrades, in the most shameful way, both sexes, and, through them, Humanity, is the last result of our much-praised civilization, the final achievement of all the efforts and struggles of hundreds of generations to improve their own situation and that of their posterity. We must either despair of mankind, and its aims and efforts, when we see all our labour and toil result in such a mockery, or we must admit that human society has hitherto sought salvation in a false direction; we must admit that so total a reversal of the position of the sexes can have come to pass only because the sexes have been placed in a false position from the beginning. If the reign of the wife over the husband, as inevitably brought about by the factory system, is inhuman, the pristine rule of the husband over the wife must have been inhuman too. If the wife can now base her supremacy upon the fact that she supplies the greater part, nay, the whole of the common possession, the necessary inference is that this community of possession is no true and rational one, since one member of the family boasts offensively of contributing the greater share. If the family of our present society is being thus dissolved, this dissolution merely shows that, at bottom, the binding tie of this family was not family affection, but private interest lurking under the cloak of a pretended community of possessions.

QUESTIONS

1. What is Engels's view of the urban life of the poor?

2. What impact does the factory system have upon women and children, according to Engels?

3. What are Engels's assumptions about the way a family ought to function? How does working-class life conflict with those assumptions?

4. Whom does Engels blame for the terrible conditions workers endure in Britain?

5. Both Engels and Edwin Chadwick, in his report for Parliament, are concerned about the poor. How do their accounts differ?

Nineteenth-Century Society and Culture

104. JANE AUSTEN

PRIDE AND PREJUDICE
(1813)

Jane Austen (1775–1817) was born the daughter of a country vicar. Her wit and insight into the pretensions and foibles of English country life made her one of the finest observers of late eighteenth-century society. Keeping her occupation secret from even close friends and neighbors, she wrote for her own enjoyment and to entertain her large family. By the time she was twelve she had written witty satires of local events but eventually turned to larger themes and longer works. Initially she had great difficulty finding a publisher; it was not until 1811 that *Sense and Sensibility* was published anonymously. It was so well received that her other novels soon were printed and *Emma* (1815) was dedicated to the Prince of Wales at his own request.

Pride and Prejudice is one of the best-loved novels of the English language. It describes the social life of a country family in unforgettable images and details a romantic relationship between two headstrong characters, Elizabeth Bennet and Mr. Darcy.

Chapter I

It is a truth universally acknowledged, that a single man in possession of a good fortune must be in want of a wife.

However little known the feelings or views of such a man may be on his first entering a neighbourhood, this truth is so well fixed in the minds of the surrounding families, that he is considered as the rightful property of some one or other of their daughters.

"My dear Mr. Bennet," said his lady to him one day, "have you heard that Netherfield Park is let at last?"

Mr. Bennet replied that he had not.

"But it is," returned she; "for Mrs. Long has just been here, and she told me all about it."

Mr. Bennet made no answer.

"Do not you want to know who has taken it?" cried his wife impatiently.

"*You* want to tell me, and I have no objection to hearing it."

This was invitation enough.

"Why, my dear, you must know, Mrs. Long says that Netherfield is taken by a young man of large fortune from the north of England; that he came down on Monday in a chaise and four to see the place, and was so much delighted with it, that he agreed with Mr. Morris immediately; that he is to take possession before Michaelmas, and some of his servants are to be in the house by the end of next week."

"What is his name?"

"Bingley."

"Is he married or single?"

"Oh! single, my dear, to be sure! A single man of large fortune; four or five thousand a-year. What a fine thing for our girls!"

"How so? how can it affect them?"

"My dear Mr. Bennet," replied his wife, "how can you be so tiresome! you must know that I am thinking of his marrying one of them."

"Is that his design in settling here?"

"Design! nonsense, how can you talk so! But it is very likely that he *may* fall in love with one of them, and therefore you must visit him as soon as he comes."

"I see no occasion for that. You and the girls may go, or you may send them by themselves, which perhaps will be still better, for as you are as handsome as any of them, Mr. Bingley might like you the best of the party."

"My dear, you flatter me. I certainly *have* had my share of beauty, but I do not pretend to be anything extraordinary now. When a woman has five grown-up daughters, she ought to give over thinking of her own beauty."

"In such cases, a woman has not often much beauty to think of."

"But, my dear, you must indeed go and see Mr. Bingley when he comes into the neighbourhood."

"It is more than I engage for, I assure you."

"But consider your daughters. Only think what an establishment it would be for one of them. Sir William and Lady Lucas are determined to go, merely on that account, for in general, you know, they visit no new-comers. Indeed you must go, for it will be impossible for *us* to visit him if you do not."

"You are over-scrupulous, surely. I dare say Mr. Bingley will be very glad to see you; and I will send a few lines by you to assure him of my hearty consent to his marrying whichever he chooses of the girls: though I must throw in a good word for my little Lizzy."

"I desire you will do no such thing. Lizzy is not a bit better than the others; and I am sure she is not half so handsome as Jane, nor half so good-humored as Lydia. But you are always giving *her* the preference."

"They have none of them much to recommend them," replied he; "they are all silly and ignorant, like other girls; but Lizzy has something more of quickness than her sisters."

"Mr. Bennet, how can you abuse your own children in such a way! You take delight in vexing me. You have no compassion on my poor nerves."

"You mistake me, my dear. I have a high respect for your nerves. They are my old friends. I have heard you mention them with consideration these twenty years at least."

"Ah! you do not know what I suffer."

"But I hope you will get over it, and live to see many young men of four thousand a-year come into the neighbourhood."

"It will be no use to us, if twenty such should come, since you will not visit them."

"Depend upon it, my dear, that when there are twenty, I will visit them all."

Mr. Bennet was so odd a mixture of quick parts, sarcastic humour, reserve, and caprice, that the experience of three-and-twenty years had been insufficient to make his wife understand his character. *Her* mind was less difficult to develop. She was a woman of mean understanding, little information, and uncertain temper. When she was discontented, she fancied herself nervous. The business of her life was to get her daughters married; its solace was visiting and news. . . .

Chapter III

Not all that Mrs. Bennet, however, with the assistance of her five daughters, could ask on the subject, was sufficient to draw from her husband any satisfactory description of Mr. Bingley [whom he had visited]. They attacked him in various ways—with barefaced questions, ingenious suppositions, and distant surmises; but he eluded the skill of them all, and they were at last obliged to accept the secondhand intelligence of their neighbour, Lady Lucas. Her report was highly favourable. Sir William had been delighted with him. He was quite young, wonderfully handsome, extremely agreeable, and, to crown the whole, he meant to be at the next assembly with a large party. Nothing could be more delightful! To be fond of dancing was a certain step towards falling in love; and very lively hopes of Mr. Bingley's heart were entertained.

"If I can but see one of my daughters happily settled at Netherfield," said Mrs. Bennet to her husband, "and all the others equally well married, I shall have nothing to wish for."

In a few days Mr. Bingley returned Mr. Bennet's visit, and sat about ten minutes with him in his library. He had entertained hopes of being admitted to a sight of the young ladies, of whose beauty he had heard much; but he saw only the father. The ladies were somewhat more fortunate, for they had the advantage of ascertaining from an upper window that he wore a blue coat, and rode a black horse.

An invitation to dinner was soon afterwards dispatched; and already had Mrs. Bennet planned the courses that were to do credit to her housekeeping when an answer arrived which deferred it all. Mr. Bingley was obliged to be in town the following day, and consequently, unable to accept the honour of their invitation, &c. Mrs. Bennet was quite disconcerted. She could not imagine what business he could have in town so soon after his arrival in Hertfordshire; and she began to fear that he might be always flying about from one place to another, and never settled at Netherfield as he ought to be. Lady Lucas quieted her fears a little by starting the idea of his being gone to London only to get a large party for the ball; and a report soon followed, that Mr. Bingley was to bring twelve ladies and seven gentlemen with him to the assembly. The girls grieved over such a number of ladies, but were comforted the day before the ball by hearing, that instead of twelve he had brought only six with him from London,—his five sisters and a cousin. And when the party entered the assembly room it consisted only of five all together,—Mr. Bingley, his two sisters, the husband of the eldest, and another young man.

Mr. Bingley was good-looking and gentleman-like; he had a pleasant countenance, and easy, unaffected manners. His sisters were fine women, with an air of decided fashion. His brother-in-law, Mr. Hurst, merely looked the gentlemen; but his friend Mr. Darcy soon drew the attention of the room by his fine, tall person, handsome features, noble mien, and the report which was in general circulation within five minutes after his entrance, of his having ten thousand a-year. The gentlemen pronounced him to be a fine figure of a man, the ladies declared he was much handsomer than Mr. Bingley, and he was looked at with great admiration for about half the evening, till his manners gave a disgust which turned the tide of his popularity; for he was discovered to be proud, to be above his company, and above being pleased; and not all his large estate in Derbyshire could then save him from having a most forbidding, disagreeable countenance, and being unworthy to be compared with his friend.

Mr. Bingley had soon made himself acquainted with all the principal people in the room; he was lively and unreserved, danced every dance, was angry that the ball closed so early, and talked of giving one himself at Netherfield. Such amiable qualities must speak for themselves. What a contrast between him and his friend! Mr. Darcy danced only once with Mrs. Hurst and once with Miss Bingley, declined being introduced to any other lady, and spent the rest of the evening in walking about the room, speaking occasionally to one of his own party. His character was decided. He was the proudest, most disagreeable man in the world, and everybody hoped that he would never come there again. Amongst the most violent against him was Mrs. Bennet, whose dislike of his general behavior was sharpened into particular resentment by his having slighted one of her daughters.

Elizabeth Bennet had been obliged, by the scarcity of gentlemen, to sit down for two dances; and during part of that time, Mr. Darcy had been standing near enough for her to overhear a conversation between him and Mr. Bingley, who came from the dance for a few minutes, to press his friend to join it.

"Come, Darcy," said he, "I must have you dance. I hate to see you standing about by yourself in this stupid manner. You had much better dance."

"I certainly shall not. You know how I detest it, unless I am particularly acquainted with my partner. At such an assembly as this it would be insupportable. Your sisters are engaged, and there is not another woman in the room whom it would not be a punishment to me to stand up with."

"I would not be so fastidious as you are," cried Bingley, "for a kingdom! Upon my honour, I never met with so many pleasant girls in my life as I have this evening; and there are several of them you see uncommonly pretty."

"*You* are dancing with the only handsome girl in the room," said Mr. Darcy, looking at the eldest Miss Bennet.

"Oh! she is the most beautiful creature I ever beheld! But there is one of her sisters sitting down just behind you, who is very pretty, and I dare say very agreeable. Do let me ask my partner to introduce you."

"Which do you mean?" and turning round he looked for a moment at Elizabeth, till catching her eye, he withdrew his own and coldly said, "She is tolerable, but not handsome enough to tempt *me;* and I am in no humour at present to give consequence to young ladies who are slighted by other men. You had better return to your partner and enjoy her smiles, for you are wasting your time with me."

Mr. Bingley followed his advice. Mr. Darcy walked off; and Elizabeth remained with no very cordial feelings towards him. She told the story, however, with great spirit among her friends; for she had a lively, playful disposition, which delighted in anything ridiculous.

The evening altogether passed off pleasantly to the whole family. Mrs. Bennet had seen her eldest daughter much admired by the Netherfield party. Mr. Bingley had danced with her twice, and she had been distinguished by his sisters. Jane was as much gratified by this as her mother could be, though in a quieter way. Elizabeth felt Jane's pleasure. Mary had heard herself mentioned to Miss Bingley as the most accomplished girl in the

neighborhood; and Catherine and Lydia had been fortunate enough to be never without partners, which was all that they had yet learnt to care for at a ball. They returned, therefore, in good spirits to Longbourn, the village where they lived, and of which they were the principal inhabitants. They found Mr. Bennet still up. With a book he was regardless of time; and on the present occasion he had a good deal of curiosity as to the event of an evening which had raised such splendid expectations. He had rather hoped that all his wife's views on the stranger would be disappointed; but he soon found that he had a very different story to hear.

"Oh! my dear Mr. Bennet," as she entered the room, "we have had a most delightful evening, a most excellent ball. I wish you had been there. Jane was so admired, nothing could be like it. Everybody said how well she looked; and Mr. Bingley thought her quite beautiful, and danced with her twice! Only think of *that,* my dear; he actually danced with her twice! and she was the only creature in the room that he asked a second time. First of all, he asked Miss Lucas. I was so vexed to see him stand up with her! but, however, he did not admire her at all; indeed, nobody can, you know; and he seemed quite struck with Jane as she was going down the dance. So he inquired who she was, and got introduced, and asked her for the two next. Then the two third he danced with Miss King, and the two fourth with Maria Lucas, and the two fifth with Jane again, and the two sixth with Lizzy and the Boulanger."

"If he had any compassion for *me,*" cried her husband impatiently, "he would not have danced half so much! For God's sake, say no more of his partners. O that he had sprained his ankle in the first dance!"

"Oh! my dear," continued Mrs. Bennet, "I am quite delighted with him. He is so excessively handsome! and his sisters are charming women. I never in my life saw anything more elegant than their dresses. I dare say the lace upon Mrs. Hurst's gown—"

Here she was interrupted again. Mr. Bennet protested against any description of finery. She was therefore obliged to seek another branch of the subject, and related, with much bitterness of spirit and some exaggeration, the shocking rudeness of Mr. Darcy.

"But I can assure you," she added, "that Lizzy does not lose much by not suiting *his* fancy; for he is a most disagreeable, horrid man, not at all worth pleasing. So high and so conceited that there was no enduring him! He walked here, and he walked there, fancying himself so very great! Not handsome enough to dance with! I wish you had been there, my dear, to have given him one of your set-downs. I quite detest the man."

QUESTIONS

1. How do married couples of the landed class relate to one another? What are the roles of husband and wife?

2. What are the most important qualifications of a prospective husband, judging from Austen's work?

3. How does courtship work among the upper classes?

4. How are unmarried women expected to behave in Miss Bennet's world? Do you think that Jane Austen was entirely happy with those expectations?

5. Jane Austen describes a lifestyle radically different from the one Chadwick and Engels investigated. Describe it.

105.   HENRIETTA-LUCY, MADAME DE LA TOUR DU PIN

MEMOIRS

(1820–1843)

Henrietta-Lucy Dillon (1770–1853) was born into the upper reaches of the French aristocracy in the waning days of the *ancien régime*. A frequent visitor at the court of Louis XVI and his wife, Marie Antoinette, she was in an excellent position to observe life at Versailles firsthand. She married her husband, the Comte de la Tour du Pin, when she was sixteen. The Comte was a soldier in the king's army and an aristocrat, and when the revolution broke out in 1789, the family faced ruin. Both Henrietta-Lucy's father and father-in-law were executed by the revolutionaries in 1794, and in order to avoid the same fate, she and her husband fled to America. While in the New World, Henrietta-Lucy lived a dramatically different life on what was then the wild frontier of upstate New York. Her husband farmed, and she performed all the duties of a frontier farmer's wife. Eventually the couple returned to France, where the Comte threw in his lot with Napoleon, rising high in the emperor's regime as a soldier and diplomat. Henrietta-Lucy followed her husband on his various postings, and eventually, after his death, retired to Italy, where she died in 1853.

Madame de la Tour du Pin's memoirs were written over a period of some twenty years. They provide an excellent view of life in France and the life of those in exile during its most turbulent period of history. In this selection, Henrietta-Lucy describes aristocratic life in the days before the revolution.

In my earliest years, I saw things which might have been expected to warp my mind, pervert my affections, deprave my character and destroy in me every notion of religion and morality. From the age of ten, I heard around me the freest conversations and the expression of the most ungodly principles. Brought up, as I was, in an Archbishop's house where every rule of religion was broken daily, I was fully aware that my lessons in dogma and doctrine were given no more importance than those in history and geography. . . .

Customs and society itself have so changed since the Revolution that I want to describe in detail what I can remember of my family's manner of life.

My uncle, the Archbishop of Narbonne, went rarely or never at all to his diocese. By virtue of his See, he was President of the States of Languedoc, but he never visited Languedoc except to preside over the meetings of the States. These lasted for six weeks during November and December and as soon as they were over my uncle returned to Paris on the pretext that the interest of the Province urgently required his presence at Court, but really in order to resume his usual life as a 'grand seigneur' in Paris and a courtier at Versailles. . . .

In those days, it was not the custom to give great dinner parties, for people dined early: at half-past two or three o'clock at the latest. By dinner-time, the ladies would sometimes have had their hair dressed, but they would still be in *déshabille*. Gentlemen, on the other hand, were nearly always formally dressed, never in a plain town coat or in uniform, but in a dress coat, either embroidered or plain, according to their age and taste. The master of the house or gentlemen who did not intend going into company later in the evening, would wear a town coat or informal dress, for to wear a hat disturbed the fragile edifice of the curled wig, which was always snow-white with powder. After dinner, people conversed; sometimes we played a game of backgammon. Then the ladies would go off to dress and the gentlemen would wait to accompany them to the theatre, if they were to be in the same box. If one stayed at home after dinner, there was a continuous stream of visitors. Supper guests did not arrive until half-past nine.

Socially, that was the really important hour of the day. There were two kinds of supper, those given by people whose supper table was open to guests on every day of the week, so that people could come when they wished, and those to which one was invited, which were numerous and brilliant. I am speaking of the days when I was a child, that is to say, between 1778 and 1784. All the toilettes, all the elegance, everything that the beautiful, fashionable society of Paris could offer in refinement and charm was to be found at these suppers. In those good days, before anyone had begun to think of national representation, a list of supper guests was a most important and carefully considered item! There were so many interests to be fostered, so many people to bring together, so many others to be kept apart! And what a social disaster for a husband to consider himself invited to a house simply because his wife was invited! One needed a very profound knowledge of convention and the current intrigues.

There were fewer balls than in later years, for the ladies' fashions of that day made dancing a form of torture: narrow heels, three inches high, which kept the foot in the same position as if standing on tiptoe to reach a book on the highest shelf in the library; a panier of stiff, heavy whalebone spreading out on either side; hair dressed at least a foot high, sprinkled with a pound of powder and pommade which the slightest movement shook down on the shoulders, and crowned by a bonnet known as a 'pouf' on which feathers, flowers and diamonds were piled pell-mell—an erection which quite spoiled the pleasure of dancing. A supper party, on the other hand, where people only talked or made music, did not disturb this edifice. . . .

My earliest visit to Versailles was in 1781. . . . In later years, when listening to tales of Queen Marie-Antoinette's sufferings and shame, my mind often went back to those days of her triumph. I was taken to watch the ball given for her by the Gardes du Corps in the Grande Salle de Spectacle at Versailles. She opened the ball with a young guardsman, wearing a blue dress strewn with sapphires and diamonds. She was young, beautiful and adored by all; she had just given France a Dauphin and it would have seemed to her inconceivable that the brilliant career on which she was launched could ever suffer a reverse. Yet she was already close to the abyss. The contrast provides much cause for reflection! . . .

This tragic Queen still betrayed, even then, a few trifling and very feminine jealousies. She had a very lovely complexion and a radiant personality, but she showed herself a little jealous of those young ladies who could bring to the hard light of noon a seventeen-year-old complexion more dazzling than her own. I was one of them, and once when she was passing through the door, the Duchesse de Duras, who was always very kind and helpful to me, whispered in my ear: 'Do not stand facing the windows.' I understood what she meant and followed her advice. But this did not prevent the Queen from sometimes passing remarks which were almost cutting about my liking for bright colours and for the poppies and brown scabious which I often wore. However, she was usually very kind to me, sometimes paying me those forthright compliments which princes have a habit of casting at young women down the whole length of a room, making the unhappy persons concerned blush to the very roots of their hair.

. . . Sunday morning audiences lasted until forty minutes past noon. Then the door opened and the footman announced: 'The King!' The Queen, who always wore Court dress, would go to meet him with a charming air of pleasure and deference. The King would incline his head to the right and the left, and speak to a few ladies whom he knew, though never to the young ones. He was so short-sighted that he could not recognise anyone at a distance of more than three paces. He was stout, about five foot six or seven inches tall, square-shouldered and with the worst possible bearing. He looked like some peasant shambling along behind his plough; there was nothing proud or regal about him. His sword was a continual embarrassment to him and he never knew what to do with his hat, yet in Court dress he looked really magnificent. He took no interest in his clothes, putting on without a glance whatever was handed to him. His coats were made of cloths suited to the various seasons, all very heavily embroidered, and he wore the diamond star of the Order of the Holy Ghost. It was only on his feast day, or on days of gala or great ceremonial that he wore the ribbon over his coat. . . .

. . . [T]he Queen entered before the chiming of the clock. Beside her door would be one of the two Curés of Versailles. He would hand her a purse and she would go around to every-one, taking up a collection and saying: 'For the poor, if you please.' Each lady had her 'écu' of six francs ready in her hand and the men had their 'louis'. The Curé would follow the Queen as she collected this small tax for her poor people, a levy which often totalled as much as one hundred 'louis' and never less than fifty.

I often heard some of the younger people, including the most spendthrift, complaining inordinately of this almsgiving being forced upon them, yet they would not have thought twice of hazarding a sum one hundred times as large in a game of chance or of spending in a morning, to no purpose at all, a sum much larger than that levied by the Queen.

It was the fashion to complain of everything. One was bored, weary of attendance at Court. The officers of the Garde du Corps, who were lodged in the Château when on duty, bemoaned having to wear uniform all day. The Ladies of the Household in attendance could not bear to miss going two or three times to Paris for supper during the eight days of their attendance at Versailles. It was the height of style to complain of duties at Court, profiting from them none the less and sometimes, indeed often, abusing the privileges they carried. All the ties were being loosened, and it was, alas, the upper classes who led the way. The Bishops did not live in their dioceses and seized on any pretext to visit Paris. Colonels, obliged to serve with their regiment for only four months of the year, would not have dreamed of staying five minutes longer than the minimum period. Unnoticed, the spirit of revolt was rampant in all classes of society. . . .

As I am not writing a history of the Revolution, I will not speak of all the conversations, discussions, or even of the arguments which differing opinions gave rise to in society. At eighteen, I found all these arguments very tedious and tried to find distraction in going as often as possible to a charming house to which I was drawn by childhood friendships which had deepened, particularly since the day I had to leave my family. This was the Hôtel de Rochechouart, one of those patriarchal houses, whose like will not be seen again, in which many generations mingled without any sense of strain, without tedium and without making exacting claims on one another. . . .

Amid all these pleasures, we were drawing near to the month of May 1789, laughing and dancing our way to the precipice. Thinking people were content to talk of abolishing all the abuses. France, they said, was about to be reborn. The word 'revolution' was never uttered. Had anyone dared to use it he would have been thought mad. In the upper classes, this illusion of security misled the wise who wanted to see an end to the abuses and to the wasting of public money. That is why so many upright and honourable people, including the King himself, who fully shared the illusion, hoped that they were about to enter a Golden Age.

Now that I have lived through so many events in the course of a long life, I am amazed at the utter blindness of the unfortunate King and his Ministers.

QUESTIONS

1. What was life like for the aristocracy before the revolution?

2. Marie Antoinette has often been portrayed as an important cause of the revolution—does the picture here justify those charges?

3. What is the role of women at Court and in the aristocracy?

4. If you were charged with defending the Court against its revolutionary critics, could you do so using Madame de la Tour du Pin's memoirs? Why or why not?

5. Madame wrote her memoirs some thirty or more years after the events she described—how do you think this might have affected her story?

106. ALEXIS SOYER

MODERN HOUSEWIFE
(1850)

ISABELLA BEETON

MRS. BEETON'S BOOK OF HOUSEHOLD MANAGEMENT
(1861)

The industrial revolution vastly expanded the ranks of the middle class in the West. With wealth came a host of new obligations for the organization and management of the home, the responsibility for which fell to women. With large families and without labor-saving devices, household management was similar to overseeing a small business. Moreover, bourgeois life was governed by a set of social conventions that could confuse even the most competent woman. The result was a profusion of etiquette and how-to books for the mistress of the middle-class home. They combined recipes and homeopathic medical advice, set the standards for manners, and provided rules about financial affairs, shopping, and management of household servants.

Alexis Soyer was a famous French chef. His *Modern Housewife* contained hundreds of recipes and sample menus with instructions for maintaining a well-ordered home. *Mrs. Beeton's Book of Household Management* was first published in 1861. It proved enormously popular; new editions were produced for over half a century. It ran to over 2000 pages and covered almost every aspect of middle-class life.

MODERN HOUSEWIFE

Household Affairs

Mrs. R.   After all the receipts and information which you have given me, there is one which you have not touched upon yet, which, perhaps, is of more importance than all the rest, it is the management of servants.

Mrs. B.   You are right, my dear, it is of great importance, and more so than many of us imagine, as for myself I do not consider that I am a good manager, being perhaps of too forgiving a disposition; but there is one good quality which I possess which makes up for the want of others, that is exactitude; by enforcing this it causes all to know their place, and perform their work.

Mrs. R.   But what surprises me is to see everything so well done and clean with so few servants; you seem to have but two maid servants, the cook, house-maid, and coachman.

Mrs. B.   Yes, that is all, and I generally find that they are enough for the work, unless I have a dinner party, and then of course, as you know, I have extra men; but I will tell you how I pass the day, and then you will be able to judge.

We are what are called early risers, that is, Mr. B. is obliged to leave home every week day at twenty minutes past nine; our breakfast is on the table at half-past eight; the breakfast parlor having previously been got ready, as the servants rise at seven. We are, when we have no visitors, our two selves, the three children, and the governess. The children, in summer time, have had a walk before breakfast, but before leaving their room they uncover their beds, and if fine open the windows, if a wet morning about two inches of the top sash is pulled down. The servants get their breakfast at the same time as we do, as we require hardly any or no waiting upon, everything being ready on the table. In a former letter I told you what was our breakfast some years since when in business, now we have placed on the table some brown bread, rolls and dry toast; the butter is in a glass butter-dish, and the eggs are brought up when we have sat down to table. The urn is placed on the table, as I make my own tea and coffee; the cocoa is made down stairs.

Mr. B. generally leaves home in the brougham, which returns in time for me; in case I should be going out, he then goes in a cab or omnibus. Whilst we are at breakfast, I generally consult Mr. B. what he would like for dinner, and if he is likely to invite any friend to dine with him; the fishmonger has previously sent his list and prices of the day. I then write with a pencil on a slip of paper the bill of fare for the nursery dinner, luncheon, should any be required, and our dinner, which I send to the cook. At ten o'clock I go down stairs into the kitchen and larder, when the cook gives me her report, that is everything that is required for the next twenty-four hours' consumption, including the servants' dinner, which report is filed in the larder and made to tally with the week's list, for I must tell you that the week's consumption of all things that will not spoil is had in on the Saturday, on which day the larder is properly scoured out, and everything put again into its proper place, there being bins for all kinds of vegetables, &c. The larder is generally kept locked, the cook and I only having keys, because it is in fact a larder, and not, as in many houses, full of emptiness; this occupies about half an hour, during which time the chambermaids have been attending to the bed-rooms and drawing-room &c. If I go out or not, I always get my toilet finished by twelve o'clock; I thus have one hour to write notes, or see tradesmen or my dressmaker, and Monday mornings check and pay my tradesmen's accounts, and to dress. If I stop at home, I amuse myself by reading, or going to see the children in the nursery, or sometimes go again into the kitchen and assist the cook on some new receipt or preparation, and often have several calls; during the course of the morning the two maids scour out alternately one or two of the rooms, according to size, except on Wednesdays, when one of them is otherwise engaged.

Mr. B. arrives home at twenty minutes to five, and at half-past five we dine: the cloth is laid, and everything prepared as if we had company; it may be a little more trouble for the servants; but when we do have any friends they find it less trouble; besides it is always uncertain but what Mr. B. may bring somebody home with him, and it prevents slovenly habits; the two maids, with the exception of Wednesdays, are always ready to attend on us. I never allow the coachman to defile our carpets with his stable shoes; all his duties in the house are—the first thing in the morning to clean the knives and forks for the day, for enough are kept out for that purpose, clean the boots and shoes, and those windows the maids cannot easily get at, and assist in the garden if required. Many have made the remark to me, that as you have a male servant why not have him wait at table. I reply that the duties of the stable are incompatible with those of the table, and if he does his duty properly he has enough to do. The servants dine at one, and have tea at quarter to five, by which time the cook has everything ready, all but to take it from the fire, and the maids the dining-room ready. The nursery dinner is at the same hour; after dinner, should we be alone, we have the children and the governess down; if we have company we do not see them; they go to bed at a

quarter to eight, and we have tea and coffee at eight; the governess comes and passes the rest of the evening with us; eleven is our usual hour of retiring, before which Mr. B. likes his glass of negus, a biscuit, or a sandwich, which is brought upon a tray.

MRS. BEETON'S BOOK OF HOUSEHOLD MANAGEMENT

The Housewife, Home Virtues, Hospitality, Good Temper, Dress and Fashion, Engaging Domestics, Wages of Servants, Visiting, Visiting Cards, Parties, Etc., Etc.

The functions of the mistress of a house resemble those of the general of an army or the manager of a great business concern. Her spirit will be seen in the whole establishment, and if she performs her duties well and intelligently, her domestics will usually follow in her path. Among the gifts that nature has bestowed on woman, few rank higher than the capacity for domestic management, for the exercise of this faculty constantly affects the happiness, comfort and prosperity of the whole family. In this opinion we are borne out by the author of *The Vicar of Wakefield*, who says: "The modest virgin, the prudent wife, and the careful matron are much more serviceable in life than petticoated philosophers, blustering heroines, or virago queans. She who makes her husband and her children happy is a much greater character than ladies described in romances, whose whole occupation is to murder mankind with shafts from the quiver of their eyes."

The housewife—Although this word may be used to describe any mistress of a household, it seems more fittingly applied to those who personally conduct their domestic affairs than to others who govern with the assistance of a large staff of well-trained servants. Times have changed since 1766, when Goldsmith wrote extolling home virtues; and in few things is the change more marked than in woman's sphere; but a woman should not be less careful in her management or blameless in her life because the spirit of the age gives her greater scope for her activities. Busy housewives should be encouraged to find time in the midst of domestic cares for the recreation and social intercourse which are necessary to the well-being of all. A woman's home should be first and foremost in her life, but if she allow household cares entirely to occupy her thoughts, she is apt to become narrow in her interests and sympathies, a condition not conducive to domestic happiness. To some overworked women but little rest or recreation may seem possible, but, generally speaking, the leisure to be enjoyed depends upon proper methods of work, punctuality, and early rising. The object of the present work is to give assistance to those who desire practical advice in the government of their home.

Early rising contributes largely to good Household Management; she who practises this virtue reaps an ample reward both in health and prosperity. When a mistress is an early riser, it is almost certain that her house will be orderly and well managed. On the contrary, if she remains in bed till a late hour, then the servants, who, as we have observed, invariably acquire some of their mistress's characteristics, are likely to become sluggards. To self-indulgence all are more or less disposed, and it is not to be expected that servants are freer from this fault than the heads of houses. Cleanliness is quite indispensable to Health, and must be studied both in regard to the person and the house, and all that it contains. Cold or tepid baths should be employed every morning.

Frugality and economy are virtues without which no household can prosper. The necessity of economy should be evident to every one, whether in possession of an income barely sufficient for a family's requirements, or of a large fortune which seems to put financial adversity out of the question. We must always remember

that to manage well on a small income is highly creditable. Economy and frugality must never, however, be allowed to degenerate into meanness.

Hospitality should be practised; but care must be taken that the love of company, for its own sake, does not become a prevailing passion; such a habit is no longer hospitality, but dissipation. A lady, when she first undertakes the responsibility of a household, should not attempt to retain all the mere acquaintances of her youth. Her true and tried friends are treasures never to be lightly lost, but they, and the friends she will make by entering her husband's circle, and very likely by moving to a new locality, should provide her with ample society.

In conversation one should never dwell unduly on the petty annoyances and trivial disappointments of the day. Many people get into

"A lady should always aim at being well and attractively dressed whilst never allowing questions of costume to establish inordinate claims on either time or purse."

the bad habit of talking incessantly of the worries of their servants and children, not realizing that to many of their hearers these are uninteresting if not wearisome subjects. From one's own point of view, also, it is well not to start upon a topic without having sufficient knowledge to discuss it with intelligence. Important events, whether of joy or sorrow, should be told to friends whose sympathy or congratulation may be welcome. A wife should never allow a word about any faults of her husband to pass her lips.

Cheerfulness—We cannot too strongly insist on the vital importance of always preserving an equable good temper amidst all the little cares and worries of domestic life. Many women may be heard to declare that men cannot realize the petty anxieties of a household. But a woman must cultivate that tact and forbearance without which no man can hope to succeed in his career. The true woman combines with mere tact that subtle sympathy which makes her the loved companion and friend alike of husband, children and all around her.

On the important subject of dress and fashion we cannot do better than quote: "Let people write, talk, lecture, satirize, as they may, it cannot be denied that, whatever is the prevailing mode in attire, let it intrinsically be ever so absurd, it will never *look* as ridiculous as another, which, however convenient, comfortable, or even becoming is totally opposite in style to that generally worn." A lady's dress should be always suited to her circumstances, and varied for different occasions. The morning dress should be neat and simple, and suitable for the domestic duties that usually occupy the early part of the day. This dress should be changed before calling hours; but it is not in good taste to wear much jewelry except with evening dress. A lady should always aim at being well and attractively dressed whilst never allowing questions of costume to establish inordinate claims on either time or purse. In purchasing her own garments, after taking account of the important detail of the length of her purse, she should aim at adapting the style of the day in such a manner as best suits the requirements of her face, figure and complexion, and never allow slavish adherence to temporary fads of fashion to overrule her own sense of what is becoming and befitting. She should also bear in mind that her different costumes have to furnish her with apparel for home wear, outdoor exercise and social functions, and try to allot due relative importance to the claims of each.

QUESTIONS

1. How does Soyer think household servants should be treated?

2. What sort of establishment did the well-run middle-class household have? How many servants were necessary, and what were their duties?

3. What was the day like for the mistress of the household? How complicated were her duties?

4. How does Mrs. Beeton characterize a good housewife?

5. How much responsibility did the middle-class woman have in her home?

107.

DOCUMENTS OF THE IRISH POTATO FAMINE

(1845–1849)

The Irish potato famine was a series of harvest failures that resulted from the appearance of a fungus that destroyed potato plants. It began in the spring of 1845 and was made worse by excessively wet weather and the slow response of farmers, landowners, and government to its severity. The reduction of one year's crop ensured the reduction of the next as there were fewer seeds to be planted, but the resilience of the fungus and the continuation of unfavorable weather conditions turned a serious situation into a catastrophe. By the middle of the nineteenth century, too many Irish peasants were wholly dependent upon the potato crop for their entire subsistence. Any harvest failure would have dire consequences. But the appearance of the fungus was unlike anything that had ever been seen in Ireland. In some areas as much as 90 percent of the crop rotted in the fields, leaving thousands of people to starve and overwhelming traditional forms of poor relief. Only dramatic government intervention might have saved lives, but government too was overwhelmed by the magnitude of the crisis and unsure of the policies that needed to be adopted. The first responsibility was that of local landowners, for most peasants were tenants, and many landowners were either absentees or were equally affected by the loss of income from their crops. Private charities sprang up to attempt to aid victims, but the scale of the problem was far beyond their abilities. The ultimate resolution of the crisis came through massive mortality and emigration. Ireland's population was reduced by more than 25 percent.

The potato famine generated considerable contemporary commentary, much of it aimed at helping the victims, some at blaming government and landlords. A representative selection of documents covering many facets of the famine follows.

From Sir Robert Peel to Sir James Graham, 13 October 1845.

The accounts of the state of the potato crop in Ireland are becoming very alarming. There is such a tendency to exaggeration and inaccuracy in Irish reports, that delay in acting upon them is always desirable. But I foresee the necessity that may be imposed upon us at an early period of considering whether there is not that well-grounded apprehension of actual scarcity that justifies and compels the adoption of every means of relief.

I have no confidence in such remedies as the prohibition of exports, or the stoppage of the distilleries. The removal of impediments to import is the only effectual remedy.

From Sir James Graham to Sir Robert Peel, 13 October 1845.

A great national risk is always incurred when a population so dense as that of Ireland subsists on the potato; for it is the cheapest and lowest food, and if it fail, no substitute can be found for starving multitudes.

Your intimate knowledge of the condition of the peasantry of Ireland, your kind and humane feeling towards them, and the fatal certainty that a famine in that quarter of the United Kingdom will be a great crisis in our national affairs, will lead you, while there is yet time, to deliberate anxiously on the course which it may be necessary for us to take.

From Sir Robert Peel to Sir James Graham, 15 October 1845.

My question on the awful question of the potato crop in Ireland will have crossed yours to me.

Interference with the due course of the laws respecting the supply of food is so momentous, and so lasting in its consequences, that we must not act without the most accurate information.

Lord Cloncurry, Chairman of Mansion House Committee, Dublin, to Sir Robert Peel, 7 November 1845.

Sir,

As Chairman of a Committee consisting of respectable gentlemen of all classes of religious and political opinions, appointed at a recent public Meeting of the citizens of Dublin, the Right Honorable the Lord Mayor in the chair.

It devolved upon me as a public duty, to address you, as responsible advisor of our Most Gracious Majesty, and which I do with unfeigned respect, and in the most anxious manner to call for your fullest and most immediate consideration to the present afflicting and most dangerous state of the people of Ireland.

We can assure you that our information is both accurate and extensive, that it reaches over all parts of Ireland, and is derived from sources altogether unaffected by any political party motive whatsoever . . .

We do solemnly assure you of our perfect knowledge that the destruction of the potatoe [sic] crop is extremely extensive, with some slight mitigation in particular localities; but, as a general calamity, is extending to all the provinces and counties in Ireland.

Nor does the evil rest here, for day after day the disease is extending; quantities of potatoes apparently in the most healthy state one day, are found on the ensuing day partially, if not entirely, unfit for human or even animal food. The disease is in its nature expansive, and is to our knowledge daily and hourly expanding; nor is there any rational evidence to show that this wide spreading rottenness will find any other limit than in the destruction of the entire potatoe crop . . .

May we respectfully refer you to Lord Devon's Report of last session, where you will find, or indeed whence we take it for granted you are already informed, that the Irish agricultural labourers and their families are calculated to amount to more than four millions of human beings, "whose only food is the potatoe, whose only drink is water, whose houses are pervious to the rain, to whom a bed or blanket is a luxury almost unknown, and who are more wretched than any other people in Europe" . . .

If then such was the condition of a large portion of the Irish people even in favourable harvests, you will, in your humanity, easily judge what must be the horrors of their situation, if the approaching famine be allowed to envelop the entire population.

We implore of you, Sir, not to allow yourself to be persuaded that we exaggerate the horrors or certainty of the approaching famine; we have no motive under heaven of misleading or misinforming you; and even if we had, you may believe we are utterly incapable of acting on such a motive; our only object is to impress on your mind what we know to be the fact—that famine and pestilence are at our door, and can be averted only by the most extensive and active precautions.

Report of Dr Playfair and Mr Lindley on the present State of the Irish Potato Crop, and on the Prospect of Approaching Scarcity. Dated 15 November 1845.

With reference to the conversation we had the honour to hold with you yesterday at the Home Office, and your wish that our individual opinions as to the extent of the Potato Disease should be communicated in writing, we have to make the following statement.

During our stay in Ireland, we completely established such official papers as were transmitted to us from the Castle; we consulted persons acquainted with the facts of the disease; we visited the district lying between Dublin and Drogheda, and inspected various Potato fields and stores in the counties of Dublin, Louth, Meath, Westmeath and part of Kildare. Judging from the evidence thus collected, and from what we have seen of the progress of the disease in England, we can come to no other conclusion than that one-half of the actual Potato crop of Ireland is either destroyed or remains in a state unfit for the food of man. We moreover feel it our duty to apprize you, that we fear this to be a low estimate.

It is doubtless true that in some places a much larger proportion of the crop is apparent-

ly safe; but, on the other hand, there are districts where it is not too much to say that the crop is lost; for example, we may mention a large field at Skerries, where not more than one Potato in twenty was found lying in a state which would admit of preservation; and another, near Oldbridge, in which, from the want of skill in the owner, all appeared to be perishing in the pits; and we have proof that these are not rare examples.

We would now add, melancholy as this picture is, that in all probability, the late rainy weather has rendered the mischief yet greater.

Of the remaining half thus assumed to be capable of preservation, there can be no doubt that the principal part may be relied on as food for the ensuing winter, provided the methods of storing which we have indicated are followed. But, considering the means, or rather the want of means, on the part of the Irish peasant, the wetness of the climate, the disputes between landlord and tenant, and perhaps the despair or other feelings of the poor cultivators, we dare not venture to hope that our plans, simple as they are, will be fully carried out; and in the meantime more of the crop will disappear.

It is also necessary to direct your attention to the quantity of Seed Potatoes which must be reserved for the coming year, if the cultivation of this plant is to be persevered in. We can state that, on an average, one-eighth of a crop is required for planting the same quantity of ground; so that in fact only three-eights of the crop can, in our view, be at this moment assumed to be available as food.

There is an opinion that, upon the whole, the Potato crop is this year a very large one. We regret that we have been unable to obtain any proof of this. On the contrary, we have seen that the crop was small; and we have it in evidence that it is below the average; but we have also seen it to be heavy, and we therefore consider that it may, perhaps, be an average crop.

We are not sufficiently acquainted with the habits of the Irish peasantry to be able to state at what time the want of food from the failure of their Potatoes may be first expected.

We have the honour,
John Lindley
Lyon Playfair.

Charles Trevelyan, Treasury, to Randolph Routh, 3 February 1846.

That indirect permanent advantages will accrue to Ireland from the scarcity, and the measures taken for its relief, I entertain no doubt; but if we were to pursue these incidental objects to the neglect of any precautions immediately required to save the people from actual starvation, our responsibilities would be fearful indeed.

Besides, the greatest improvement of all which could take place in Ireland would be, to teach the people to depend upon themselves for developing the resources of the country, instead of having recourse to the assistance of the Government on every occasion. Much has been done of late years to put this important matter on its proper footing; but if a firm stand is not made against the prevailing disposition to take advantage of this crisis to break down all barriers, the true permanent interests of the country will, I am convinced, suffer in a manner which will be irreparable in our time.

Isaac Butt writing in the Dublin University Magazine (1847).

What can be more absurd, what can be more wicked, than for men professing attachment to an imperial Constitution to answer claims now put forward for state assistance to the unprecedented necessities of Ireland, by talking of Ireland being a drain upon the *English* treasury? . . . If the union be not a mockery, there exists no such thing as an English treasury . . . when calamity falls upon us, are [we] to be told that we then recover out separate existence as a nation, just so far as to disentitle us to the state assistance which any portion of a nation vis-

ited with such a calamity had a right to expect from the governing power? If Cornwall had been visited with the scenes that have desolated Cork, would similar arguments have been used? Would men have stood up and denied that Cornwall was entitled to have the whole country share the extraordinary loss?

All our measures are based on the principle that this calamity ought to be regarded as an imperial one, and borne by the empire at large. If this be not conceded—if the state be not, as we have said, our government—if we are not to receive the assistances which government can render upon such an occasion—what alternative is there for any Irishman but to feel that the united parliament has abdicated the functions of government for Ireland, and to demand for his country that separate legislative existence, the necessity of which will be fully proved.

Report of the British Relief Association.

The response, which this appeal received, was as prompt as the emergency required. Her Majesty the Queen immediately directed that her name should be placed at the head of a list of donors for a contribution of £2000 with a most gracious promise of such further amount as the exigency might demand: and the demand was liberally followed by every member of the Royal Family, including His Majesty the King of Hanover.

A circular, issued by the Right Honorable the Lord Mayor of London to the chief magistrates of the provincial cities and boroughs of England and Wales, met with an equally ready response. Public meetings were called in several important towns; subscription lists were opened at nearly all the banks and principle mercantile establishments of the country; and these lists afford conclusive evidence of the anxiety of Englishmen, whatever their sphere or station, to contribute, to the utmost extent of their means, towards the relief of their suffering fellow-subjects.

At a subsequent period, the subjects of the Crown of Great Britain, scattered not only in the colonies, but in foreign states, entered into public subscriptions for the same purpose. Nor were the contributions limited to British subjects. In the list of donors will be found the name of His Imperial Majesty the Sultan, a subscriber of £1000, whose munificent example was followed in his own and other states by many, whose sole ties with the people of Great Britain were those of sympathy, humanity, and the brotherhood of mankind.

The Belfast Ladies' Association 1847.

Resolutions.

A meeting convened by a circular, was held in Mr Hall's Large Room, Commercial Buildings, on Friday, January 1st, 1847, which was attended by a large and influential assemblage of Ladies, of all religious denominations.

Miss Kowles having been called to the Chair, the following resolutions were passed unanimously:

Resolved—1st. That this meeting do form itself into a Society, for the purpose of raising a fund by subscription, and otherwise as may be resolved upon, to be applied to the relief of such of the afflicted districts throughout Ireland as may appear to the Committee, now to be appointed, most in need of relief, being guided by the urgency of the case without reference to religious distinctions . . .

3rd. That a subscription list be opened, for the above purpose; and that the Committee do divide the Town into districts, and appoint Collectors, to solicit subscriptions to their funds, from those who have not already subscribed ...

5th. That for the purpose of raising further funds, a Bazaar of Ladies' Work be opened, in this town, in the course of the Spring—the time and place to be arranged by the Ladies of the Committee; and that the Ladies of this meeting, and their friends, be requested to exert themselves to assist, by contribution of their work . . .

Report.

One of the first public efforts of the Committee was to prepare and publish, from the documents collected by the Corresponding Committee, a Circular or Appeal, giving a short account of the objects of the Association, and some extracts from authentic communications, shewing the awful intensity of the destitution, and calculated to engage the sympathies and exertions of the benevolent, to aid the Committee in their efforts to afford relief to the unfortunate sufferers.

Most generous was the response to this appeal. Not only from our own neighbourhood, but from other places in Ireland, from Scotland, and, above all, from England, subscriptions have been forwarded to the Committee, the magnitude and promptitude of which sufficiently shew the impression made on their minds by the short and simple, but authentic, tales of horror revealed in the circular. Upwards of £2,000 have already been collected in money, and a large amount has been received in clothes, and in materials to be made into clothing.

At first (except in one instance), the sole cry of those who sent forward appeals for relief to the Committee, was for food. Thousands were in a state which daily threatened starvation; it was impossible for the Committee to shut their ears against the cry of the famishing pleading for aid. The first grants, necessarily, were for the purchase of food, to be distributed to the hungry and helpless. Clothes were also given to those who, for want of raiment, could neither seek for work, nor engage in any labour that required them to leave their homes . . .

The following extracts are taken from letters addressed to the correspondents. The first, dated 8th January, was received exactly one week after the formation of the Association, and is given, as shewing the gradual increase of destitution, from that to the present time (6th March, 1847):

"From the Rev. James Ovens, Inniskeil Glebe, Ardara, County Donegal, 8th. January 1847.
I have once to bring under the kind consideration of the Ladies' Society of Belfast the state and circumstances of the parish of Inniskeil,

with a population of nearly twelve thousand; four thousand applicants to the Relief Committee for work; eight hundred helpless persons, from age, sickness, and infirmity, unable to enter on laborious work. I have not, in this parish, in extent thirty miles, chiefly mountain and all inhabited, a resident landed proprietor; and from the absentee landlords I have only received the sum of £45. It would be painful to enter into a detail of the destitute families of six, eight or ten, subsisting on a quantity of food, daily, almost incredible. This locality is forty-five miles from Derry, the only sure market we have for supplies. The greatest difficulty and expense attend the transit of provisions" . . .

"From the Rev. Francis M'Clure, Carrigart, County Donegal, 27th. February 1847.
Your donation will do much good in this locality —a locality where famine is besieging almost every cottage, and disease following hard in its footsteps, and rapidly carrying off its victims.

Yesterday, twelve from this neighbourhood were borne to their lonely graves. Today, I have been informed, that almost an equal number bade adieu to the cares and troubles of this life.

Dysentery is the disease, which is most fatal, and it is as infectious as fever. The £20 which I also received, for the purpose of relieving distress, by giving employment to females, will do a very great deal of good. It will give relief to at least fifty for a period of three months; and I hope, by that time, should relief not have come from some other source, that your praiseworthy Association will be enabled once more to extend its benevolent and liberal hand to those greatest of all objects of charity, whom God hath put into your kind hearts to save from horrors of famine."

James Hack Tuke, *A Visit to Connaught in the Autumn of 1847.*

The landlords of Mayo, as well as of many other portions of Connaught, as a class (there are many noble exceptions who feel and see the impolicy and evil of such proceedings) are pursuing a course which cannot fail to add to the universal wretchedness and poverty which exist. The corn crops, bountiful as they may be, are not sufficient to meet the landlords' claim for rent and arrears contracted during the last two years of famine, and it is at least not unnatural for the tenant to be unwilling to give up that, without which he must certainly perish. In every direction, the agents of the landlords, armed with the full powers of the law, are at work— everywhere one sees the driver or bailiff 'canting' the small patches of oats or potatoes— or keepers, whose exorbitant charges must be paid by the unfortunate tenant, placed over the crop. Even the produce of seed, distributed through the agency of benevolent associations, has been totally swept away. To add to the universal distress caused by this system of seizure, eviction is in many cases practiced, and not a few of the roofless dwellings which meet the eye, have been destroyed at the insistence of landlords, after turning adrift the miserable inmates; and this even at a time like the present, when the charity of the whole world has been turned towards the relief of this starving peasantry . . .

What prospects are there for these miserable outcasts? Death, indeed must be the portion of some, for their neighbours, hardly richer than themselves, were principally subsisting on turnip tops; whilst the poor house of the union of Westport is nearly forty miles distant. Turnips taken, can we say stolen, from the fields, as they wearily walk thither, would be their only chance of support. Some indeed would never reach their destination—death would relieve them of their sufferings, and the landlord of his burden.

QUESTIONS

1. What were the concerns of the British government at the beginning of the famine?

2. What roles did private philanthropy play during the famine?

3. Was Ireland helped or hurt by its union with England and Scotland during the famine?

4. How did the structure of landownership affect the results of the famine?

Political Critiques

108.   J. S. MILL

ON LIBERTY
(1859)

John Stuart Mill (1806–73) was trained from infancy to be a philosopher and reformer in the tradition of the Benthamites. When he was only three, his father, one of the original Utilitarians, began his education, teaching him languages and classics. At the age of seventeen Mill entered the service of the East India Company, where he rose to the important post of chief examiner. While with the East India Company he wrote a number of works on social and economic questions and edited the *London Review*. When the company was dissolved in 1858, Mill turned to writing full-time. His own philosophy moved away from that of his father, becoming more idealistic as time passed. In 1865 he was elected a member of Parliament, where he voted with the radicals and advocated the extension of the franchise to women. He died in France in 1873.

On Liberty was the product of many years of thought about the nature of freedom. Mill advocated individual rights over those of the state, and carefully delineated personal and social liberty.

The object of this Essay is to assert one very simple principle, as entitled to govern absolutely the dealings of society with the individual in the way of compulsion and control, whether the means used be physical force in the form of legal penalties, or the moral coercion of public opinion. That principle is, that the sole end for which mankind are warranted, individually or collectively, in interfering with the liberty of action of any of their number, is self-protection. That the only purpose for which power can be rightfully exercised over any member of a civilized community, against his will, is to prevent harm to others. His own good, either physical or moral, is not a sufficient warrant. He cannot rightfully be compelled to do or forbear because it will be better for him to do so, because it will make him happier, because, in the opinions of others, to do so would be wise, or even right. These are good reasons for remonstrating with him, or reasoning with him, or persuading him, or entreating him, but not for compelling him, or visiting him with any evil in case he do otherwise. To justify that, the conduct from which it is desired to deter him must be calculated to produce evil to some one else. The only part of the conduct of any one, for which he is amenable to society, is that which concerns others. In the part which merely concerns himself, his independence is, of right, absolute. Over himself, over his own body and mind, the individual is sovereign.

This, then, is the appropriate region of human liberty. It comprises, first, the inward domain of consciousness; demanding liberty of conscience, in the most comprehensive sense; liberty of thought and feeling; absolute freedom of opinion and sentiment on all subjects, practical or speculative, scientific, moral, or theological. The liberty of expressing and publishing opinions may seem to fall under a different principle, since it belongs to that part of the conduct of an individual which concerns other people; but, being almost of as much importance as the liberty of thought itself, and resting in great part on the same reasons, is practically inseparable from it. Secondly, the principle requires liberty of tastes and pursuits; of framing the plan of our life to suit our own character; of doing as we like, subject to such consequences as may follow: without impediment from our fellow creatures, so long as what we do does not harm them, even though they should think our conduct foolish, perverse, or wrong. Thirdly, from this liberty of each individual, follows the liberty, within the same limits, of combination among individuals; freedom to unite, for any purpose not involving harm to others; the persons combining being supposed to be of full age, and not forced or deceived.

No society in which these liberties are not, on the whole, respected, is free, whatever may be its form of government; and none is completely free in which they do not exist absolute and unqualified. The only freedom which deserves the name, is that of pursuing our own good in our own way, so long as we do not attempt to deprive others of theirs, or impede their efforts to obtain it. Each is the proper guardian of his own health, whether bodily, or mental and spiritual. Mankind are greater gainers by suffering each other to live as seems good to themselves, than by compelling each to live as seems good to the rest.

Apart from the peculiar tenets of individual thinkers, there is also in the world at large an increasing inclination to stretch unduly the powers of society over the individual, both by the force of opinion and even by that of legislation: and as the tendency of all the changes taking place in the world is to strengthen society, and diminish the power of the individual, this encroachment is not one of the evils which tend spontaneously to disappear, but, on the contrary, to grow more and more formidable. The disposition of mankind, whether as rulers or as fellow-citizens, to impose their own opinions and inclinations as a rule of conduct on others, is so energetically supported by some of the best and by some of the worst feelings incident to human nature, that it is hardly ever kept under restraint by anything but want of power; and as the power is not declining, but growing, unless a strong barrier of moral conviction can be raised against the mischief, we must expect, in the present circumstances of the world, to see it increase.

Of Individuality

No one pretends that actions should be as free as opinions. On the contrary, even opinions lose their immunity, when the circumstances in which they are expressed are such as to constitute their expression a positive instigation to some mischievous act. An opinion that corn-dealers are starvers of the poor, or that private property is robbery, ought to be unmolested when simply circulated through the press, but may justly incur punishment when delivered orally to an excited mob assembled before the house of a corn-dealer, or when handed about among the same mob in the form of a placard. Acts, of whatever kind, which, without justifiable cause, do harm to others, may be, and in the more important cases absolutely require to be, controlled by the unfavourable sentiments, and, when needful, by the active interference of mankind. The liberty of the individual must be thus far limited; he must not make himself a nuisance to other people. But if he refrains from molesting others in what concerns them, and merely acts according to his own inclination and judgment in things which concern himself, the same reasons which show that opinion should be free, prove also that he should

Portrait of English philosopher and economist John Stuart Mill (1806–73).

be allowed, without molestation, to carry his opinions into practice at his own cost. That mankind are not infallible; that their truths, for the most part, are only half-truths; that unity of opinion, unless resulting from the fullest and freest comparison of opposite opinions, is not desirable, and diversity not an evil, but a good, until mankind are much more capable than at present of recognizing all sides of the truth, are principles applicable to men's modes of action, not less than to their opinions. As it is useful that while mankind are imperfect there should be different opinions, so is it that there should be different experiments of living; that free scope should be given to varieties of character, short of injury of others; and that the worth of different

modes of life should be proved practically, when any one thinks fit to try them. It is desirable, in short, that in things which do not primarily concern others, individuality should assert itself. Where, not the person's own character, but the traditions or customs of other people are the rule of conduct, there is wanting one of the principal ingredients of human happiness, and quite the chief ingredient of individual and social progress.

In maintaining this principle, the greatest difficulty to be encountered does not lie in the appreciation of means towards an acknowledged end, but in the indifference of persons in general to the end itself. If it were felt that the free development of individuality is one of the leading essentials of well-being; that it is not only a coordinate element with all that is designated by the terms of civilization, instruction, education, culture, but is itself a necessary part and condition of all those things; there would be no danger that liberty should be under-valued, and the adjustment of the boundaries between it and social control would present no extraordinary difficulty. But the evil is, that individual spontaneity is hardly recognized by the common modes of thinking, as having any intrinsic worth, or deserving any regard on its own account. The majority, being satisfied with the ways of mankind as they now are (for it is they who make them what they are), cannot comprehend why those ways should not be good enough for everybody; and what is more, spontaneity forms no part of the ideal of the majority of moral and social reformers, but is rather looked on with jealousy, as a troublesome and perhaps rebellious obstruction to the general acceptance of what these reformers, in their own judgment, think would be best for mankind.

Limits to the Authority of Society

What, then, is the rightful limit to the sovereignty of the individual over himself? Where does the authority of society begin? How much of human life should be assigned to individuality, and how much to society?

Each will receive its proper share, if each has that which more particularly concerns it. To individuality should belong the part of life in which it is chiefly the individual that is interested; to society, the part which chiefly interests society.

Though society is not founded on a contract, and though no good purpose is answered by inventing a contract in order to deduce social obligations from it, every one who receives the protection of society owes a return for the benefit, and the fact of living in society renders it indispensable that each should be bound to observe a certain line of conduct towards the rest. This conduct consists, first, in not injuring the interests of one another; or rather certain interests, which, either by express legal provision or by tacit understanding, ought to be considered as rights; and secondly, in each person's bearing his share (to be fixed on some equitable principle) of the labours and sacrifices incurred for defending the society or its members from injury and molestation. These conditions society is justified in enforcing, at all costs to those who endeavor any molestation. These conditions society is justified in enforcing, at all costs to those who endeavor to withhold fulfillment. Nor is this all that society may do. The acts of an individual may be hurtful to others, or wanting in due consideration for their welfare, without going the length of violating any of their constituted rights. The offender may then be justly punished by opinion, though not by law. As soon as any part of a person's conduct affects prejudicially the interests of others, society has jurisdiction over it, and the question whether the general welfare will or will not be promoted by interfering with it, becomes open to discussion. But there is no room for entertaining any such question when a person's conduct affects the interests of no persons besides himself, or needs not affect them unless they like (all the persons concerned being of full age, and the ordinary amount of understanding). In all such cases there should be perfect freedom, legal and social, to do the action and stand the consequences.

It would be a great misunderstanding of this doctrine, to suppose that it is one of selfish indifference, which pretends that human beings have no business with each other's conduct in life, and that they should not concern themselves about the well-doing or well-being of one another, unless their own interest is involved. Instead of any diminution, there is need of a great increase of disinterested exertion to promote the good of others. But disinterested benevolence can find other instruments to persuade people to their good, than whips and scourges, either of the literal or the metaphorical sort. I am the last person to undervalue the self-regarding virtues; they are only second in importance, if even second, to the social. It is equally the business of education to cultivate both. But even education works by conviction and persuasion as well as by compulsion, and it is by the former only that, when the period of education is past, the self-regarding virtues should be inculcated. Human beings owe to each other help to distinguish the better from the worse, and encouragement to choose the former and avoid the latter. They should be for ever stimulating each other to increased exercise of their higher faculties, and increased direction of their feelings and aims towards wise instead of foolish, elevating instead of degrading, objects and contemplations. But neither one person, nor any number of persons, is warranted in saying to another human creature of ripe years, that he shall not do with his life for his own benefit what he chooses to do with it.

QUESTIONS

1. When is society justified in restricting liberty?

2. What conditions must be satisfied before Mill would describe a society as truly free?

3. How might Mill respond to the arguments of reformers who demand state intervention in the economy and society?

4. How does Mill distinguish between the sort of liberty that is allowable and the sort that is not?

5. Mill saw his vision of freedom as beneficial, but others criticized it as unrealistic and even inhumane. Why?

109.   PIERRE PROUDHON

WHAT IS PROPERTY?
(1840)

Pierre Joseph Proudhon (1809–65), a radical French socialist, achieved fame as an advocate of anarchy as a political system. Proudhon's political ideas were colored by his upbringing as the son of a poor and irresponsible peasant. Forced to leave school at an early age, Proudhon began his career as a printer's apprentice. He learned to read and write on the job. As his interests became more political, he became a writer and journalist. Proudhon scandalized France with his declaration that "Property is theft" and was subjected to constant political harassment after the publication of *What Is Property?* His newspaper, *Representative of the People,* was closed down, and he was jailed for several years before being exiled. He returned to France after being pardoned by Napoleon III and in his last years became an influential leader of the Parisian working class.

What Is Property? was Proudhon's first and most important book. Proudhon believed that anarchy—a radical individualism in which there was no room for the state—was the only logical solution to social inequality and injustice.

From the right of the strongest springs the exploitation of man by man, or bondage; usury, or the tribute levied upon the conquered by the conqueror; and the whole numerous family of taxes, duties, monarchical prerogatives, house-rents, farm-rents, &c.; in one word—property.

Force was followed by artifice, the second manifestation of justice; from artifice sprang the profits of manufacturers, commerce, and banking, mercantile frauds, and pretensions which are honored with the beautiful names of *talent* and *genius,* but which ought to be regarded as the last degree of knavery and deception; and, finally, all sorts of social inequalities.

In those forms of robbery which are prohibited by law, force and artifice are employed alone and undisguised; in the authorized forms, they conceal themselves within a useful product, which they use as a tool to plunder their victim.

The direct use of violence and stratagem was early and universally condemned; but no nation has yet got rid of that kind of robbery which acts through talent, labor, and possession, and which is the source of all the dilemmas of casuistry and the innumerable contradictions of jurisprudence.

The right of force and the right of artifice—glorified by the rhapsodists in the poems of the "Iliad" and the "Odyssey"—inspired the legislation of the Greeks and Romans, from which they passed into our morals and codes. Christianity has not changed at all. The Gospel should not be blamed, because the priests, as stupid as the legists, have been unable either to expound or to understand it. The ignorance of councils and popes upon all questions of morality is equal to that of the market-place and the money-changers; and it is this utter ignorance of right, justice, and society, which is killing the Church, and discrediting its teachings for ever. The infidelity of the Roman Church and other Christian churches is flagrant; all have disregarded the precept of Jesus; all have erred in moral and doctrinal points; all are guilty of teaching false and absurd dogmas, which lead straight to wickedness and murder. Let it ask pardon of God and men,—this church which called itself infallible, and which has grown so corrupt in morals; let its reformed sisters humble themselves, . . . and the people, undeceived, but still religious and merciful, will begin to think.

The development of right has followed the same order, in its various expressions, that property has in its forms. Every where we see justice driving robbery before it and confining it within narrower and narrower limits. Hitherto the victories of justice over injustice, and of equality over inequality, have been won by instinct and the simple force of things; but the final triumph of our social nature will be due to our reason, or else we shall fall back into feudal chaos. Either this glorious height is reserved for our intelligence, or this miserable depth for our baseness.

The second effect of property is despotism. Now, since despotism is inseparably connected with the idea of legitimate authority, in explaining the natural causes of the first, the principle of the second will appear.

What is to be the form of government in the future? I hear some of my younger readers reply: "Why, how can you ask such a question? You are a republican." "A republican! Yes; but that word specifies nothing. *Res publica;* that is, the public thing. Now, whoever is interested in public affairs—no matter under what form of government—may call himself a republican. Even kings are republicans."—"Well! you are a democrat?"—"No."—"What! you would have a monarchy."—"No."—"A constitutionalist?"—"God forbid!"—"You are then an aristocrat?"—"Not at all."—"You want a mixed government?"—"Still less."—"What are you, then?"—"I am an anarchist."

"Oh! I understand you; you speak satirically. This is a hit at the government."—"By no means. I have just given you my serious and well-considered profession of faith. Although a firm friend of order, I am (in the full force of the term) an anarchist. Listen to me."

By means of self-instruction and the acquisition of ideas, man acquires the idea of *science*—that is, of a system of knowledge in harmony with the reality of things, and inferred from observation. He searches for the science, or the system, of inanimate bodies—the system of organic bodies, the system of the human mind, and the system of the universe: why should he not also search for the system of society? But, having reached this height, he comprehends that political truth, or the science of politics, exists quite independently of the will of sovereigns, the opinion of majorities, and popular beliefs—that kings, ministers, magistrates, and nations, as wills, have no connection with the science, and are worthy of no consideration. He comprehends, at the same time, that, if man is born a sociable being, the authority of his father over him ceases on the day when, his mind being formed and his education finished, he becomes the associate of his father; that his true chief and his king is the demonstrated truth; that politics is a science, not a stratagem; and that the function of the legislator is reduced, in the last analysis, to the methodical search for truth.

Thus, in a given society, the authority of man over man is inversely proportional to the stage of intellectual development which that society has reached; and the probable duration of that authority can be calculated from the more or less general desire for a true government—that is, for a scientific government. And just as the right of force and the right of artifice retreat before the steady advance of justice, and must finally be extinguished in equality, so the sovereignty of the will yields to the sovereignty of the reason, and must at least be lost in scientific socialism. Property and royalty have been crumbling to pieces ever since the world began. As man seeks justice in equality, so society seeks order in anarchy.

Anarchy—the absence of a master, of a sovereign—such is the form of government to which we are every day approximating, and which our accustomed habit of taking man for our rule, and his will for law, leads us to regard as the height of disorder and the expression of chaos. The story is told, that a citizen of Paris in the seventeenth century having heard it said that in Venice there was no king, the good man could not recover from his astonishment, and nearly died from laughter at the mere mention of so ridiculous a thing. So strong is our prejudice. The most advanced among us are those who wish the greatest possible number of sovereigns. Soon, undoubtedly, some one will say, "Everybody is king." But, when he has spoken, I will say, in my turn, "Nobody is king; we are, whether we will or no, associated." Every question of domestic politics must be decided by departmental statistics; every question of foreign politics is an affair of international statistics. The science of government rightly belongs to one of the sections of the Academy of Sciences, whose permanent secretary is necessarily prime minister; and, since every citizen may address a memoir to the Academy, every citizen is a legislator. But, as the opinion of no one is of any value until its truth has been proven, no one can substitute his will for reason—nobody is king.

All questions of legislation and politics are matters of science, not of opinion. The legislative power belongs only to the reason, methodically recognized and demonstrated. To attribute to any power whatever the right of veto or of sanction, is the last degree of tyranny. Justice and legality are two things as independent of our approval as is mathematical truth. To compel, they need only to be known; to be known, they need only to be considered and studied. What, then, is the nation, if it is not the sovereign—if it is not the source of the legislative power? The nation is the guardian of the law—the nation is the *executive power*. Every citizen may assert: "This is true; that is just"; but his opinion controls no one but himself. That the truth which he proclaims may become a law, it must be recognized. Now, what is it to recognize a law? It is to verify a mathematical or a metaphysical calculation; it is to repeat an experiment, to observe a phenomenon, to establish a fact. Only the nation has the right to say, "Be it known and decreed."

I confess that this is an overturning of received ideas, and that I seem to be attempting to revolutionize our political system; but I beg the reader to consider that, having begun with a paradox, I must, if I reason correctly, meet with paradoxes at every step, and must end with paradoxes. For the rest, I do not see how the liberty of citizens would be endangered by entrusting to their hands, instead of the pen of the legislator, the sword of the law. The executive power, belonging properly to the will, cannot be confided to too many proxies. That is the true sovereignty of the nation.

The proprietor, the robber, the hero, the sovereign—for all these titles are synonymous—imposes his will as law, and suffers neither contradiction nor control; that is, he pretends to be the legislative and the executive power at once. Accordingly, the substitution of the scientific and true law for the royal will is accomplished only by a terrible struggle; and this constant substitution is, after property, the most potent element in history, the most prolific source of political disturbances. Examples are too numerous and too striking to require enumeration.

The old civilization has run its race; a new sun is rising, and will soon renew the face of the earth. Let the present generation perish, let the old prevaricators die in the desert! The holy earth shall not cover their bones. Young man, exasperated by the corruption of the age, and absorbed in your zeal for justice! If your country is dear to you, and if you have the interests of humanity at heart, have the courage to espouse the cause of liberty! Cast off your old selfishness, and plunge into the rising flood of popular equality! There your regenerate soul will acquire new life and vigor; your enervated genius will recover unconquerable energy; and your heart, perhaps already withered, will be rejuvenated! Every thing will wear a different look to your illuminated vision; new sentiments will engender new ideas within you; religion, morality, poetry, art, language will appear before you in nobler and fairer forms; and thenceforth, sure of your faith, and thoughtfully enthusiastic, you will hail the dawn of universal regeneration!

And you, sad victims of an odious law! You, whom a jesting world despoils and outrages! You, whose labor has always been fruitless, and whose rest has been without hope, take courage! Your tears are numbered! The fathers have sown in affliction, the children shall reap in rejoicings!

O God of liberty! God of equality! Thou who didst place in my heart the sentiment of justice, before my reason could comprehend it, hear my ardent prayer! Thou hast dictated all that I have written; Thou hast shaped my thought; Thou hast directed my studies; Thou hast weaned my mind from curiosity and my heart from attachment, that I might publish Thy truth to the master and the slave. I have spoken with what force and talent Thou hast given me: it is Thine to finish the work. Thou knowest whether I seek my welfare or Thy glory, O God of liberty! Ah! perish my memory, and let humanity be free! Let me see from my obscurity the people at last instructed; let noble teachers enlighten them; let generous spirits guide them! Abridge, if possible, the time of our trial; stifle pride and avarice in equality; annihilate this love of glory which enslaves us; teach these poor children that in the bosom of liberty there are neither heroes nor great men! Inspire the powerful man, the rich man, him whose name my lips shall never pronounce in Thy presence, with a horror of his crimes; let him be the first to apply for admission to the redeemed society; let the promptness of his repentance be the ground of his forgiveness! Then, great and small, wise and foolish, rich and poor, will unite in an ineffable fraternity; and, singing in unison a new hymn, will rebuild Thy altar, O God of liberty and equality!

QUESTIONS

1. Why does Proudhon maintain that property is theft?

2. What is the author's solution for the problems of his age?

3. Politics, Proudhon argues, is a science, not an art. What does he mean?

4. What will anarchy bring to society? What will this new society look like?

5. What is Proudhon trying to do in his work? Is he offering a practical blueprint for society?

110.

THE GREAT CHARTER
(1842)

The Great Charter was a petition from a broad-based movement for political and social reform that dominated British politics in the 1840s. The Chartists were a loose confederation of middle-class shopkeepers, tradesmen, artisans, and all varieties of workers. They demanded political reform of the franchise and the process of parliamentary elections. Chartism was both a popular and a national movement, joining together Irish and Scottish reformers with English ones. Its greatest leader was the Irishman Feargus O'Connor.

The Charter delivered to the House of Commons in 1842 contained over 3 million signatures. In 1848 an effort was made to double that number and to bring over half a million people to London for its presentation. In the end, only 50,000 appeared, and as economic prosperity returned to England after 1848, Chartism diminished in importance. Although the major points of the Charter were not achieved, the agitation was important to the many franchise reforms that followed.

The People's Charter—Petition

[A Petition from the working classes throughout the kingdom, of the presentation of which Mr. Thomas Duncombe had previously given notice, was brought down to the House, by a procession consisting of a vast multitude. Its bulk was so great, that the doors were not wide enough to admit it, and it was necessary to unroll it, to carry it into the House. When unrolled, it spread over a great part of the floor and rose above the level of the Table.]

Mr. T. Duncombe, in presenting it to the House, said,—Looking at the vast proportions of this petition—looking, too, at the importance attaching to it, not only from the matter it contains, but from the millions who have signed it, I am quite satisfied, that if I were to ask the House to relax the rules which it has laid down to govern the presentation of petitions, it would grant me the indulgence; but as I have given notice of a motion for tomorrow, that the petition should be taken into the serious consideration of the House, and that those who have signed it, should by their counsel and agents, be heard at the Bar of your House, in support of the allegations which the petition contains, I shall not ask the House to grant me that indulgence, but will keep myself strictly within the limits which have been laid down for the presentation of all petitions. I beg respectfully to offer to the acceptance of this House, a petition signed by 3,315,752 of the industrious classes of this country. The petition proceeds from those upon whose toil, upon whose industry, upon whose affection, and upon whose attachment, I may say, every institution, every law, nay, even the very Government, and the whole property and commerce of the country depend. These persons now most respectfully come before you, to state the manifold grievances under which they are suffering. . . .

The petition was read by the Clerk, as follows:

"TO THE HONOURABLE THE COMMONS OF
GREAT BRITAIN AND IRELAND,
IN PARLIAMENT ASSEMBLED.

"The petition of the undersigned people of the United Kingdom,

"Sheweth—That Government originated from, was designed to protect the freedom and promote the happiness of, and ought to be responsible to, the whole people.

"That the only authority on which any body of men can make laws and govern society, is delegation from the people.

"That as Government was designed for the benefit and protection of, and must be obeyed and supported by all, therefore all should be equally represented.

"That any form of Government which fails to effect the purposes for which it was designed, and does not fully and completely represent the whole people, who are compelled to pay taxes to its support and obey the laws resolved upon by it, is unconstitutional, tyrannical, and ought to be amended or resisted.

"That your honourable House, as at present constituted, has not been elected by, and acts irresponsibly of, the people; and hitherto has only represented parties, and benefitted the few, regardless of the miseries, grievances, and

petitions of the many. Your honourable House has enacted laws contrary to the expressed wishes of the people, and by unconstitutional means enforced obedience to them, thereby creating an unbearable despotism on the one hand, and degrading slavery on the other.

"That if your honourable House is of opinion that the people of Great Britain and Ireland ought not to be fully represented, your petitioners pray that such opinion may be unequivocally made known, that the people may fully understand what they can or cannot expect from your honourable House; because if such be the decision of your honourable House, your petitioners are of opinion that where representation is denied, taxation ought to be resisted.

"That your petitioners instance, in proof of their assertion, that your honourable House has not been elected by the people; that the population of Great Britain and Ireland is the present time about twenty-six millions of persons; and that yet, out of this number, little more than nine hundred thousand have been permitted to vote in the recent election of representatives to make laws to govern the whole.

"That the existing state of representation is not only extremely limited and unjust, but unequally divided, and gives preponderating influence to the landed, and monied interests, to the utter ruin of the small-trading and labouring classes.

"That bribery, intimidation, corruption, perjury, and riot, prevail at all parliamentary elections, to an extent best understood by the Members of your honourable House.

"That your petitioners complain that they are enormously taxed to pay the interest of what is termed the national debt, a debt amounting at present to £800,000,000, being only a portion of the enormous amount expended in cruel and expensive wars for the suppression of all liberty, by men not authorised by the people, and who, consequently, had no right to tax posterity for the outrages committed by them upon mankind. And your petitioners loudly complain of the augmentation of that debt, after twenty-six years of almost uninterrupted peace, and whilst poverty and discontent rage over the land.

"That taxation, both general and local, is at this time too enormous to be borne; and in the opinion of your petitioner is contrary to the spirit of the Bill of Rights, wherein it is clearly expressed that no subject shall be compelled to contribute to any tax, talliage, or aid, unless imposed by common consent in Parliament.

"That in England, Ireland, Scotland, and Wales, thousands of people are dying from actual want; and your petitioners, whilst sensible that poverty is the great exciting cause of crime, view with mingled astonishment and alarm the ill provision made for the poor, the aged, and infirm; and likewise perceive, with feelings of indignation, the determination of your honourable House to continue the Poor-law Bill in operation, notwithstanding the many proofs which have been afforded by sad experience of the unconstitutional principle of that bill, of its unchristian character, and of the cruel and murderous effects produced upon the wages of working men, and the lives of the subjects of this realm."

"That your petitioners conceive that bill to be contrary to all previous statutes, opposed to the spirit of the constitution, and an actual violation of the precepts of the Christian religion; and, therefore, your petitioners look with apprehension to the results which may flow from its continuance.

"That your petitioners would direct the attention of your honourable House to the great disparity existing between the wages of the producing millions, and the salaries of those whose comparative usefulness ought to be questioned, where riches and luxury prevail amongst the rulers, and poverty and starvation amongst the ruled.

"That your petitioners, with all due respect and loyalty, would compare the daily income of the Sovereign Majesty with that of thousands of the working men of this nation; and whilst your petitioners have learned that her Majesty receives daily for her private use the sum of £164 17s. 10d., they have also ascertained that many thousands of the families of the labourers are only in the receipt of 3¾ d. per head per day.

"That your petitioners have also learned that his royal Highness Prince Albert receives each day the sum of £104 2s., whilst thousands have to exist upon 3d. per head per day.

"That your petitioners have also heard with astonishment, that the King of Hanover daily receives £57 10s. whilst thousands of the tax-payers of this empire live upon 2¾ d. per head per day.

"That your petitioners have, with pain and regret, also learned that the Archbishop of Canterbury is daily in the receipt of £52 10s. per day, whilst thousands of the poor have to maintain their families upon an income not exceeding 2d. per head per day.

"That notwithstanding the wretched and unparalleled condition of the people, your honourable House has manifested no disposition to curtail the expenses of the State, to diminish taxation, or promote general prosperity.

"That unless immediate remedial measures be adopted, your petitioners fear the increasing distress of the people will lead to results fearful to contemplate; because your petitioners can produce evidence of the gradual decline of wages, at the same time that the constant increase of the national burdens must be apparent to all.

"That your petitioners know that it is the undoubted constitutional right of the people, to meet freely, when, how, and where they choose, in public places, peaceably, in the day, to discuss their grievances, and political or other subjects, or for the purpose of framing discussing, or passing any vote, petition, or remonstrance, upon any subject whatsoever.

"That your petitioners complain that the right has unconstitutionally been infringed; and 500 well disposed persons have been arrested, excessive bail demanded, tried by packed juries, sentenced to imprisonment, and treated as felons of the worst description.

"That an unconstitutional police force is distributed all over the country, at enormous cost, to prevent the due exercise of the people's rights. And your petitioners are of opinion that the Poor-law Bastilles and the police stations, being co-existent, have originated from the same cause, viz., the increased desire on the part of the irresponsible few to oppress and starve the many.

"That your petitioners complain that the hours of labour, particularly of the factory workers, are protracted beyond the limits of human endurance, and that the wages earned, after unnatural application to toil in heated and unhealthy workshops, are inadequate to sustain the bodily strength, and supply those comforts which are so imperative after an excessive waste of physical energy.

"That your petitioners also direct the attention of your honourable House to the starvation wages of the agricultural labourer, and view with horror and indignation the paltry income of those whose toil gives being to the staple food of this people.

"That your petitioners believe all men have a right to worship God as may appear best to their consciences, and that no legislative enactments should interfere between man and his Creator.

"That your petitioners maintain that it is the inherent, indubitable, and constitutional right, founded upon the ancient practice of the realm of England, and supported by well approved statutes, of every male inhabitant of the United Kingdom, he being of age and of sound mind, non-convict of crime, and not confined under any judicial process, to exercise the elective franchise in the choice of Members to serve in the Commons House of Parliament.

"That your petitioners can prove, that by the ancient customs and statutes of this realm, Parliament should be held once in each year.

"That your petitioners maintain that Members elected to serve in Parliament ought to be the servants of the people, and should, at short and stated intervals, return to their constituencies, to ascertain if their conduct is approved of, and to give the people power to reject all who have not acted honestly and justly.

"That your petitioners complain that possession of property is made the test of men's qualification to sit in Parliament.

"That your petitioners can give proof that such qualification is irrational, unnecessary, and not in accordance with the ancient usages of England.

"That your petitioners complain, that by influence, patronage, and intimidation, there is at present no purity of election; and your petitioners contend for the right of voting by ballot.

"That your petitioners complain that seats in your honourable House are sought for at a most extravagant rate of expense; which proves an enormous degree of fraud and corruption.

"That your petitioners, therefore, contend, that to put an end to secret political traffic, all representatives should be paid a limited amount for their services.

"That your petitioners complain of the inequality of representation; and contend for the division of the country into equal electoral districts.

"That your petitioners, therefore, exercising their just constitutional right, demand that your honourable House do remedy the many gross and manifest evils of which your petitioners complain, do immediately, without alteration, deduction, or addition, pass into a law the document entitled, 'The People's Charter,' which embraces the representation of male adults, vote by ballot, annual Parliaments, no property qualification, payment of members, and equal electoral districts.

"And that your petitioners, desiring to promote the peace of the United Kingdom, security of property, and prosperity of commerce, seriously and earnestly press this, their petition, on the attention of your honourable House."

QUESTIONS

1. The presentation of the Great Charter to Parliament was meant to make a powerful impression upon the British people. What message do you think the presentation conveyed?

2. The petition's name was meant to echo the famous Magna Carta of the thirteenth century. Why? Why would reformers choose to make their point with a petition?

3. What is the political philosophy of the Chartists? What, according to them, makes a government legitimate?

4. How does the Charter propose to reform the British government?

5. Many people thought the Charter was a revolutionary document. Would you agree?

III.   **WILLIAM II**

LETTER TO THE SHOGUN
(1844)

BAKUFU

REPLY TO THE
GOVERNMENT OF HOLLAND
(1845)

William II (1792–1849) became king of the Netherlands in 1840 after an adventurous youth. The victorious armies of France drove his father from his country in 1795, and so the prince was raised in exile and developed a burning desire to defeat the French and return home. William joined the British army, and served under the Duke of Wellington in his struggles against Napoleon I. He commanded the Dutch troops in Wellington's army at the decisive battle of Waterloo in 1815, where he earned the admiration of his contemporaries for his courage under fire. Although William was wounded at Waterloo, he survived the defeat of Napoleon to return home to Holland. He succeeded his father as King in 1840 and presided somewhat reluctantly over the transformation of the Netherlands into a constitutional monarchy. William was a popular monarch despite his conservative political views, and he skillfully steered his kingdom through a turbulent decade. In the 1840s, changes unleashed by rapid industrialization and the growth of political conflict between social classes made the lot of a European sovereign an unenviable one, but William managed to keep the Netherlands at peace with its neighbors and itself throughout his reign.

Reproduced here are a letter William dispatched to the Japanese government in 1844 and the Shogun's reply. European expansionism, fueled by the growth of industry, had already made its presence felt in Asia when Britain forced China to open its markets to British goods in the Opium War of 1842. An even more resolutely isolationist Japan continued to resist the blandishments of Westerners eager to enter the Japanese market. Dutch traders had enjoyed exclusive—but very limited—access to Japan for decades, and William's letter was part of an attempt by the king to force the Japanese government to deal more openly with the West.

LETTER OF KING WILLIAM II OF HOLLAND TO THE *SHOGUN* OF JAPAN, FEBRUARY 15, 1844

We, William the Second by the Grace of God, King of the Netherlands, Prince of Orange and Nassau, Grand Duke of Luxemburg etc., write this our royal letter with a faithful heart to our friend, the very noble, most serene, and all-powerful sovereign of the great Empire of Japan, who has his seat in the imperial palace of Edo, the abode of peace.

May this epistle be duly delivered into the hands of our imperial friend and find him in good health and peace. More than two centuries ago by imperial order of Your Majesty's serene ancestor, the celebrated Gongen Ijejas [Tokugawa Ieyasu], permission was granted to the Dutch to come with their trading ships to Japan; and in virtue of this imperial order, the Dutch, our subjects, are still received and treated with all kindness in Japan, and moreover the leading men in that trade have been granted the honour of paying homage in person to Your Majesty.

This unfaltering goodwill exhibited towards our subjects fills us with kindly feelings towards Japan and the desire to do all that is possible for the furtherance of peace within your imperial domain and for the prosperity of your subjects.

There never has been any correspondence between the sovereigns of the Netherlands and Japan. There was no necessity, for commercial affairs and general news were communicated by the government which under our control rules over Batavia and all the islands belonging to our dominion in Asia.

But now we feel drawn to terminate this silence. There are important matters worthy of communication. They do not concern the trade of our subjects with Japan, but the political interests of the Empire. They relate to matters worthy to be treated of between king and king.

The future of Japan causes us much anxiety. May we succeed in averting imminent disaster by our good counsel.

From the communications that our vessels bring from year to year to Nagasaki, Your Majesty will have learnt that the King of England has lately been waging a violent war against the Chinese Empire.

The mighty Emperor of China after a long but fruitless resistance, was finally compelled to succumb to the superior power of European military tactics, and in the consequent treaty of peace, agreed to conditions by which the ancient Chinese policy has undergone great alteration, and whereby five Chinese ports have been opened to European trade.

When, thirty years ago, the war which had been waged in Europe, was terminated, all nations began to work for peace.

The kings remembering the lesson of the wise opened to their subjects every channel for trade.

Populations were on the increase. The discoveries in machinery and physics rendered manual labour less necessary.

Commerce and industry rapidly increased everywhere, but, nevertheless, there was in many countries, a lack of the necessities of life.

This was especially the case in mighty England, notwithstanding the wealth, the resources and the enterprising spirit of the inhabitants. Restlessly seeking new channels for their trade, in their efforts to do so, they sometimes came in conflict with foreign nations. The English government by force of circumstances was then compelled to assist and protect its subjects by force.

In this way quarrels occurred between the English merchants and the Chinese officials at Canton. From that quarrel war arose. That war was fatal to China, for many thousand Chinese were killed, many cities were taken and devastated, many millions in treasure were yielded as indemnity to the conquerors.

Such disasters now threaten the Japanese Empire. A mere mischance might precipitate a conflict. The number of all sorts of vessels sailing the Japanese seas will be greater than ever before, and how easily might a quarrel occur between the crews of those vessels and the inhabitants of Your Majesty's dominion!

The thought that such quarrels may end in war fills us with solicitude. The wisdom that characterizes Your Majesty's government will, we hope, know how to avert these dangers.

This wisdom was already evident in the mandate, which was read by the government of Nagasaki to the Netherlands Supreme Official on the thirteenth of the eighth month of the year 1842, ordering the kindly treatment of all foreign vessels. But is that mandate sufficient?

Only such vessels are mentioned, as are driven on to the Japanese coast by hurricane or lack of provisions. What will be done with vessels that come for other and friendly reasons to visit the Japanese coast?

Are these to be repulsed by force or unfriendly treatment? Will quarrels arise? Quarrels lead to war, and war leads to destruction. Those are the disasters which we wish to avert from Japan. It is our desire as a token of gratefulness for the hospitality enjoyed by our subjects for more than two hundred years. The philosopher says: "In security, we must guard against danger; in peace, against confusion."

We have watched the course of events with serious attention. The intercourse between the different nations of the earth is increasing with great rapidity. An irresistible power is drawing them together. Through the invention of steamships distances have become shorter. A nation preferring to remain in isolation at this time of increasing relationships could not avoid hostility with many others.

We know that the laws of Your Majesty's serene ancestors were issued with a view rigorously to restrict intercourse with foreign nations. But (says Lao Tseu) "when wisdom is seated on the throne, she will excel in maintaining peace." When in the strict observance of old laws, peace might be disturbed, wisdom will succeed in smoothing difficulties.

This, Allpowerful Emperor, is our friendly advice, ameliorate the laws against the foreigners, lest happy Japan be destroyed by war. We give Your Majesty this advice with honest intentions, free from political self-interest.

We hope that wisdom will make the Japanese government realize that peace can only be maintained through friendly relations, and that these are only created by commercial relations. . . .

Given at our royal palace at The Hague the 15th day of February 1844, in the fourth year of our reign.

REPLY OF THE *SHOGUN'S* GOVERNMENT (BAKUFU) TO THE GOVERNMENT OF HOLLAND, JULY 5, 1845

In the seventh month of the last year a letter from Your Excellencies' Sovereign despatched by a Dutch vessel arrived at the port of Nagasaki in our province of Hizen. The chief magistrate of that port, Izawa Mimasaka-no-kami, on receipt thereof forwarded it to Edo and it has been attentively read by our Lord.

That Your Excellencies' Sovereign in view of the trade relations which have subsisted for the past two hundred years should from so great a distance take into consideration the interests of our country and offer suggestions was most certainly evidence of hearty good will. Moreover, our Lord gratefully appreciates and returns thanks for the various precious gifts which have been presented.

Although the suggestions offered are worthy of adoption, there are reasons why this cannot be. When the founder of our dynasty entered upon his career, intercourse and trade with countries beyond the sea were in an unsettled condition. Later when the time came for determining with what countries intercourse should be permitted, intercourse was limited to Korea and Loo Choo, and trade to Your Excellencies' country and China. Aside from these countries all intercourse was entirely disallowed.

If now it were desired to extend these limits, it would be in contravention of the ancestral law.

Hence we communicate this decision to Your Excellencies and thus inform Your Excellencies' Sovereign. Although this may appear discourteous, such is the strictness of the ancestral law, that no other course is open to us. . . .

Now since the ancestral law has been once fixed, posterity must obey. Henceforth, pray cease correspondence. If not, although it should be attempted a second or a third time, communications cannot be received. Pray do not be surprised at this. Letters from Your Excellencies also will have the same treatment and will receive no response.

Nevertheless, the trade of Your Excellencies' country will remain unchanged. In this also the ancestral law will be carefully observed. Pray communicate this to Your Excellencies' Sovereign.

Notwithstanding what we have stated, our Lord in no wise fails in respect towards Your Excellencies' Sovereign, but on the contrary deeply appreciates, his sincere loyalty. Hence we his officials make this announcement. We may have inadequately expressed our Lord's real purpose, but we trust Your Excellencies will understand it.

2nd year of Koka, the year of Wood-Serpent, 6th month, 1st day.

QUESTIONS

1. Why does King William think Japan should open its ports to Westerners?

2. How does the Japanese government respond to the Dutch letter?

3. These letters illustrate the impending collision of two profoundly different cultures. Judging from the letters themselves, how would you say the two sides are different?

4. Westerners firmly believed that opening Japan to the world would be beneficial for both Japan and the West. Why? Why would the Shogun resist the supposed benefits of contact with European culture?

5. These letters are part of a diplomatic exchange—what might they tell us about the conduct of international relations in the nineteenth century?

112. KARL MARX AND FRIEDRICH ENGELS

THE COMMUNIST MANIFESTO

(1848)

Karl Marx (1818–83) was born in Prussia, the son of a lawyer and public official. He was trained as a philosopher and received a doctorate in 1841. It was his interest in history and public law, however, that led him to become a social reformer. Marx worked as a journalist, writing for liberal and radical papers in Germany, France, and Belgium. He became a supporter of the French socialist movement and began a lifelong collaboration with Friedrich Engels. By the 1850s Marx was working on his sustained analysis of the capitalist system, which resulted in the publication of his three-volume work, *Capital* (1867–94). He died in London in 1883.

The Communist Manifesto is one of the definitive documents of modern political organization. With it, the communist movement, which would ultimately result in the Russian Revolution, was generated. Marx and Engels wrote the *Manifesto* as a platform for the Communist League, an international workers' organization that they had joined the previous year. The *Manifesto* was both a statement of belief and a resounding call to action.

Bourgeois and Proletarians

The history of all hitherto existing society is the history of class struggles.

Freeman and slave, patrician and plebeian, lord and serf, guildmaster and journeyman, in a word, oppressor and oppressed, stood in constant opposition to one another, carried on an uninterrupted, now hidden, now open fight, a fight that each time ended, either in a revolutionary reconstitution of society at large, or in the common ruin of the contending classes.

In the earlier epochs of history, we find almost everywhere a complicated arrangement of society into various orders, a manifold gradation of social rank. In ancient Rome we have patricians, knights, plebeians, slaves; in the Middle Ages, feudal lords, vassals, guildmasters, journeyman, apprentices, serfs; in almost all of these classes, again, subordinate gradations.

The modern bourgeois society that has sprouted from the ruins of feudal society, has not done away with class antagonisms. It has but established new classes, new conditions of oppression, new forms of struggle in place of the old ones.

Our epoch, the epoch of the bourgeoisie, possesses, however, this distinctive feature: It has simplified the class antagonisms. Society as a whole is more and more splitting up into two great hostile camps, into two great classes directly facing each other—bourgeoisie and proletariat.

Proletarians and Communists

The immediate aim of the Communists is the same as that of all the other proletarian parties; Formation of the proletariat into a class, overthrow of bourgeois supremacy, conquest of political power by the proletariat.

The distinguishing feature of Communism is not the abolition of property generally, but the abolition of bourgeois property. But modern bourgeois private property is the final and most complete expression of the system of producing and appropriating products that is based on class antagonisms, on the exploitation of the many by the few.

In this sense, the theory of the Communists may be summed up in the single sentence: abolition of private property.

We Communists have been reproached with the desire of abolishing the right of personally acquiring property as the fruit of man's own labour, which property is alleged to be the groundwork of all personal freedom, activity and independence.

Hard-won, self-acquired, self-earned property! Do you mean the property of the petty artisan and of the small peasant, a form of property that preceded the bourgeois form? There is no need to abolish that; the development of industry has to a great extent already destroyed it, and is still destroying it daily.

Or do you mean modern bourgeois private property?

But does wage-labour create any property for the labourer? Not a bit. It creates capital, *i.e.,* that kind of property which exploits wage-labour, and which cannot increase except upon condition of begetting a new supply of wage-labour for fresh exploitation. Property, in its present form, is based on the antagonism of capital and wage-labour. Let us examine both sides of this antagonism.

To be a capitalist, is to have not only a purely personal, but a social *status* in production. Capital is a collective product, and only by the united action of many members, nay, in the last resort, only by the united action of all members of society, can it be set in motion.

Capital is therefore not a personal, it is a social, power.

When, therefore, capital is converted into common property, into the property of all members of society, personal property is not thereby transformed into social property. It is only the social character of the property that is changed. It loses its class character.

Let us now take wage-labour.

The average price of wage-labour is the minimum wage, *i.e.,* that quantum of the means of subsistence which is absolutely requisite to keep the labourer in bare existence as a labourer. What, therefore, the wage-labourer appropriates by means of his labour, merely suffices to prolong and reproduce a bare existence. We by no means intend to abolish this personal appropriation of the products of labour, an appropriation that is made for the maintenance and reproduction of human life, and that leaves no surplus wherewith to command the labour of others. All that we want to do away with is the miserable character of this appropriation, under which the labourer lives merely to increase capital, and is allowed to live only insofar as the interest of the ruling class requires it.

In bourgeois society, living labour is but a means to increase accumulated labour. In Communist society, accumulated labour is but a means to widen, to enrich, to promote the existence of the labourer.

In bourgeois society, therefore, the past dominates the present; in Communist society, the present dominates the past. In bourgeois society capital is independent and has individuality, while the living person is dependent and has no individuality.

And the abolition of this state of things is called by the bourgeois, abolition of individuality and freedom! And rightly so. The abolition of bourgeois individuality, bourgeois independence, and bourgeois freedom is undoubtedly aimed at.

By freedom is meant, under the present bourgeois conditions of production, free trade, free selling and buying.

But if selling and buying disappears, free selling and buying disappears also. This talk about free selling and buying, and all the other "brave words" of our bourgeois about freedom in general, have a meaning, if any, only in contrast with restricted selling and buying, with the fettered traders of the Middle Ages, but have no meaning when opposed to the Communist abolition of buying and selling, of the bourgeois conditions of production, and of the bourgeoisie itself.

You are horrified at our intending to do away with private property. But in your existing society, private property is already done away with for nine-tenths of the population; its existence for the few is solely due to its non-existence in the hands of those nine-tenths. You reproach us, therefore, with intending to do away with a form of property, the necessary condition for whose existence is the non-existence of any property for the immense majority of society.

In a word, you reproach us with intending to do away with your property. Precisely so; that is just what we intend.

From the moment when labour can no longer be converted into capital, money, or rent, into a social power capable of being monopolised, *i.e.,* from the moment when individual property can no longer be transformed into bourgeois property, into capital, from that moment, you say, individuality vanishes.

You must, therefore, confess that by "individual" you mean no other person than the bourgeois, than the middle class owner of property. This person must, indeed, be swept out of the way, and made impossible.

But you Communists would introduce community of women, screams the whole bourgeoisie in chorus.

The bourgeois sees his wife as a mere instrument of production. He hears that the instruments of production are to be exploited in common, and, naturally, can come to no other conclusion that the lot of being common to all will likewise fall to the woman.

He has not even a suspicion that the real point aimed at is to do away with the status of women as mere instruments of production.

For the rest, nothing is more ridiculous than the virtuous indignation of our bourgeois at the community of women which, they pretend, is to be openly and officially established by the Communists. The Communists have no need to introduce community of women; it has existed almost from time immemorial.

Our bourgeois, not content with having the wives and daughters of their proletarians at their disposal, not to speak of common prostitutes, take the greatest pleasure in seducing each other's wives.

Bourgeois marriage is in reality a system of wives in common and thus, at the most, what the

Communists might possibly be reproached with is that they desire to introduce, in substitution for a hypocritically concealed, an openly legalised community of women. For the rest, it is self-evident, that the abolition of the present system of production must bring with it the abolition of the community of women springing from that system, *i.e.,* of prostitution both public and private.

The Communists are further reproached with desiring to abolish countries and nationality.

The workingmen have no country. We cannot take from them what they have not got. Since the proletariat must first of all acquire political supremacy, must rise to be the leading class of the nation, must constitute itself *the* nation, it is, so far, itself national, though not in the bourgeois sense of the word.

National differences and antagonisms between peoples are vanishing gradually from day to day, owing to the development of the bourgeoisie, to freedom of commerce, to the world market, to uniformity in the mode of production and in the conditions of life corresponding thereto.

The supremacy of the proletariat will cause them to vanish still faster. United action, of the leading civilised countries at least, is one of the first conditions for the emancipation of the proletariat.

In proportion as the exploitation of one individual by another is put an end to, the exploitation of one nation by another will also be put an end to. In proportion as the antagonism between classes within the nation vanishes, the hostility of one nation to another will come to an end.

"Undoubtedly," it will be said, "religion, moral, philosophical and juridical ideas have been modified in the course of historical development. But religion, morality, philosophy, political science, and law, constantly survived this change."

"There are, besides, eternal truths, such as Freedom, Justice, etc., that are common to all states of society. But Communism abolishes eternal truths, it abolishes all religion, and all morality, instead of constituting them on a new basis; it therefore acts in contradiction to all past historical experience."

What does this accusation reduce itself to? The history of all past society has consisted in the development of class antagonisms, antagonisms that assumed different forms at different epochs.

But whatever form they may have taken, one fact is common to all past ages, *viz.,* the exploitation of one part of society by the other. No wonder, then, that the social consciousness of past ages, despite all the multiplicity and variety it displays, moves within certain common forms, or general ideas, which cannot completely vanish except with the total disappearance of class antagonisms.

The Communist revolution is the most radical rupture with traditional property relations; no wonder that its development involves the most radical rupture with traditional ideas.

The Communists disdain to conceal their views and aims. They openly declare that their ends can be attained only by the forcible overthrow of all existing social conditions. Let the ruling classes tremble at a Communist revolution. The proletarians have nothing to lose but their chains. They have a world to win.

Workingmen of all countries, unite!

QUESTIONS

1. In the Marxist view, what has been the course of history? What was the state of politics when the *Manifesto* was composed?

2.   What is the Communist party's relation to the working class?

3.   What is the Party's goal? How will this end be achieved?

4.   Marx and Engels scoffed at those who denounced communism as inimical to freedom. Why? What is freedom, according to the *Manifesto*?

5.   Why would the nation-state disappear under communism?

113.   ALEXANDER II AND PRINCE KROPOTKIN

THE EMANCIPATION OF THE SERFS
(1861)

Alexander II (1818–81) became emperor of Russia upon the death of his father, Nicholas I. Unlike his rigidly conservative father, Alexander was determined to use his autocratic power to reform Russia. He instituted a series of educational and administrative reforms and worked to simplify the legal system. Convinced of the importance of economic modernization, Alexander encouraged the building of railroads. He also did much to improve Russia's inadequate banking system. He was most famous, however, for his decision to free the serfs. Bound to their land and masters, Russian serfs were little better than slaves. Convinced that serfdom stood in the way of economic advance and relying upon his God-given authority as emperor, Alexander abolished the institution. In a speech before the State Council in 1861, Alexander confronted reluctant aristocrats with the inevitability of his decision to abolish serfdom. Hailed as the "Tsar Liberator" and beloved by his people, Alexander, ironically, was assassinated by terrorists demanding even greater social reforms.

Prince Peter Kropotkin (1842–1921) was one of the young nobles who had a firsthand view of the impact of the emancipation. In his later years, Kropotkin was a famous revolutionary and anarchist, but in 1861 when Alexander abolished serfdom he was a student in the exclusive Corps of Pages, a school for the sons of the aristocracy. In his memoirs he gave an eyewitness account of the events following the tsar's proclamation.

Alexander's Address in the State Council, January 28, 1861

The matter of the liberation of the serfs, which has been submitted for the consideration of the State Council, I consider to be a vital question for Russia, upon which will depend the development of her strength and power. I am sure that all of you, gentlemen, are just as convinced as I am of the benefits and necessity of this measure. I have another conviction, which is that this matter cannot be postponed; therefore I demand that the State Council finish with it in the first half of February so that it can be announced before the start of work in the fields; . . . I repeat—and this is my absolute will—that this matter should be finished right away.

For four years now it has dragged on and has been arousing various fears and anticipations among both the estate owners and the peasants. Any further delay could be disastrous to the state. I cannot help being surprised and happy, and I am sure all of you are happy, at the trust and calm shown by our good people in this matter. Although the apprehensions of the nobility are to a certain extent understandable, for the closest and material interests of each are involved, not withstanding all this, I have not forgotten and shall never forget that the approach to the matter was made on the initiative of the nobility itself, and I am happy to be able to be a witness to this before posterity. In my private conversations with the *guberniia* marshals of the nobility, and during my travels about Russia, when receiving the nobility, I did not conceal the trend of my thoughts and opinions on the question that occupies us all and said everywhere that this transformation cannot take place without certain sacrifices on their part and that all my efforts consist in making these sacrifices as little weighty and burdensome as possible for the nobility. I hope, gentlemen, that on inspection of the drafts presented to the State Council, you will assure yourselves that all that can be done for the protection of the interests of the nobility has been done; if on the other hand you find it necessary in any way to alter or to add to the present work, then I am ready to receive your comments; but I ask you only not to forget that the basis of the whole work must be the improvement of the life of the peasants—an improvement not in words alone or on paper but in actual fact.

Before proceeding to a detailed examination of this draft itself, I would like to trace briefly the historical background of this affair. You are acquainted with the origin of serfdom. Formerly it did not exist among us; this law was established by autocratic power and only autocratic power can abolish it, and that is my sincere will.

My predecessors felt all the evils of serfdom and continually endeavored, if not to destroy it completely, to work toward the gradual limitation of the arbitrary power of the estate owners.

. . . My late father [Nicholas I] was continuously occupied with the thought of freeing the serfs. Sympathizing completely with this thought, already in 1856, before the coronation, while in Moscow I called the attention of the leaders of the nobility of the Moscow *guberniia* to the necessity for them to occupy themselves with improving the life of the serfs, adding that serfdom could not continue forever and that it would therefore be better if the transformation took place from above rather than from below. . . .

The Editorial Commissions worked for a year and seven months and, notwithstanding all the reproaches, perhaps partly just, to which the commissions were exposed, they finished their work conscientiously and presented it to the Main Committee. The Main Committee, under the chairmanship of my brother [Grand Duke Konstantin Nikolaevich], toiled with indefatigable energy and zeal. I consider it my duty to thank all the members of the committee, especially my brother, for their conscientious labors in this matter.

There may be various views on the draft presented, and I am willing to listen to all the different opinions. But I have the right to demand one thing from you: that you, putting aside all personal interests, act not like estate owners but like imperial statesmen invested with my trust. Approaching this important matter I have not concealed from myself all those difficulties that awaited us and I do not conceal then now; but, firmly believing in the grace of God and being convinced to the sacredness of this matter, I trust that God will not abandon us but will bless us to finish it for the future prosperity of our beloved fatherland. . . .

Kropotkin's Memoir

We went to the parade; and when all the military performances were over, Alexander II, remaining on horseback, loudly called out, "The officers to me!" They gathered round him, and he began, in a loud voice, a speech about the great event of the day.

"The officers . . . the representatives of the nobility in the army"—these scraps of sentences reached our ears—"an end has been put to centuries of injustice . . . I expect sacrifices from the nobility . . . the loyal nobility will gather round the throne" . . . and so on. Enthusiastic hurrahs resounded amongst the officers as he ended.

We ran rather than marched back on our way to the corps, hurrying to be in time for the Italian opera, of which the last performance in the season was to be given that afternoon; some manifestation was sure to take place then. Our military attire was flung off with great haste, and several of us dashed, lightfooted, to the sixth-story gallery. The house was crowded.

During the first entr'acte the smoking-room of the opera filled with excited young men, who all talked to one another, whether acquainted or not. We planned at once to return to the hall, and to sing, with the whole public in a mass choir, the hymn "God Save the Tsar."

However, sounds of music reached our ears, and we all hurried back to the hall. The band of the opera was already playing the hymn, which was drowned immediately in enthusiastic hurrahs coming from all parts of the hall. I saw Bavéri, the conductor of the band, waving his stick, but not a sound could be heard from the powerful band. Then Bavéri stopped, but the hurrahs continued. I saw the stick waved again in the air; I saw the fiddle-bows moving, and musicians blowing the brass instruments, but again the sound of voices overwhelmed the band. Bavéri began conducting the hymn once more, and it was only by the end of that third repetition that isolated sounds of brass instruments pierced through the clamor of human voices.

The same enthusiasm was in the streets. Crowds of peasants and educated men stood in front of the palace, shouting hurrahs, and the Tsar could not appear without being followed by demonstrative crowds running after his carriage. Herzen was right when, two years later, as Alexander was drowning the Polish insurrection in blood, and "Muravioff the Hanger" was strangling it on the scaffold, he wrote, "Alexander Nikolaevich, why did you not die on that day? Your name would have been transmitted in history as that of a hero."

Where were the uprisings which had been predicted by the champions of slavery? Conditions more indefinite that those which had been created by the Polozhenie (the emancipation law) could not have been invented. If anything could have provoked revolts, it was precisely the perplexing vagueness of the conditions created by the new law. And yet, except in two places where there were insurrections, and a very few other spots where small disturbances entirely due to misunderstandings and immediately appeased took place, Russia remained quiet—more quiet than ever. With their usual good sense, the peasants had understood that serfdom was done away with, that "freedom had come," and they accepted the conditions imposed upon them, although these conditions were very heavy.

I was in Nikolskoye [a Kropotkin estate in the Kaluga *guberniia*] in August 1861, and again in the summer of 1862, and I was struck with the quiet, intelligent way in which the peasants had accepted the new conditions.

They knew perfectly well how difficult it would be to pay the redemption tax for the land, which was in reality an indemnity to the nobles in lieu of the obligations of serfdom. But they so much valued the abolition of their personal enslavement that they accepted the ruinous charges—not without murmuring, but as a hard necessity—the moment that personal freedom was obtained.

When I saw our Nikolskoye peasants, fifteen months after the liberation, I could not but admire them. Their inborn good nature and softness remained with them, but all traces of servility had disappeared. They talked to their masters as equals talk to equals, as if they never had stood in different relations. Besides, such men came out from among them as could make a stand for their rights.

QUESTIONS

1. Judging from the tsar's speech to his council, what sort of generalizations might you make about the monarch's power in the Russian state?

2. What appears to be the chief obstacle in the way of liberating the serfs? How does Alexander handle this problem?

3. How was the tsar's act received in Saint Petersburg?

4. What was the reaction of the peasants to their liberation?

114.   OTTO VON BISMARCK

REFLECTIONS AND REMINISCENCES
(1898)

SPEECH TO THE REICHSTAG
(1879)

Otto von Bismarck (1815–98) was one of the most successful statesmen of the nineteenth century. His political and diplomatic talents made possible the unification of Germany under the leadership of Prussia. Born into a minor aristocratic family, Bismarck was prepared for a legal career and began his work as an officer of the courts. During the upheavals of 1848 Bismarck emerged as an inflexible champion of conservatism. When revolutionaries met in Frankfurt in an abortive attempt to create a unified Germany, along liberal lines, the king dispatched Bismarck as one of Prussia's delegates. He ultimately rose to become prime minister, a post he held for thirty years. Unlike the liberals of 1848, Bismarck's goal was the unification of the diverse German states under conservative Prussian leadership, and he accomplished this through diplomacy and war. In 1871 he became the first chancellor of Germany.

Bismark's political career was a very long one, but his principles and policies were quite consistent. His early life, a portion of which is recounted here from his memoirs, was passed amid the political turmoil of mid-nineteenth-century Prussia, when Liberals and Conservatives struggled to control the destiny of the state. The second selection comes from a speech made after German unification. At that time, as chancellor, Bismarck was the most powerful figure in the German state. Delivered before the Reichstag, this speech reveals the heart of his political philosophy: German unity over all.

REFLECTIONS AND REMINISCENCES

I left school at Easter 1832, a normal product of our state system of education; a Pantheist, and, if not a Republican, at least with the persuasion that the Republic was the most rational form of government; reflecting too upon the causes which could decide millions of men permanently to obey *one man,* when all the while I was hearing from grown up people much bitter or contemptuous criticism of their rulers. Moreover, I had brought away with me 'German-National' impressions from Plamann's preparatory school, conducted on Jahn's drill-system, in which I lived from my sixth to my twelfth year. These impressions remained in the stage of theoretical reflections, and were not strong enough to extirpate my innate Prussian monarchical sentiments. My historical sympathies remained on the side of authority. . . . Every German prince who resisted the Emperor before the Thirty Years' war roused my ire; but from the Great Elector onwards I was partisan enough to take an anti-imperial view, and to find it natural that things should have been in readiness for the Seven Years' war. Yet the German-National feeling remained so strong in me that, at the beginning of my University life, I at once entered into relations with the *Burschenschaft,* or group of students which made the promotion of a national sentiment its aim. But after personal intimacy with its members, I disliked their refusal to 'give satisfaction,' as well as their want of breeding in externals and of acquaintance with the forms and manners of good society; and a still closer acquaintance bred an aversion to the extravagance of their political views, based upon a lack of either culture or knowledge of the conditions of life which historical causes had brought into existence, and which I, with my seventeen years, had had more opportunities of observing than most of these students, for the most part older than myself. Their ideas gave me the impression of an association between Utopian theories and defective breeding. Nevertheless, I retained my own private National sentiments, and my belief that in the near future events would lead to German unity; in fact, I made a bet with my American friend Coffin that this aim would be attained in twenty years.

In my first half-year at Göttingen occurred the Hambach festival (May 27, 1832), the 'festal ode' of which still remains in my memory; in my third the Frankfort outbreak (April 3, 1833). These manifestations revolted me. Mob interference with political authority conflicted with my Prussian schooling, and I returned to Berlin with less Liberal opinions than when I quitted it. . . .

The impressions that I had received in my childhood were little adapted to make a squire of me. In Plamann's educational establishment, conducted on the systems of Pestalozzi and Jahn, the 'von' before my name was a disadvantage, so far as my childish comfort was concerned, in my intercourse with my fellow-pupils and my teachers. Even at the high school at the Grey Friars I had to suffer, as regards individual teachers, from that hatred of nobility which had clung to the greater part of the educated *bourgeoisie* as a reminiscence of the days before 1806. But even the aggressive tendency which occasionally appeared in *bourgeois* circles never gave me any inducement to advance in the opposite direction. My father was free from aristocratic prejudices, and his inward sense of equality had been modified, if at all, by his youthful impressions as an officer, but in no way by any over-estimate of inherited rank. My mother was the daughter of Mencken, Privy Councillor to Frederick the Great, Frederick William II, and Frederick William III, who sprang from a family of Leipzig professors, and was accounted in those days a Liberal. The later generations of the Menckens—those immediately preceding me—had found their way to Prussia in the Foreign Office and about the Court. Baron von Stein has quoted my grandfather Mencken as an honest, strongly Liberal official. Under these circumstances, the views which I imbibed with my mother's milk were Liberal rather than reactionary; and if my mother had lived to see my ministerial activity, she would scarcely have been in accord with its direction, even though she

would have experienced great joy in the external results of my official career. She had grown up in bureaucratic and court circles; Frederick William IV spoke of her as 'Mienchen,' in memory of childish games. I can therefore declare it an unjust estimate of my views in my younger years, when 'the prejudices of my rank' are thrown in my teeth and it is maintained that a recollection of the privileges of the nobility has been the startingpoint of my domestic policy.

Moreover, the unlimited authority of the old Prussian monarchy was not, and is not, the final word of my convictions. As to that, to be sure, this authority of the monarch constitutionally existed in the first United Diet, but accompanied by the wish and anticipation that the unlimited power of the King, without being overturned, might fix the measure of its own limitation. Absolutism primarily demands impartiality, honesty, devotion to duty, energy, and inward humility in the ruler. These may be present, and yet male and female favourites (in the best case the lawful wife), the monarch's own vanity and susceptibility to flattery, will nevertheless diminish the fruits of his good intentions, inasmuch as the monarch is not omniscient and cannot have an equal understanding of all branches of his office. As early as 1847 I was in favour of an effort to secure the possibility of public criticism of the government in parliament and in the press, in order to shelter the monarch from the danger of having blinkers put on him by women, courtiers, sycophants, and visionaries, hindering him from taking a broad view of his duties as monarch, or from avoiding and correcting his mistakes. This conviction of mine became all the more deeply impressed upon me in proportion as I became better acquainted with Court circles, and had to defend the interest of the state from their influences and also from the opposition of a [provincial] patriotism. The interests of the state alone have guided me, and it has been a calumny when publicists, even well-meaning, have accused me of having ever advocated an aristocratic system. I have never regarded birth as a substitute for want of ability; whenever I have come forward on behalf of landed property, it has not been in the interests of proprietors of my own class, but because I see in the decline of agriculture one of the greatest dangers to our permanence as a state. . . .

. . . I had a critical disposition, and was consequently Liberal, in the sense in which the word was then used among landed proprietors to imply discontent with the bureaucracy, the majority of whom on their side were men more liberal than myself, though in another sense.

I again slipped off the rails of my parliamentary Liberal tendencies, with regard to which I found little understanding or sympathy in Pomerania, but which in Schönhausen met with the acquiescence of men in my own district, like Count Wartensleben of Karow, Schierstädt-Dahlen, and others (the same men of whom some were among the party of Church patrons in the New Era subsequently condemned). This was the result of the style, to me unsympathetic, in which the opposition was conducted in the first United Diet, to which I was summoned, only for the last six weeks of the session, as substitute for Deputy von Brauchitsch, who was laid up with illness. The speeches of the East Prussians, Saucken-Tarputschen and Alfred Auerswald, the sentimentality of Beckerath, the Gallo-Rhenish Liberalism of Heydt and Mevissen, and the boisterous violence of Vincke's speeches, disgusted me; and even at this date when I read the proceedings they give me the impression of imported phrases made to pattern. I felt that the King was on the right track, and could claim to be allowed time, and not be hurried in his development.

I came into conflict with the Opposition the first time I made a longer speech than usual, on May 17, 1847, when I combated the legend that the Prussians had gone to war in 1813 to get a constitution, and gave free expression to my natural indignation at the idea that foreign domination was in itself no adequate reason for fighting. It appeared to me undignified that the nation, as a set-off to its having freed itself, should hand in to the King an account payable in the paragraphs of a constitution. My performance produced a storm. I remained in the tribune turning over the leaves of a newspaper which lay there, and then, when the commotion had subsided, I finished my speech.

SPEECH TO THE GERMAN REICHSTAG, 9 JULY 1879

Since I have been a Minister, I have never belonged to a faction, nor could I have belonged to one, as I have successively been loved by only a few and hated by all. Each has had its turn. When I first took over the post of Prussian Minister President in 1862, all had remembrances which—I can well attest—raised hatred toward me to anti-patriotic heights. . . . I have not allowed myself to be misled by this and have also never attempted to avenge myself for it; from the beginning of my career I have had only one lodestar: to unify Germany, taking any path, and employing any means, and so far as this has been achieved, to strengthen this unity, further it and shape it, so that through the free will of all participants it will endure. I consider the government one of these participants, and regard it as an extraordinarily great advantage in comparison with other countries which have a national constitution that the [Prussian] monarchy also has power beyond Prussia . . . and that if we wanted to unilaterally destroy it, we could not replace it with another equally strong binding force. I do not want everyone to share the same conviction, I do not want to persuade anyone, I only want to explain how I came to my position against factions. When we returned from the war in 1866, it would have been very easy for me . . . to say: Now that Prussia has become bigger, the [old] constitution is no longer appropriate, and we must negotiate it anew; in short, propelled by the aura of success that still clung to everything after [the victory at] Königgrätz, [it would have been easy for me] to pursue with full sail the cleverest and most trenchant reactionary policies. You know that I did the opposite, and that thereby I at first incurred the disapprobation of a great part of my old political friends, and that securing . . . the continuance of the constitutional system cost me many arduous battles. Did I do this for love of the constitutional system? Gentlemen, I will not portray myself better that I am; I must certainly completely deny that. I am no opponent of the constitutional system, on the contrary, I consider it the only feasible form of government—but if I had believed that a dictatorship, that absolutism in Prussia, would have been more useful in furthering the process of German unification, I would have unquestioningly and unscrupulously defended absolutism. But I have decided after careful reflection—and I had to struggle against inclinations close to my heart and influences difficult to combat—that no, we must keep to the path of constitutionality, which incidentally corresponds to my inner feelings and my belief in the overall practicability of our policies. The solicitousness, then, which I showed to opponents who reconciled themselves with me . . . thus prepared the ground for my later break with the conservative party. Then, actually as a result of the relationship of the question of the [Catholic] Church to the Polish [question], the conflict over church matters arose. This battle robbed me of the natural support of the conservative party, which I had been able to count on, and had the conservative party not left me in the lurch then, I would probably have had to take a different path to consolidate the constitution of the German Empire. . . . It came to a hard fight, which caused a momentary flaring up of the thousand-year-old controversy between church and state. . . . I fought this battle with the same passion that I hope will remain characteristic of me in all my dealings with subjects that involve my convictions and the well-being of my fatherland and the rights

of my king, so long as I live. But I must also say here: I consider it well, under [certain] conditions, to fight conflicts courageously to their end, but I have never [considered conflicts] desirable as lasting institutions, and if ways and means are offered, to moderate the sharpness of the opposition, without affecting the principles involved in the actual controversy, if opposing sides get to know one another and through common work toward common and higher goals learn to respect one another, yes, then it probably does not lie within my rights as Minister [President] to stand in the way of or reject such a course.

If after 1871 I was, for a time, drawn closer to the liberal faction through these events and conflicts beyond my control, it is perhaps excusable for the Minister [President] and for the Reichschancellor. In so far as it was possible, I have made it impossible for this situation to last forever by means of cultivating my relationships to other circles within the Empire and amongst the population. I believed . . . that we—from right to left—would make up three batallions, and perhaps could march separately but fight together. This early prognostication of mine has regrettably not been born out, and conditions, not my will, have so contorted things, that the gentlemen who previously often and in their own way supported me, join in the battles and fall on me in their journals, their most prestigious and highly accredited journals with such rage and in such language as to completely disgust and mislead me. Similar proceedings have taken place before the assembled Reichstag, in which the Reichschancellor was scolded by a single excellent deputy in a way that, I must say, a member of a friendly faction would never have done without the disapproval of the faction. (Laughter)

All of the foregoing are the reasons that I have in opposition to my earlier, and I hope someday also future, allies adopted the disposition that they denounce me for and publically proclaim me 'cold to the very heart.' I cannot—the government cannot—run after any single faction, but it must go its own way, the way it thinks right; in this fashion it will be subject to decisions made by the Reichstag, it will need the support of factions, but it can never be subjected to the domination of a single faction! . . .

I would like also to add, here, an admonition to these gentlemen, not to resurrect old quarrels between the clans over such simple and uncontentious issues as tariffs, economic matters, and financial and budgetary concerns. That is not now in the offing, but in the strict segregation that takes place in the forming of factions, we risk putting the factions in the place of the clans. Perhaps later on all the bonds, even all the family ties between the different factions will actually fall away, and every individual faction will reconstitute itself as a separate clan—hopefully this day will never come. But I would like to request that high politics and the fear that any sort of political machinations lie behind these simple measures not be brought to bear on these matters and that the furious battle of the factions not be pursued so far that the interests of the Reich suffer. . . . From the side of the government, I can definitely assure you, that it will not stray from the path it has chosen because of attacks which are, in my opinion, irrelevant, and I will for my part, follow to the end the path that in the interests of the fatherland I believe to be the right one, undeterred—for whether I reap hatred or love, that is, to me, a matter of indifference! (Right: Bravo!)

QUESTIONS

1. What is Bismarck's view of politics? Who is suited for making political decisions?

2. What appear to be Bismarck's main political principles? What does he believe in?

3. Bismarck has been described as the Iron Chancellor. Does his speech lend credence to that view?

4. What occupies a higher place in Bismarck's thought: the German nation or the German people? Is there a difference between the two?

5. What is Bismarck's view of political parties (or "factions," as he calls them) and constitutions?

115.

115.   **POPE LEO XIII**

RERUM NOVARUM
(THE CONDITION OF LABOR)
(1891)

Gioaccino Pecci (1810–1903), Pope Leo XIII from 1878–1903, was born in Carpineto, Italy. His parents were of the lower nobility, and he received a Jesuit education and a doctorate in theology in 1832. He was trained as a diplomat at the church-run Academy of Noble Ecclesiastics, and also studied canon and civil law. At the age of 27 he was appointed governor of a papal town in Sicily, Benevento. He succeeded in suppressing a long-standing problem with bandits, and was rewarded with a promotion in 1841. In 1843 he was appointed Papal nuncio (ambassador) to Belgium, where he served for three years. He was eventually recalled, after making himself unwelcome by his strong stand against Belgian liberals. After his return to Italy, he served as Bishop of Perugia. In 1853 he became a cardinal, and in 1878 was elected to the papacy as Leo XIII. Leo was an active pope, issuing eighty-five encyclicals dealing with a wide range of issues. He supported the creation of many new Catholic universities, particularly in the United States, and he was the first pope to open the Vatican archive to scholars.

Leo's pontificate was a difficult one; the unification of Italy had deprived the papacy of temporal power, and it was challenged by the spread of secularism throughout the world. Class conflict and political assaults upon the Church threatened its mission, and *Rerum Novarum,* excerpted here, was Leo's attempt to address some of the most significant social problems of his day.

1. It is not surprising that the spirit of revolutionary change, which has long been predominant in the nations of the world, should have passed beyond politics and made its influence felt in the cognate field of practical economy. The elements of a conflict are unmistakable: the growth of industry, and the surprising discoveries of science; the changed relations of masters and workmen; the enormous fortunes of individuals and the poverty of the masses; the increased self-reliance and the closer mutual combination of the working population; and, finally, a general moral deterioration. The momentous seriousness of the present state of things just now fills every mind with painful apprehension; wise men discuss it; practical men propose schemes; popular meetings, legislatures, and sovereign princes, all are occupied with it—and there is nothing which has a deeper hold on public attention.

The Condition of Labor

It is a matter on which we have touched once or twice already. But in this Letter the responsibility of the Apostolic office urges Us to treat the question expressly and at length, in order that there may be no mistake as to the principles which truth and justice dictate from its settlement. The discussion is not easy, nor is it free from danger. It is not easy to define the relative rights and the mutual duties of the wealthy and of the poor, of capital and of labor. And the danger lies in this, that crafty agitators constantly make use of these disputes to pervert men's judgments and to stir up the people to sedition.

2. But all agree, and there can be no question whatever, that some remedy must be found, and quickly found, for the misery and wretchedness which press so heavily at this moment on the large majority of the very poor. The ancient workmen's Guilds were destroyed in the last century, and no other organization took their place. Public institutions and the laws have repudiated the ancient religion. Hence by degrees it has come to pass that Working Men have been given over, isolated and defenseless, to the callousness of employers and the greed of unrestrained competition. The evil has been increased by rapacious Usury, which, although more than once condemned by the Church, is nevertheless, under a different form but with the same guilt, still practiced by avaricious and grasping men. And to this must be added the custom of working by contract, and the concentration of so many branches of trade in the hands of a few individuals, so that a smaller number of very rich men have been able to lay upon the masses of the poor a yoke little better than slavery itself.

3. To remedy these evils the *Socialists,* working on the poor man's envy of the rich, endeavor to destroy private property, and maintain that individual possessions should become the common property of all, to be administered by the State or by municipal bodies. They hold that, by thus transferring property from private persons to the community, the present evil state of things will be set to rights, because each citizen will then have his equal share of whatever there is to enjoy. But their proposals are so clearly futile for

all practical purposes, that if they were carried out the working man himself would be among the first to suffer. Moreover they are emphatically unjust, because they would rob the lawful possessor, bring the State into a sphere that is not its own, and cause complete confusion in the community.

Private Ownership

4. It is surely undeniable that, when a man engages in remunerative labor, the very reason and motive of his work is to obtain property, and to hold it as his own private possession. If one man hires out to another his strength or his industry, he does this for the purpose of receiving in return what is necessary for food and living; he thereby expressly proposes to acquire a full and real right, not only to the remuneration, but also to the disposal of that remuneration as he pleases. Thus, if he lives sparingly, saves money, and invests his savings, for greater security, in land, the land in such a case is only his wages in another form; and, consequently, a working man's little estate thus purchased should be as completely at his own disposal as the wages he receives for his labor. But it is precisely in this power of disposal that ownership consists, whether the property be land or movable goods. The *Socialists,* therefore, in endeavoring to transfer the possessions of individuals to the community, strike at the interests of every wage earner, for they deprive him of the liberty of disposing of his wages, and thus of all hope and possibility of increasing his stock and of bettering his condition in life.

5. What is of still greater importance, however, it that the remedy they propose is manifestly against justice. For every man has by nature the right to possess property as his own. This is one of the *chief points of distinction* between man and the animal creation. For the brute has no power of self-direction, but is governed by two chief instincts, which keep his powers alert, move him to use his strength, and determine him to action

without the power of choice. These instincts are self-preservation and the propagation of the species. Both can attain their purpose by means of things which are close at hand; beyond their surrounding the brute creation cannot go, for they are moved to action by sensibility alone, and by the things which sense perceives. But with man it is different indeed. He possesses, on the one hand, the full perfection of animal nature, and therefore he enjoys, at least, as much as the rest of the animal race, the fruition of the things of the body. But animality, however perfect, is far from being the whole of humanity, and is indeed humanity's humble handmaid, made to serve and obey. It is the mind, or the reason, which is the chief thing in us who are human beings; it is this which makes a human being human, and distinguishes him essentially and completely from the brute. And on this account—*viz.*, that man alone among animals possesses reason—it must be within his right to have things not merely for temporary and momentary use, as other living beings have them, but in stable and permanent possession; he must have not only things which perish in the using, but also those which, though used, remain for use in the future.

Employer and Employee

15. The great mistake that is made in the matter now under consideration, is to possess oneself of the idea that class is naturally hostile to class; that rich and poor are intended by nature to live at war with one another. So irrational and so false is this view, that the exact contrary is the truth. Just as the symmetry of the human body is the result of the disposition of the members of the body, so in a State it is ordained by nature that these two classes should exist in harmony and agreement, and should, as it were, fit into one another, so as to maintain the equilibrium of the body politic. Each requires the other; capital cannot do without labor, nor labor without capital. Mutual agreement results

in pleasantness and good order; perpetual conflict necessarily produces confusion and outrage. Now, in preventing such strife as this, and in making it impossible, the efficacy of Christianity is marvelous and manifold.

16. First of all, there is nothing more powerful that Religion (of which the Church is the interpreter and guardian) in drawing rich and poor together, by reminding each class of its duties to the other, and especially of the duties of justice. Thus Religion teaches the laboring man and the workman to carry out honestly and well all equitable agreements freely made, never to injure capital, nor to outrage the person of an employer; never to employ violence in representing his own cause, nor to engage in riot and disorder; and to have nothing to do with men of evil principles, who work upon the people with artful promises, and raise foolish hopes which usually end in disaster and in repentance when too late. Religion teaches the rich man and the employer that their work people are not their slaves; that they must respect in every man his dignity as a man and as a Christian; that labor is nothing to be ashamed of, if we listen to right reason and to Christian philosophy, but is an honorable employment, enabling a man to sustain his life in an upright and creditable way; and that it is shameful and inhuman to treat men like chattels to make money by, or to look upon them merely as so much muscle or physical power. Thus, again Religion teaches that, as among the workmen's concerns are Religion herself, and things spiritual and mental, that employer is bound to see that he has time for the duties of piety; that he be not exposed to corrupting influences and dangerous occasions; and that he be not led away to neglect his home and family or to squander his wages. Then, again, the employer must never tax his workpeople beyond their strength, nor employ them in work unsuited to their sex or age.

17. His great and principal obligation is to give to every one that which is just. Doubtless before we can decide whether wages are adequate

many thing have to be considered; but rich men and masters should remember this—that to exercise pressure for the sake of gain, upon the indigent and destitute, and to make one's profit out of the need of another, is condemned by all laws, human and divine. To defraud any one of wages that are his due is a crime which cries to the avenging anger of Heaven. "Behold, the hire of the laborers. . . which by fraud has been kept back by you, crieth; and the cry of them hath entered the ears of the Lord of Sabaoth."[5] Finally, the rich must religiously refrain from cutting down the workman's earnings, either by force, fraud, or by usurious dealing; and with the more reason because the poor man is weak and unprotected, and because his slender means should be sacred in proportion to their scantiness.

Were these precepts carefully obeyed and followed would not strife die out and cease?

The Dignity of Labor

20. As for those who do not possess the gifts of fortune, they are taught by the Church that, in God's sight poverty is no disgrace, and that there is nothing to be ashamed of in seeking one's bread by labor. This is strengthened by what we see in Christ Himself, "Who whereas He was rich, for our sakes became poor";[17] and who, being the Son of God, and God Himself chose to seem and to be considered the son of a carpenter (nay, did not disdain to spend a great part of His life as a carpenter Himself. "Is not this the Carpenter the son of Mary?"[18] From the contemplation of this Divine example, it is easy to understand that the true dignity and excellence of man lies in his moral qualities, that is, in virtue; that virtue is the common inheritance of all, equally within the reach of high and low, rich and poor; and that virtue, and virtue alone, whereever found, will be followed by the rewards of everlasting happiness, Nay, God Himself seems to incline more to those who suffer evil; for Jesus Christ calls the poor blessed;[19] He lovingly invites those in labor and grief to come to Him for solace;[20] and He displays the tenderest charity to the lowly and oppressed. These reflections cannot fail to keep down the pride of those who are well off, and to cheer the spirit of the afflicted; to incline the former to generosity, and the latter to tranquil resignation. Thus the separation which pride would make tends to disappear, nor will it be difficult to make rich and poor join hands in friendly concord.

21. But, if Christian precepts prevail, the two classes will not only be united in the bonds of friendship, but also those of brotherly love. For they will understand and feel that all men are the children of the common Father, that is, of God; that all have the same end, which is God Himself, who alone can make either men or angels absolutely and perfectly happy; that all at each death are redeemed by Jesus Christ, and raised to the dignity of children of God, and are thus united in brotherly ties both with each other and with Jesus Christ, "the first born among many brethren"; that the blessings of nature and the gifts of grace belong in common to the whole human race, and that to all, except to those who are unworthy, is promised the inheritance of the kingdom of Heaven. "If sons, heirs also; heirs indeed of God, and co-heirs of Christ."[21]

Such is the scheme of duties and of rights which is put forth to the world by the Gospel. Would it not seem that strife must quickly cease were society penetrated with ideas like these?

---

[5]St. James v. 4.

[17]2 Cor. vii. 9.

[18]St. Mark vi. 3.

[19]St. Matt. v. 3: "Blessed are the poor in spirit."

[20]Ibid., xi. 28: "Come to Me all you that labor and are burdened, and I will refresh you."

[21]Rom. viii. 17.

The Workman's Rights

31. When work-people have recourse to a strike, it is frequently because the hours of labor are too long, or the work too hard, or because they consider their wages insufficient. The grave inconvenience of this not uncommon occurrence should be obviated by public remedial measures; for such paralysis of labor not only affects the masters and their work-people, but is extremely injurious to trade, and to the general interests of the public. Moreover, on such occasions, violence and disorder are generally not far off, and thus it frequently happens that the public peace is threatened. The laws should be beforehand, and prevent these troubles from arising; they should lend their influence and authority to the removal in good time of the courses which lead to conflicts between masters and those whom they employ.

32. But if the owners of property must be made secure, the work-man, too has property and possessions in which he must be protected; and, first of all, there are his spiritual and mental interests. Life on earth, however good and desirable in itself, is not the final purpose for which man is created; it is only the way and the means to that attainment of truth, and that practice of goodness in which the full life of the soul consists. It is the soul which is made after the image and likeness of God; it is in the soul that sovereignty resides, in virtue of which man is commanded to rule the creatures below him, and to use all the earth and ocean for his profit and advantage. "Fill the earth and subdue it; and rule over the fishes of the sea and the fowls of the air, and all living creatures which move upon the earth."[27] In this respect all men are equal; there is no difference between rich and poor, master and servant, ruler and ruled, "for the same is Lord over all."[28] No man may outrage with impunity that human dignity which God Himself treats with reverence, nor stand in the way of that higher life which is the preparation for the eternal life of Heaven. Nay, more; a man has here no power over himself. To consent to any treatment which is calculated to defeat the end and purpose of his being is beyond his right; he cannot give up his soul to servitude; for it is not man's own rights which are here in question, but the rights of God, most sacred and inviolable.

From this follows the obligation of the cessation of work and labor on Sundays and certain festivals. This rest from labor is not to be understood as mere idleness; much less must it be an occasion of spending money and a vicious excess, as many would desire it to be; but it should be rest from labor consecrated by Religion. Repose united with religious observance disposes man to forget for a while the business of this daily life, and to turn his thoughts to heavenly things and to the worship which he so strictly owes to the Eternal Deity. It is this, above all, which is the reason and motive for the Sunday rest; a rest sanctioned by God's great law of the ancient covenant, "Remember thou keep holy the Sabbath day,"[29] And taught to the world by His own mysterious "rest" after the creation of man, "He rested on the seventh day from all His work which He had done."[30]

Hours of Labor

33. If we turn now to things exterior and corporal, the first concern of all is to save the poor workers from the cruelty of grasping speculators, who use human beings as mere instruments for making money. It is neither justice nor humanity so to grind men down with excessive labor as to stupefy their minds and wear out their bodies. Man's powers, like his general nature, are limited, and beyond these limits he cannot go. His strength is developed and increased by use and exercise, but

---

[27]Gen. i. 28.

[28]Rom. x. 12.

[29]Exod. xx. 8.

[30]Gen. ii. 2.

only on condition of due intermission and proper rest. Daily labor, therefore, must be so regulated that it may not be protracted during longer hours than strength admits. How many and how long the intervals of rest should be, will depend upon the nature of the work, on circumstances of time and place, and on the health and strength of the workman. Those who labor in mines and quarries, and in work within the bowels of the earth, should have shorter hours in proportion, as their labor is more severe and more trying to health. Then, again, the season of the year must be taken in account; for not unfrequently a kind of labor is easy at one time which at another is intolerable or very difficult. Finally, work which is suitable for a strong man cannot reasonably be required from a woman or a child.

Child Labor

And in regard to children, great care should be taken not to place them in workshops and factories until their bodies and minds are sufficiently mature. For just as rough weather destroys buds of spring, so too early an experience of life's hard work blights the young promise of a child's powers, and makes any real education impossible. Women, again, are not suited to certain trades; for a woman is by nature fitted for home-work, and it is that which is best adapted at once to preserve her modesty, and to promote the good bringing up of children and the well-being of the family. As a general principle, it may be laid down, that a workman ought to have leisure and rest in proportion to the wear and tear of his strength; for the waste of strength must be repaired by the cessation of work.

In all agreements between masters and work-people, there is always the condition, expressed or understood, that there be allowed proper rest for soul and body. To agree in any other sense would be against what is right and just; for it can never be right or just to require on the one side, or to promise on the other, the giving up of those duties which a man owes to his God and to himself.

Just Wages

34. We now approach a subject of very great importance and one on which, if extremes are to be avoided, right ideas are absolutely necessary. Wages, we are told, are fixed by free consent; and, therefore, the employer when he pays what was agreed upon, has done his part, and is not called upon for anything further. The only way, it is said, in which injustice could happen, would be if the master refused to pay the whole of the wages, or the workman would not complete the work undertaken; when this happens the State should intervene, to see that each obtains his own, but not under any other circumstances.

This mode of reasoning is by no means convincing to a fair-minded man, for there are important considerations which it leaves out of view altogether. To labor is to exert one's self for the sake of procuring what is necessary for the purposes of life, and most of all for self-preservation. "In the sweat of thy brow thou shalt eat bread."[31] Therefore, a man's labor has two notes or characters. First of all, it is *personal*; for the exertion of individual power belongs to the individual who puts it forth, employing this power for that personal profit for which it was given. Secondly, a man's labor is *necessary*; for without the results of labor a man cannot live; and self-conservation is a law of nature, which it is wrong to disobey. Now, if we were to consider labor merely so far as it is *personal*, doubtless it would be within the workman's right to accept any rate of wages whatever; for in the same way as he is free to work or not, so he is free to accept a small remuneration or even none at all. But this is a mere abstract supposition; the labor of the working man is not only his personal attribute, but it is *necessary*; and this makes all the difference. The preservation of life is the bounden

---

[31]Gen. iii. 1.

duty of each and all, and to fail therein is a crime. It follows that each one has a right to procure what is required in order to live; and the poor can procure it in no other way than by work and wages.

Let it be granted, then, that, as a rule, workman and employer should make free agreements, and in particular should freely agree as to wages; nevertheless, there is a dictate of nature more imperious and more ancient than any bargain between man and man, that the remuneration must be enough to support the wage-earner in reasonable and frugal comfort. If through necessity or fear of a worse evil, the workman accepts harder conditions because an employer or contractor will give him no better, he is the victim of force and injustice.

Conclusion

45. We have now laid before you, Venerable Brethren, who are the persons, and what are the means, by which this most difficult question must be solved. Every one must put his hand to work which falls to his share, and that at once and immediately, lest the evil which is already so great may by delay become absolutely beyond remedy. Those who rule the State must use the law and the institutions of the country; masters and rich men must remember their duty; the poor, whose interests are at stake, must make every lawful and proper effort; since Religion alone, as We said at the beginning, can destroy the evil at its root, all men must be persuaded that the primary thing needful is to return to real Christianity, in the absence of which all the plans and devices of the wisest will be of little avail.

As far as regards the Church, its assistance will never be wanting, be the time or the occasion what it may; and it will intervene with great effect in proportion as its liberty of action is the more unfettered; let this be carefully noted by those whose office it is to provide for the public welfare. Every minister of holy Religion must throw into the conflict all the energy of his mind, and all the strength of his endurance; with your authority, Venerable Brethren, and by your example, they must never cease to urge upon all men of every class, upon the high as well as the lowly, the Gospel doctrines of Christian life; by every means in their power they must strive for the good of the people; and above all they must earnestly cherish in themselves, and try to arouse in others, Charity, the mistress and queen of virtues. For the happy results we all long for must be chiefly brought about by the plenteous outpouring of Charity; of that true Christian Charity which is the fulfilling of the whole Gospel law, which is man's surest antidote against worldly pride and immoderate love of self; that Charity whose office is described and whose Godlike features are drawn by the Apostle St. Paul in these words: "Charity is patient, is kind, . . . (seeketh not her own, . . . (suffereth all things, . . . (endureth all things." [39]

On each of you, Venerable Brethren, and on your clergy and people, as an earnest of God's mercy and a mark of Our affection, We lovingly in the Lord bestow the Apostolic Benediction.

Given at St. Peter's in Rome, the fifteenth day of May, 1891, the fourteenth year of Our Pontificate.

---

[39] I Cor. xiii. 4–7.

QUESTIONS

1. What is the condition of the working class, according to Leo?

2. Why is private property important?

3. What is Leo's view of socialism? Does he believe that it will work? Why or why not?

4. What are the responsibilities of employers and the rich towards their workers?

5. What is Leo's solution for the ills of society?

Emancipating the Mind and the Body

THE DESCENT OF MAN
(1871)

Charles Darwin (1809–82) pioneered the biological theory of evolution. He was born into a prominent middle-class English family. His grandfather was Josiah Wedgwood, whose ceramic potteries were celebrated by Samuel Smiles. Darwin was not a distinguished student and failed at both medical and divinity studies. By chance in 1832 he was signed on to a naval expedition whose purpose was to catalog plant and animal life in South America and the Pacific. During the voyage, Darwin became an accomplished naturalist. His observations led him to the theory of natural selection, adaptation, and eventually to evolution itself. He published a number of volumes based on his discoveries while at sea and he worked secretly to provide a convincing explanation of his theory of evolution. After the publication of *On the Origin of Species by Means of Natural Selection* he became a celebrated—though controversial—scientific leader in Britain. On his death in 1882 he was buried in Westminster Abbey.

    The Descent of Man is a continuation of Darwin's earlier *Origin of Species,* one of the seminal works of modern biology. *Descent* extends the theory of evolution to humans, and so invited a storm of protest from the leaders of the Anglican church. Evolutionary theory remains a topic of discussion to this day.

The main conclusion here arrived at, and now held by many naturalists who are well competent to form a sound judgment, is that man is descended from some less highly organised form. The grounds upon which this conclusion rests will never be shaken, for the close similarity between man and the lower animals in embryonic development, as well as in innumerable points of structure and constitution, both of high and of the most trifling importance,—the rudiments which he retains, and the abnormal reversions to which he is occasionally liable,—are facts which cannot be disputed. They have long been known, but until recently they told us nothing with respect to the origin of man. Now when viewed by the light of our knowledge of the whole organic world, their meaning is unmistakable. The great principle of evolution stands up clear and firm, when these groups or facts are considered in connection with others, such as the mutual affinities of the members of the same group, their geographical distribution in past and present times, and their geological succession. It is incredible that all these facts should speak falsely. He who is not content to look, like a savage, at the phenomena of nature as disconnected, cannot any longer believe that man is the work of a separate act of creation. He will be forced to admit that the close resemblance of the embryo of man to that, for instance, of a dog—the construction of his skull, limbs and whole frame on the same plan with that of other mammals, independently of the uses to which the parts may be put—. . . all point in the plainest manner to the conclusion that man is the co-descendant with other mammals of a common progenitor. . . .

Through the means just specified, aided perhaps by others as yet undiscovered, man has been raised to his present state. But since he attained to the rank of manhood, he has diverged into distinct races, or as they may be more fitly called, sub-species. Some of these, such as the Negro and European, are so distinct that, if specimens had been brought to a naturalist without any further information, they would undoubtedly have been considered by him as good and true species. Nevertheless all the races agree in so many unimportant details of structure and in so many mental peculiarities, that these can be accounted for only by inheritance from a common progenitor; and a progenitor thus characterised would probably deserve to rank as man. . . .

By considering the embryological structure of man,—the homologies which he presents with the lower animals,—the rudiments which he retains,—and the reversions to which he is liable, we can partly recall in imagination the former condition of our early progenitors; and can approximately place them in their proper place in the zoological series. We thus learn that man is descended from a hairy, tailed quadruped, probably arboreal in its habits, and an inhabitant of the Old World. This creature, if its whole structure had been examined by a naturalist, would have been classed amongst the Quadrumana, as surely as the still more ancient progenitor of the Old and New World monkeys. The Quadrumana and all the higher mammals are probably derived from an ancient marsupial animal, and this through a long line of diversified forms, from some amphibian-like creature, and this again from some fish-like animal. In the dim obscurity of the past we can see that the early progenitor of all the Vertebrata must have been an aquatic animal, provided with branchiæ, with the two sexes united in the same individual,

and with the most important organs of the body (such as the brain and heart) imperfectly or not at all developed. This animal seems to have been more like the larvæ of the existing marine Ascidians than any other known form.

The high standard of our intellectual powers and moral disposition is the greatest difficulty which presents itself, after we have been driven to this conclusion on the origin of man. But every one who admits the principle of evolution, must see that the mental powers of the higher animals, which are the same in kind with those of man, though so different in degree, are capable of advancement. Thus the interval between the mental powers of one of the higher apes and of a fish, or between those of an ant and scale-insect, is immense; yet their development does not offer any special difficulty; for with our domesticated animals, the mental faculties are certainly variable, and the variations are inherited. No one doubts that they are of the utmost importance to animals in a state of nature. Therefore the conditions are favourable for their development through natural selection. The same conclusion may be extended to man; the intellect must have been all-important to him, even at a very remote period, as enabling him to invent and use language, to make weapons, tools, traps, &c., whereby with the aid of his social habits, he long ago became the most dominant of all living creatures. . . .

The belief in God has often been advanced as not only the greatest, but the most complete of all the distinctions between man and the lower animals. It is however impossible, as we have seen, to maintain that this belief is innate or instinctive in man. On the other hand a belief in all-pervading spiritual agencies seems to be universal; and apparently follows from a considerable advance in man's reason, and from a still greater advance in his faculties of imagination, curiosity and wonder. I am aware that the assumed instinctive belief in God has been used by many persons as an argument for His existence. But this is a rash argument, as we should thus be compelled to believe in the existence of many cruel and malignant spirits, only a little more powerful than man; for the belief in them is far more general than in a beneficent Deity. The idea of a universal and beneficent Creator does not seem to arise in the mind of man, until he has been elevated by long-continued culture. . . .

I am aware that the conclusions arrived at in this work will be denounced by some as highly irreligious; but he who denounces them is bound to shew why it is more irreligious to explain the origin of man as a distinct species by descent from some lower form, through the laws of variation and natural selection, than to explain the birth of the individual through the laws of ordinary reproduction. The birth both of the species and of the individual are equally parts of that grand sequence of events, which our minds refuse to accept as the result of blind chance. The understanding revolts at such a conclusion, whether or not we are able to believe that every slight variation of structure,—the union of each pair in marriage,—the dissemination of each seed,—and other such events, have all been ordained for some special purpose. . . .

The main conclusion arrived at in this work, namely that man is descended from some lowly organised form, will, I regret to think, be highly distasteful to many. But there can hardly be a doubt that we are descended from barbarians. The astonishment which I felt on first seeing a party of Fuegians on a wild and broken shore will never be forgotten by me, for the reflection at once rushed into my mind—such were our ancestors. These men were absolutely naked and bedaubed with paint, their long hair was tangled, their mouths frothed with excitement, and their expression was wild, startled, and distrustful. They possessed hardly any arts, and like wild animals lived on what they could catch; they had no government, and were merciless to every one not of their own small tribe. He who has seen a savage in his native land will not feel much shame, if forced to acknowledge that the blood of some more humble creature flows in his veins. For my own part I would as soon be descended from that heroic little monkey, who braved his dreaded enemy in order to save the life of his keeper, or from that old baboon, who descending from the mountains, carried away in triumph his young comrade from a crowd of astonished dogs—as from a savage who delights to torture his enemies, offers up bloody sacrifices, practises infanticide without remorse, treats his wives like slaves, knows no decency, and is haunted by the grossest superstitions.

Man may be excused for feeling some pride at having risen, though not through his own exertions, to the very summit of the organic scale; and the fact of his having thus risen, instead of having been aboriginally placed there, may give him hope for a still higher destiny in the distant future. But we are not here concerned with hopes or fears, only with the truth as far as our reason permits us to discover it; and I have given the evidence to the best of my ability. We must, however, acknowledge, as it seems to me, that man with all his noble qualities, with sympathy which feels for the most debased, with benevolence which extends not only to other men but to the humblest living creature, with his god-like intellect which has penetrated into the movements and constitution of the solar system—with all these exalted powers—Man still bears in his bodily frame the indelible stamp of his lowly origin.

QUESTIONS

1.   What is evolution? How does it work, and what purpose does it serve?

2.   What sort of picture does Darwin give of nature?

3. Darwin's work has sometimes been used to justify racial discrimination. Why?

4. What evidence does Darwin offer for evolution?

5. Galileo, in his letter to Christina, defends his science from religious critics. Compare his defense with Darwin's. Are they similar? How do they differ?

---

117.   **FRIEDRICH NIETZSCHE**

BEYOND GOOD AND EVIL

(1886)

Friedrich Nietzsche (1844–1900) was one of the nineteenth century's most significant philosophers, whose ideas had an important influence upon Western society. He was born in eastern Germany, the son of a Protestant minister. He studied classics at the Universities of Bonn and Leipzig, and in 1869 became a professor of classics at the University of Basel, in Switzerland. Although he became a Swiss citizen, and in later years had no love for the German Empire, he nevertheless served as a medical orderly in the Franco-Prussian War of 1870–71. He published his first book, *The Birth of Tragedy,* in 1872. Like most of the rest of his published work during his life, it was badly received.

In 1879, suffering from poor health, Nietzsche resigned his position, and devoted himself to his writing. Over the next decade he wrote a series of important works of philosophy, including *Thus Spoke Zarasthustra* (1883–84) and *The Geneaology of Morals* (1887). In 1889 he lost his sanity, probably the result of a long-standing syphilitic infection. He lived eleven years more, but never recovered from his illness.

Beyond Good and Evil, excerpted here, was Nietzsche's attempt to systematize his philosophy. The current selection concerns his views of modern society and democracy.

199

Inasmuch as at all times, as long as there have been human beings, there have also been herds of men (clans, communities, tribes, peoples, states, churches) and always a great many people who obeyed, compared with the small number of those commanding—considering, then, that nothing has been exercised and cultivated better and longer among men so far than obedience—it may fairly be assumed that the need for it is now innate in the average man, as a kind of *formal conscience* that commands: "thou shalt unconditionally do something, unconditionally not do something else," in short, "thou shalt." This need seeks to satisfy itself and to fill its form with some content. According to its strength, impatience, and tension it seizes upon things as a rude appetite, rather indiscriminate, and accepts whatever is shouted into its ears by someone who issues commands (parents, teachers, laws, class prejudices, public opinions).

The strange limits of human development, the way it hesitates, takes so long, often turns back, and moves in circles, is due to the fact that the herd instinct of obedience is inherited best, and at the expense of the art of commanding. If we imagined this instinct progressing for once to its ultimate excesses, then those who command and are independent would eventually be lacking altogether; or they would secretly suffer from a bad conscience and would find it necessary to deceive themselves before they could command (as if they, too, merely obeyed). This state is actually encountered in Europe today: I call it the moral hypocrisy of those commanding. They know no other way to protect themselves against their bad conscience than to pose as the executors of more ancient or higher commands (of ancestors, the constitution, of right, the laws, or even of God). Or they even borrow herd maxims from the herd's way of thinking such as "first servants of their people" or "instruments of the common weal."

On the other side, the herd man in Europe today gives himself the appearance of being the only permissible kind of man, and glorifies his attributes, which make him tame, easy to get along with, and useful to the herd, as if they were the truly human virtues: namely, public spirit, benevolence, consideration, industriousness, moderation, modesty, indulgence, and pity. In those cases, however, where one considers leaders and bellwethers indispensable, peo-ple today make one attempt after another to add together clever herd men by way of replacing commanders: all parliamentary constitutions, for example, have this origin. Nevertheless, the appearance of one who commands unconditionally strikes these herd-animal Europeans as an immense comfort and salvation from a gradually intolerable pressure, as was last attested in a major way by the effect of Napoleon's appearance. The history of Napoleon's reception is almost the history of the higher happiness attained by this whole century in its most valuable human beings and moments.

200

In an age of disintegration that mixes races indiscriminately, human beings have in their bodies the heritage of multiple origins, that is, opposite, and often not merely opposite, drives and value standards that fight each other and rarely permit each other any rest. Such human beings of late cultures and refracted lights will on the average be weaker human beings: their most profound desire is that the war they *are* should come to an end. Happiness appears to them, in agreement with a tranquilizing (for example, Epicurean or Christian) medicine and way of thought, pre-eminently as the happiness of resting, of not being disturbed, of satiety, of finally attained unity, as a "sabbath of sabbaths," to speak with the holy rhetorician Augustine who was himself such a human being.

But when the opposition and war in such a nature have the effect of one more charm and incentive of life—and if, moreover, in addition to his powerful and irreconcilable drives, a real mastery and subtlety in waging war against oneself, in other words, self-control, self-outwitting, has been inherited or cultivated, too—then those magical, incomprehensible, and unfathomable ones arise, those enigmatic men predestined for victory and seduction, whose most beautiful expression is found in Alcibiades and Caesar (to whose company I should like to add that *first* European after my taste, the Hohenstaufen Frederick II), and among artists perhaps Leonard Da Vinci. They appear in precisely the same ages when that weaker type with its desire for rest comes to the fore: both types belong together and owe their origin to the same causes.

201

As long as the utility reigning in moral value judgments is solely the utility of the herd, as long as one considers only the preservation of the community, and immorality is sought exactly and exclusively in what seems dangerous to the survival of the community—there can be no morality of "neighbor love." Supposing that even there was a constant little exercise of consideration, pity, fairness, mildness, reciprocity of assistance; supposing that even in that state of society all those drives are active that later receive the honorary designation of "virtues" and eventually almost coincide with the concept of "morality"—in that period they do not yet at all belong in the realm of moral valuations; they are still *extra-moral*. An act of pity, for example, was not considered either good or bad, moral or immoral, in the best period of the Romans; and even when it was praised, such praise was perfectly compatible with a kind of disgruntled disdain as soon as it was juxtaposed with an action that served the welfare of the whole, of the *res publica.*

In the last analysis, "love of the neighbor" is always something secondary, partly conventional and arbitrary-illusory in relation to *fear of the neighbor.* After the structure of society is fixed on the whole and seems secure against external dangers, it is this fear of the neighbor that again creates new perspectives of moral valuation. Certain strong and dangerous drives, like an enterprising spirit, foolhardiness, vengefulness, craftiness, rapacity, and the lust to rule, which had so far not merely been honored insofar as they were socially useful—under different names, to be sure, from those chosen here—but had to be trained and

cultivated to make them great (because one constantly needed them in view of the dangers to the whole community, against the enemies of the community), are now experienced as doubly dangerous, since the channels to divert them are lacking, and, step upon step, they are branded as immoral and abandoned to slander.

Now the opposite drives and inclinations receive moral honors; step upon step, the herd instinct draws its conclusions. How much or how little is dangerous to the community, dangerous to equality, in an opinion, in a state or affect, in a will, in a talent—that now constitutes the moral perspective: here, too, fear is again the mother of morals.

The highest and strongest drives, when they break out passionately and drive the individual far above the average and the flats of the herd conscience, wreck the self-confidence of the community, its faith in itself, and it is as if its spine snapped. Hence just these drives are branded and slandered most. High and independent spirituality, the will to stand alone, even a powerful reason are experienced as dangers; everything that elevates an individual above the herd and intimidates the neighbor is henceforth called *evil*; and the fair, modest, submissive, conforming mentality, the *mediocrity* of desires attains moral designations and honors. Eventually, under very peaceful conditions, the opportunity and necessity for educating one's feeling to severity and hardness is lacking more and more; and every severity, even in justice, begins to disturb the conscience; any high and hard nobility and self-reliance is almost felt to be an insult and arouses mistrust; the "lamb," even more the "sheep," gains in respect.

There is a point in the history of society when it becomes so pathologically soft and tender that among other things it sides even with those who harm it, criminals, and does this quite seriously and honestly. Punishing somehow seems unfair to it, and it is certain that imagining "punishment" and "being supposed to punish" hurts it, arouses fear in it. " Is it not enough to render him *undangerous?* Why still punish? Punishing itself is terrible." With this question, herd morality, the morality of timidity, draws its ultimate consequence. Supposing that one could altogether abolish danger, the reason for fear, this morality would be abolished, too *eo ipso:* it would no longer be needed, it would no longer *consider itself* necessary.

Whoever examines the conscience of the European today will have to pull the same imperative out of a thousand moral folds and hideouts—(the imperative of herd timidity: "we want that some day there should be *nothing any more to be afraid of!*") Throughout Europe, the will and way to this day is now called "progress."

202

Let us immediately say once more what we have already said a hundred times, for today's ears resist such truths—*our* truths. We know well enough how insulting it sounds when anybody counts man, unadorned and without metaphor, among the animals; but it will be charged against us as almost a *guilt* that precisely for the men of "modern ideas" we constantly employ such expressions as "herd," "herd instincts," and so forth. What can be done about it? We cannot do anything else; for here exactly lies our novel insight. We have found that in all major moral judgments Europe is now of one mind, including even the countries dominated by the influence of Europe: plainly, one now *knows* in Europe what Socrates thought he did not know and what that famous old serpent once promised to teach—today one "knows" what is good and evil.

Now it must sound harsh and cannot be heard easily when we keep insisting: that which here believes it knows, that which here glorifies itself with its praises and reproaches, calling itself good, that is the instinct of the herd animal, man, which has scored a breakthrough and

attained prevalence and predominance over other instincts—and this development is continuing in accordance with the growing physiological approximation and assimilation which it is the symptom. *Morality in Europe today is herd animal morality*—in other words, as we understand it, merely one type of human morality besides which, before which, and after which many other types of, above all *higher* moralities, are or ought to be, possible. But this morality resists such a "possibility," such an "ought" with all its power: it says stubbornly and inexorably, "I am morality itself, and nothing besides is morality." Indeed, with the help of a religion which indulged and flattered the most sublime herd animals desires, we have reached the point where we find even in political and social institutions an ever more visible expression of their morality: the *democratic* movement is the heir of the Christian movement.

But there are indications that its tempo is still much too slow and sleepy for the more impatient, for the sick, the suffers of the instinct mentioned: witness the ever madder howling of the anarchist dogs who are baring their fangs more and more obviously and roam through the alleys of European culture. They seem opposites of the peacefully industrious democrats and ideologists of revolution, and even more so of the doltish philosophasters and brotherhood enthusiasts who call themselves socialists and want a "free society"; but in fact they are at one with the lot in their thorough and instinctive hostility to every other form of society except that of the *autonomous* herd (even to the point of repudiating the very concepts of "master" and "servant"—*ni dieu ni maître*[19] runs a socialist formula). They are at one in their tough resistance to every special claim, every special right and privilege (which means in the last analysis, *every* right: for once all are equal nobody needs "rights" any more). They are at one in their mistrust of punitive justice (as

---

[19]"Neither god nor master"; cf. section 22 above.

if it were a violation of those who are weaker, a wrong against the *necessary* consequence of all previous society). But they are also at one in the religion of pity, in feeling with all who feel, live, and suffer (down to the animal, up to "God"— the excess of a "pity with God" belongs in a democratic age). They are at one, the lot of them, in the cry and the impatience of pity, in their deadly hatred of suffering generally, in their almost feminine inability to remain spectators, to *let* someone suffer. They are at one in their involuntary plunge into gloom and unmanly tenderness under whose spell Europe seems threatened by a new Buddhism. They are at one in their faith in the morality of *shared* pity, as if that were morality in itself, being the height, the *attained* height of man, the sole hope of the future, the consolation of present man, the great absolution from all former guilt. They are at one, the lot of them, in their faith in the community as the *savior*, in short, in the herd in "themselves"—

203

We have a different faith; to us the democratic movement is not only a form of the decay of political organization but a form of the decay, namely, the diminution, of man, making him mediocre and lowering his value. Where, then, must we reach with our hopes?

Toward *new philosophers*; there is no choice; toward spirits strong and original enough to provide the stimuli for opposite valuations and to revalue and invert "eternal values"; toward forerunners, toward men of the future who in the present tie the knot and constraint that forces the will of millennia upon the *new* tracks. To teach man the future of man as his *will*, as dependent on human will, and to prepare great ventures and over-all attempts of discipline and cultivation by way of putting an end to that gruesome dominion of nonsense and accident that has so far been called "history"— the nonsense of the "greatest number" is mere-

ly its ultimate form: at some time new types of philosophers and commanders will be necessary for that, and whatever has existed on earth of concealed, terrible, and benevolent spirits, will look pale and dwarfed by comparison. It is the image of such leaders that *we* envisage: may I say this out loud, you free spirits? The conditions that one would have partly to create and partly to exploit for their genesis; the probable ways and tests that would enable a soul to grow to such a height and force that it would feel the *compulsion* for such tasks; a revaluation of values under whose new pressure and hammer a conscience would be steeled, a heart turned to bronze, in order to endure the weight of such responsibility; on the other hand, the necessity of such leaders, the frightening danger that they might fail to appear or that they might turn out badly or degenerate—these are *our* real worries and gloom—do you know that, you free spirits? —these are the heavy distant thoughts and storms that pass over the sky of *our* life.

There are few pains as sore as once having seen, guessed, felt how an extraordinary human being strayed from his path and degenerated. But anyone who has the rare eye for the over-all danger that "man" himself *degenerates*; anyone who, like us, has recognized the monstrous fortuity that has so far had its way and play regarding the future of man—a game in which no hand, and not even a finger, of God took part as a player; anyone who fathoms the calamity that lies concealed in the absurd guilelessness and blind confidence of "modern ideas" and even more in the whole Christian-European morality—suffers from an anxiety that is past all comparisons. With a single glance he sees what, given a favorable accumulation and increase of forces and tasks, might yet *be made of man*; he knows with all the knowledge of his conscience how man is still unexhausted for the greatest possibilities and how often the type "man" has already confronted enigmatic decisions and new paths—he knows still better from his most painful memories what wretched things have so far usually broken a being of the highest rank that was in the process of becoming, so that it broke, sank, and became contemptible.

The *over-all degeneration of man* down to what today appears to the socialist dolts and flatheads as their "man of the future"—as their ideal—this degeneration and diminution of man into the perfect herd animal (or, as they say, to the man of the "free society"), this animalization of man into the dwarf animal of equal rights and claims, is *possible,* there is no doubt of it. Anyone who has once thought through this possibility to the end knows one kind of nausea that other men don't know—but perhaps also a new *task!*—

QUESTIONS

1.   What is the "herd," what does it believe?

2.   When Nietzsche talks about "the good" what does he mean? Is it a good thing?

3.   What is the role of a hero like Napoleon in Nietzsche's philosophy?

4.   What are the "new philosophers"? How do they differ from the "old philosophers"?

5.   Few thinkers had as great an impact upon the late nineteenth and early twentieth centuries as Nietzsche. Why do you think he was so popular?

118.   SIGMUND FREUD

THE INTERPRETATION OF DREAMS
(1899)

Sigmund Freud (1856–1939) was an Austrian medical doctor whose work forms the basis of the discipline of psychology. Born in a provincial town in what is now the Czech Republic, Freud came from an assimilated middle-class Jewish family. He studied medicine at the University of Vienna, and after graduation decided to specialize in psychiatry. Opening his own practice, Freud began to work on the theories that were to make him a household name. In the 1890s he developed the technique that he labeled psychoanalysis, introducing a number of terms that have passed into common parlance, including *ego, id,* and *Oedipus complex.* He also pioneered work on the unconscious. Freud lived in Vienna until it was occupied by Hitler's troops in 1938. He fled to London, where he died the following year.

Freud's best-known and most important work was *The Interpretation of Dreams,* in which he uncovered the ways in which the unconscious operates and posited the now-familiar theory of dreams as wish-fulfillment.

I am proposing to show that dreams are capable of interpretation; and any contributions to the solution of the problem which have already been discussed will emerge only as possible by-products in the accomplishment of my special task. On the hypothesis that dreams are susceptible of interpretation, I at once find myself in disagreement with the prevailing doctrine of dreams—in fact, with all the theories of dreams, excepting only that of Scherner, for "to interpret a dream" is to specify its "meaning," to replace it by something which takes its position in the concatenation of our psychic activities as a link of definite importance and value. But, as we have seen, the scientific theories of the dream leave no room for a problem of dream-interpretation; since, in the first place, according to these theories, dreaming is not a psychic activity at all, but a somatic process which makes itself known to the psychic apparatus by means of symbols. Lay opinion has always been opposed to these theories. It asserts its privilege of proceeding illogically, and although it admits that dreams are incomprehensible and absurd, it cannot summon up the courage to deny that dreams have any significance. Led by a dim intuition, it seems rather to assume that dreams have a meaning, albeit a hidden one; that they are intended as a substitute for some other thought-process, and that we have only to disclose this substitute correctly in order to discover the hidden meaning of the dream.

The unscientific world, therefore, has always endeavored to "interpret" dreams, and by applying one or the other of two essentially different methods. The first of these envisages the dream-content as a whole, and seeks to replace it by another content, which is intelligible and in certain respects analogous. This is symbolic dream-interpretation; and of course it goes to pieces at the very outset in the case of those dreams which are not only unintelligible but confused. The construction which the biblical Joseph placed upon the dream of Pharaoh furnishes an example of this method. The seven fat kine, after which came seven lean ones that devoured the former, were a symbolic substitute for seven years of famine in the land of Egypt, which according to the prediction were to consume all the surplus that seven fruitful years had produced. Most of the artificial dreams contrived by the poets are intended for some such symbolic interpretation, for they reproduce the thought conceived by the poet in a guise not unlike the disguise which we are wont to find in our dreams.

The idea that the dream concerns itself chiefly with the future, whose form it surmises in advance—a relic of the prophetic significance with which dreams were once invested—now becomes the motive for translating into the future the meaning of the dream which has been found by means of symbolic interpretation.

A demonstration of the manner in which one arrives at such a symbolic interpretation cannot, of course, be given. Success remains a matter of ingenious conjecture, of direct intuition, and for this reason dream-interpretation has naturally been elevated into an art which seems to depend upon extraordinary gifts. The second of the two popular methods of dream-interpretation entirely abandons such claims. It might be described as the "cipher method," since it treats the dream as a kind of secret code in which every sign is translated into another sign of known meaning, according to an established key. For example, I have dreamt of a letter, and also of a funeral or the like; I consult a "dream-book," and I find that "letter" is to be translated by "vexation" and "funeral" by "engagement." It now remains to establish a connection, which I am again to assume as pertaining to the future, by means of the rigmarole which I have deciphered.

An ancient and stubbornly retained popular belief seems to have come nearer to the truth of the matter than the opinion of modern science. I must insist that the dream actually does possess a meaning, and that a scientific method of dream-interpretation is possible.

When, after passing through a narrow defile, one suddenly reaches a height beyond which the ways part and a rich prospect lies outspread in different directions, it is well to stop for a moment and consider whither one shall turn next. We are in somewhat the same position after we have mastered this first interpretation of a dream. We find ourselves standing in the light of a sudden discovery. The dream is not comparable to the irregular sounds of a musical instrument, which, instead of being played by the hand of a musician, is struck by some external force; the dream is not meaningless, not absurd, does not presuppose that one part of our store of ideas is dormant while another part begins to awake. It is a perfectly valid psychic phenomenon, actually a wish-fulfilment; it may be enrolled in the continuity of the intelligible psychic activities of the waking state; it is built up by a highly complicated intellectual activity. But at the very moment when we are about to rejoice in this discovery a host of problems besets us. If the dream, as this theory defines it, represents a fulfilled wish, what is the cause of the striking and unfamiliar manner in which this fulfilment is expressed?

It is easy to show that the wish-fulfillment in dreams is often undisguised and easy to recognize, so that one may wonder why the language of dreams has not long since been understood. There is, for example, a dream which I can evoke as often as I please, experimentally, as it were. If, in the evening, I eat anchovies, olives, or other strongly salted foods, I am thirsty at night, and therefore I wake. The waking, however, is preceded by a dream, which has always the same content, namely, that I am drinking. I am drinking long draughts of water; it tastes as delicious as only a cool drink can taste when one's throat is parched; and then I wake, and find that I have an actual desire to drink. The cause of this dream is thirst, which I perceive when I wake. From this sensation arises the wish to drink, and the dream shows me this wish as fulfilled. It thereby serves a function, the nature of which I soon surmise. I sleep well, and am not accustomed to being waked by a bodily need. If I succeed in appeasing my thirst by means of the dream that I am drinking, I need not wake up in order to satisfy that thirst. It is thus a *dream of convenience*. The dream takes the place of action, as elsewhere in life.

If I now declare that wish-fulfilment is the meaning of *every* dream, so that there cannot be any dreams other than wish-dreams, I know beforehand that I shall meet with the most emphatic contradiction. Nevertheless, it is not difficult to parry these objections. It is merely necessary to observe that our doctrine is not based upon the estimates of the obvious dream-content but relates to the thought-content, which, in the course of interpretation, is found to lie behind the dream. Let us compare and contrast the *manifest* and the *latent dream-content*. It is true that here are dreams the manifest content of which is of the most painful nature. But has anyone ever tried to interpret these dreams—to discover their latent thought-content? If not, the two objections to our doctrine are no longer valid; for there is always the possibility that even our painful and terrifying dreams may, upon interpretation, prove to be wish-fulfilments.

She puts a candle into a candlestick; but the candle is broken, so that it does not stand up. The girls at school say she is clumsy; but she replies that it is not her fault.

Here, too, there is an actual occasion for the dream; the day before she had actually put a candle into a candlestick; but this one was not broken. An obvious symbolism has here been employed. The candle is an object which excites the female genitals; its being broken, so that it does not stand upright, signifies impotence on the man's part (*it is not her fault*). But does this young woman, carefully brought up, and a stranger to all obscenity, know of such an application of the candle? By chance she is able to tell how she came by this information. While paddling a canoe on the Rhine, a boat passed her which contained some students, who were singing rapturously, or rather yelling: "When the Queen of Sweden, behind closed shutters, with the candles of Apollo. . . ."

She does not hear or else understand the last word. Her husband was asked to give her the required explanation. These verses are then replaced in the dream-content by the innocent recollection of a task which she once performed *clumsily* at her boarding-school, because of the *closed shutters*. The connection between the theme of masturbation and that of impotence is clear enough. "Apollo" in the latent dream-content connects this dream with an earlier one in which the virgin Pallas figured. All this is obviously not innocent.

Sigmund Freud (1856–1939).

The Dream-Work

All other previous attempts to solve the problems of dreams have concerned themselves directly with the manifest dream-content as it is retained in the memory. They have sought to obtain an interpretation of the dream from this content, or, if they dispensed with an interpretation, to base their conclusions concerning the dream on the evidence provided by this content. We, however, are confronted by a different set of data; for us a new psychic material interposes itself between the dream-content and the results of our investigations: the *latent* dream-content, or dream-thoughts, which are obtained only by our method. We develop the solution of the dream from this latent content, and not from the manifest dream-content. We are thus confronted with a new problem, an entirely novel task—that of examining and tracing the relations between the latent dream-thoughts and the manifest dream-content, and the processes by which the latter has grown out of the former.

The dream-thoughts and the dream-content present themselves as two descriptions of the same content in two different languages; or, to put it more clearly, the dream-content appears to us as a translation of the dream-thoughts into another mode of expression, whose symbols and laws of composition we must learn by comparing the origin with the translation. The dream-thoughts we can understand without further trouble the moment we have ascertained them. The dream-content is, as it were, presented in hieroglyphics, whose symbols must be translated, one by one, into the language of the dream-thoughts.

And what of the value of dreams in regard to our knowledge of the future? That, of course, is quite out of the question. One would like to substitute the words: "in regard to our knowledge of the past." For in every sense a dream has its origin in the past. The ancient belief that dreams reveal the future is not indeed entirely devoid of truth. By representing a wish as fulfilled the dream certainly leads us into the future; but this future, which the dreamer accepts as his present, has been shaped in the likeness of the past by the indestructible wish.

QUESTIONS

1. What are the popular types of dream interpretation?

2. How does Freud's method of interpreting dreams differ from previous techniques?

3. What, according to Freud, is a dream? Why do we have them?

4. Why are dreams important?

5. Freud criticized traditional dream interpretation as unscientific, yet his own methods have been questioned. How might Freud's own experience and circumstances have affected his theories?

119.   E. SYLVIA PANKHURST

HISTORY OF THE SUFFRAGE MOVEMENT

(1912)

Sylvia Pankhurst (1882–1960) came from a British family that dedicated its collective energies to the enfranchisement of women. Her mother, Emmeline, was the founder of the Women's Franchise League and leader of the suffragettes, a group that campaigned with increasing militancy for voting rights for all women. Sylvia's sister Christabel led the middle-class wing of the movement, while Sylvia devoted her energies to women workers. She founded a political movement in the East End of London among the poorest and most oppressed female workers.

In *History of the Suffrage Movement*, Sylvia Pankhurst vividly portrays the lengths to which both government and supporters of female suffrage went in their struggle. The imprisonments and hunger strikes that the campaign engendered deeply shocked the sensibilities of the nation. So too did the campaign of civil disobedience that the suffragettes pursued in the years prior to the First World War. It was not until 1928 that British women finally achieved full rights of political participation.

Author's Preface

This history of Women's Suffrage agitation is written at a time when the question is in the very forefront of British politics. What the immediate future holds for those women who are most actively engaged in fighting for their political freedom no one can foretell, but one thing is certain: complete victory for their cause is not far distant.

When the long struggle for the enfranchisement of women is over, those who read the history of the movement will wonder at the blindness that led the Government of the day to obstinately resist so simple and obvious a measure of justice.

The men and women of the coming time will, I am persuaded, be filled with admiration for the patient work of the early pioneers and the heroic determination and persistence in spite of coercion, repression, misrepresentation, and insult of those who fought the later militant fight.

Perhaps the women born in the happier days that are to come, while rejoicing in the inheritance that we of today are preparing for them, may sometimes wish that they could have lived in the heroic days of stress and struggle and have shared with us the joy of battle, the exaltation that comes of sacrifice of self for great objects and the prophetic vision that assures us of the certain triumph of this twentieth-century fight for human emancipation.

The First Women's Parliament in the Caxton Hall and the Sending Out of the Mounted Police to Drive Away the Women's Deputation.

And now again the thoughts of all the women who wanted votes were turning towards the opening of Parliament. The old fashioned Suffragists had held their demonstration during the recess but that of the Suffragettes was still to come and it had been announced that on February 13th, 1907, a Parliament of women would sit in the Caxton Hall to consider the provision of the King's speech to be read in the Nation's Parliament on the previous day. It was but a year since Annie Kenney had set off to rouse London and since Mrs. Pankhurst had feared that we should neither fill the Caxton Hall nor induce a body of women to march for the sake of a vote through the London streets, but the tickets were now sold off so rapidly that the Exeter Hall in the Strand was also requisitioned, and we could now firmly rely on hundreds of women who were ready and eager, not merely to walk in procession, but if need be to risk imprisonment for the Cause.

Parliament met on Tuesday the 12th, and we soon learnt that the King's speech had made no mention of Votes for Women. Therefore when the Women's Parliament met at three o'clock next day, it did so ready for decisive action. Mrs. Pankhurst was in the Chair, and throughout the proceedings there were manifestations of an enthusiasm such as the women of our time had before then never learnt to show. A Resolution expressive of indignation that Votes for Women had been omitted from the King's speech and calling upon the House of Commons to insist that precedence should be given to such a measure, was moved in stirring words and carried with every demonstration of fervent eagerness. A motion that the resolution should be taken to the Prime Minister by a deputation from the meeting was greeted with cheering and waving of handkerchiefs. Then the watchword, "Rise up women!" was sounded, and the answer came in a great unanimous shout, "Now," while hundreds of women volunteers ready for Parliament or Prison sprang to their feet.

Mrs. Despard was chosen to lead the deputation, and, as each woman marched out of the Caxton Hall, a copy of the Resolution for the Prime Minister was put into her hand. We formed up in orderly procession, and, amid the cheers of the thousands of men and women who had gathered in sympathy, and with police walking in front of us, we marched into Victoria Street and on towards the House of Commons.

It was cold but a shimmering dainty day, the sky a delicate rain-washed blue and the sunshine gleaming on the fine gilded points on the roof of the tall clock tower. We stepped out smartly and all seemed to be going well, but when those who were in front reached the green in front of the Abbey, a body of police barred their way and an Inspector called to them to turn back, and ordered his men to break up the procession. The police strode through and through our ranks, but the women at once united again and pressed bravely on. A little further we went thus, when suddenly, a body of mounted police came riding up. In an instant Mrs. Despard and several others in the front ranks were arrested, and the troopers were urging their horses into the midst of the women behind, scattering them right and left.

Still we strove to reach our destination, and returned again and again. Those of us who

rushed from the roadway on to the pavement were pressed by the horses closer and closer against the walls and railings until at last we retreated or were forced away by the constables on foot. Those of us who took refuge in doorways were dragged roughly down the steps and hurled back in front of the horses. When even this failed to banish us, the foot constables rushed at us and, catching us fiercely by the shoulders, turned us round again and then seizing us by the back of the neck and thumping us cruelly between the shoulders forced us at a running pace along the streets until we were far from the House of Commons. They had been told to drive us away and to make as few arrests as possible. Still we returned again, until at last sixty-five women and two men, all of them bruised and dishevelled, had been taken to the police station, and those who had not been arrested were almost fainting from fatigue. Then, after ten o'clock, the police succeeded in clearing the approaches to the House of Commons, and the mounted men were left galloping about in the empty square till midnight, when the House rose.

In spite of the fierce battle to keep them out, fifteen of the Suffragettes succeeded by strategy in making their way into the Strangers' Lobby of the House of Commons and at about six o'clock attempted to hold a meeting there. The police, of course, rushed to put them out and, in the confusion that ensued one of the women succeeded in getting past the barriers and making her way down the passage leading to the beautiful white inner lobby which opens into the sacred chamber of debate. She had just reached the first set of swing-doors when a Member of Parliament dashed up and slammed them against her with such force that she was thrown to the ground and carried out in a fainting condition.

Next morning all the world was talking of the mêlée, and in the newspapers there were long accounts and startling headlines describing the scenes that had taken place. These were very much more favourable to the women than any which had been published hitherto, for, though the Press was still far from admitting the extreme urgency of the cause of Women's Suffrage, or the need for the militant tactics as a means of obtaining the Parliamentary vote, still a large section of both Press and public were unanimous in condemning the Government for the violent measures which it had employed to suppress the women's deputation. Many compared the sending out of mounted police against a procession of unarmed women to the employment of Cossacks in Russia, and the Liberal *Daily Chronicle* published a cartoon called "The London Cossack" which showed a portly policeman riding off with a trophy of ladies' hats.

Very great precautions were taken to prevent the Suffragettes approaching Mr. Asquith when he visited Leeds to speak at the Coliseum on the afternoon of Saturday, October 10th. From 7 o'clock in the morning the police had been massed around the hall and cordons, both on foot and mounted men were drawn up outside the railway station and along the road by which the Prime Minister was to pass. But, in spite of all the force to guard him, as Mr. Asquith emerged, Mrs. Baines, a little fragile figure, with face ashen white and dark, blazing eyes, a creature compounded of zeal and passion, threw herself in front of him, crying, "Votes for Women, and down with tyranny!" and the crowd cheered her, though she was at once rudely hurled aside by the police. Then, followed by thousands of people, she made her way to Cockridge Street outside the Coliseum, where she had already announced that she would hold an open air meeting simultaneously with that of Mr. Asquith, inside. A great crowd had gathered there to hear her and when she put to them a resolution that she and her Suffragette comrades should go to the Coliseum to demand an interview with the Prime Minister, a forest of hands shot up in favour. Then declaring, "If these tyrants won't come to us, we must go to them and compel a hearing," she jumped down

from the carriage which had served her as a platform, and, followed by a number of other women and more slowly by the crowd itself, she moved on towards the Coliseum. Half way across the road the police barred the way and an inspector asked her where she was going. "Don't be foolish, Mrs. Baines," he said when she told him, but she was not to be deterred and, running round one of the mounted police, was arrested by a constable on foot. The other women still pressed forward and one by one five of them were arrested and taken to the Town Hall, where they were charged with disorderly conduct, whilst Mr. Asquith left the meeting by a back exit amid the hisses and groans of the crowd.

On Monday morning the others were each sent to prison for five days on refusing to be bound over to keep the peace, but the case against Mrs. Baines was held over until the following Wednesday. She was then charged with inciting to riot and unlawful assembly. Her case was to be held over until the Assizes, in November, and the opportunity of being tried by Judge and Jury which Mrs. Pankhurst, Christabel Pankhurst, and Mrs. Drummond had claimed in vain was thus to fall to her lot. The Grand Jury, having returned a True Bill against Mrs. Baines, Mr. Pethick Lawrence, who was defending her, served subpoenas to give evidence at the trial upon Mr. Asquith and Mr. Herbert Gladstone; but the Cabinet Ministers had no intention of allowing themselves to be examined by the Suffragettes and to be made into a Suffragette advertisement a second time. They applied to the Divisional Court for a Rule to set aside the subpoenas, and did not scruple to take advantage of their position as members of the Government to employ both the Attorney General, Sir William Robson, K.C., and the Solicitor General, Sir Samuel Evans, K. C., to plead their case in opposition to Mr. Pethick Lawrence. Though no precedent for setting aside a subpoena in criminal cases could be found, it was decided that neither Mr. Asquith nor Mr. Gladstone should be called upon to give evidence.

On Thursday and Friday, November 19th and 20th, the actual trial took place in the Leeds Town Hall. Mrs. Baines freely admitted that she had used the words, "if these tyrants will not come to us, we must go to them and compel a hearing," and that her intention had been to get into the meeting and secure an interview with the Prime Minister, but she protested that she had had no intention of injuring him or anyone and when Mr. Bairstow, K. C., the Counsel for the prosecution, asked if she had carried any weapons, she replied, "Oh, my tongue is weapon enough!" When asked to give an account of her life, she said that she was the daughter of a working man and had begun to help in earning the family living at eleven years of age. After her marriage she had continued to be a wage-earner, though she was the mother of five children, because her husband, who was a shoemaker, was only able to earn 25 shillings a week. Nevertheless she had done much public and social work as she had been a Salvation Army lieutenant, an evangelist to a working-men's mission, a member of the Stockport unemployed committee and committee for the feeding of school children, and a worker in the temperance cause. When asked to give some account of her speech to the crowd on the 10th of October, she said, "I wanted the men and women of Leeds to understand why we were there to protest against Mr. Asquith's refusal to give us the vote. I said that that afternoon Mr. Asquith would be dealing with the Licensing question; that this was more a woman's question than it was a man's, because we women suffered most through intemperance, and that no real temperance reform would ever be brought about until women had a voice in the matter. The unemployed question was also more a woman's question than it was a man's, because it was the women who really suffered most. Mr. Asquith had never known what it was, as I have done, to go without food or to go to school hungry. We wanted to see Mr. Asquith and we wanted to know when we were going to have access to Mr. Asquith."

After the evidence on both sides had been heard Mr. Lawrence made an eloquent speech for the defence, but it was nevertheless decided that Mrs. Baines was guilty of unlawful assembly. The Judge then asked her to enter into her own recognisances to be of good behaviour, explaining that if she agreed she would merely be promising not to use violence or to incite to violence in future. Mrs. Baines steadfastly maintained that she had had no intention of using violence, but felt that she could not conscientiously agree to be bound over to keep the peace. Mr. Justice Pickford then said that though he was reluctant to do so, he must pass sentence upon her and ordered that she should be imprisoned for six weeks in the Second Division. In the result, however, she was only kept in prison for three weeks because, though she had gone free meanwhile, the fortnight during which she had awaited trial at the Assizes was counted as part of her sentence, and in addition she was entitled to one week's remission of sentence for good behaviour.

QUESTIONS

1. What sort of tactics did the suffragists use in their pursuit of the right to vote?

2. The suffragists organized themselves into a women's parliament. Why?

3. How were the suffragists treated when they marched on Parliament? Why did violence erupt?

4. What was the political world's general reaction to the suffragists' cause?

5. Pankhurst's memoir is obviously biased in favor of the suffragists. How might an opponent of women's suffrage have described some of the same events?

120.   BEATRICE WEBB

WOMEN AND THE FACTORY ACTS

(1896)

Beatrice Potter Webb (1858–1947) was the eighth daughter of a Gloucester businessman. She had little formal education and after an unsuccessful love affair moved to London, where she worked on a massive study of the London poor under the direction of her cousin, the social reformer Charles Booth. Her sympathy for the plight of the wretched Londoners and the condition of working people led to her initial political involvement. In 1892 she married Sidney Webb who shared her interests in politics and socialism. They were among the founders of the Fabian Socialists, a group that included George Bernard Shaw and H. G. Wells. The Fabians advocated gradual reform that would transform Britain into a socialist democracy. The Webbs were early members of the Labor Party. Among their more lasting achievements was the establishment of the London School of Economics.

Beatrice Webb was consistently interested in the plight of workers. In *Women and the Factory Acts* she turned her attention to the conditions peculiar to women in the work force. This was published as an official Fabian Socialist tract, number 67 in the series.

The discussions on the Factory Act of 1895 raised once more all the old arguments about Factory legislation, but with a significant new cleavage. This time legal regulation was demanded, not only by all the organizations of working women whose labor was affected, but also by, practically, all those actively engaged in Factory Act administration. The four women Factory Inspectors unanimously confirmed the opinion of their male colleagues. Of all the classes having any practical experience of Factory legislation, only one—that of the employers—was ranged against the Bill, and that not unanimously. But the employers had the powerful aid of most of the able and devoted ladies who have usually led the cause of women's enfranchisement, and whose strong theoretic objection to Factory legislation caused many of the most important clauses in the Bill to be rejected.

Now those who object to further Factory legislation are right in asserting that the issue cannot be decided by harrowing accounts of factory tyranny, or particular cases of cruelty or hardship. I shall not trouble you with the long list of calamities in the unregulated trades, on which the official report of the Chief Inspector of Factories lays so much stress—the constitutions ruined by long hours in dressmakers' workrooms or insanitary laundries, the undermining of family life by the degradation of the home into a workshop, the diseases and deaths caused by white lead and lucifer matches. And, I hope, no one in the discussion will think it any argument against Factory Acts that some poor widow might find it more difficult to get bread for her starving children if she were forbidden to work at the white lead factory; that some sick man's daughter would not be allowed to earn the doctor's fee by taking extra work home after her factory day; or that some struggling laundress might find it impossible to make a living if she could not employ her girls for unlimited hours. Either way there must be hard cases, and individual grievances. The question is whether, taking the whole population and all considerations into account, the evils will be greater under regulation or under free competition.

The student of past Factory agitations sees the same old bogeys come up again and again. Among these bogeys the commonest and most obstructive has always been that of foreign competition, that is to say, the risk that the regulated workers will be supplanted by "free labor"— whether of other countries or of other classes at home. At every step forward in legal regulation the miner and the textile worker have been solemnly warned that the result of any raising of their standard of sanitation, safety, education or leisure would be the transference of British capital to China or Peru. And to my mind it is only another form of the same fallacy when capitalists' wives and daughters seek to alarm working women by prophesying, as the result of further Factory legislation, the dismissal of women and girls from employment, and their replacement by men. The opposition to Factory legislation never comes from workers who have any practical experience of it. Every existing organization of working women in the kingdom has declared itself in favor of Factory legislation. Unfortunately, working women have less power to obtain legislation than middle-class women have to obstruct it. Unfortunately, too, not a few middle-class women have allowed their democratic sympathies and Collectivist principles to be overborne by this fear of handicapping women in their struggle for employment. Let us, therefore, consider, as seriously as we can, this terror lest the capitalist employing women and girls at from five to twelve shillings a week, should, on the passage of a new Factory Act, replace them by men at twenty or thirty shillings.

First let us realize the exact amount of the inequality between the sexes in our Factory Acts. All the regulations with respect to safety, sanitation, employers' liability, and age apply to men and women alike. The only restriction of any importance in our Labor Code which bears unequally on men and women is that relating to the hours of labor. Up to now there has been sufficient influence among the employers, and sufficient prejudice and misunderstanding among legislators, to prevent them expressly legislating, in so many words, about the hours of labor of adult men. That better counsels are now prevailing is shown by the fact that Parliament in 1892 gave power to the Board of Trade to prevent excessive hours of work among railway servants, and that the Home Secretary has now a similar power in respect of any kind of manual labor which is injurious to health or dangerous to life and limb. I need hardly say that I am heartily in favor of regulating, by law, the hours of adult men, wherever and whenever possible. But although the prejudice is breaking down, it is not likely that the men in the great staple industries will be able to secure for themselves the same legal limitation of hours and prohibition of overtime that the women in the textile manufactures have enjoyed for nearly forty years. And thus it comes about that some of the most practical proposals for raising the condition of the women in the sweated trades must take the form of regulations applying to women only.

It is frequently asserted as self-evident that any special limitation of women's labor must militate against their employment. If employers are not allowed to make their women work overtime, or during the night, they will, it is said, inevitably prefer to have men. Thus, it is urged, any extension of Factory legislation to trades at present unregulated must diminish the demand for women's labor. But this conclusion, which seems so obvious, really rests on a series of assumptions which are not borne out by facts.

The first assumption is, that in British industry to-day, men and women are actively competing for the same employment. I doubt whether any one here has any conception of the infinitesimal extent to which this is true. We are so accustomed, in the middle-class, to see men and women engaged in identical work, as teachers, journalists, authors, painters, sculptors, comedians, singers, musicians, medical practitioners, clerks, or what not, that we almost inevitably assume the same state of things to exist in manual labor and manufacturing industry. But this is very far from being the case. To begin with, in over nine-tenths of the industrial field there is no such thing as competition between men and women: the men do one thing, and the women do another. There is no more chance of our having our houses built by women than of our getting our floors scrubbed by men. And even in those industries which employ both men and women, we find them sharply divided in different departments, working at different processes, and performing different operations. In the tailoring trade, for instance, it is often assumed that men and women are competitors. But in a

detailed investigation of that trade I discovered that men were working at entirely separate branches to those pursued by the women. And when my husband, as an economist, lately tried to demonstrate the oft-repeated statement that women are paid at a lower rate than men, he found it very difficult to discover any trade whatever in which men and women did the same work. As a matter of fact, the employment of men or women in any particular industry is almost always determined by the character of the process. In many cases the physical strength or endurance required, or the exposure involved, puts the work absolutely out of the power of the average woman. No law has hindered employers from engaging women as blacksmiths, steel-smelters, masons, or omnibus-drivers. The great mass of extractive, constructive, and transport industries must always fall to men. On the other hand, the women of the wage-earning class have hitherto been distinguished by certain qualities not possessed by the average working man. For good or for evil they eat little, despise tobacco, and seldom get drunk; they rarely strike or disobey orders; and they are in many other ways easier for an employer to deal with. Hence, where women can really perform a given task with anything like the efficiency of a man, they have, owing to their lower standard of expenditure, a far better chance than the man of getting work. The men, in short, enjoy what may be called a "rent" of superior strength and endurance; the women, on their side, in this preference for certain employments, what may be called a "rent" of abstemiousness.

I do not wish to imply that there are absolutely no cases in British industry in which men and women are really competing with each other. It is, I believe, easy to pick out an instance here and there in which it might be prophesied that the removal of an existing legal restriction might, in the first instance, lead to some women being taken on in place of men. In the book and printing trade of London, for instance, it has been said that if women were allowed by law to work all through the night, a certain number of exceptionally strong women might oust some men in book-folding and even in compositors' work. We must not overlook these cases; but we must learn to view them in their proper proportion to the whole field of industry. It would clearly be a calamity to the cause of women's advancement if we were to sacrifice the personal liberty and economic independence of three or four millions of wage-earning women in order to enable a few hundreds or a few thousands to supplant men in certain minor spheres of industry.

The second assumption is, that in the few cases in which men and women may be supposed really to compete with each other for employment, the effect of any regulation of women's hours is pure loss to them, and wholly in favor of their assumed competitors who are unrestricted. This, I believe, is simply a delusion. Any investigator of women's work knows full well that what most handicaps women is their general deficiency in industrial capacity and technical skill. Where the average woman fails is in being too much of an amateur at her work, and too little of a professional. Doubtless it may be said that the men are to blame here: it is they who induce women to marry, and thus divert their attention from professional life. But though we cannot cut at the root of this, by insisting, as I once heard it gravely suggested, on "three generations of unmarried women," we can do a great deal to encourage the growth of professional spirit and professional capacity among women workers, if we take care to develop our industrial organization along the proper lines. The first necessity is the exclusion of illegitimate competitors. The real enemies of the working woman are not the men, who always insist on higher wages, but the "amateurs" of her own sex. So long as there are women, married or unmarried, eager and able to take work home, and do it in the intervals of another profession, domestic service, we shall

never disentangle ourselves from that vicious circle in which low wages lead to bad work, and bad work compels low wages. The one practical remedy for this disastrous competition is the extension of Factory legislation, with its strict limitation of women's hours, to all manufacturing work wherever carried on. It is no mere coincidence that the only great industry in which women get the same wages as men— Lancashire cotton weaving—is the one in which precise legal regulation of women's hours has involved the absolute exclusion of the casual amateur. No woman will be taken on at a cotton mill unless she is prepared to work the full factory hours, to come regularly every day, and put her whole energy into her task. In a Lancashire village a woman must decide whether she will earn her maintenance by working in the mill or by tending the home: there is no "betwixt and between." The result is a class of women wage-earners who are capable of working side by side with men at identical tasks; who can earn as high wages as their male competitors; who display the same economic independence and professional spirit as the men; and who are, in fact, in technical skill and industrial capacity, far in advance of any other class of women workers in the kingdom. If we want to bring the women wage-earners all over England up to the level of the Lancashire cotton weavers, we must subject them to the same conditions of exclusively professional work.

There is another way in which the extension of the Factory Acts to the unregulated trades is certain to advance women's industrial position. We have said that the choice of men or women as workers is really determined by the nature of the industrial process. Now these processes are constantly changing; new inventions bring in new methods of work, and often new kinds of machinery. This usually means an entire revolution in the character of the labor required. What to-day needs the physical strength or the life-long apprenticeship of the skilled handicraftsman may, tomorrow, by a new machine, or the use of motive power, be suddenly brought within the capacity of the nimble fingers of a girl from the Board School. It is in this substitution of one process for another that we discover the real competition between different classes or different sexes in industry.

Now this evolution of industry leads inevitably to an increased demand for women's labor. Immediately we substitute the factory, with its use of steam power, and production on a large scale, for the sweater's den or the domestic workshop, we get that division of labor and application of machinery which is directly favorable to the employment of women. It is to "the factory system, and the consequent growth of the ready-made trade," declares Miss Collet, that must "be traced the great increase in the number of girls employed in the tailoring trade." The same change is going on in other occupations. Miss Collet notices that the employment of female labor has specially increased in the great industry of boot and shoemaking. But, as in the analogous case of the tailoring trade, the increase has not been in the number of the unregulated women workers in the sweaters' dens. Formerly we had a man working in his own room, and employing his wife and daughter to help him at all hours. Some people might have argued that anything which struck at the root of this system would deprive women of employment. As a matter of fact, the result has been, by division of labor in the rapidly growing great boot factories, to substitute for these few hundreds of unpaid assistants, many thousands of independent and regularly employed women operatives. For we must remember that when these changes take place, they take place on a large scale. Whilst the Society for Promoting the Employment of Women is proud to secure new openings for a few scores or a few hundreds, the industrial evolution which I have described has been silently absorbing, in one trade or another, hundreds of thousands of women of all classes. It is therefore infinitely more important for the friends of women's employment to enquire how

an extension of the Factory Acts would influence our progress towards the factory system, than how it would affect, say, the few hundred women who might be engaged in night-work book-folding.

We can now sum up the whole argument. The case for Factory legislation does not rest on harrowing tales of exceptional tyranny, though plenty of these can be furnished in support of it. It is based on the broad facts of the capitalist system, and the inevitable results of the Industrial Revolution. A whole century of experience proves that where the conditions of the wage-earner's life are left to be settled by "free competition" and individual bargaining between master and man, the worker's "freedom" is delusive. Where he bargains, he bargains at a serious disadvantage, and on many of the points most vital to himself and to the community he cannot bargain at all. The common middle-class objection to Factory legislation—that it interferes with the individual liberty of the operative—springs from ignorance of the economic position of the wage-earner. Far from diminishing personal freedom, Factory legislation positively increases the individual liberty and economic independence of the workers subject to it. No one who knows what life is among the people in Lancashire textile villages on the one hand, and among the East End or Black Country unregulated trades on the other, can ever doubt this.

All these general considerations apply more forcibly to women wage-earners than to men. Women are far more helpless in the labor market, and much less able to enforce their own common rule by Trade Unionism. The only chance of getting Trade Unions among women workers lies through the Factory Acts. We have before us nearly forty years' actual experience of the precise limitation of hours and the absolute prohibition of overtime for women workers in the cotton manufacture; and they teach us nothing that justifies us in refusing to extend the like protection to the women slaving for irregular and excessive hours in laundries, dressmakers' workrooms, and all the thousand and one trades in which women's hours of work are practically unlimited.

Finally, we have seen that the fear of women's exclusion from industrial employment is wholly unfounded. The uniform effect of Factory legislation in the past has been, by encouraging machinery, division of labor, and production on a large scale, to increase the employment of women, and largely to raise their status in the labor market. At this very moment the neglect to apply the Factory Acts effectively to the domestic workshop is positively restricting the demand for women workers in the clothing trades. And what is even more important, we see that it is only by strict regulation of the conditions of women's employment that we can hope for any general rise in the level of their industrial efficiency. The real enemy of the woman worker is not the skilled male operative, but the unskilled and half-hearted female "amateur" who simultaneously blacklegs both the workshop and the home. The legal regulation of women's labor is required to protect the independent professional woman worker against these enemies of her own sex. Without this regulation it is futile to talk to her of the equality of men and women. With this regulation, experience teaches us that women can work their way in certain occupations to a man's skill, a man's wages, and a man's sense of personal dignity and independence.

QUESTIONS

1. Webb notes that one of the groups that opposed further regulation of women's work was the suffragists. Why did they oppose this type of reform?

2. Opponents of regulation maintained that reform would reduce the number of women workers. How does Webb answer this argument?

3. Why do women not compete well with men in the labor market? What must they do to succeed?

4. Why have the Factory Acts been good for female workers? What was the argument against them?

5. How does Webb's socialism affect her arguments about the needs and status of women?

Thoughts on Empire

IMPERIALISM

(1902)

John A. Hobson (1858–1940) was the son of a prosperous English newspaper owner. He inherited his father's liberalism as well as his considerable fortune. Hobson graduated from Oxford University and began a career in politics and journalism. His chief interests were economic and social reform. He became an important figure in the progressive circles that were making themselves felt in early twentieth-century politics. He opposed the erosion of civil liberties brought on by the First World War; after the war he joined the Labour Party, where he remained an influential figure, especially active in the creation of the League of Nations.

Imperialism was one of Hobson's most important works and one that has become a benchmark of the subject. The author had observed the British imperial system firsthand in South Africa and had fought against it from the beginning. He was one of the first to link imperialism's social and economic effects with its cultural effects and to argue the case that imperialism corrupted both rulers and ruled.

I

If Imperialism may no longer be regarded as a blind inevitable destiny, is it certain that imperial expansion as a deliberately chosen line of public policy can be stopped?

We have seen that it is motived, not by the interests of the nation as a whole, but by those of certain classes, who impose the policy upon the nation for their own advantage. The amalgam of economic and political forces which exercises this pressure has been submitted to close analysis. But will the detection of this confederacy of vicious forces destroy or any wise abate their operative power? For this power is a natural outcome of an unsound theory in our foreign policy. Put into plain language, the theory is this, that any British subject choosing, for his own private pleasure or profit, to venture his person or his property in the territory of a foreign State can call upon this nation to protect or avenge him in case he or his property is injured either by the Government or by any inhabitant of this foreign State. Now this is a perilous doctrine. It places the entire military, political, and financial resources of this nation at the beck and call of any missionary society which considers it has a peculiar duty to attack the religious sentiments or observances of some savage people, or of some reckless explorer who choose just those spots of earth known to be inhabited by hostile peoples ignorant of British power; the speculative trader or the mining prospector gravitates naturally towards dangerous and unexplored countries, where the gains of a successful venture will be quick and large. All these men, missionaries, travellers, sportsmen, scientists, traders, in no proper sense the accredited representatives of this country, but actuated by private personal motives, are at Liberty to call upon the British nation to spend millions of money and thousands of lives to defend them against risks which the nation has not sanctioned. It is only right to add that unscrupulous statesmen have deliberately utilised these insidious methods of encroachment, seizing upon every alleged outrage inflicted on these private adventurers or marauders as a pretext for a punitive expedition which results in the British flag waving over some new tract of territory. Thus the most reckless and irresponsible individual members of our nation are permitted to direct our foreign policy. Now that we have some four hundred million British subjects, any one of whom in theory or in practice may call upon the British arms to extricate him from the results of this private folly, the prospects of a genuine *pax Britannica* are not particularly bright.

But those sporadic risks, grave though they have sometimes proved, are insignificant when compared with the dangers associated with modern methods of international capitalism and finance. It is not long since industry was virtually restricted by political boundaries, the economic intercourse of nations being almost wholly confined to commercial exchanges of goods. The recent habit of investing capital in a foreign country has now grown to such an extent that the well-to-do and politically powerful classes in Great Britain to-day derive a large and ever larger proportion of their incomes from capital invested outside the British Empire. This growing stake of our wealthy classes' in countries over which they have no political control is a revolutionary force in modern politics; it means a constantly growing tendency to use their political power as citizens of this State to interfere with the political condition of those States where they have an industrial stake.

II

Analysis of Imperialism, with its natural supports, militarism, oligarchy, bureaucracy, protection, concentration of capital and violent trade fluctuations, has marked it out as the supreme danger of modern national States. The power of the imperialist forces within the nation to use the national resources for their private gain, by operating the instrument of the State, can only be overthrown by the establishment of a genuine democracy, the direction of public policy by the people for the people through representatives over whom they exercise a real control. Whether this or any other nation is yet competent for such a democracy may well be a matter of grave doubt, but until and unless the external policy of a nation is "broad-based upon a people's will" there appears little hope of remedy. The scare of a great recent war may for a brief time check the confidence of these conspirators against the commonwealth, and cause them to hold their hands, but the financial forces freshly generated will demand new outlets, and will utilise the same political alliances and the same social, religious, and philanthropic supports in their pressure for new enterprises. The circumstances of each new imperialist exploit differ from those of all preceding ones: whatever ingenuity is requisite for the perversion of the public intelligence, or the inflammation of the public sentiment, will be forthcoming.

The chief economic source of Imperialism has been found in the inequality of industrial opportunities by which a favoured class accumulates superfluous elements of income which, in their search for profitable investments press ever farther afield: the influence on State policy of these investors and their financial managers secures a national alliance of other vested interests which are threatened by movements of social reform: the adoption of Imperialism thus serves the double purpose of securing private material benefits for favoured classes of investors and traders at the public cost, while sustaining the general cause of conservatism by diverting public energy and interest from domestic agitation to external employment.

To term Imperialism a national policy is an impudent falsehood: the interests of the nation are opposed to every act of this expansive policy. Every enlargement of Great Britain in the tropics is a distinct enfeeblement of true British nationalism. Indeed, Imperialism is commended in some quarters for this very reason, that by breaking the narrow bounds of nationalities it facilitates and forwards internationalism. There are even those who favour or condone the forcible suppression of small nationalities by larger ones under the impulse of Imperialism, because they imagine that this is the natural approach to a world-federation and eternal peace. A falser view of political evolution it is difficult to conceive.

The claim that an imperial State forcibly subjugating other peoples and their lands does so for the purpose of rendering services to the conquered equal to those which she exacts is notoriously false: she neither intends equivalent services nor is capable of rendering them, and the pretence that such benefits to the governed form a leading motive or result of Inperialism implies a degree of moral or intellectual obliquity so grave as itself to form a new peril for any nation fostering so false a notion of the nature of its conduct. "Let the motive be in the deed, not in the event," says a Persian proverb.

Imperialism is a depraved choice of national life, imposed by self-seeking interests which appeal to the lusts of quantitative acquisitiveness and of forceful domination surviving in a nation from early centuries of animal struggle for existence. Its adoption as a policy implies a deliberate renunciation of that cultivation of the higher inner qualities which for a nation as for an individual constitutes the ascendency of reason over brute impulse. It is the besetting sin of all successful States, and its penalty is unalterable in the order of nature.

QUESTIONS

1. What, according to Hobson, is the main thrust of British foreign policy? What is wrong with that policy?

2. Why is imperialism dangerous?

3. Who benefits most from imperialism, according to Hobson?

4. Some imperialists claimed that expansion was in the interests of colonial subjects as well as the mother country. How does Hobson respond to this argument?

5. How might a dedicated imperialist answer Hobson's criticisms?

122.   CECIL RHODES

CONFESSION OF FAITH

(1877)

Cecil Rhodes (1853–1902) was one of the greatest of all the European empire builders. He left his mark on the continent of Africa with the De Beers diamond mines and founded the white-dominated state of Rhodesia (now Zimbabwe). Rhodes was a sickly child who went to South Africa in hope of improving his health. Once there, he became caught up in diamond fever. He began by forming partnerships and staking claims. By 1891 he owned 90 percent of all the diamond-producing mines in South Africa. His investments in gold mines were equally lucrative, and he became one of the richest men in the world. Rhodes was heavily involved in British political policy in South Africa and was forced to resign his offices after the abortive Jameson Raid. He died in 1902, leaving most of his fortune to philanthropic projects, including the establishment of the Rhodes scholarships that send American and German students to England.

Rhodes's *Confession of Faith* is in the form of a final testament. It expounds his views on racial supremacy, religion, and imperialism.

It often strikes a man to inquire what is the chief good in life; to one the thought comes that it is a happy marriage, to another great wealth, and as each seizes on his idea, for that he more or less works for the rest of his existence. To myself thinking over the same question the wish came to render myself useful to my country. I then asked myself how could I and after reviewing the various methods I have felt that at the present day we are actually limiting our children and perhaps bringing into the world half the human beings we might owing to the lack of country for them to inhabit that if we had retained America there would at this moment be millions more of English living. I contend that we are the finest race in the world and that the more of the world we inhabit the better it is for the human race. Just fancy those parts that are at present inhabited by the most despicable specimens of human beings what an alteration there would be if they were brought under Anglo-Saxon influence, look again at the extra employment a new country added to our

dominions gives. I contend that every acre added to our territory means in the future birth to some more of the English race who otherwise would not be brought into existence. Added to this the absorption of the greater portion of the world under our rule simply means the end of all wars, at this moment had we not lost America I believe we could have stopped the Russian-Turkish war by merely refusing money and supplies. Having these ideas what scheme could we think of to forward this object. I look into history and I read the story of the Jesuits I see what they were able to do in a bad cause and I might say under bad leaders.

The idea gleaming and dancing before one's eyes like a will-of-the-wisp at last frames itself into a plan. Why should we not form a secret society with but one object the furtherance of the British Empire and the bringing of the whole uncivilised world under British rule for the recovery of the United States for the making the Anglo-Saxon race but one Empire. What a dream, but yet it is probable, it is possible. I once heard it argued by a fellow in my own college, I am sorry to own it by an Englishman, that it was a good thing for us that we have lost the United States. There are some subjects on which there can be no arguments, and to an Englishman this is one of them, but even from an American's point of view just picture what they have lost, look at their government, are not the frauds that yearly come before the public view a disgrace to any country and especially theirs which is the finest in the world. Would they have occurred had they remained under English rule great as they have become how infinitely greater they would have been with the softening and elevating influences of English rule, think of those countless 1000's of Englishmen that during the last 100 years would have crossed the Atlantic and settled and populated the United States. Would they have not made without any prejudice a finer country of it than the low class Irish and German emigrants? All this we have lost and that country loses owing to whom? Owing to two or three ignorant pigheaded statesmen of the last century, at their door lies the blame. Do you ever feel mad? Do you ever feel murderous. I think I do with those men. I bring facts to prove my assertion. Does an English father when his sons wish to emigrate ever think of suggesting emigration to a country under another flag, never—it would seem a disgrace to suggest such a thing I think that we all think that poverty is better under our own flag than wealth under a foreign one.

Put your mind into another train of thought. Fancy Australia discovered and colonised under the French flag, what would it mean merely several millions of English unborn that at present exist we learn from the past and to form our future. We learn from having lost to cling to what we possess. We know the size of the world we know the total extent. Africa is still lying ready for us it is our duty to take it. It is our duty to seize every opportunity of acquiring more territory and we should keep this one idea steadily before our eyes that more territory simply means more of the Anglo-Saxon race more of the best the most human, most honourable race the world possesses.

To forward such a scheme what a splendid help a secret society would be a society not openly acknowledged but who would work in secret for such an object.

I contend that there are at the present moment numbers of the ablest men in the world who would devote their whole lives to it. I often think what a loss to the English nation in some respects the abolition of the Rotten Borough System has been. What thought strikes a man entering the House of Commons, the assembly that rules the whole world? I think it is the mediocrity of the men but what is the cause. It is simply—an assembly of wealth of men whose lives have been spent in the accumulation of money and whose time has been too much engaged to be able to spare any for the study of past history. And yet in the hands of such men rest our destinies. Do men like the great Pitt, and Burke and Sheridan not now exist[?] I contend they do. There are men now living [who] live and die unused, unemployed. What has been the main cause of the success of the Romish Church? The fact that every enthusiast, call it if you like every madman finds employment in it. Let us form the same kind of society a Church for the extension of the British Empire. A society which should have its members in every part of the British Empire working with one object and one idea we should have its members placed at our universities and our schools and should watch the English youth passing through their hands just one perhaps in every thousand would have the mind and feelings for such an object, he should be tried in every way, he should be tested whether he is endurant, possessed of eloquence, disregardful of the petty details of life, and if found to be such, then elected and bound by oath to serve for the rest of his life in his Country. He should then be supported if without means by the Society and sent to that part of the Empire where it was felt he was needed.

Take another case, let us fancy a man who finds himself his own master with ample means on attaining his majority whether he puts the question directly to himself or not, still like the old story of virtue and vice in the Memorabilia a fight goes on in him as to what he should do. Take if he plunges into dissipation there is nothing too reckless he does not attempt but after a time his life palls on him, he mentally says this is not good enough, he changes his life, he reforms, he travels, he thinks now I have found the chief good in life, the novelty wears off, and he tires, to change again, he goes into the far interior after the wild game he thinks at last I've found that in life of which I cannot tire, again he is disappointed. He returns he thinks is there nothing I can do in life? Here I am with means, with a good house, with everything that is to be envied and yet I am not happy I am tired of life[;] to such a man the Society should go, should test, and should finally show him the greatness of the scheme and list him as a member.

Take one more case of the younger son with high thoughts, high aspirations, endowed by nature with all the faculties to make a great man, and with the sole wish in life to serve his Country but he lacks two things the means and the opportunity, ever troubled by a sort of inward deity urging him on to high and noble deeds, he is compelled to pass his time in some occupation which furnishes him with mere existence, he lives unhappily and dies miserably. Such men as these the Society should search out and use for the furtherance of their object.

In every Colonial legislature the Society should attempt to have its members prepared at all times to vote or speak and advocate the closer union of England and the colonies, to crush all disloyalty and every movement for the severance of our Empire. The Society should inspire and even own portions of the press for the press rules the mind of the people. The Society should always be searching for members who might by their position in the world by their energies or character forward the object but the ballot and test for admittance should be severe.

Once make it common and it fails. Take a man of great wealth who is bereft of his children perhaps having his mind soured by some bitter disappointment who shuts himself up separate from his neighbours and makes up his mind to a miserable existence. To such men as these the Society should go gradually disclose the greatness of their scheme and entreat him to throw in his life and property with them for this object. I think that there are thousands now existing who would eagerly grasp at the opportunity. Such are the heads of my scheme.

For fear that death might cut me off before the time for attempting its development I leave all my worldly goods in trust to S. G. Shippard and the Secretary for the Colonies at the time of my death to try to form such a Society with such an object.

QUESTIONS

1. What was the goal of Rhodes's life, according to his testament?

2. What reasons does Rhodes give for supporting imperial expansion?

3. How does Rhodes propose to advance Anglo-Saxon world domination?

4. What role would the native peoples in new colonies play once Anglo-Saxon rule was established?

5. The confession was written for posterity and was not published until after Rhodes's death. What sort of impression do you think Rhodes wanted to create with this document?

123.   CARL VELTIN

SOCIAL LIFE OF THE SWAHILIS
(late 19th century)

Carl Veltin was a German professor of African and Oriental languages who spent a number of years as the official interpreter for the governor of the German East African territories. He worked among the Swahilis, mostly Bantu tribesmen who lived in Mrima, the coast opposite Zanzibar. Veltin was interested in Swahili customs and folklore and appears to have interviewed village elders and recorded their responses. He also made transcripts of accounts of Swahili travelers, including an unusual diary of an ivory trader. When he returned to Berlin in 1896 he translated and published his notes. He published his accounts in the original Swahili so that his own (and subsequent) translations would not distort the experiences he tried to record.

The selections printed here are related to Swahili customs regarding the raising of children until marriage. They provide an intimate glimpse into the lives of ordinary Africans and demonstrate the importance of ceremony and ritual in a predominantly oral culture.

A child (baby) is fed on millet, and the millet is pounded into a flour and ladled into earthen pitchers to keep it from dust and sand. Each morning they draw out enough for the child's food, and it is cooked with sugar and the child is fed. As to the feeding, they put some gruel in a small cooking-pot and it is cooled off and then put on a small plate. Holding the child, the mother puts some gruel on the palm of her hand and feeds the child with her finger and the child swallows (the gruel). When it has eaten she gives it some water or suckles it. Then the child goes to sleep.

When he wakes up, the child has his face washed and antimony is applied to his face. Then *muru* medicine is ground and the child is given the *muru* water to drink by another person, and they anoint the child's whole body with it, for this is children's medicine for intestinal worms. And when he sleeps a knife is placed under his pillow and his feet are wrapped in asafoetida for fear of being possessed by a great bird. In a house where there is a small child a crab is hung up in the roof on the wood in the middle of the ridge pole for fear of evil diseases. . . .

And the person who comes with the medicine for convulsions agrees to place the child under a charm, that is he fastens medicine (a charm) on the child in case the child 'be broken in body' because of the people who commit adultery and the people who look at the child with 'the evil eye'. He brings *jimbo* medicine and it is placed on a large cooking-pot, and the water from it is used for washing the child morning and evening. Unless they do this, the adulterers will get hold of him, and he will have rickets

When the child is about to grow teeth *fungo* medicine is made for him, this is to make the teeth firm so that they do not grow badly, in case the upper teeth come first. The old men and women make this medicine; they dig up the tubers of the nut-grass weed, and a charm is prepared for wearing round the (child's) neck until the teeth are grown.

If the teeth are slow in growing the child is treated by medicine-men; he is given *jimbo* medicines for bathing and anointing. Also *hoza* medicine is gathered; these are certain leaves from the forest, and the child is anointed. After a few days the teeth appear.

If the child grows his upper teeth (first), in the old days they would not bring the child up, and even now some people do not like to do so. Others say, 'I can't throw away my own blood, I will bring it up.' And some nurture the child, but have no joy in it. A child like this is called *kibi*, but afterwards he is given a name just like other children. Some people are afraid to give their hand to a child like this, because they fear death or illness (as a consequence). A child born with feet first is also called *kibi*. They do not bring him up, they will kill him or they will take him to the mosque and leave him inside. At day-break when the people who come to pray find him they know that this child was badly born. It may happen that someone will take him and bring him up, he will make him his son; the reason for refusing to nurture him is that they fear death. This custom amongst the Swahilis is held also among the Zaramu.

In Mrima country there are children who turn out very white, but their parents are black. They believe that such a child has been exchanged for a child of an evil spirit. During the first seven days his mother went to the toilet at night, and left him by himself; she did not put a necklace or a knife under the pillow nor fasten asafoetida on the child's arm. The evil one saw the child by itself and exchanged him; leaving the child of an evil spirit, he took away the human being.

Or others say, 'When his mother was pregnant she was possessed by an evil spirit, and so she bore a white child.' This is why Swahilis, when there children are small, fasten asafoetida on their arms; asafoetida has a bad smell, and an evil spirit does not like it. And these albino children,

when Swahilis see them they are very startled and do not like them. Some want to kill them, but if they bring them up, when they are big, they (the albinos) do not shake hands with people, (it is) as if they had a skin disease or leprosy.

Up to the age of seven a girl is called *kigori*, and when she is fifteen she is called *mwari*. It is usual for these children to stay in the house. First their ears are pierced with thorns. And on the day of the piercing they rejoice with her just like at a wedding. The child is taught how to behave (lit. very good manners) at home; she washes the utensils, plates and bowls, and when she has finished she is given the beginning of a leaf-strip to plait. Each day her work is plaiting mats and being taught to cook. She is not allowed to go out, but at night she may go to visit people connected with her, but she does not go alone, she is chaperoned by a female slave or a woman elder. But if she is a gad-about, she is beaten by her parents, and she finds it difficult get a husband, for people say, 'So-and-So' girl is a gad-about, she knows every place.'

When she is in the house and a visitor comes to the door, male or female, and her parents do not know about it, she must hide in another room without conversing with the visitor. If her parents hear her conversing they go for her, saying to her, 'When you hear someone at the door, do you peep out so that everyone can see your face?' And if people hear that she does not hide her face, they speak against her in the village, 'So-and-So's girl, her face has dried her up, she is not modest, she is not a suitable person to be married; she may possibly get a husband, but it will take a long time.'

And when the girl is ten there comes a woman who is her confidential advisor, and she puts a string of beads around the girl's loins. This woman is her special friend for always. A woman who has no string of beads, people say of her that her loins are withered.

When they bring up a child, especially when he gets to the age of six or seven, they teach him good manners. And he must listen carefully to the commands of his parents. If they have refused him something, he must obey.

They teach him to greet people; especially if he sees an important person with his parents, he should greet him. He is taught to approach adults with respect and good manners. If he begs ha'pennies from every person passing, he is beaten. When a child is in the company of adults, he should not sit down before the adults are seated. If he is in company, it is not customary (for him) to say this or that. When a young person goes with an elder in public or to a feast, and he is sitting with them as they converse, it is his duty to be perfectly quiet, listening to whatever command they wish to give him. It is not good manners to laugh now with this person and then with that. Unless of course he is with friends of his own age, then he can converse and laugh and make as much noise as he likes.

When a child accompanies his father, it is not right for that child to lead the way, but the father should be in front. Or if he goes out with his teacher, likewise the teacher should go in front. Unless the child does this he has insulted his father and teacher, and he has abused his own reputation, for people will ask him, 'Did not your father teach you good manners, nor your teacher, that you should be so unmannerly?'

In the same way, it is not right for a child to point out people's failings, for example, 'So-and-So's wife does not cook properly', or, 'Today they have gone to bed hungry, they have no food, their house is dark, they have no lamp.' If a child says things like this, people know he has no manners. Then a child is often told by his parents, 'If ever you are told a secret, you must hide it, for it is not right to tell it to every Tom, Dick, and Harry.'

And when visitors are come to the house and they are eating together, a child is told not to wash his hands before the adults have done so. If there is no one in the house to serve at the meal, the child takes the water-jug and brings the people water to wash their hands. And when they are eating, it is not mannerly to take the meat all the time, but only when they give the child permission to eat the meat. When he is eat-

ing and takes a piece of meat with every ball of food, people look at him, and say afterwards, 'That child has no manners, another day, don't take him out in public, he brings shame.'

Every child must obey commands from three sources (lit. of three people) if he wants the blessing of God. First, the command of the ruler (lit. king), and secondly of his two parents, and thirdly of his teacher. Laws from these three he must closely obey. And if he scorns these commands, he has disobeyed the law of God.

A female child of seven years of seven years of age is called *kigori*, but when she is about thirteen years old people say, 'Such-and-such a *kigori* has become a *mwari*.' When her parents find out that she has begun her puberty, news is sent at once to her *kungwi*, and she comes to the girl's house to take her to her own home to be confined there. And the girl does not appear before strangers, but (is seen) only by her *kungwi* and her relatives; she stays at her *kungwi*'s house for six months or a whole year, but some (girls) stay only a month and then return to their parents.

And at her *kungwi*'s house she is taught to look after herself properly, and to live properly, respecting people; she is taught to cook and to plait mats and when she is married to live properly with her husband. Her *kungwi* gives her a *msio* stone; this is a coral stone from the top of a reef on the coast, (which) is dressed by an expert so that it becomes soft and round. A young girl receives this stone to grind mixtures like *tibu* perfume, *dalia* powder, *maua maulidi* scent, and every kind of perfume with which she massages herself. The same stone is used on her wedding day, and when it is taken to the wedding, or when a woman goes to her friend to borrow it, the stone is not carried unless it is covered, it is covered with a cloth for people not to see it; but when it is kept in the house after being used it is not covered, everybody can see it.

When the time for staying at the *kungwi*'s is over, the *kungwi* tells her parents, 'We want to take the girl to the *muyombo* tree.' Her elders brew fermented and unfermented beer. At the *muyombo* tree many women gather together, and other young girls are there (lit. come). Sometimes they go into a house if it is big enough there in the country (i.e. away from the town), at other times they build a hut. And these girls are taken by night so that people should not see them; they are also carried pick-a-back by the women. The *kungwi* has her former clients, perhaps six or seven of them; she invites them, saying, 'Tomorrow we are going to the *muyombo* tree, so come along and carry your friend.' And they are obliged to go (lit. come), because a girl does not neglect (lit. leave) the bidding of her *kungwi;* she obeys the bidding of her *kungwi* more than that of her mother.

After they have taken the girl to the lodge, a dance takes place call *unyago*. And at the *unyago* dance the drums are played, and some women dance to show the girls, so that the girls may dance just as the gown-ups do, for unless they know how to do it they must be taught. And they sing initiation-songs. Something is put down behind the girl's back, and she takes it up by her mouth bending backwards and moving her hips, while a drum is beaten and a song is sung.

If the *makungwi* have sung and the girl is unable to recognize the meaning of such-and-such a song, or if she is given instructions without being able to comprehend it, she is beaten, (but) also she is told the meaning of it. If she knows the instruction, all the women say with a loud voice, '*Chiriku, chiriku,'* and this means, 'Oh my child, my beautiful child.'

On the seventh day the girls are taken to the *muyombo* tree. All the *makungwi* and the girls stay beating the drums and dancing, and if there is beer they drink it. In the evening the girls have their hair shaved, some of them have a tuft (left) on the crown, they have their eyes blackened, and on their heads they apply *dalia* powder, because of being shaven. Then they are dressed in new clothes and decked with silver orna- ments. In the evening they are brought to the

village; there is no singing as they are brought. The free-born children are given a present at home by their relatives, they bring them all sorts of things there. Some give them mats, others bracelets, others again rings, and some give them money, And the slave-girls are paraded round the villages, and they are dressed up just like the free-born girls; they are led around by their *makungwi*. If they see a man they know, they give him their hand, and he puts out money to give them a present; and if they see a woman they know the fall down at her feet, that is the proper greeting, and the woman produces something to give them. And they are not allowed to speak with anyone except the persons who has given a present. They are paraded for three days. The fine dress is taken off and they get everyday clothes.

When a man wants to marry first he makes a proposal of marriage, and for his proposal he sends someone, a relative of the bride-to-be (lit. that woman), to take a message to the girl's father, and the one who is sent is called a go-between or an ambassador. Some send the go-between to speak with the girl's father, and others write a letter. When they have agreed, the suitor and the go-between, the go-between replies, 'Give mea kerchief and I will wporite a letter.' So the suitor gives a kerchief, and the go-between writes a letter like this:

> My ancient one So-and-So son of So-and-So, I inform you that So-and-So's son has come and he wants to marry your daughter, and these are happy matters. A daughter (is) a perishable commodity (lit. rotten goods) like gunpowder and fire, or like cotton and fire, or like an onion. Please if you read this letter, I want a reply, and excuse me. Greetings, &c.

When the letter is finished the kerchief is its envelope, for that is great respect. When the girl's father has read the letter he will call his rel- atives, men and women, to advise them. Some will accept, others will refuse. Those who refuse want to be given a little something by the suitor, and he will produce something to give to the contentious ones. Then they will say, 'The matter is settled, this is indeed the man.'

The go between will inform the suitor that his (future) in-laws are all content, and the suitor will buy every (kind of) gift to send to his sweetheart, like a nice cloth or nice just-ripe fruits, but they do not meet, from the day when money is sent to the wedding-day, whether it be a period of a month or a year.

The go-between will go back again to the in-laws and ask the father, 'How much will your marriage payments be?' The girl's father will reply, 'My *kilemba* will be so much and the dowry so much.' The go-between goes back, he gives the suitor the information from the in-laws, and if he accepts and has the money, at once he counts out the marriage payment to give it to the go-between to take to his in-law. If the in-law has died, his brother or his elder (the girl's grandparent) receives it, and if these are not (alive) they look for people in the family (lit. house), connected with the girl, but one who is a man. If there is no one at all, the woman herself receives it.

When the father has received the money he calls his relatives to show them the money, and they divide it between them. The mother gets her *uweleko* and her *kondawi*. If there is an aunt, she receives a little, and if there is a grandmother, she gets a little. Every person amongst the relations get a little, because this is respect. All the money that is left the father takes. And this money is called 'the door shutter' or 'the courtship clincher,' meaning that the girl may not be sought in marriage by another person.

After payment of the proposal money the in-laws will want the woman's marriage payment. If the man has no marriage payment they will agree about a period (for payments), like a year or more, so that he can give it to them afterwards. If they accept he must write a note to guarantee before witnesses that the agreement really is such.

After a few days the man will want his wife; he tells his go-between, 'At the new moon I want to get married.' The go-between takes the news to the in-laws,' and they reply, 'Very well, we are ready.' The girl's father tells the people concerned, 'On such-and-such a day I have a cup of coffee.' This message is the responsibility of the girl's father, and if he is unable, if he is poor, the suitor does it, if he is a person of substance.

The wedding usually takes place in the house of the bride's parents until the seven days are over. On the morning of the wedding the house is decorated, it is arranged neatly with dishes and chairs and mirrors, and it is fumigated with aromatic aloe wood and (sprinkled) with a bottle of rose-water. At the beginning of the afternoon the women friends of the bride and others on her side come to make her ready; they take to the toilet, bathe her, and comb her hair, and they massage her whole body with *tibu* perfume, then she is censed, they plait her hair and cut it, that is they cut the hair a little (in a small patch, but lit. on the face), this is called *denge*. They also apply antimony to the eyes (i.e. the eyebrows and the lashes) and a little on the face, and they sing as they do this.

When the toilet is finished the bridegroom is brought after sunset to the bride's house by her friends, with rejoicing and merriment. And he has adorned himself with a calico garment, a cloth cloak, a turban and shoes, a curved dagger and perhaps a sword or a stick in the hand. When he reaches the wedding-house and wants to go in, the women prevent him at the door, they want their *kingia* (due for entering), and he gives them a certain amount of money. Of he tries (lit. wants) to deceive them, saying, 'Allow me to see my bride (lit. wife), and then I will give you your *kingia* gift.' But the women do not agree.

When he goes inside, the *makungwi* give him his wife (to-be), and she gives him her hand and greets him. And this is when they meet for the first time. The woman does not speak to the groom until he first gives the *kono* and *kipakasa* and *fichuo* gifts, the *kono* because she gave him her hand, she wants the gift due for this in (his) taking a new woman. And *kipakasa* is for (his) embracing (her), and the *fichuo* is for speaking with her, because formerly he had not seen her face nor heard her voice, this is why these dues are wanted. And the groom gives (the gifts); for example, he gives her a ring for her *kono*, or a bracelet for her *kipakasa*, and a metal chain for her *fichuo*, or else he gives her as much money as he can.

When he has made these customary gifts, the groom goes to the reception-hall, and his bride stays in her room, and the groom goes to partake of the 'wedding-dish'; he breaks off some cooked rice and puts it on a plate with some meat; his bride is sent this to eat; it is called 'the gift-rice.' Meanwhile, the young women play their small drums and cymbals, they sing their wedding-songs. And when the people have partaken of the wedding-dish, they read the first chapter of the Quran. The bridal pair, the man and woman, have already been married by the Muslim teacher on the day preferred by the bridegroom, but some are married by the teacher on the wedding-day itself in the morning.

The people at the wedding pray to God for the bridal couple, and they say:

God grant you a good home for speaking and listening; may He greatly increase your prosperity, may He take away from you sickness in your home, may He give you male and female offspring. May God protect you from enemies, through His loving kindness.

When they have eaten, and read the first chapter of the Quran, the bridegroom undresses and puts on two cloths, because he is about to have his feet washed; one cloth he wears around the lower half of his body, and one he covers himself with (i.e. over the head). He sits on a chair, and his feet are in a tray or a flat wooden platter. The bride's *kungwi* will wash his feet, and a slave-girl holds a water-jug. The *kungwi* sings a song and the women respond, like this: 'let us wash the master's feet with water from Zemzem,' or, 'The dish-shaped gong of the song-leaders, let them enter the dance in pairs,' or 'And let the money be placed on the Swahillis' gong.'

If the young people hear this song, everyone arranges to put something on the gong, everyone according as he is able. The *kungwi* will count the money obtained. Then she will call the parents of the bride for them to divide the money in three parts; one part for the *kungwi*, the second part the parents will receive, and the third goes to the bridal couple, but the money taken by the *kungwi* and the parents will not be used (i.e. for themselves), they will buy necessaries for the honeymoon period of six days.

When the honeymoon period is over, the wife is taken to her husband, and a screen is made for her, and this screen is a canopy. A big screen is made and the bride goes into is with other women. The slave-girls hold cymbals, and some have a buffalo horn, and they go along singing songs. When she gets to the house her husband invites the women relatives of both sides to show them the bride's kitchen. And they are shown this by having a lot of food made for them, and he invites anyone he likes to eat his food, and it is called, 'The Kitchen Hint.' After this no further meal is prepared, for this is the end of the wedding.

QUESTIONS

1. How are children acculturated in a Swahili community?

2. What is the role of science and medicine in bringing up children? Why did the Swahilis practice infanticide?

3.   What is the role of the Kungwi in the education of women?

4.   How are marriages arranged among the Swahilis?

---

124.   **RUDYARD KIPLING**

"THE WHITE MAN'S BURDEN"
(1899)

Rudyard Kipling (1865–1936) was one of the most celebrated authors of the era. Born in India the son of a civil servant, he was involved from the beginning with the British Empire. His parents sent him to England to attend boarding school, where he was lonely and unhappy. As soon as he could, he returned to India to write novels and stories, including *The Jungle Book* (1894–95) and *Kim* (1901). He won the Nobel Prize for Literature in 1907. Kipling's patriotism was placed in the service of the state during World War I, though the battlefield death of his only son deeply affected him.

Kipling's work stresses imperial themes; "The White Man's Burden" (1899) is a succinct summary of his view on the duties of empire. It was actually addressed to Americans after their victory in the Spanish-American War.

The White Man's Burden

Take up the White Man's burden—
    Send forth the best ye breed—
Go bind your sons to exile
    To serve your captives' need;
To wait in heavy harness,
    On fluttered folk and wild—
Your new-caught, sullen peoples,
    Half-devil and half-child.

Take up the White Man's burden—
    In patience to abide,
To veil the threat of terror
    And check the show of pride;
By open speech and simple,
    An hundred times made plain,
To seek another's profit,
    And work another's gain.

Take up the White Man's burden—
    The savage wars of peace—
Fill full the mouth of Famine
    And bid the sickness cease;
And when your goal is nearest
    The end for others sought,
Watch Sloth and heathen Folly
    Bring all your hope to nought.

Take up the White Man's burden—
    No tawdry rule of kings,
But toil of serf and sweeper—
    The tale of common things.
The ports ye shall not enter,

The roads ye shall not tread,
Go make them with your living,
   And mark them with your dead.

Take up the White Man's burden—
   And reap his old reward:
The blame of those ye better,
   The hate of those ye guard—
The cry of hosts ye humour
   (Ah, slowly!) toward the light:—
"Why brought ye us from bondage,
   "Our loved Egyptian night?"

Take up the White Man's burden—
   Ye dare not stoop to less—

Nor call too loud on Freedom
   To cloak your weariness;
By all ye cry or whisper,
   By all ye leave or do,
The silent, sullen peoples
   Shall weigh your Gods and you.

Take up the White Man's burden—
   Have done with childish days—
The lightly proffered laurel,
   The easy, ungrudged praise.
Comes now, to search your manhood
   Through all the thankless years,
Cold, edged with dear-bought wisdom,
   The judgment of your peers!

QUESTIONS

1.   What is the "White Man's Burden"? What are the responsibilities of the imperialist toward his subjects?

2.   How do colonial subjects repay their masters, according to Kipling?

3.   What assumptions does Kipling make about other peoples?

4.   Compare Kipling's view of race with that of Rhodes. Are they alike or different?

125.   **GEORGE ORWELL**

"SHOOTING AN ELEPHANT"

(1936)

George Orwell is the pseudonym of Eric Blair (1903–50), who was born into a civil servant's household in India. Although the family had relatively high social status, neither parent had much of an income. Orwell had to make his way by his wits, eventually earning a scholarship at Eton, one of the most prestigious English private schools. Although he distinguished himself intellectually, Orwell shunned an academic career and instead enlisted in the Burmese police force. His firsthand experiences with British imperialism shocked him deeply, and he began a lifelong identification with the under-privileged and outcasts of society. Returning to England, Orwell began to write for a living, surviving mostly on fees from journalism and a small income from novels. It was not until the very end of his life that he achieved fame and financial security. His last two novels, *Animal Farm* (1945) and *Nineteen Eighty-Four* (1949), have become classics. He died of tuberculosis in 1950.

"Shooting an Elephant" is largely autobiographical in content. It is a story at once simple and complex about rulers and ruled, domination and subordination, freedom and responsibility.

In Moulmein, in Lower Burma, I was hated by large numbers of people—the only time in my life that I have been important enough for this to happen to me. I was sub-divisional police officer of the town, and in an aimless, petty kind of way anti-European feeling was very bitter. No one had the guts to raise a riot, but if a European woman went through the bazaars alone somebody would probably spit betel juice over her dress. As a police officer I was an obvious target and was baited whenever it seemed safe to do so. When a nimble Burman tripped me up on the football field and the referee (another Burman) looked the other way, the crowd yelled with hideous laughter. This happened more than once. In the end the sneering yellow faces of young men that met me everywhere, the insults hooted after me when I was at a safe distance, got badly on my nerves. The young Buddhist priests were the worst of all. There were several thousands of them in the town and none of them seemed to have anything to do except stand on street corners and jeer at Europeans.

All this was perplexing and upsetting. For at that time I had already made up my mind that imperialism was an evil thing and the sooner I chucked up my job and got out of it the better. Theoretically—and secretly, of course—I was all for the Burmese and all against their oppressors, the British. As for the job I was

doing, I hated it more bitterly than I can perhaps make clear. In a job like that you see the dirty work of Empire at close quarters. The wretched prisoners huddling in the stinking cages of the lock-ups, the grey, cowed faces of the long-term convicts, the scarred buttocks of the men who had been flogged with bamboos—all these oppressed me with an intolerable sense of guilt. But I could get nothing into perspective. I was young and ill-educated and I had had to think out my problems in the utter silence that is imposed on every Englishman in the East. I did not even know that the British Empire is dying, still less did I know that it is a great deal better than the younger empires that are going to supplant it. All I knew was that I was stuck between my hatred of the empire I served and my rage against the evil-spirited little beasts who tried to make my job impossible. With one part of my mind I thought of the British Raj as an unbreakable tyranny, as something clamped down, *in saecula saeculorum,* upon the will of prostrate peoples; with another part I thought that the greatest joy in the world would be to drive a bayonet into a Buddhist priest's guts. Feelings like these are the normal by-products of imperialism; ask any Anglo-Indian official, if you can catch him off duty.

One day something happened which in a roundabout way was enlightening. It was a tiny incident in itself, but it gave me a better glimpse than I had had before of the real nature of imperialism—the real motives for which despotic governments act. Early one morning the sub-inspector at a police station the other end of the town rang me up on the phone and said that an elephant was ravaging the bazaar. Would I please come and do something about it? I did not know what I could do, but I wanted to see what was happening and I got on to a pony and started out. I took my rifle, an old .44 Winchester and much too small to kill an elephant, but I thought the noise might be useful *in terrorem*. Various Burmans stopped me on the way and told me about the elephant's doings. It was not, of course, a wild elephant, but a tame one which had gone 'must.' It had been chained up as tame elephants always are when their attack of 'must' is due, but on the previous night it had broken its chain and escaped. Its mahout, the only person who could manage it when it was in that state, had set out in pursuit, but he had taken the wrong direction and was now twelve hours' journey away, and in the morning the elephant had suddenly reappeared in the town. The Burmese population had no weapons and were quite helpless against it. It had already destroyed somebody's bamboo hut, killed a cow and raided some fruit-stalls and devoured the stock; also it had met the municipal rubbish van, and, when the driver jumped out and took to his heels, had turned the van over and inflicted violence upon it.

The Burmese sub-inspector and some Indian constables were waiting for me in the quarter where the elephant had been seen. It was a very poor quarter, a labyrinth of squalid bamboo huts, thatched with palm-leaf, winding all over a steep hillside. I remember that it was a cloudy stuffy morning at the beginning of the rains. We began questioning the people as to where the elephant had gone, and, as usual, failed to get any definite information. That is invariably the case in the East; a story always sounds clear enough at a distance, but the nearer you get to the scene of events the vaguer it becomes. Some of the people said that the elephant had gone in one direction,

some said that he had gone in another, some professed not even to have heard of any elephant. I had almost made up my mind that the whole story was a pack of lies, when we heard yells a little distance away. There was a loud, scandalized cry of 'Go away, child! Go away this instant!' and an old woman with a switch in her hand came round the corner of a hut, violently shooing away a crowd of naked children. Some more women followed, clicking their tongues and exclaiming; evidently there was something there that the children ought not to have seen. I rounded the hut and saw a man's dead body sprawling in the mud. He was an Indian, a black Dravidian coolie, almost naked, and he could not have been dead many minutes. The people said that the elephant had come suddenly upon him round the corner of the hut, caught him with his trunk, put its foot on his back and ground him into the earth. This was the rainy season and the ground was soft, and his face had scored a trench a foot deep and a couple of yards long. He was lying on his belly with arms crucified and head sharply twisted to one side. His face was coated with mud, the eyes wide open, the teeth bared and grinning with an expression of unendurable agony. (Never tell me, by the way, that the dead look peaceful. Most of the corpses I have seen looked devilish.) The friction of the great beast's foot had stripped the skin from his back as neatly as one skins a rabbit. As soon as I saw the dead man I sent an orderly to a friend's house near by to borrow an elephant rifle. I had already sent back the pony, not wanting it to go mad with fright and throw me if it smelled the elephant.

The orderly came back in a few minutes with a rifle and five cartridges, and meanwhile some Burmans had arrived and told us that the elephant was in the paddy fields below, only a few hundred yards away. As I started forward practically the whole population of the quarter flocked out of their houses and followed me. They had seen the rifle and were all shouting excitedly that I was going to shoot the elephant. They had not shown much interest in the elephant when he was merely ravaging their homes, but it was different now that he was going to be shot. It was bit of fun to them, as it would be to an English crowd; besides, they wanted the meat. It made me vaguely uneasy, I had no intention of shooting the elephant—I had merely sent for the rifle to defend myself if necessary—and it is always unnerving to have a crowd following you. I marched down the hill, looking and feeling a fool, with the rifle over my shoulder and an ever-growing army of people jostling at my heels. At the bottom when you got away from the huts there was a metalled road and beyond that a miry waste of paddy fields a thousand yards across, not yet ploughed but soggy from the first rains and dotted with coarse grass. The elephant was standing eighty yards from the road, his left side towards us. He took not the slightest notice of the crowd's approach. He was tearing up bunches of grass, beating them against his knees to clean them and stuffing them into his mouth.

I had halted on the road. As soon as I saw the elephant I knew with perfect certainty that I ought not to shoot him. It is a serious matter to shoot a working elephant—it is comparable to destroying a huge and costly piece of machinery—and obviously one ought not to do it if it can possibly be avoided. And at that distance, peacefully eating, the elephant looked no more dangerous than a cow. I thought then and I think now that his attack of 'must' was already passing off; in which case he would merely wander harmlessly about until the mahout came back and caught him. Moreover, I did not in the least want to shoot him. I decided that I would watch him for a little while to make sure that he did not turn savage again, and then go home.

But at that moment I glanced round at the crowd that had followed me. It was an immense crowd, two thousand at the least and growing every minute. It blocked the road for a long distance on either side. I looked at the sea of yellow faces above the garish clothes—faces all happy and excited over this bit of fun, all certain that the elephant was going to be shot. They were watching me as they would watch a conjurer about to perform a trick. They did not like me, but with the magical rifle in my hands I was momentarily worth watching. And suddenly I realized that I should have to shoot the elephant after all. The people expected it of me and I had got to do it; I could feel their two thousand wills pressing me forward, irresistibly. And it was at this moment, as I stood there with the rifle in my hands, that I first grasped the hollowness, the futility of the white man's dominion in the East. Here was I, the white man with his gun, standing in front of the unarmed native crowd—seemingly the leading actor of the piece; but in reality I was only an absurd puppet pushed to and fro by the will of those yellow faces behind. I perceived in this moment that when the white man turns tyrant it is his own freedom that he destroys. He becomes a sort of hollow, posing dummy, the conventionalized figure of a sahib. For it is the condition of his rule that he shall spend his life in trying to impress the 'natives' and so in every crisis he has got to do what the 'natives' expect of him. He wears a mask, and his face grows to fit it. I had got to shoot the elephant. I had committed myself to doing it when I sent for the rifle. A sahib has got to act like a sahib; he has got to appear resolute, to know his own mind and do definite things. To come all that way, rifle in hand, with two thousand people marching at my heels, and then to trail feebly away, having done nothing—no, that was impossible. The crowd would laugh at me. And my whole life, every white man's life in the East, was one long struggle not to be laughed at.

But I did not want to shoot the elephant. I watched him beating his bunch of grass against his knees, with that preoccupied grandmotherly air that elephants have. It seemed to me that it would be murder to shoot him. At that age I was not squeamish about killing animals, but I had never shot an elephant and never wanted to. (Somehow it always seems worse to kill a *large* animal.) Besides, there was the beast's owner to be considered. Alive, the elephant was worth at least a hundred pounds; dead, he would only be worth the value of his tusks—five pounds, possibly. But I had got to act quickly. I turned to some experienced-looking Burmans who had been there when we

George Orwell was the pseudonym of English author Eric Blair (1903–50).

arrived, and asked them how the elephant had been behaving. They all said the same thing: he took no notice of you if you left him alone, but he might charge if you went too close to him.

It was perfectly clear to me what I ought to do. I ought to walk up to within, say, twenty-five yards of the elephant and test his behaviour. If he charged I could shoot, if he took no notice of me it would be safe to leave him until the mahout came back. But also I knew that I was going to do no such thing. I was a poor shot with a rifle and the ground was soft mud into which one would sink at every step. If the elephant charged and I missed him, I should have about as much chance as a toad under a steam-roller. But even then I was not thinking particularly of my own skin, only the watchful yellow faces behind. For at that moment, with the crowd watching me, I was not afraid in the ordinary sense, as I would have been if I had been alone. A white man mustn't be frightened in front of 'natives'; and so, in general, he isn't frightened. The sole thought in my mind was that

if anything went wrong those two thousand Burmans would see me pursued, caught, trampled on and reduced to a grinning corpse like that Indian up the hill. And if that happened it was quite probable that some of them would laugh. That would never do. There was only one alternative. I shoved the cartridges into the magazine and lay down on the road to get a better aim.

The crowd grew very still, and a deep, low, happy sigh, as of people who see the theatre curtain go up at last, breathed from innumerable throats. They were going to have their bit of fun after all. The rifle was a beautiful German thing with cross-hair sights. I did not then know that in shooting an elephant one should shoot to cut an imaginary bar running from ear-hole to ear-hole. I ought therefore, as the elephant was sideways on, to have aimed straight at his ear-hole; actually I aimed several inches in front of this, thinking the brain would be further forward.

When I pulled the trigger I did not hear the bang or feel the kick—one never does when a shot goes home—but I heard the devilish roar of glee that went up from the crowd. In that instant, in too short a time, one would have thought, even for the bullet to get there, a mysterious, terrible change had come over the elephant. He neither stirred nor fell, but every line of his body had altered. He looked suddenly stricken, shrunken, immensely old, as though the frightful impact of the bullet had paralysed him without knocking him down. At last, after what seemed a long time—it might have been five seconds, I dare say—he sagged flabbily to his knees. His mouth slobbered. An enormous senility seemed to have settled upon him. Once could have imagined him thousands of years old. I fired again into the same spot. At the second shot he did not collapse but climbed with desperate slowness to his feet and stood weakly upright, with legs sagging and head drooping. I fired a third time. That was the shot that did for him. You could see the agony of it jolt his whole body and knock the last remnant of strength from his legs. But in falling he seemed for a moment to rise, for as his hind legs collapsed beneath him he seemed to tower upwards like a huge rock toppling, his trunk reaching skyward like a tree. He trumpeted, for the first and only time. And then down he came, his belly towards me, with a crash that seemed to shake the ground even where I lay.

I got up. The Burmans were already racing past me across the mud. It was obvious that the elephant would never rise again, but he was not dead. He was breathing very rhythmically with long rattling gasps, his great mound of a side painfully rising and falling. His mouth was wide open—I could see far down into caverns of pale pink throat. I waited a long time for him to die, but his breathing did not weaken. Finally I fired my two remaining shots into the spot where I thought his heart must be. The thick blood welled out of him like red velvet, but still he did not die. His body did not even jerk when the shots hit him, the tortured breathing continued without a pause. He was dying, very slowly and in great agony, but in some world remote from me where not even a bullet could damage him further. I felt that I had got to put an end to that dreadful noise. It seemed dreadful to see the great beast lying there, powerless to move and yet powerless to die, and not even to be able to finish him. I sent back for my small rifle and poured shot after shot into his heart and down his throat. They seemed to make no impression. The tortured gasps continued as steadily as the ticking of a clock.

In the end I could not stand it any longer and went away. I heard later that it took him half an hour to die. Burmans were arriving with dahs and baskets even before I left, and I was told they had stripped his body almost to the bones by the afternoon.

Afterwards, of course, there were endless discussions about the shooting of the elephant. The owner was furious, but he was only an Indian and could do nothing. Besides, legally I had done the right thing, for a mad elephant has to be killed, like a mad dog, if its owner fails to control it. Among the Europeans opinion was divided. The older men said I was right, the younger men said it was a damn shame to shoot an elephant for killing a coolie, because an elephant was worth more than any damn Coringhee coolie. And afterwards I was very glad that the coolie had been killed; it put me legally in the right and it gave me a sufficient pretext for shooting an elephant. I often wondered whether any of the others grasped that I had done it solely to avoid looking a fool.

QUESTIONS

1. What were relations like between the Burmese and Europeans? Why were they so difficult?

2. What is the ambivalence Orwell feels about imperialism?

3. Why did Orwell shoot the elephant?

4. What did the incident reveal to Orwell about the nature of imperialism?

5. How does Orwell's experience in Burma fit with the views of Rhodes and Kipling?

Part VI
TWENTIETH-CENTURY EUROPE

(continued)

THE TRANSFORMATION OF EASTERN EUROPE

TOWARD A NEW WORLD

War and Revolution

126.

VOICES FROM THE
BATTLE OF THE SOMME
(1916)

One of the bloodiest battles in the history of warfare took place in north-eastern France in the summer of 1916. The western front of the Great War had settled into a stalemate with huge armies dug into trenches facing each other. Fighting took the form of forays into no man's land, booby trapped with wire, primitive land mines, and fixed position machine guns. For months, dispatches reported "all quiet on the western front." But then the Germans decided to throw all of the might they had against the massively fortified French position at Verdun. Their hope was not to take the fortress, but to bleed the French of men, ammunition and supplies. It is estimated that over a million shells were expended on the first day of the battle and nearly 600,000 men died in the carnage. In order to relieve the German pressure on Verdun, the British army attacked along the river Somme in July 1916. On the first day, 57,000 British troops were killed and the toll for the entire three-month push was staggering. French and British allies lost 600,000 men, the Germans a mere half million. The allied "victory" was an advance of seven miles.

The Battle of the Somme became a by-word for the futility of the First World War and many works of literature were created against its backdrop. The accounts produced here, however, are from participants during the actual fighting. They come from letters and diaries kept contemporaneously with the events and capture the immediacy of its horror.

I was shell-shocked, I suppose. At any rate, I wasn't much use—inclined to cry, if anything. In fact, I couldn't stop and, being rather young, I was somewhat ashamed of it. But it had been a total shambles. The first two companies had got across and, about an hour after they started, I was told to take B Company across to support them. We had no idea that the whole attack was a diversion. We thought that we were going forward. We had maps and plans of Gommecourt—we knew from information we'd got from the local people exactly where every house was. But the trouble was that Gommecourt stuck out in the middle of the line and we didn't attack it directly. We attacked on one side of the château park and the 46th Division were attacking on the other. We were supposed to encircle it and link up behind. But what we didn't know was that the Germans had so manoeuvred and organized their line that this part which we weren't to attack was really their strongpoint, and they simply had a clear field of fire on either side and nothing to bother about in front. And the shellfire was absolutely appalling. They were simply pouring shells down. We just couldn't get across. We didn't even get as far as the trench we'd dug—well, there was no trench left. It was all hammered to blazes. We got just about as far as our old front line and then it became quite impossible. The company in front of me said, 'It's no use. We can't get over.'

We got orders to turn and try to make our way back to the village. One of my subalterns was newly out. Such a nice chap. He must have had money and we used to tease him a bit because his batman was the family butler! This young officer jumped out of the trench to try to organize the men, pass the word and get them moving to the communication trench, and he was promptly killed. Just disappeared in an explosion. The whole of the valley was being swept with machine-gun fire and hammered with shells. We got the men organised as best we could—those of us who were left. So many gone, and we'd never even got past our own front-line trench! And then we found we couldn't get back. The trenches were indescribable! We were simply treading on the dead. Eventually my Sergeant and I got out on top—we were at the back of the Company. I heard a shell coming. I remember thinking, 'Imagine! Just imagine hearing a single shell in the middle of all this din!' It burst just above my head. The Sergeant was blown one way and I was blown the other. He was killed. I don't know how I got back. I simply don't know how I got back. It was murder.

• • •

It was like all hell let loose—an absolute inferno! It was like someone throwing fire crackers into a fire, but multiplied a million times. All the ammunition was exploding in the heat and flying over our heads. There were no officers there and no order was given.

There were three of us stood in a trench and, of course, the top of the trench was crumbling in all the time until our ankles were covered and I screamed at this NCO even though he was a bombardier. I took charge. 'We'll get killed whatever happens!' I screamed. 'We'll be killed whether we stop here or whether we run away. For God's sake let's be killed trying to get out of it.' And he said, 'Right-o George.'

It was every man for himself. We ran like hell. The dump was blazing, lighting up the sky, and there was nothing else to do but run because, as soon as the Germans spotted it—and you could see it for miles around—all their guns would be trained on it.

There was a young officer staggering round blinded and screaming and, as we ran, I saw our cook—just his head sticking out of the earth where he'd been buried, and he was screaming too. Not that you could hear anything in the terrible roaring of all these explosives, but you could see by men's faces if they were screaming. And you could see that this man had gone stark staring mad by the frenzy in his face.

You couldn't do anything for him. The idea of digging amidst all that would have been sheer lunacy and everyone was running just to get out of it. I didn't expect to get out of it. I didn't expect to be alive a few seconds afterwards. We ran like hell until we were out of range. Then we dropped down and lay on the ground and watched this thing—a great lurid light, lighting up the whole sky. Blazing!

• • •

It was the waiting to go over that was the worst, because we didn't go over until almost three o'clock in the afternoon. There was a whole brigade waiting to go over on a battalion front, so we were crowded up like anything. During the morning, the Sergeant came round with the old rum jar and gave us a dessert spoonful of rum, just to put Dutch courage in us. It was strong, that Army rum, and I think he had two or three spoonfuls to our one—or more!

We really needed that rum, waiting to go over the top! Our own guns had put down this terrific barrage but, because we were a bit higher up than the Germans, in order to hit them they'd had to sight the guns so that they would just skim the top of our trenches and there we were, crouching in this terrible noise, and these terrible shells going over us just inches above. You can't describe the feeling! You can't describe the noise! A couple of our own chaps were killed. One fellow had the top of his head took off with one of our own shells. His brains were all over the place. But the artillery couldn't help it. They had a terrible job to get the elevation right and just had to try and skim the top of our trenches and this poor chap Dixon got it. He was only five or six yards away from me. It didn't do much for us to see that sort of thing before we went over!

Five minutes after we went over the top we were finished! The German machine-guns went through our lines just like a mow goes through a field of corn. I don't think we got two hundred yards before we were so mucked up that we just had to lay out in No Man's Land. I was in a shell-hole with the Sergeant—the one who'd been sampling the rum. We were absolutely pinned down but he kept jumping up and shouting, 'Why don't we advance? Why don't we advance?' He was absolutely hollering. How could you advance when there was three of you there and you couldn't see anybody else? I shouted back at him, 'Why don't you keep down? You'll be drawing the guns on us!'

D Company had gone across first and C Company were supposed to be following behind us. From this shell-hole we looked back and we could see C Company there lying on the ground spread out in extended order, just as they'd gone across. We couldn't understand why they weren't coming up to support us. There was just the three of us in the shell-hole—the Platoon Sergeant and Jack Hall, who was the Lance-Corporal, and myself. And the Sergeant said, 'Why the hell don't they come

on and give us a hand? We can't go in there on our own!'

This old Sergeant wasn't half going on, nothing would keep him quiet. He was an enlisted man—he wasn't a Regular. There was only two of us Regulars in The 7th Battalion, but the Sergeant had been in the Marines before the war, so he should have known better. Of course he had all this rum in him. Then the third time he jumped up they got him! A bullet went straight in his ear and blew half his face away. Me and Jack had to lay there with him. We lay there for hours and hours and hours with all this clatter going on around us and when it got dusk we started to crawl back.

• • •

Lieutenant Hall was alive, but only just. He said, 'Can you help me! I've got a bad wound in my hip. I can't move.' I said to Jack 'Can you hold my rifle and I'll pick him up?'

I picked him up and I carried him back to the trench—it was all of a hundred yards and it took a long, long time, because we had to be careful moving; the whole thing was still like an inferno although it was getting well dark. When we got into the trench, I laid him on the fire step. A few yards beyond him, laying out there we'd come across a chap we called Corporal Gussie—a machine-gunner. He was badly shot in the stomach and I didn't suppose there was much hope for him, but he was in a bad way. I couldn't do anything, having the Lieutenant with me, but I said to the Corporal, 'I'll come back for you, Gussie.' So, when I'd laid the Lieutenant down and someone else came to see to him, I said, 'Right. I'm going out again.' But the officer wouldn't let me go. I felt very badly about it, because I'd promised Gussie I would go back, but the officer said, 'No you're not. You've had quite enough for one day.' It was nine o'clock at night by then, so I suppose, in a way, he was right. But I tried to insist and, I remember he said to me, 'Anyone who's left out there isn't worth picking up now!'

He was right. There were twenty-three of us left alive out of my whole company. I don't know how they missed us. It was a miracle! It was a miracle that any of us got back. I don't believe I've ever cried in my life, but, when I got back and found out what had happened, how many men we'd lost, I cried then. I was a Regular and they were all Volunteers, but we was all mucked in together. I cried then.

. . .

I thought I was a goner. I didn't think I'd get back. I didn't think I'd *ever* get back.

Lying out there that morning I were within twenty-five or thirty yards of the German front line, looking through this telescopic sight at the gap in their trench. I could have touched it. I had my finger in the trigger all the time, not moving, and I saw a few of them laid to rest. But it didn't do our lads much good. As soon as they started across the machine-guns opened up. It seemed like hours before they got up near to me, but they kept on coming. I still dursn't move. These bullets are flying all over the place. It were Maxims they were firing and they were shooting across each other, with this hissing noise as they went past. I dursn't turn round, but I heard the noise behind me and I knew our fellows were coming. Some of them were getting hit and they were yelling and shouting, but they came on, and when the first wave got up to me I jumped up.

I were in the first row and the first one I saw were my chum, Clem Cunnington. I don't think we'd gone twenty yards when he got his straight through the breast. Machine-gun bullets. He went down. I went down. We got it in the same burst. I got it through the shoulder. I hardly noticed it, at the time, I were so wild when I saw that Clem were finished. We'd got orders: 'Every man for himself and no prisoners!' It suited me that, after I saw Clem lying there.

I got up and picked up my rifle and got through the wire into their trench and straight in front there was this dugout—full of Jerries,

and one big fellow was on the steps facing me. I had this Mills bomb. Couldn't use my arm. I pulled the pin with my teeth and flung it down and I were shooting at them, I were that wild. 'There you are! Bugger yourselves! Share that between you!' Then I were off! It was hand to hand! I went round one traverse and there was one—face to face. I couldn't fire one-handed, but I could use the bayonet. It was him or me—and I went first! Jab! Just like that. It were my job. And from there I went on. Oh, I were wild! Seeing Clem like that!

We were climbing out of the trench, making for the second line, and that's where they got me again just as I were climbing out, through the fingers this time, on the same arm. I still managed to get on. I kept up with the lads nearly to the second line. Then I got another one. It went through my tin hat and down straight through my foot. Well, that finished it!

After a bit, lying there, I saw two fellows drop into some shell-hole. I crawled after them and, of course, you couldn't see much for the smoke but, next thing we *did* know, the Germans had taken back all their front line again. There were no more of our fellows about. So there we had to stop. When night came I were in a deuce of a state. I must have been fainting off and on, what with the loss of blood. You'd no idea of the passage of time. I didn't know where I were. I only knew there were Germans in front and Germans behind and I had no idea which way were the British lines.

What with having nothing to eat and nothing to drink all day, my tongue was getting as big as two. I could hardly close my mouth. My water-bottle was gone. I couldn't realise where I was. Lights going up all the time. All this noise. Them shelling from their side and us shelling from ours, and machine-guns in between. What worried me was getting caught in our own shell-fire. I bothered more about that. Well, they dropped in front of me and they dropped behind me but they never put one into the shell-hole.

• • •

Orders came along, 'We're to move off at a certain time and we'll advance on the village of Pozières.' Our artillery guns were mounted in a place called Sausage Valley and they were continually firing and, of course, we had to go through them. The main impact of an 18-pounder gun firing is the compression of the shell leaving the muzzle as it goes forward. When you were in front of the guns, you got into that compression. Of course the shell was going up in the air but you got the full blast, where you were, and it was a very hard experience to put up with.

Then we came into the counter-fire of the Germans. The shells were lobbing all over the place. We didn't know where on earth we were. We got into a chalk pit and guides met us there, fellows who were trained for the purpose. They led each party up. There was no front line as such, just a series of shell-holes and timber—no front, no back, no lines of demarcation. It was just an open devastated area. The companies didn't know where they were. You had to put yourself in position and say, 'Well, where are we?' And our CO said, 'Well, you take up fifty yards from here to here—say down to that broken-off tree—and the next company will have to take on from there and co-ordinate it that way.'

That went on all night, with the shelling still going on and they were throwing over big stuff. We got into this Gibraltar HQ—I had to be with HQ because I was a signaler. We weren't in there ten minutes when a nine-inch shell landed on top of it. There were about twenty or thirty of our fellows down below in there—and down fifteen or twenty feet in a very solid concrete-lined job. But the compression was terrific. All night long they were calling for stretcher-bearers. Every time a salvo came over, after the explosion, you could hear these calls going up outside, 'Stretcher-bearer! Stretcher-bearer!' We took an awful lot of casualties that night, even before the boys went over.

The night we took over we had a terrible time going up the line. There was a tremendous bombardment going on and we were getting nearer and nearer to it. We had to move into a gun position to the right of Trones Wood, alongside the road, with Guillemont just in front and the battery we were taking over from was firing right up to the last minute. Then they pulled out and we pulled in and started firing. We only had five guns to fire with, because even before we started one gun was knocked out. I was in the Signallers' dugout, so I didn't see it, but we heard the shell exploding and saw a stretcher being carried past. A little while later, we got a signal through from Dublin Trench. It said *Please send down a burial party at once to 1/3 West Lancashire Field Ambulance Regimental Aid Post* and it was signed by the Medical Officer of the 277 Brigade, a Major Reilly. It was naïve of him really. But it was his first night in there and he probably didn't realise the situation. We had no one to spare to send a burial party for one man! When the daylight came, there were bodies all over the place—bloated bodies, they hadn't been able to clear away. The guns were literally wheel to wheel and we were firing, firing, firing twenty-four hours a day. There were gun lines everywhere—a continuous row of them. There was no end to them—and all of them were firing almost non-stop, right round the clock.

It began to get on your nerves after a while. It wasn't so much that we were being shelled—although we were, because the Germans used to put over these big 5.9 shells and then they'd follow them up with shrapnel shells to catch anyone who was running away. But what really began to get me was the sound of our own guns. The sound waves were going over your head all the time, like a tuning fork being struck on your steel helmet. A terrible sound—ping, ping, ping—this terrible vibration day and night and this noise in your head, just like a tuning fork being rung again and again. It went right through you. You couldn't get away from it. It went right down into your nerves.

• • •

There was a terrific smell. It was so awful it nearly poisoned you. A smell of rotten flesh. The old German front line was covered with bodies—they were seven and eight deep and they had all gone black. The smell! These people had been laying since the First of July. Wicked it was! Colonel Pinney got hold of some stretchers and our job was to put the bodies on them and, with a man at each end, we *threw* them into that crater. There must have been over a thousand bodies there. I don't know how many we buried. I'll never forget that sight. Bodies all over the place. I'll never forget it. I was only eighteen, but I thought, 'There's something wrong here!'

My job was to take the identity discs off the dead men. Other people were detailed off to collect the rifles and other people collected the equipment and then there was a band of stretcher-bearers who picked up these dead gentlemen and took them to the edge of this crater and tipped them over, rolled them down and they buried themselves in the chalk before they got to the bottom.

My lot, we had to collect the bodies off the old German wire. Over 200 we counted. And we dumped them in the crater. All the time we were getting shelled, and casualties were happening of course. Some of us was hoping they'd happen. I know I didn't mind it happening! Then I got it! I'd just jumped in a trench between two men, Gomer Evans and Dick Darling, and as I jumped in there was this terrific crash. I didn't know any more until I woke up a few minutes later, and there was old Gomer Evans, he'd got the top of his nut blown off, and Dick Darling, he'd got it in the back. His kidneys blown out. We had to bury them both. But we didn't put them in the crater. We buried them just to the side of it.

As far as you could see there were all these bodies lying out there—literally thousands of them, just where they'd been caught on the First of July. Some were without legs, some were legs without bodies, arms without bodies. A terrible sight. They'd been churned up by shells even after they were killed. We were just dumping them into the crater—just filling them over. It didn't seem possible. It didn't get inside me or scare me, but it just made me wonder that these could have been men. It made me wonder what it was all about. And far away in the distance we could see nothing but a line of bursting shells. It was continuous. You wouldn't have thought that anybody could have existed in it, it was so terrific. And yet we knew we were going up into it, with not an earthly chance.

QUESTIONS

1. What was the experience of "shell shock"?

2. How did the loss of friends affect some soldiers?

3. What did the soldier mean when he reflected that he was only eighteen years old?

4. How did the attitude toward death differ between veterans of the trenches and newcomers?

127.   ERNST JÜNGER

STORM OF STEEL
(1920)

Ernst Jünger (1895–1998) left his middle-class German home in 1912 in search of adventure. Military life attracted him, so he enlisted in the renowned French Foreign Legion. On the outbreak of the First World War, he returned to Germany, where at the age of nineteen he enlisted in the forces and became a lieutenant on the western front. Jünger served in the trenches throughout the war and received a medal for bravery. Afterwards, he studied philosophy and natural science. When Jünger first began to write, his work brought him to the attention of the newly formed Nazi party, but he did not join and did not support many of the Nazi causes. He again enlisted in World War II and was one of the officers involved in the abortive attempt on Hitler's life in 1944. After the war Jünger's militarist attitudes changed radically, and he became an active campaigner for peace and European unity.

Storm of Steel was Jünger's first novel. A memoir of his days in the trenches, it graphically portrays the lives of the soldiers—both the privations they suffered and the bonds that they built up together.

The Author's Preface

I was a nineteen-year-old lieutenant in command of a platoon, and my part of the line was easily recognizable from the English side by a row of tall shell-stripped trees that rose from the ruins of Monchy. My left flank was bounded by the sunken road leading to Berles-au-Bois, which was in the hands of the English; my right was marked by a sap running out from our lines, one that helped us many a time to make our presence felt by means of bombs and rifle grenades.

Today there is no secret about what those trenches concealed, and a book such as this may, like a trench map years after the event, be read with sympathy and interest by the other side. But here not only the blue and red lines of the trenches are shown, but the blood that beat and the life that lay hid in them.

Time only strengthens my conviction that it was a good and strenuous life, and that the war,

for all its destructiveness, was an incomparable schooling of the heart. The front-line soldier whose foot came down on the earth so grimly and harshly may claim this at least, that it came down cleanly. Warlike achievements are enhanced by the inherent worth of the enemy.

On the 23d of August we were transported in lorries to Le Mesnil. Our spirits were excellent, though we knew we were going to be put in where the battle of Somme was at its worst. Chaff and laughter went from lorry to lorry. We marched from Le Mesnil at dusk to Sailly-Saillisel, and here the battalion dumped packs in a large meadow and paraded in battle order.

Artillery fire of a hitherto unimagined intensity rolled and thundered on our front. Thousands of twitching flashes turned the western horizon into a sea of flowers. All the while the wounded came trailing back with white, dejected faces, huddled into the ditches by the gun and ammunition columns that rattled past.

A man in a steel helmet reported to me as guide to conduct my platoon to the renowned Combles, where for the time we were to be in reserve. Sitting with him at the side of the road, I asked him, naturally enough, what it was like in the line. In reply I heard a monotonous tale of crouching all day in shell holes with no one on either flank and no trenches communicating with the rear, of unceasing attacks, of dead bodies littering the ground, of maddening thirst, of wounded and dying, and of a lot besides. The face half-framed by the steel rim of the helmet was unmoved; the voice accompanied by the sound of battle droned on, and the impression they made on me was one of unearthly solemnity. One could see that the man had been through horror to the limit of despair and there had learned to despise it. Nothing was left but supreme and superhuman indifference.

"Where you fall, there you lie. No one can help you. No one knows whether he will come back alive. They attack every day, but they can't get through. Everybody knows it is life and death."

As far as we could see in the darkness, Combles was utterly shot to bits. The damage seemed to be recent, judging from the amount of timber among the ruins and the contents of the houses slung over the road. We climbed over numerous heaps of débris—rather hurriedly, owing to a few shrapnel shells—and reached our quarters. They were in a large, shot-riddled house. Here I established myself with three sections. The other two occupied the cellar of a ruin opposite.

At 4 a.m. we were aroused from our rest on the fragments of bed we had collected, in order to receive steel helmets. It was also the occasion of discovering a sack of coffee beans in a corner of the cellar; whereupon there followed a great brewing of coffee.

After breakfast I went out to have a look round. Heavy artillery had turned a peaceful little billeting town into a scene of desolation in the course of a day or two. Whole houses had been flattened by single direct hits or blown up so that the interiors of the rooms hung over the chaos like the scenes on a stage. A sickly scent of dead bodies rose from many of the ruins, for many civilians had been caught in the bombardment and buried beneath the wreckage of their homes. A little girl lay dead in a pool of blood on the threshold of one of the doorways.

The square in front of the ruins of the church had been particularly hard hit. Here was the entrance to the catacombs, a very ancient underground passage with recesses here and there in which were crowded the staffs of all the units engaged. It was said that the civilians had opened up the entrance with pickaxes when the bombardment began. It had been walled up and kept secret from the Germans during the whole of their occupation. The streets were reduced to narrow paths winding circuitously round and over heaps of timber and masonry. Quantities of fruit and vegetables were going to waste in the churned-up gardens.

A plentiful supply of "iron rations" provided us with a dinner that we cooked in the kitchen, and concluded, needless to say, with strong coffee. I then settled myself in an armchair upstairs. From letters scattered about I saw that the house belonged to a brewer, Lesage. Cupboards and chests of drawers were thrown open; there was an overturned washstand, a sewing machine, and a perambulator. The pictures and the looking glasses on the walls were all broken. Drawers had been pulled out and emptied, and a yard deep all over the floor were underclothes, corsets, books, papers, bedroom tables, broken glass, bottles, notebooks, chair legs, coats, cloaks, lamps, curtains, window frames, doors torn from their hinges, lace, photographs, oil paintings, albums, broken boxes, hats, flower pots, and torn wall paper, all tangled up together in wild confusion.

In the course of the afternoon the firing increased to such a degree that single explosions were no longer audible. There was nothing but one terrific tornado of noise. From seven onward the square and the houses round were shelled at intervals of half a minute with fifteen-centimeter shells. There were many duds among them, which all the same made the houses rock. We sat all this while in our cellar, round a table, on armchairs covered in silk, with our heads propped on our hands, and counted the seconds between the explosions. Our jests became less frequent, till at last the foolhardiest of us fell silent, and at eight o'clock two direct hits brought down the next house.

From nine to ten the shelling was frantic. The earth rocked and the sky boiled like a gigantic cauldron.

Hundreds of heavy batteries were concentrated on and round Combles. Innumerable shells came howling and hurtling over us. Thick smoke, ominously lit up by Very lights, veiled everything. Head and ears ached violently, and we could only make ourselves understood by shouting a word at a time. The power of logical thought and the force of gravity seemed alike to be suspended. One had the sense of something as unescapable and as unconditionally fated as a catastrophe of nature. An N.C.O. of No. 3 platoon went mad.

At ten this carnival of hell gradually calmed down and passed into a steady drum fire. It was still certainly impossible to distinguish one shell from another.

At last we reached the front line. It was held by men cowering close in the shell holes, and their dead voices trembled with joy when they heard that we were the relief. A Bavarian sergeant major briefly handed over the sector and the Very-light pistol.

My platoon formed the right wing of the position held by the regiment. It consisted of a shallow sunken road which had been pounded by shells. It was a few hundred meters left of Guillemont and a rather shorter distance right of Bois-de-Trônes. We were parted from the troops on our right, the Seventy-sixth Regiment of Infantry, by a space about five hundred meters wide. This space was shelled so violently that no troops could maintain themselves there.

As I had no idea how far off the enemy were, I warned my men to be ready for the worst. We all remained on guard. I spent the night with my batman and two orderlies in a hole perhaps one yard square and one yard deep.

When day dawned we were astonished to see, by degrees, what a sight surrounded us.

The sunken road now appeared as nothing but a series of enormous shell holes filled with pieces of uniform, weapons, and dead bodies. The ground all round, as far as the eye could see, was plowed by shells. You could search in vain for one wretched blade of grass. This churned-up battlefield was ghastly. Among the living lay the dead. As we dug ourselves in we found them in layers stacked one upon the top of another. One company after another had been shoved into the drum fire and steadily annihilated. The corpses were covered with the masses of soil turned up by the shells, and the next company advanced in the place of the fallen.

The sunken road and the ground behind were full of German dead; the ground in front, of English. Arms, legs, and heads stuck out stark above the lips of the craters. In front of our miserable defenses there were torn-off limbs and corpses over many of which cloaks and ground sheets had been thrown to hide the fixed stare of their distorted features. In spite of the heat no one thought for a moment of covering them with soil.

The village of Guillemont was distinguished from the landscape around it only because the shell holes there were of a whiter color by reason of the houses which had been ground to powder. Guillemont railway station lay in front of us. It was smashed to bits like a child's plaything. Delville Wood, reduced to matchwood, was farther behind.

Day had scarcely dawned when an English flying man descended on us in a steep spin and circled round incessantly like a bird of prey, while we made for our holes and cowered there. Nevertheless, the observer's sharp eyes must have spied us out, for a siren sounded its deep, long-drawn notes above us at short intervals. After a little while it appeared that a battery had received the signal. One heavy shell after another came at us on a flat trajectory with incredible fury. We crouched in our refuges and could do nothing. Now and then we lit a cigar and threw it away again. Every moment we expected a rush of earth to bury us. The sleeve of Schmidt's coat was torn by a big splinter.

At three in the afternoon the men came in from the left flank and said they could stick it no longer, as their shelters were shot to bits. It cost me all my callousness to get them back to their posts.

Just before ten at night the left flank of the regimental front was heavily shelled, and after twenty minutes we came in for it too. In a brief space we were completely covered in dust and smoke, and yet most of the hits were just in front or just behind. While this hurricane was raging I went along my platoon front. The men were standing, rifle in hand, as though carved in stone, their eyes fixed on the ground in front of them. Now and then by the light of a rocket I saw the gleam of helmet after helmet, bayonet after bayonet, and I was filled with pride at commanding this handful of men that might very likely be pounded into the earth but could not be conquered. It is in such moments that the human spirit triumphs over the mightiest demonstrations of material force. The fragile body, steeled by the will, stands up to the most terrific punishment.

QUESTIONS

1. When he wrote *Storm of Steel* Jünger believed that his experience had been a positive one. Why?

2. What was the average soldier's experience in the trenches like?

3. How did the war affect those caught up in it?

4. Judging from Jünger's account, why was the First World War so devastating? How was it different?

5. Is this an antiwar novel?

128.   **WOODROW WILSON**

THE FOURTEEN POINTS

(1918)

Woodrow Wilson (1856–1924), twenty-eighth president of the United States, brought America into the First World War on the side of the Allied Powers. Wilson was born in Virginia, but he was educated in the north, where he later made his home. A brilliant student, he became a professor of political economy, first at Weslyan University and later at Princeton. His abilities led him into administration, and in 1902 he was named president of Princeton. Wilson's credentials as a reformer were impressive enough to win him the governorship of New Jersey in 1910. Two years later he was elected president on the Democratic ticket. He was reelected in 1916 on the platform that he had kept America out of the European conflict, but by the next year he was persuaded to throw American might behind Britain and France. Wilson's change of policy was founded on his idealism—in the belief that the war would make the world safe for democracy and would eliminate forever the need for war. His dream of a League of Nations to settle world problems by debate rather than gunfire was achieved; but the U.S. Senate refused to ratify the Treaty of Versailles, so America never joined the League of Nations.

The Fourteen Points neatly summarize the principles for which Wilson believed the First World War was fought.

We have entered this war because violations of right had occurred which touched us to the quick and made the life of our own people impossible, unless they were corrected, and the world secured once for all against their recurrence.

What we demand in this war, therefore, is nothing peculiar to ourselves. It is that the world be made fit and safe to live in, and particularly that it be made safe for every peace-loving nation which, like our own, wishes to live its own free life, determine its own institutions, be assured of justice and fair dealing by the other peoples of the world, as against force and selfish aggression. All the peoples of the world are in effect partners in this interest, and for our own part we see very clearly that unless justice be done to others it will not be done to us.

The program of the world's peace, therefore, is our program; and that program, the only possible one as we see it, is this:

I. Open covenants of peace, openly arrived at, after which there shall be no private international understandings of any kind, but diplomacy shall proceed always frankly and in the public view.

II. Absolute freedom of navigation upon the seas, outside territorial waters, alike in peace and in war, except as the seas may be closed in whole or in part by international action for the enforcement of international covenants.

III. The removal, so far as possible, of all economic barriers and the establishment of an equality of trade conditions among all the nations consenting to the peace and associating themselves for its maintenance.

IV. Adequate guarantees given and taken that national armaments will be reduced to the lowest point consistent with domestic safety.

V. A free, open-minded, and absolutely impartial adjustment of all colonial claims, based upon a strict observance of the principle that in determining all such questions of sovereignty the interests of the populations concerned must have equal weight with the equitable claims of the Government whose title is to be determined.

VI. The evacuation of all Russian territory, and such a settlement of all questions affecting Russia as will secure the best and freest cooperation of the other nations of the world in obtaining for her an unhampered and unembarrassed opportunity for the independent determination of her own political development and national policy, and assure her of a sincere welcome into the society of free nations under institutions of her own choosing; and, more than a welcome, assistance also of every kind that she may need and may herself desire. The treatment accorded Russia by her sister nations in the months to come will be the acid test of their good will, of their comprehension of her needs as distinguished from their own interests, and of their intelligent and unselfish sympathy.

VII. Belgium, the whole world will agree, must be evacuated and restored without any attempt to limit the sovereignty which she enjoys in common with all other free nations. No other single act will serve as this will serve to restore confidence among the nations in the laws which they have themselves set and determined for the government of their relations with one another. Without this healing act the whole structure and validity of international law is forever impaired.

VIII. All French territory should be freed and the invaded portions restored; and the wrong done to France by Prussia in 1871 in the matter of Alsace-Lorraine, which has unsettled the peace of the world for nearly fifty years, should be righted, in order that peace may once more be made secure in the interest of all.

IX. A readjustment of the frontiers of Italy should be effected along clearly recognizable lines of nationality.

X. The peoples of Austria-Hungary, whose place among the nations we wish to see safeguarded and assured, should be accorded the freest opportunity of autonomous development.

XI. Rumania, Serbia, and Montenegro should be evacuated; occupied territories restored; Serbia accorded free and secure access to the sea; and the relations of the several Balkan states to one another determined by friendly counsel along historically established lines of allegiance and nationality; and international guarantees of the political and economic independence and territorial integrity of the several Balkan states should be entered into.

XII. The Turkish portions of the present Ottoman Empire should be assured a secure

Woodrow Wilson (1856–1924) served as the twenty-eighth president of the United States.

sovereignty, but the other nationalities which are now under Turkish rule should be assured an undoubted security of life and an absolutely unmolested opportunity of autonomous development, and the Dardanelles should be permanently opened as a free passage to the ships and commerce of all nations under international guaranties.

XIII. An independent Polish state should be erected which should include the territories inhabited by indisputably Polish populations, which should be assured a free and secure access to the sea, and whose political and economic independence and territorial integrity should be guaranteed by international covenant.

XIV. A general association of nations must be formed, under specific covenants, for the purpose of affording mutual guaranties of political independence and territorial integrity to great and small states alike.

In regard to these essential rectifications of wrong and assertions of right we feel ourselves to be intimate partners of all the Governments and peoples associated together against the imperialists. We cannot be separated in interest or divided in purpose. We stand together until the end.

QUESTIONS

1. Why, according to Wilson, had the United States entered the war?

2. A number of points of Wilson's plan touch on questions of national borders. Who, according to the president, should have the greatest role in deciding such questions?

3. What was to be the function of "general association of nations"?

4. The Fourteen Points were a masterful piece of political propaganda, but Wilson was less successful at translating them into reality. Why?

5. Do the Fourteen Points reflect any peculiarly American characteristics? Would the plan have been different if written by a French or British statesman?

129.   V. I. LENIN

WHAT IS TO BE DONE?

(1902)

Vladimir Ilich Ulyanov (1870–1924) took his famous pseudonym after he began his career as a professional revolutionary. Lenin was from a middle-class family and was strongly influenced by his older brother, who also was engaged in revolutionary politics. In 1887 his brother was captured by the tzarist regime and executed. From that moment, Lenin dedicated himself to the overthrow of the Russian government. He became a Marxist and joined the underground movement. In 1895 Lenin, too, was arrested and briefly imprisoned in Siberia. After 1900 he lived abroad, the exiled leader of the Bolshevik wing of the Social Democratic Party. It was not until the outbreak of the First World War that Lenin was able to return to Russia and begin the work of creating a Marxist revolution. In February 1917 the feeble government of the tzar was overthrown and eventually replaced by a provisional government led by Alexander Kerensky. It was Kerensky's government that Lenin worked to remove, tirelessly advocating its replacement by a truly revolutionary Marxist workers' regime. He succeeded in November 1917 and spent the rest of his life consolidating power in the new Soviet Union.

What Is to Be Done? is an early statement of Lenin's belief in the need for a truly socialist revolution. Against those who advocated a democratic trade union movement, as had developed in the Western democracies, Lenin called for a socialist revolution led by a cadre of party professionals. Only these revolutionaries could create the fundamental change that Lenin believed was necessary for Russia.

We have said that *there could not yet be* Social-Democratic consciousness among the workers. It could only be brought to them from without. The history of all countries shows that the working class, exclusively by its own effort, is able to develop only trade union consciousness, i.e., the conviction that it is necessary to combine in unions, fight the employers and strive to compel the government to pass necessary labour legislation, etc. The theory of Socialism, however, grew out of the philosophic, historical and economic theories that were elaborated by the educated representatives of the propertied classes, the intellectuals. According to their social status, the founders of modern scientific Socialism, Marx and Engels, themselves belonged to the bourgeois intelligentsia.

Since there can be no talk of an independent ideology being developed for the masses of the workers themselves in the process of their movement the *only* choice is: either the bourgeois or the socialist ideology. There is no middle course (for humanity has not created a "third" ideology, and, moreover, in a society torn by class antagonisms there can never be a non-class or above-class ideology). Hence, to belittle the socialist ideology *in any way,* to *turn away from it in the slightest degree* means to strengthen bourgeois ideology. There is a lot of talk about spontaneity, but the *spontaneous* development of the working-class movement leads to its becoming

subordinated to the bourgeois ideology, *leads to its developing according to the program* of the *Credo,* for the spontaneous working-class movement is trade unionism, and trade unionism means the ideological enslavement of the workers by the bourgeoisie. Hence, our task, the task of Social-Democracy, is to *combat spontaneity,* to *divert* the working-class movement from this spontaneous, trade-unionist striving to come under the wing of the bourgeoisie, and to bring it under the wing of revolutionary Social-Democracy.

As a matter of fact, it is possible to "raise the activity of the masses of the workers" *only* provided this activity *is not restricted* to "political agitation on an economic basis." And one of the fundamental conditions for the necessary expansion of political agitation is the organization of *comprehensive* political exposure. The masses *cannot* be trained in political consciousness and revolutionary activity in any other way except by means of such exposures. Hence, activity of this kind is one of the most important functions of international Social-Democracy as a whole, for even the existence of political liberty does not in the least remove the necessity for such exposures; it merely changes somewhat the sphere against which they are directed.

We are not children to be fed on the thin gruel of "economic" politics alone; we want to know everything that others know, we want to learn the details of *all* aspects of political life and to take part *actively* in every single political event. In order that we may do this, the intellectuals must talk to us less of what we already know, and tell us more about what we do not yet know and what we can never learn from our factory and "economic" experience, that is, you must give us political knowledge. You intellectuals can acquire this knowledge, and it is your *duty* to bring it to us in a hundred and a thousand times greater measure than you have done up to now; and you must bring it to us, not only in the form of arguments, pamphlets and articles which sometimes—excuse our frankness!—are rather dull, but precisely in the form of live *exposures* of what our government and our governing classes are doing at this very moment in all spheres of life. Just devote more zeal to carrying out this duty, and *talk less about "raising the activity of the masses of the workers!"* We are far more active than you think, and we are quite able to support, by open, street fighting, demands that do not promise any "palpable results" whatever! And it is not for you to "raise" our activity, because *activity is precisely the thing you yourselves lack!* Bow less in worship to spontaneity, and think more about raising *your own* activity, gentlemen!

A workers' organization must in the first place be a trade organization; secondly, it must be as broad as possible; and thirdly, it must be as little clandestine as possible (here, and further on, of course, I have only autocratic Russia in mind). On the other hand, the organizations of revolutionaries must consist first, foremost and mainly of people who make revolutionary activity their profession (that is why I speak of organizations of *revolutionaries*, meaning revolutionary Social-Democrats). In view of this common feature of the members of such an organization, *all distinctions as between workers and intellectuals,* and certainly distinctions of trade and profession, must be *utterly obliterated.* Such an organization must of necessity be not too extensive and as secret as possible.

As I have already said time and again that by "wise men," in connection with organization, I mean *professional revolutionaries,* irrespective of whether they are trained from among students or workingmen. I assert: 1) that no revolutionary movement can endure without a stable organization of leaders that maintains continuity; 2) that the wider the masses spontaneously drawn into the struggle, forming the basis of the movement and participating in it, the more urgent the need of such an organization, and the more solid this organization must be (for it is much easier for demagogues to sidetrack the more backward sections of the masses); 3) that such an organization must consist chiefly of people professionally engaged in revolutionary activity; 4) that in an autocratic state, the more we *confine* the membership of such an organization to people who are professionally engaged in revolutionary activity and who have been professionally trained in the art of combating the political police, the more difficult will it be to wipe out such an organization, and 5) the *greater* will be the number of people of the working class and of the other classes of society who will be able to join the movement and perform active work in it.

To concentrate all secret functions in the hands of as small a number of professional revolutionaries as possible does not mean that the latter will "do the thinking for all" and that the crowd will not take an active part in the *movement.* On the contrary, the crowd will advance from its ranks increasing numbers of professional revolutionaries; for it will know that it is not enough for a few students and for a few workingmen waging the economic struggle, to gather together and form a "committee," but that it takes years to train oneself to be a professional revolutionary; the crowd will "think" not of amateurish methods alone but of such training. The centralization of the secret functions of the *organization* by no means implies the centralization of all the functions of the *movement.* The active participation of the widest mass in the illegal press will not diminish because a "dozen" professional revolutionaries centralize the secret functions connected with this work; on the contrary, it will *increase* tenfold. In this way, and in this way alone, will we ensure that reading of illegal literature, writing for it, and to some extent even distributing it, will *almost cease to be secret work,* for the police will soon come to realize the folly and futility of setting the whole judicial and administrative machine into motion to intercept every copy of publication that is being broadcast in thousands. This applies not only to the press, but to every function of the movement, even to demonstrations. The active and widespread participation of the masses will not suffer; on the contrary, it will benefit by the fact that a "dozen" experienced revolutionaries, trained professionally no less than the police, will centralize all the secret aspects of the work—drawing up leaflets, working out approximate plans and appointing bodies of leaders for each urban district, for each factory district and for each educational institution, etc. (I know that exception will be taken to my "undemocratic" views, but I shall reply fully to this anything but intelligent objection later on.) The centralization of the most secret functions in an organization of revolutionaries will not diminish, but rather increase the extent and quality of the activity of a large number of other organizations which are intended for a broad public and are therefore as loose and as nonsecret as possible, such as workers' trade unions, workers' self-education circles and circles for reading illegal literature, socialist and also democratic circles among *all* other sections of the population, etc., etc. We must have such circles, trade unions and organizations everywhere in *as large a number as possible* and with the widest variety of functions; but it would be absurd and dangerous to *confuse* them with the organization of *revolutionaries,* to obliterate the border line between them, to dim still more the masses' already incredibly hazy appreciation of the fact that in order to "serve" the mass movement we must have people who will devote themselves exclusively to Social-Democratic activities, and that such people must *train* themselves patiently and steadfastly to be professional revolutionaries.

QUESTIONS

1. What is Lenin's view of dissent? How closely must people adhere to socialist thought?

2. Why does Lenin reject trade unionism for the working class?

3. What must a revolutionary movement have to succeed?

4. Lenin argues that revolutionary activity must be centralized. Why? How does this reflect his own interests?

5. Lenin ultimately succeeded in his goal of overthrowing the Russian government. Is *What Is to Be Done?* an effective blueprint for would-be revolutionaries?

The Second World War

130.   **J. M. KEYNES**

THE ECONOMIC CONSEQUENCES
OF THE PEACE
(1919)

John Maynard Keynes (1883–1946), one of the most distinguished modern economists, was born into an English academic family. He was educated at Eton and at King's College, Cambridge. Almost from the beginning he was marked out as a brilliant student, especially in mathematics and classics. At Cambridge he had a stunning career and was elected to the "Apostles," one of the most privileged of all undergraduate societies. His connection with the London Bloomsbury Group, which included Vanessa Bell and Virginia Woolf, brought his interest in mathematics toward the practical science of economics. Keynes made a career in government and as a university professor at Cambridge. His reputation was built upon his *General Theory of Employment, Interest, and Money* (1935–36), a technical work that advocated government intervention to lessen unemployment and developed the relationship between demand and overall economic conditions.

Attached to the British delegation at the Versailles conference after World War I, Keynes became so disillusioned with the proceedings that he resigned his post and published *The Economic Consequences of the Peace*. He was the first to argue that the reparations demanded of Germany would be counterproductive to the regeneration of Europe.

In England the outward aspect of life does not yet teach us to feel or realize in the least that an age is over. We are busy picking up the threads of our life where we dropped them, with this difference only, that many of us seem a good deal richer than we were before. Where we spent millions before the war, we have now learnt that we can spend hundreds of millions and apparently not suffer for it. Evidently we did not exploit to the utmost the possibilities of our economic life. We look, therefore, not only to a return to the comforts of 1914, but to an immense broadening and intensification of them. All classes alike thus build their plans, the rich to spend more and save less, the poor to spend more and work less.

But perhaps it is only in England (and America) that it is possible to be so unconscious. In continental Europe the earth heaves and no one but is aware of the rumblings. There it is not just a matter of extravagance or "labor troubles?"; but of life and death, of starvation and existence, and of the fearful convulsions of a dying civilization.

In the first place, the vast expenditures of the war, the inflation of prices, and the depreciation of currency, leading up to a complete instability of the unit of value, have made us lose all sense of number and magnitude in matters of finance. What we believed to be the limits of possibility have been so enormously exceeded, and those who founded their expectations on the past have been so often wrong, that the man in the street is now prepared to believe anything which is told him with some show of authority, and the larger the figure the more readily he swallows it.

There are no precedents for the indemnity imposed on Germany under the present Treaty; for the money exactions which formed part of the settlement after previous wars have differed in two fundamental respects from this one. The sum demanded has been determinate and has been measured in a lump sum of money; and so long as the defeated party was meeting the annual instalments of cash no consequential interference was necessary.

But for reasons already elucidated, the exactions in this case are not yet determinate, and the sum when fixed will prove in excess of what can be paid in cash and in excess also of what can be paid at all. It was necessary, therefore, to set up a body to establish the bill of claim, to fix the mode of payment, and to approve necessary abatements and delays. It was only possible to place this body in a position to exact the utmost year by year by giving it wide powers over the internal economic life of the enemy countries, who are to be treated henceforward as bankrupt estates to be administered by and for the benefit of the creditors. In fact, however, its powers and functions have been enlarged even beyond what was required for this purpose, and the Reparation Commission has been established as the final arbiter on numerous economic and financial issues which it was convenient to leave unsettled in the Treaty itself.

I cannot leave this subject as though its just treatment wholly depended either on our own pledges or on economic facts. The policy of reducing Germany to servitude for a generation, of degrading the lives of millions of human beings, and of depriving a whole nation of happiness should be abhorrent and detestable,— abhorrent and detestable, even if it were possible, even if it enriched ourselves, even if it did not sow the decay of the whole civilized life of Europe. Some preach it in the name of Justice. In the great events of man's history, in the unwinding of the complex fates of nations Justice is not so simple. And if it were, nations are not authorized, by religion or by natural morals, to visit on the children of their enemies the misdoings of parents or of rulers.

The essential facts of the situation, as I see them, are expressed simply. Europe consists of the densest aggregation of population in the history of the world. This population is accustomed to a relatively high standard of life, in which, even now, some sections of it anticipate improvement rather than deterioration. In relation to other continents Europe is not self-sufficient; in particular it cannot feed itself. Internally the population is not evenly distributed, but much of it is crowded into a relatively small number of dense industrial centers. This population secured for itself a livelihood before the war, without much margin of surplus, by means of a delicate and immensely complicated organization, of which the foundations were supported by coal, iron, transport, and an unbroken supply of imported food and raw materials from other continents. By the destruction of this organization and the interruption of the stream of supplies, a part of this population is deprived of its means of livelihood. Emigration is not open to the redundant surplus. For it would take years to transport them overseas, even, which is not the case, if countries could be found which were ready to receive them. The danger confronting us, therefore, is the rapid depression of the standard of life of the European populations to a point which will mean actual starvation for some (a point already reached in Russia and approximately reached in Austria). Men will not always die quietly. For starvation, which brings to some lethargy and a helpless despair, drives other temperaments to the nervous instability of hysteria and to a mad despair. And these in their distress may overturn the remnants of organization, and submerge civilization itself in their attempts to satisfy desperately the overwhelming needs of the individual. This is the danger against which all our resources and courage and idealism must now co-operate.

Lenin is said to have declared that the best way to destroy the Capitalist System was to debauch the currency. By a continuing process of inflation, governments can confiscate, secretly and unobserved, an important part of the wealth of their citizens. By this method they not only confiscate, but they confiscate *arbitrarily;* and, while the process impoverishes many, it actually enriches some. The sight of this arbitrary rearrangement of riches strikes not only at security, but at confidence in the equity of the existing distribution of wealth. Those to whom the system brings windfalls, beyond their deserts and even beyond their expectations or desires, become "profiteers," who are the object of the hatred of the bourgeoisie, whom the inflationism has impoverished, not less than of the proletariat. As the inflation proceeds and the real value of the currency fluctuates wildly from month to month, all permanent relations between debtors and creditors, which form the ultimate foundation of capitalism, become so utterly disordered as to be almost meaningless; and the process of wealth-getting degenerates into a gamble and a lottery.

Lenin was certainly right. There is no subtler, no surer means of overturning the existing basis of society than to debauch the currency. The process engages all the hidden forces of economic law on the side of destruction, and does it in a manner which not one man in a million is able to diagnose.

In the latter stages of the war all the belligerent governments practised, from necessity or incompetence, what a Bolshevist might have done from design. Even now, when the war is over, most of them continue out of weakness the same malpractices. But further, the Governments of Europe, being many of them at this moment reckless in their methods as well as weak, seek to direct on to a class known as "profiteers?" the popular indignation against the more obvious consequences of their vicious methods. These "profiteers?" are, broadly speaking, the entrepreneur class of capitalists, that is to say, the active and constructive element in the whole capitalist society, who in a period of rapidly rising prices cannot help but get rich quick whether they wish it or desire it or not. If prices are continually rising, every trader who has purchased for stock or owns property and plant inevitably makes profits. By directing hatred against this class, therefore, the European Governments are carrying a step further the fatal process which the subtle mind of Lenin had consciously conceived. The profiteers are a consequence and not a cause of rising prices. By combining a popular hatred of the class of entrepreneurs with the blow already given to social security by the violent and arbitrary disturbance of contract and of the established equilibrium of wealth which is the inevitable result of inflation, these Governments are fast rendering impossible a continuance of the social and economic order of the nineteenth century. But they have no plan for replacing it.

We are thus faced in Europe with the spectacle of an extraordinary weakness on the part of the great capitalist class, which has emerged from the industrial triumphs of the nineteenth century, and seemed a very few years ago our all-powerful master. The terror and personal timidity of the individuals of this class is now so great, their confidence in their place in society and in their necessity to the social organism so diminished, that they are the easy victims of intimidation. This was not so in England twenty-five years ago any more than it is now in the United States.

Then the capitalists believed in themselves, in their value to society, in the propriety of their continued existence in the full enjoyment of their riches and the unlimited exercise of their power. Now they tremble before every insult;—call them pro-Germans, international financiers, or profiteers, and they will give you any ransom you choose to ask not to speak of them so harshly. They allow themselves to be ruined and altogether undone by their own instruments, governments of their own making, and a press of which they are the proprietors. Perhaps it is historically true that no order of society ever perishes save by its own hand.

QUESTIONS

1. How has the Great War affected European society?

2. Why does Keynes oppose the extraction of war reparations from Germany?

3. Keynes identifies inflation as an important danger to economic and political stability. Why?

4. What, according to Keynes, has happened to the once-confident class of capitalist entrepreneurs in Europe?

5. Woodrow Wilson saw World War I as a crusade for democracy and peace. From Keynes's work, would you say that the outcome of the war had promoted those values?

131.   **WINIFRED HOLTBY**

WOMEN AND A CHANGING CIVILIZATION
(1934)

Winifred Holtby (1898–1935) was a novelist, poet, and journalist who was associated with British feminist and pacifist causes in the early part of the twentieth century. Born into a farming family, Holtby was strongly influenced by her mother who was the first woman country councilor in the East Riding of Yorkshire. She was educated locally and attended Sommerville College, Oxford where she read for a History degree between stints as a volunteer in the Women's Auxiliary during the First World War. At Oxford she began a lifelong friendship with Vera Brittain with whom she lived after moving to London. Her early career was as a journalist and she wrote for many of the leading newspapers of the day including the liberal Manchester Guardian. In 1926 she became editor of the feminist weekly magazine, *Time and Tide*. By then Holtby was a published novelist whose work retained a socialist bite and a Yorkshire flavor. After women were given the vote in Britain she worked tirelessly to educate them, publishing *A New Voter's Guide to Party Programs* (1929). After a trip to South Africa she set two of her novels there and continued to write both imaginative and sociological studies. Her appreciation of Virginia Woolf (1932) helped revive interest in Bloomsbury's women writers and her most important work, *South Riding* (1936) was published shortly after her death. It has twice been filmed as a movie and as a television serial. She died in 1935.

Women and a Changing Civilization (1934) was one of Holtby's sociological works which demonstrates her training as journalist. She was profoundly affected by the Great Depression (which contemporaries still called "the slump") and worried that it would cause deterioration in the recent gains made by British women.

The Slump Complex

These disadvantages are further accentuated by a group of reactions which I shall call the "slump complex." They have been particularly conspicuous during the past five years, and affect especially those young men and women who grew into maturity since the Armistice. Their condition is natural; it is directly attributable to the circumstances of their epoch, but they are apt to overlook this and mistake it for an unalterable law of nature ignored with naïve ignorance by their elders.

The effect of the slump upon women's economic position is most obvious, not only in the problems of unemployment among both industrial and professional women, but still more in the bitterness surrounding the question of married women's paid employment, "pin money" office girls, unorganised casual female factory labour, and claims to alimony, maintenance and separation allowances. These are the dilemmas of scarcity. It is here that the shoe pinches when national purchasing power has failed to distribute adequately the products of industry.

During the War, women entered almost every branch of industry and most of the professions. Even the Diplomatic Service, still, when this book is written, closed to women (though a

committee is inquiring into future possibilities) was temporarily invaded by the adventurous Gertrude Bell who, under the modest title of Temporary Assistant Political Officer, really acted as British representative in Iraq. In transport, engineering, chemicals, textiles, tailoring and woodwork, women took the places which, ever since the sorting-out process which followed the first disorganized scramble of the Industrial Revolution, had been reserved to men. They took and they enjoyed them.

Then the men returned, and on demobilization demanded again the jobs which they had left. The position was not simple.

Some of the men had received promises that their work should be kept for them; but of these, some did not return. Some women surrendered their shovels, lathes and hoes without a grievance. Their work had been "for the duration of the war" and they had no desire to retain it.

But others thought differently. Women, they told themselves, had been excluded from the more highly-skilled and better-paid industrial posts for two or more generations. They had been told that certain processes were beyond their power. It was a lie. During the war they had proved it to be so, by their own skill and efficiency. Why surrender without a word opportunities closed to them by fraud and falsehood? They had as much right to wheel, loom or cash-register as any man. Why then pretend that they were intruders in a world which was as much their own as their brothers'?

Some of these malcontents were nevertheless driven out; some stayed because their employers found them cheaper, and became unwilling blacklegs. One notable example of this was the case of "writing assistants" in the Civil Service, the lowest-graded category of clerks, engaged on purely mechanical and routine tasks. Organisations of ex-service men repeatedly petitioned that men should be admitted to this work; but the refusal was justified on the grounds that the work—besides being inadequately paid—was "too mechanical" for men.

The boom came; the new industries of the South sprang up like mushrooms; cities grew. For six or seven years it seemed as though production was infinite in expansion and the presence of women at unfamiliar tasks; though arousing occasional local criticism, not nationally disturbing.

The slump changed all that. After 1928, jobs became not duties which war-time propaganda taught girls that it was patriotic to perform, but privileges to be reserved for potential bread-winners and father of families. Women were commanded to go back to the home.

The bitterness began which has lasted ever since—the women keeping jobs and the men resenting it—the men regaining the jobs and the women resenting it.

On November 14th, 1933, the Central Hall, Westminster, was crowded for a mass meeting of women's organizations to proclaim the right of married women to paid employment. The crowds, the banners, the enthusiasm, echoed, faintly but unmistakably the sprit of pre-war suffrage meetings. The following March the Hall was nearly filled again when a similar demand was made for "Equal Pay for Equal Work."

In January 1934 the *New-Chronicle* published an article on Women Secretaries by a well-know writer, pleading the advantages of higher payment in order that the girls might not only be better fed and housed, but neater in appearance, more self-respecting and therefore more efficient. On the next day a correspondent had written in to the paper, bitterly complaining: "Better pay and smarter clothes for women: unemployment and patched pants for men."

The men have a real grievance. So long as women are content to accept lower wages, to remain unorganised, and to regard wage-earning as a "meanwhile" occupation till marriage, their cheap labour will continue to blackleg; and during any widespread contraction of trade, under a system of competitive capitalism, employers will deliberately use them for this purpose.

But the trouble is complex. The slump did not only depress the economic life of the country; it depressed its political, its intellectual and spiritual life.

Just after the war, society was infected by a rush of idealism to the head. Democracy and reason, equality and co-operation were acclaimed as uncontested virtues. In the new constitutions of Europe and America were incorporated splendid statements about the freedom of opinion, equality of the sexes, accessibility of education. We were about to build a brave new world upon the ruins of catastrophe.

The children who to-day are young men and women were assured at school of a good time coming. Everything evil was the result of four years' war; that horror had passed; they were to inherit the benefits purchased by sacrifice. Old hampering conventions had broken down; superstitions were destroyed; the young had come into their kingdom.

It was under the influence of this optimism that young women cherished ambitions for the wider exercise of their individual powers, and saw no limit to the kind and quality of service which they might offer to the community.

About 1926, after the General Strike in England and its failure, after the entry of Germany into the League of Nations and the delay by the Powers in making good their promises, the slump in idealism began to set in. Reason, democracy, the effort of the individual human will, liberty and equality were at a discount. As economic opportunities shrank, so the hopefulness and idealism of the early post-war period dwindled.

In Italy, Germany and Ireland a new dream of natural instinctive racial unity was arising, which designed for women a return to their "natural" functions of housekeeping and childbearing; while in the English-speaking countries a new anti-rational philosophy combined with economic fatalism, militated against the ebullient hopes which an earlier generation had pinned to education, effort, and individual enterprise.

All generalisations are false. In every civilised country are little groups of older women with memories of suffrage struggles, and young women who grew up into the post-war optimism, and whose ideas remain unchanged by the fashions of the hour. It is they who still organise protests against reaction; who in national and international societies defend the political, civil and economic equality of man and women; who invade new territories of achievement; who look towards a time when there shall be no wrangling over rights and wrongs, man's place and woman's place, but an equal and co-operative partnership, the individual going unfettered to the work for which he is best suited, responsibilities and obligations shared alike.

But these groups of professional women, organisers, artists, writers, members of societies like the Equal Rights International, the Open Door Council, the National Women's Party of America, the Women's International League of Peace and Freedom, are now in a minority and they know it.

The younger women more closely resemble a description recently given of the newly-adult generation in modern France. "They are fatalists. They are sensible. They are not interested in ideas. They believe that a war is coming against Germany which will destroy all individual plans, and the say 'Que Faire?' They do not choose their work. They have to take what they can get and be glad of that. They marry early, feeling that life being so short and uncertain they must make sure of posterity while they can. They are completely indifferent to large general principles or long-distance hopes of social amelioration. They have stoical courage but no enterprise, no hope, and no idealism. They ask for discipline, not freedom; for security, not for opportunity. Many of them are returning to orthodox religion; but few of them seem to have experienced religious ardour."

One man I know, an ex-minister of the Crown in this country, gave an explanation that the young generation just recently adult has grown up in a time of huge impersonal events—the War, the Boom, the Slump. News is reported daily of immense catastrophes over which they can have no control, the Japanese and Indian earthquakes, Chinese famine, African drought. The cheap daily press and wireless bring these facts vividly home to them in a way their ancestors never knew. The individual will seems unimportant, the individual personality is dwarfed, by happenings on so large a scale. The world is too much for them. They give it up, content to be passive passengers in a vehicle which they cannot steer.

This is the slump complex—this narrowing of ambition, this closing-in alike of ideas and opportunities. Somewhere, a spring of vitality and hope has failed. As though it required too great an effort against such odds to assume responsibility for their own individual destiny, they fall back upon tradition, instinct, orthodoxy. The slump is really a general resignation by humanity of its burden of initiative, and women fall under its influence as much as men.

QUESTIONS

1. What does Holtby mean by the "slump complex"?

2. What was the role of women in labor during the Great War?

3. How are women played off against the men in the labor market?

4. Why does Holtby think young women are fatalists?

---

132.   **BENITO MUSSOLINI**

FASCIST DOCTRINE
(1932)

Benito Mussolini (1883–1945) was the son of a blacksmith with socialist leanings in northern Italy. Educated at great financial sacrifice to his family, he chose a career as a political journalist. His talents led to his advancement to the position of editor of the official socialist newspaper in Rome. Mussolini broke with the party over Italy's role in the First World War. He served as a soldier in the Italian army and learned firsthand about his skills as a leader among the common people. After the war he formed the Fascist party, and by 1923 was the undisputed leader of Italy; his writings and ideas influenced Adolf Hitler. Although Mussolini believed that he could control the younger German leader, Italy became a satellite state of Germany by the end of the 1930s. Mussolini led Italy into the Second World War, invading Ethiopia and joining the Axis alliance. In 1943 he was deposed and two years later executed in Milan.

Fascist Doctrine is a statement of Mussolini's principles. His political program combined nationalism and anticommunism.

Fundamental Ideas

. . . Anti-individualistic, the Fascist conception of life stresses the importance of the State and accepts the individual only in so far as his interests coincide with those of the State. . . . It is opposed to classical liberalism which arose as a reaction to absolutism and exhausted its historical function when the State became the expression of the conscience and will of the people. Liberalism denied the State in the name of the individual; Fascism reasserts the rights of the State as expressing the real essence of the individual. And if liberty is to be the attribute of living men and not of abstract dummies invented by individualistic liberalism, then Fascism stands for liberty, and for the only liberty worth having, the liberty of the State and of the individual within the State. The Fascist conception of the State is all-embracing;

outside of it no human or spiritual values can exist, much less have value. Thus understood, Fascism is totalitarian, and the Fascist State—a synthesis and a unit inclusive of all values—interprets, develops, and potentiates the whole life of a people.

No individuals or groups (political parties, cultural associations, economic unions, social classes), exist outside the State. Fascism is therefore opposed to Socialism to which unity within the State (which amalgamates classes into a single economic and ethical reality) is unknown, and which sees in history nothing but the class struggle. Fascism is likewise opposed to trade-unionism as a class weapon. But when brought within the orbit of the State, Fascism recognises the real needs which give rise to socialism and trade-unionism, giving them due weight in the guild or corporative system in which divergent interests are coordinated and harmonised in the unity of the State.

Grouped according to their several interests, individuals form classes; they form trade-unions when organised according to their several economic activities; but first and foremost they form the State, which is no mere matter of numbers, the sum of the individuals forming the majority. Fascism is therefore opposed to that form of democracy which equates a nation to the majority, lowering it to the level of the largest number; but it is the purest form of democracy if the nation be considered—as it should be—from the point of view of quality rather than quantity, as an idea . . . expressing itself in a people as the conscience and will of the few, if not, indeed of one. . . .

Political and Social Doctrine

Fascism is now clearly defined not only as a régime but as a doctrine. . . .

First of all, as regards the future development of mankind—and quite apart from all present political considerations—Fascism does not, generally speaking, believe in the possibility or utility of perpetual peace. It therefore discards pacifism as a cloak for cowardly supine renunciation in contra-distinction to self-sacrifice. War alone keys up all human energies to their maximum tension and sets the seal of nobility on those peoples who have the courage to face it. . . . Therefore all doctrines which postulate peace at all costs are incompatible with Fascism. Equally foreign to the spirit of Fascism, even if accepted as useful in meeting special political situations—are all internationalistic or League superstructures which, as history shows, crumble to the ground whenever the heart of nations is deeply stirred by sentimental, idealistic or practical considerations. . . .

. . . Fascism [*is*] the resolute negation of the doctrine underlying so-called scientific and Marxian socialism, the doctrine of historic materialism which would explain the history of mankind in terms of the class-struggle and by changes in the processes and instruments of production, to the exclusion of all else.

That the vicissitudes of economic life . . . have their importance, no one denies; but that they suffice to explain human history to the exclusion of other factors is absurd. Fascism believes now and always in sanctity and heroism, that is to say in acts in which no economic motive—remote or immediate—is at work. Having denied historic materialism, which sees in men mere puppets on the surface of history, appearing and disappearing on the crest of the waves while in the depths the real directing forces move and work, Fascism also denies the immutable and irreparable character of the class struggle which is the natural outcome of this economic conception of history; above all it denies that the class struggle is the preponderating agent in social transformations. . . . [*Finally,*] Fascism denies the materialistic conception of happiness. . . . This means that Fascism denies the equation: well-being = happiness, which sees in men mere animals, content when they can feed and fatten, thus reducing them to a vegetative existence pure and simple.

After socialism, Fascism trains its guns on the whole block of democratic ideologies, and rejects both their premises and their practical applications and implements. Fascism denies that numbers, as such, can be the determining factor in human society; it denies the right of numbers to govern by means of periodical consultations; it asserts the irremediable and fertile and beneficent inequality of men who cannot be levelled by any such mechanical and extrinsic device as universal suffrage. Democratic régimes may be described as those under which the people are, from time to time, deluded into the belief that they exercise sovereignty, while all the time real sovereignty resides in and is exercised by other and sometimes irresponsible and secret forces. Democracy is a kingless régime infested by many kings who are sometimes more exclusive, tyrannical, and destructive than one, even if he be a tyrant. . . .

. . . In rejecting democracy Fascism rejects the absurd conventional lie of political equalitarianism, the habit of collective irresponsibility, the myth of felicity and indefinite progress. . . .

Fascism is definitely and absolutely opposed to the doctrines of liberalism, both in the political and the economic sphere. . . .

The liberal century, after piling up innumerable Gordian knots, tried to cut them with the sword of the world war. Never has any religion claimed so cruel a sacrifice. Were the Gods of liberalism thirsting for blood?

Now liberalism is preparing to close the doors of its temples, deserted by the peoples who feel that the agnosticism it professed in the sphere of economics and the indifferentism of which it has given proof in the sphere of politics and morals, would lead the world to ruin in the future as they have done in the past.

This explains why all the political experiments of our day are antiliberal. . . .

A party governing a nation "totalitarianly" is a new departure in history. . . . We are free to believe that this is the century of authority, a century tending to the "right," a Fascist century. If the nineteenth century was the century of the individual (liberalism implies individualism), we are free to believe that this is the "collective" century, and therefore the century of the State. . . . All doctrines aim at directing the activities of men towards a given objective. . . . A doctrine must therefore be a vital act and not a verbal display. Hence the pragmatic strain in Fascism, its will to power, its will to live, its attitude toward violence, and its value.

The keystone of the Fascist doctrine is its conception of the State, of its essence, its functions, and its aims. For Fascism the State is absolute, individuals and groups relative. . . . Instead of directing the game and guiding the material and moral progress of the community, the liberal State restricts its activities to recording results. The Fascist State is wide awake and has a will of its own. For this reason it can be described as "ethical." At the first quinquennial assembly of the régime, in 1929, I said:

"The Fascist State is not a night-watchman, solicitous only of the personal safety of its citizens; nor is it organized exclusively for the purpose of guarantying a certain degree of material prosperity and relatively peaceful conditions of life; a board of directors would do as much. Neither is it exclusively political, divorced from practical realities and holding itself aloof from the multifarious activities of the citizens and the nation. The State, as conceived and realised by Fascism is a spiritual and ethical entity for securing the political, juridical, and economic organization of the nation, an organisation which in its origin and growth is a manifestation of the spirit. The State guarantees the internal and external safety of the country, but it also safeguards and transmits the spirit of the people, elaborated down the ages in its language, its customs, its faith. The State is not only the present, it is also the past and above all the future. Transcending the individual's brief spell of life, the State stands for the immanent conscience of the nation. The forms in which it finds expression change, but the need for it remains. The State educates the citizens to civism, makes them aware of their mission, urges them to unity; its justice harmonises their divergent interests; it transmits to future generations the conquests of the mind in the fields of science, art, law, human solidarity; it leads men up from primitive tribal life to that highest manifestation of human power, imperial rule. The State hands down to future generations the memory of those who laid down their lives to ensure its safety or to obey its laws; it sets up as examples and records for future ages the names of the captains who enlarged its territory and of the men of genius who have made it famous. Whenever respect for the State declines and the disintegrating and centrifugal tendencies of individuals and groups prevail, nations are headed for decay."

Since 1929 economic and political developments have everywhere emphasised these truths. The importance of the State is rapidly growing. The so-called crisis, (depression) can only be settled by State action and within the orbit of the State. . . .

If liberalism spells individualism, Fascism spells government. The Fascist State is, however, a unique and original creation. It is not reactionary but revolutionary, for it anticipates the solution of certain universal problems which have been raised elsewhere, in the political field by the splitting-up of parties, the usurpation of power by parliaments, the irresponsibility of assemblies; in the economic field by the increasingly numerous and important functions discharged by trade-unions and trade associations with their disputes and ententes, affecting both capital and labor; in the ethical field by the need felt for order, discipline, obedience to the moral dictates of patriotism.

Fascism desires the State to be strong and organic, based on broad foundations of popular support. The Fascist State lays claim to rule in the economic field no less than in others; it makes its action felt throughout the length and breadth of the country by means of its corporative, social, and educational institutions, and all the political, economic, and spiritual forces of the nation, organised in their respective associations, circulate within the State.

A State based on millions of individuals who recognise its authority, feel its action, and are ready to serve its ends is not the tyrannical state of mediaeval lordling. It has nothing in common with the despotic States existing prior to or subsequent to 1789. Far from crushing the individual, the Fascist State multiplies his energies, just as in a regiment a soldier is not diminished but multiplied by the number of his fellow soldiers.

The Fascist State organises the nation, but it leaves the individual adequate elbow room. It has curtailed useless or harmful liberties while preserving those which are essential. In such matters the individual cannot be the judge, but the State only.

The Fascist State is not indifferent to religious phenomena in general nor does it maintain an attitude of indifference to Roman Catholicism, the special, positive religion of Italians. The State has not got a theology but it has a moral code. The Fascist State sees in religion one of the deepest of spiritual manifestations and for this reason it not only respects religion but defends and protects it. The Fascist State does not attempt, as did Robespierre at the height of the revolutionary delirium of the Convention, to set up a "god" of its own; nor does it vainly seek, as does Bolshevism, to efface God from the soul of man. Fascism respects the God of ascetics, saints, and heroes, and it also respects God as conceived by the ingenuous and primitive heart of the people, the God to whom their prayers are raised.

The Fascist State expresses the will to exercise power and to command. Here the Roman tradition is embodied in a conception of strength. . . . Fascism sees in the imperialistic spirit—i.e. in the tendency of nations to expand—a manifestation of their vitality. In the opposite tendency, which would limit their interests to the home country, it sees a symptom of decadence. Peoples who rise or rearise are imperialistic; renunciation is characteristic of dying peoples. The Fascist doctrine is that best suited to the tendencies and feelings of a people which, like the Italian, after lying fallow during centuries of foreign servitude, is now reasserting itself in the world.

But imperialism implies discipline, the coordination of efforts, a deep sense of duty and a spirit of self-sacrifice. This explains many aspects of the practical activity of the régime, and the direction taken by many of the forces of the State, as also the severity which has to be exercised towards those who would oppose this spontaneous and inevitable movement of twentieth century Italy by agitating outgrown ideologies of the nineteenth century, ideologies rejected wherever great experiments in political and social transformations are being dared.

Never before have the peoples thirsted for authority, direction, order, as they do now. If each age has its doctrine, then innumerable symptoms indicate that the doctrine of our age is the Fascist. . . .

Fascism has now acquired throughout the world that universality which belongs to all doctrines which by achieving self-expression represent a moment in the history of human thought.

QUESTIONS

1. What is liberty in the Fascist state? Why does the state have total power?

2. Mussolini would have argued that the Fascist state was democratic. Why?

3. What is the Fascist view of war?

4. Why do Fascists reject socialism and liberal democracy?

5. Mussolini claimed that fascism enhanced the life of the individual. How so?

---

133.   **ADOLF HITLER**

MEIN KAMPF

(1923)

Adolf Hitler (1889–1945) was the leader of one of the most powerful and brutal dictatorships in Western history. His father was a minor customs official in Austria, so Adolf grew up in a provincial town on the German border. His early years were spent pursuing an unsuccessful career as an artist against his father's wishes. In 1913 he left Austria in order to avoid military conscription and settled in Munich where, paradoxically, he became so caught up in war fever that he joined the German army. Hitler served in

France, where he was wounded several times and eventually decorated for bravery. The war was the happiest period of his life; when he was demobilized after the German defeat, he joined and eventually led the right-wing National Socialist German Workers Party. His politics were a mixture of nationalism and racism that appealed especially to former soldiers who shared Hitler's view that Germany had not lost the First World War, but had been betrayed by its leaders. By 1932 the Nazi party was the largest in Germany; Hitler was named chancellor in 1933. Once in power, he began an economic and military recovery that restored Germany to its former position as one of the leading states in Europe. His territorial ambitions, however, led directly to the Second World War, and his racial attitudes led directly to the Holocaust. When Germany's military situation became hopeless, Hitler committed suicide in Berlin in 1945.

Mein Kampf was written while Hitler was in jail after an attempt to overthrow the German government. The title means "My Struggle"; this very long and turgid work is a combination of a memoir and a statement of political philosophy. It includes some of Hitler's characteristic racist and anti-Semitic ideas.

It is a futile enterprise to argue which race or races were the original bearers of human culture and, with it, the actual founders of what we sum up with the word "mankind." It is simpler to put this question to oneself with regard to the present, and here the answer follows easily and distinctly. What we see before us of human culture today, the results of art, science, and techniques, is almost exclusively the creative product of the Aryan. But just this fact admits of the not unfounded conclusion that he alone was the founder of higher humanity as a whole, thus the prototype of what we understand by the word "man." He is the Prometheus of mankind, out of whose bright forehead springs the divine spark of genius at all times, forever rekindling that fire which in the form of knowledge lightened up the night of silent secrets and thus made man climb the path towards the position of master of the other beings on this earth. Exclude him—and deep darkness will again fall upon the earth, perhaps even, after a few thousand years, human culture would perish and the world would turn into a desert.

If one were to divide mankind into three groups: culture-founders, culture-bearers, and culture-destroyers, then, as representative of the

first kind, only the Aryan would come in question. It is from him that the foundation and the walls of all human creations originate, and only the external form and color depend on the characteristics of the various peoples involved. He furnishes the gigantic building-stones and also the plans for all human progress, and only the execution corresponds to the character of the people and races in the various instances. In a few decades, for instance, the entire east of Asia will call a culture its own, the ultimate bases of which will be Hellenic spirit and Germanic technique, just as is the case with us. Only the *external* form will (at least partly) bear the features of Asiatic character. It is not the case, as some people claim, that Japan adds European techniques to her culture, but European science and techniques are trimmed with Japanese characteristics. But the basis of actual life is no longer the special Japanese culture, although it determines the color of life (because outwardly, in consequence of its inner difference, it is more visible to European eyes), but it is the enormous scientific and technical work of Europe and America, that is, of Aryan peoples. Based on these achievements alone the East is also able to follow general human progress. This creates the basis for the fight for daily bread, it furnishes weapons and tools for it, and only the external makeup is gradually adapted to Japanese life.

But if, starting today, all further Aryan influence upon Japan should stop, and supposing that Europe and America were to perish, then a further development of Japan's present rise in science and technology could take place for a little while longer; but in the time of a few years the source would dry out, Japanese life would gain, but its culture would stiffen and fall back into the sleep out of which it was startled seven decades ago by the Aryan wave of culture. Therefore, exactly as the present Japanese development owes its life to Aryan origin, thus also in the dim past foreign influence and foreign spirit were the awakener of the Japanese culture. The best proof of this is the fact that the latter stiffened and became completely paralyzed later on. This can only happen to a people when the originally creative race nucleus was lost, or when the external influence, which gave the impetus and the material for the first development in the cultural field, was lacking later on. But if it is ascertained that a people receives, takes in, and works over the essential basic elements of its culture from other races, and if then, when a further external influence is lacking, it stiffens again and again, then one can perhaps call such a race a "*culture-bearing*" one but never a "*culture-creating*" one.

We see this most clearly in that race that cannot help having been, and being, the supporter of the development of human culture—the Aryans. As soon as Fate leads them towards special conditions, their latent abilities begin to develop in a more and more rapid course and to mold themselves into tangible forms. The cultures which they found in such cases are nearly always decisively determined by the available soil, the climate, and—by the subjected people. The latter, however, is the most decisive of all factors. The more primitive the technical presumptions for a cultural activity are, the more necessary is the presence of human auxiliary forces which then, collected and applied with the object of organization, have to replace the force of the machine. Without this possibility of utilizing inferior men, the Aryan would never have been able to take the first steps towards his later culture; exactly as, without the help of various suitable animals which he knew how to tame, he would never have arrived at a technology which now allows him to do without these very animals. The words *"Der Mohr hat seine Schuldigkeit getan, er kann gehen"* [The Moor has done his duty, he may go] has unfortunately too deep a meaning. For thousands of years the horse had to serve man and to help in laying the foundations of a development which now, through the motor-car, makes the horse itself superfluous. In a few years it will have ceased its activity, but without its former cooperation man would hardly have arrived at where he stands today.

Therefore, for the formation of higher cultures, the existence of inferior men was one of the most essential presumptions, because they alone were able to replace the lack of technical means without which a higher development is unthinkable. The first culture of mankind certainly depended less on the tamed animal, but rather on the use of inferior people.

Only after the enslavement of subjected races, the same fate began to meet the animals, and not *vice versa*, as many would like to believe. For first the conquered walked behind the plow—and after him, the horse. Only pacifist fools can again look upon this as a sign of human baseness, without making clear to themselves that this development had to take place in order to arrive finally at that place from where today these apostles are able to sputter forth their drivel into the world.

The progress of mankind resembles the ascent on an endless ladder; one cannot arrive at the top without first having taken the lower steps. Thus the Aryan had to go the way which reality showed him and not that of which the imagination of a modern pacifist dreams. The way of reality, however, is hard and difficult, but it finally ends where the other wishes to bring mankind by dreaming, but unfortunately removes it from, rather than brings it nearer to, it.

Therefore, it is no accident that the first cultures originated in those places where the Aryan, by meeting lower peoples, subdued them and made them subject to his will. They, then, were the first technical instrument in the service of a growing culture.

With this the way that the Aryan had to go was clearly lined out. As a conqueror he subjected the lower peoples and then he regulated their practical ability according to his command and his will and for his aims. But while he thus led them towards a useful, though hard activity, he not only spared the lives of the subjected, but perhaps he even gave them a fate which was better than that of their former so-called "freedom." As long as he kept up ruthlessly the master's standpoint, he not only really remained "master" but also the preserver and propagator of the culture. For the latter was based exclusively on his abilities, and, with it, on his preservation in purity. But as soon as the subjected peoples themselves began to rise (probably) and approached the conqueror linguistically, the sharp separating wall between master and slave fell. The Aryan gave up the purity of his blood and therefore he also lost his place in the Paradise which he had created for himself. He became submerged in the race-mixture, he gradually lost his cultural ability more and more, till at last not only mentally but also physically he began to resemble more the subjected and aborigines than his ancestors. For some time he may still live on the existing cultural goods, but then petrifaction sets in, and finally oblivion.

In this way cultures and realms collapse in order to make room for new formations.

The blood-mixing, however, with the lowering of the racial level caused by it, is the sole cause of the dying-off of old cultures; for the people do not perish by lost wars, but by the loss of that force of resistance which is contained only in the pure blood.

All that is not race in this world is trash.

All world historical events, however, are only the expression of the races' instinct of self-preservation in its good or in its evil meaning.

The Jew forms the strongest contrast to the Aryan. Hardly in any people of the world is the instinct of self-preservation more strongly developed than in the so-called "chosen people." The fact of the existence of this race alone may be looked upon as the best proof of this. Where is the people that in the past two thousand years has been exposed to so small changes of the inner disposition, of character, etc., as the Jewish people? Which people finally has experienced greater changes than this one—and yet has always come forth the same from the most colossal catastrophes of mankind? What an infinitely persistent will for life, for preserving the race do these facts disclose!

Also the intellectual abilities were schooled in the course of centuries. Today the Jew is looked upon as "clever," and in a certain sense he has been so at all times. But his reason is not the result of his own development, but that of object lessons from without.

Never did the reverse process take place.

For, even if the Jewish people's instinct of self-preservation is not smaller, but rather greater, than that of other nations, and even if his spiritual abilities very easily create the impression as though they were equal to the intellectual disposition of the other races, yet the most essential presumption for a cultured people is completely lacking, the idealistic disposition.

But how far the Jew takes over foreign culture, only imitating, or rather destroying, it, may be seen from the fact that he is found most frequently in that art which also appears directed least of all towards invention of its own, the art of acting. But here, too, he is really only the "juggler," or rather the ape; for here, too, he lacks the ultimate touch of real greatness; here, too, he is not the ingenious creator, but the outward imitator, whereby all the turns and tricks he applies cannot deceive us concerning the inner lack of lowers man, and never again can its consequences be removed from body and mind.

Only upon examining and comparing, in the face of this sole question, all the other problems of life, one will be able to judge how ridiculously small the latter are as compared with the former. How all of them are only temporal, while the question of the preservation of the blood is one of human eternity.

All really important symptoms of decay of the pre-War time ultimately go back to racial causes.

QUESTIONS

1. What is the role of the Aryan race in human history, according to Hitler?

2. Why are the Japanese, in Hitler's theories, a "culture-bearing" rather than a "culture-creating" people?

3. Hitler believed that cultural progress was necessarily aggressive. Why? How might these views have applied to his own policies in later years?

4. How are Jews said to destroy cultures?

5. Did Hitler view the defeat in World War I as inevitable? Was the Allied victory a good or a bad thing, in Hitler's view?

134.

MEMORIES OF THE HOLOCAUST

(1938–1945)

The following selections are the recollections of three survivors of the Holocaust. Sam Bankhalter was born to a Jewish family in Lodz, Poland; Fred Baron to an Austrian Jewish family; and Reidar Dittmann was a Protestant Norwegian. Although from very different backgrounds and countries, they all had one thing in common: they were deemed enemies of the Nazi state. Bankhalter and Baron were Jews, and Dittmann was a political dissident. All three were very lucky in that unlike most of the others who fell into the hands of the S.S., they survived.

Baron and Bankhalter were deported to the infamous death camp at Auschwitz in occupied Poland, and Dittmann was held in the German camp at Buchenwald. They were rescued at the end of the war by Allied forces.

[Sam Bankhalter's father was a manufacturer of prefabricated wooden houses, a Hebrew scholar, and an ardent Zionist who helped young Poles who wanted to go to Palestine. Sam was running an errand for his father when the Nazis caught him and sent him to Auschwitz.]

There was always anti-Semitism in Poland. The slogan even before Hitler was "Jew, get out of here and go to Palestine." As Hitler came to power, there was not a day at school I was not spit on or beaten up.

I was at camp when the Germans invaded Poland. The camp directors told us to find our own way home. We walked many miles with airplanes over our heads, dead people on the streets. At home there were blackouts. I was just a kid, tickled to death when I was issued a flashlight and gas mask. The Polish army was equipped with buggies and horses, the Germans were all on trucks and tanks. The war was over in ten days.

THE GHETTO The German occupation was humiliation from day one. If Jewish people were wearing the beard and sidecurls, the Germans were cutting the beard, cutting the sidecurls, laughing at you, beating you up a little bit. Then the Germans took part of Lodz and put on barbed wire, and all the Jews had to assemble in this ghetto area. You had to leave in five or ten minutes or half an hour, so you couldn't take much stuff with you.

The Jewish community chose my father to run the cemetery, to organize burials and clean up the streets, because dead people started smelling on the streets. They brought in frozen Jewish soldiers, hundreds and hundreds. I helped bury them.

AUSCHWITZ We were the first ones in Auschwitz. We built it. What you got for clothing was striped pants and the striped jacket, no underwear, no socks. In wintertime you put paper in your shoes, and we used to take empty cement sacks and put a string in the top, put two together, one in back and one in front, to keep warm.

If they told you to do something, you went to do it. There was no yes or no, no choices. I worked in the crematorium for about eleven months. I saw Dr. Mengele's experiments on children, I knew the kids that became vegetables. Later in Buchenwald I saw Ilse Koch with a hose and regulator, trying to get pressure to make a hole in a woman's stomach. I saw them cutting Greek people in pieces. I was in Flossenburg for two weeks, and they shot 25,000 Russian soldiers, and we put them down on wooden logs and burned them. Every day the killing, the hanging, the shooting, the crematorium smell, the ovens, and the smoke going out.

I knew everybody, knew every trick to survive. I was one of the youngest in Auschwitz, and I was like "adopted" by a lot of the older people, especially the fathers. Whole families came into Auschwitz together, and you got to Dr. Mengele, who was saying "right, left, left, right," and you knew, right there, who is going to the gas chamber and who is not. Most of the men broke down when they knew their wives and their kids—three-, five-, nine-year-olds—went into the gas chambers. In fact, one of my brothers committed suicide in Auschwitz because he couldn't live with knowing his wife and children are dead.

I was able to see my family when they came into Auschwitz in 1944. I had a sister, she had a little boy a year old. Everybody that carried a child went automatically to the gas chamber, so my mother took the child. My sister survived, but she still suffers, feels she was a part of killing my mother.

I waved to my mother and I went over to my father and said, "Dad, where's God? They kill rabbis, priests, ministers, the more religious, the faster they go! What has happened?" His only answer to me was, "This is the way God wants it." This was the last time I spoke to my father. . . .

[Fred Baron was fifteen when the Germans marched into Vienna in 1938. His parents were well-to-do assimilated Jews; both died in the Holocaust.]

Jews rounded up in the Warsaw Ghetto, World War II.

. . . In March 1938 the Germans marched into Austria. What had evolved in Germany over five years happened in Austria within a matter of weeks.

THE OCCUPATION One of my best friends became overnight an outspoken Austrian Nationalist and an anti-Semite. I was kicked out of high school. My father's store was closed down. Bank accounts were closed, people lost their jobs, Jews were not allowed to practice as professionals. We were penniless, forced to share our apartment with other Jews.

Jews could not go to any public building or any parks. We could not go to a library or movie. We were not allowed to ride on public transportation except under certain conditions, and then only on the rear platform. We could not go into a store, except one hour a day. Even if we had money we were not allowed to buy many things, including some foods, because they were just not sold to Jews. I went to a soup kitchen every day to bring home our only meal.

September 1, 1939, war broke out with Poland, and after a few weeks they took Jewish people on trains and dumped them in ghettoes in Polish cities. Many of our friends were taken this way. My father saw his family, everything, going down the drain. He became very sick, and there was no medical treatment for Jews, so he didn't get any treatment and soon died.

My mother and I were hiding one night here and one night there, with non-Jewish friends. Anybody hiding a Jew was subject to terrible penalties, so to ask even a close friend to hide you was not an easy thing to do. We also tried to hide in Jewish apartments where the people were already deported.

Then I found work at the railroad station and was given security for myself and my mother. I worked carrying pig-iron on my shoulders.

In fall of 1941 the German extermination policy really got running. Transports to the east were increasing, so my mother and I went over the border at night to Hungary.

In Hungary I was trying to get legal documentation so we could get food stamps. I traveled to a little town where somebody with connections was supposedly able to give us the necessary papers. But a crime was committed in the town, and as soon as they saw me, a stranger, they put me in jail. The judge said I was innocent but wanted to send me back to Austria! I tried to explain that being sent back there was like a death sentence, and finally the judge dismissed me because I had some papers from my father, who was a volunteer and an officer in the Austro-Hungarian army in the first World War. I was given papers that I was a legal resident of Hungary and could get food tickets.

Then the Hungarian authorities got hold of my mother and put her in jail in Budapest. Because we entered the country without papers, they told her they would deport her unless I would join her.

This was December 1941. We were sent to an internment camp in northeastern Hungary. There were separate buildings for men and women, but I saw my mother from time to time. Later all the male Jews were sent to a prison camp near the Slovakian border, and my mother was freed to live with relatives in Hungary. She sent me letters, a package containing some clothing, even a cake. Then the German S.S. completed the occupation of Hungary in the spring of 1944, my mother again was put into a camp, and that was the last I heard from her.

DEPORTATION I was marched with the local Jewish population—men, women, and children—eight or ten hours, to a small railroad station. Nobody told us where we were going. We were forced into railroad cars, 100 to 120 in one car, like sardines, without food, without water, without any sanitary facility. The cars were sealed and we stood there for maybe half a day before even moving. Finally, began the slow trip to nowhere.

There were children in our car, and old people. People got sick, died, and some went insane. It was an absolute, indescribable hell. I really don't know how many days and nights we were in that living hell on wheels.

When we finally stopped, they tore open the railroad cars and we were blinded by light, because our eyes were just not used to light any more. We saw funny-looking characters wearing striped pajama-like uniforms with matching caps, with great big sticks in their hands. They were screaming and yelling in all languages to jump out of the cars.

I didn't know where I was. All around us were barracks and barbed wire and machine gun towers, and in the distance I saw what looked like a huge factory with black smoke coming out of chimneys. I noticed a peculiar smell in the air and also a fine dust, subduing the light. The sunshine was not bright but there were birds singing. It was a beautiful day.

We were marched through a meadow filled with yellow flowers and one of the fellows next to me just turned and walked straight into the meadow. The guards cried out to him to stop, but he didn't hear or he didn't want to. He just kept slowly marching into the meadow, and then they opened up with machine guns and the man fell down dead. And that was my reception to Auschwitz.

AUSCHWITZ We were separated, men and women, and formed rows of fives. I found myself in front of a very elegantly dressed German officer. He was wearing boots and white gloves and he carried a riding whip, and with the whip he was pointing left or right, left or right. Whichever direction he pointed, guards pushed the person in front of him either left or right. I was twenty-one years old and in pretty good shape, but older people were sent to the other side and marched away.

We had to undress and throw away all belongings except our shoes. We were chased through a cold shower, and we stood shivering in the night air until we were told to march to a barracks. We were handed prisoner uniforms—a jacket, pants, and a sort of beanie—and a metal dish. We didn't really know what happened yet. We were absolutely numb.

A non-Jewish kapo, an Austrian with a hard, weather-beaten face, told us, "You have arrived at hell on earth." He had been in prison since 1938, and he gave us basic concepts on how to stay alive.

"Don't trust anybody," he said, "don't trust your best friend. Look out for yourself. Be selfish to the point of obscenity. Try and stay alive from one minute to the other one. Don't let down for one second. Always try and find out where the nearest guards are and what they are doing. Don't volunteer for anything. And don't get sick, or you will be a goner in no time."

Auschwitz was gigantic—rows and rows of barracks as far as the eye could see, subdivided by double strings of electric barbed wire. There were Hungarians and Polish Jews and a great number of Greeks, many Dutch Jews, some French, Germans.

Food was our main interest in life. In the morning we received what they called coffee— black water. We worked until noon, then we got a bowl of soup. In the evening we received another bowl of either vegetable or soup, a little piece of bread, and sometimes a tiny little piece of margarine or sugar or some kind of sausage. And that was the food for the day.

Suicides happened all the time, usually by hanging, at night. One fellow threw himself in front of a truck. It just broke his arm, but the S.S. guards beat him to a pulp, and in the morning he was dead.

A tremendous number of transports were coming in. The gas chambers could not keep up,

so they were burning people in huge pits. Some of the smaller children were thrown in alive. We could hear the screams day and night, but sometimes the human mind can take just so much and then it just closes up and refuses to accept what is happening just 100, 200 feet away. . . .

[*Reidar Dittmann was a Lutheran. He was only eighteen, a music student studying choral conducting, when the Germans occupied his country in April 1940.*]

I was the first political prisoner in the history of my home town, and my home town is 1,100 years old! In October of 1940 I demonstrated against the Germans by leading 4,000 young people singing anti-German songs, and I was arrested and given a six-week jail term. But my father came, and the judge let him take me home.

When the underground was organized that same fall, it became reasonable for the organizers to use someone who had already showed his loyalty. As a clerk in a shipyard building ships for the Germans, my task as a member of the resistance was to see to it that work would go very slowly. One day a major merchant vessel was being officially baptized by the admiral of the German fleet in Norway. His wife cracked the champagne bottle on the prow, the ship sailed down the bedding—and then it sank! We had removed the plates the night before. I was sentenced to life imprisonment for that and sent to build coastal fortifications.

Then the puppet premier of Norway, Vidkun Quisling, pardoned 1,000 political prisoners according to age, and since I was only nineteen, I was sent home. I immediately got back into the underground, and I was apprehended again. This time I was sent to Germany, to Buchenwald.

BUCHENWALD The first concentration camps in Germany were built to get members of the political opposition out of the way. The senior inmate in my barracks was a German Social Democrat, a member of the city council in Kassel. He was imprisoned on April 15, 1933, six weeks after the Nazi takeover! He was a professional survivor, number 431. I had number 32,232.

The corpse carriers were one of the more active working teams in Buchenwald. From 800 to 2,000 people died every day. We estimated that if you were Norwegian, Dutch, Danish, you might survive. If you were Belgian or French, your chances were slightly poorer. If you were Czechoslovakian or Hungarian, they were even poorer. As a Polish prisoner, you had a life expectancy of three weeks. The Jews, of course, were a totally separate category, brought into Buchenwald for the express purpose of being exterminated.

We wore our numbers in a triangle on our left breast pocket. A red triangle meant political prisoner, and we had *NO*, which meant *Norwegian*. Criminals were wearing green triangles. Jewish prisoners had a purple triangle. The tattooing of numbers was reserved for Jewish prisoners.

On my card was written "Germanic intellectual material." I was Lutheran, Protestant, I was a university student, I was "Germanic"—blue eyes, blond hair. I was like an S.S. recruitment poster! So in a sense, that card said I was destined to survive. . . .

Everything you did in camp, you did through responding to the public address system. One morning we were informed that roll call was delayed. We could hear the grinding of trucks, the mobile gas chambers that were waiting. And we knew that the night before some 10,000 Jews had arrived from Hungary.

We were hovering out in front of our barracks, and we heard this shuffling of wooden shoes against the gravel, from the lower part of the camp. The sound came closer and closer, and in the grayness of this November morning we saw masses of people shuffling toward the roll-call area.

They were all males. There were some so old they couldn't walk by themselves but had to be supported by younger individuals. And there were some so young they hadn't yet learned to walk, and they were carried in the arms of their fathers, their uncles, their grandfathers. They were all walking toward annihilation.

And on this particular day, the smoke poured forth so voluminously from the crematory chimney that daylight didn't break through.

As the war approached its end in the spring of 1945, we hardly got any food at all. I was convinced I wouldn't survive, because we were all thinking, "The Germans are not going to let us get out and tell about it."

LIBERATION To be called to the gate meant to be exterminated. On March 18, 1945, the announcement came over the public address system, "All Norwegians to the gate." We were 349 Norwegians. We shuffled up the walk to the roll-call area, and the commander-in-chief—he was hanged in Nuremberg—came in with two people in dusty uniforms. He was smiling. To see him frown was horrible. To see him smile was even worse.

One of the two young men in the dusty uniforms said to us in Swedish, "I have come to take you to neutral Sweden." We didn't believe it. We thought that this is a trick. And then he said, "Go back to your barracks and pick up your belongings."

If he had been part of the system, he would certainly have known that we had nothing but our striped suits, and a triangle with a number, and our wooden shoes! So we shuffled back to the barracks, and into the barracks, and out again, and back to the roll-call area. And there they were, the two in the dusty uniforms, and the commander was gone. And the same young man said, "All right, boys. Let's go. . . ."

I weighed ninety-two pounds.

QUESTIONS

1. Extermination became Nazi policy for the Jewish people in 1941. How did the regime deal with Jews before that date?

2. Some Jews survived the Holocaust by eluding capture. How did Fred Baron manage to escape captivity for so long?

3. What were conditions in the camps like? What could a prisoner do to survive?

4. Nazi racial policy dictated different treatment for different nationalities—how does this document illustrate this point?

5. Compare these accounts with the testimony of Adolf Eichmann, the man who organized the transport of Jews to the camps (pp. 281–284). How different are they?

135.   **WINSTON CHURCHILL**

SPEECHES

(1940)

Winston Churchill (1874–1965), artist, writer, historian, journalist, and prime minister of England from 1940 to 1945 and again from 1951 to 1955, was born at Blenheim, the ancestral home of his family since the eighteenth century. His father was Lord Randolph Churchill, one of the rising stars in the Conservative party during the 1880s. Winston attended Harrow and the Royal Military Academy at Sandhurst, where he prepared for a career as an officer. He fought in India and Africa before returning to England to enter politics. First elected to Parliament in 1901, by 1911 he was first lord of the admiralty, where he was instrumental in rebuilding the British navy prior to World War I. After the war he abandoned his political career and turned to writing both histories and journalism. He opposed Chamberlain's policy of appeasement and did not return to government until the war broke out in 1939; the following year he became prime minister.

Churchill was one of the greatest orators of his day. His speeches in the House of Commons and those broadcast to the nation over the BBC provided encouragement to the British people during the darkest periods of the war. His familiar cigar and "V" for victory sign were known throughout the world.

Blood, Toil, Tears and Sweat

May 13, 1940

On Friday evening last I received His Majesty's Commission to form a new Administration. It was the evident wish and will of Parliament and the nation that this should be conceived on the broadest possible basis and that it should include all parties, both those who supported the late Government and also the parties of the Opposition. I have completed the most important part of this task. A War Cabinet has been formed of five Members, representing, with the Opposition Liberals, the unity of the nation. The three party Leaders have agreed to serve, either in the War Cabinet or in high executive office. The three Fighting Services have been filled. It was necessary that this should be done in one single day, on account of the extreme urgency and rigour of events. A number of other positions, key positions, were filled yesterday, and I am submitting a further list to His Majesty tonight. I hope to complete the appointment of the principal Ministers during tomorrow. The appointment of the other Ministers usually takes a little longer, but I trust that, when Parliament meets again, this part of my task will be completed, and that the administration will be complete in all respects.

I considered it in the public interest to suggest that the House should be summoned to meet today. Mr. Speaker agreed, and took the necessary steps, in accordance with the powers conferred upon him by the Resolution of the House. At the end of the proceedings today, the Adjournment of the House will be proposed until Tuesday, 21st May, with, of course, provision for earlier meeting, if need be. The business to be considered during that week will be notified to Members at the earliest opportunity. I now invite the House, by the Motion which stands in my name, to record its approval of the steps taken and to declare its confidence in the new Government.

To form an Administration of this scale and complexity is a serious undertaking in itself, but it must be remembered that we are in the preliminary stage of one of the greatest battles in history, that we are in action at many other points in Norway and in Holland, that we have to be prepared in the Mediterranean, that the air battle is continuous and that many preparations, such as have been indicated by my hon. Friend below the Gangway, have to be made here at home. In this crisis I hope I may be pardoned if I do not address the House at any length today. I hope that any of my friends and colleagues, or former colleagues, who are affected by the political reconstruction, will make allowance, all allowance, for any lack of ceremony with which it has been necessary to act. I would say to the House, as I said to those who have joined this Government: "I have nothing to offer but blood, toil, tears and sweat."

We have before us an ordeal of the most grievous kind. We have before us many, many long months of struggle and of suffering. You ask, what is our policy? I can say: It is to wage war, by sea, land and air, with all our might and with all the strength that God can give us; to wage war against a monstrous tyranny, never surpassed in the dark, lamentable catalogue of human crime. That is our policy. You ask, what is our aim? I can answer in one word: It is victory, victory at all costs, victory in spite of all terror, victory, however long and hard the road may be; for without victory, there is no survival. Let that be realised; no survival for the British Empire, no survival for all that the British Empire has stood for, no survival for the urge and impulse of the ages, that mankind will move forward towards its goal. But I take up my task with buoyancy and hope. I feel sure that our cause will not be suffered to fail among men. At this time I feel entitled to claim the aid of all, and I say, "Come then, let us go forward together with our united strength."

War Situation

August 20, 1940

Almost a year has passed since the war began, and it is natural for us, I think, to pause on our journey at this milestone and survey the dark, wide field.

Rather more than a quarter of a year has passed since the new Government came into power in this country. What a cataract of disaster has poured out upon us since then. The trustful Dutch overwhelmed; their beloved and respected Sovereign driven into exile; the peaceful city of Rotterdam the scene of a massacre as hideous and brutal as anything in the Thirty Years' War. Belgium invaded and beaten down; our own fine Expeditionary Force, which King Leopold called to his rescue, cut off and almost captured, escaping as it seemed only by a miracle and with the loss of all its equipment; our Ally, France, out; Italy in against us; all France in the power of the enemy, all its arsenals and vast masses of military material converted or convertible to the enemy's use; a puppet Government set up at Vichy which may at any moment be forced to become our foe; the whole Western seaboard of Europe from the North Cape to the Spanish frontier in German hands; all the ports, all the airfields on this immense front, employed against us as potential springboards of invasion. Moreover, the German air power, numerically so far outstripping ours, has been brought so close to our Island that what we used to dread greatly has come to pass and the hostile bombers not only reach our shores in a few minutes and from many directions, but can be escorted by their fighting aircraft. Why Sir, if we had been confronted at the beginning of May

with such a prospect, it would have seemed incredible that at the end of a period of horror and disaster, or at this point in a period of horror and disaster, we should stand erect, sure of ourselves, masters of our fate and with the conviction of final victory burning unquenchable in our hearts. Few would have believed we could survive; none would have believed that we should today not only feel stronger but should actually be stronger than we have ever been before.

Let us see what has happened on the other side of the scales. The British nation and the British Empire finding themselves alone, stood undismayed against disaster. No one flinched or wavered; nay, some who formerly thought of peace, now think only of war. Our people are united and resolved, as they have never been before. Death and ruin have become small things compared with the shame of defeat or failure in duty. We cannot tell what lies ahead. It may be that even greater ordeals lie before us. We shall face whatever is coming to us. We are sure of ourselves and of our cause and here then is the supreme fact which has emerged in these months of trial.

Meanwhile, we have not only fortified our hearts but our Island. We have rearmed and hope—indeed I pray—that we shall not be found unworthy of our victory if after toil and tribulation it is granted to us. For the rest, we have to gain the victory. That is our task.

For my own part, looking out upon the future, I do not view the process with any misgivings. I could not stop it if I wished; no one can stop it. Like the Mississippi, it just keeps rolling along. Let it roll. Let it roll on full flood, inexorable, irresistible, benignant, to broader lands and better days.

QUESTIONS

1.   What was the government's policy at the start of Churchill's premiership?

2.   What was Britain's situation after a year of war against the Axis?

3. How does Churchill characterize Britain's military situation? Is he optimistic or pessimistic?

4. Churchill was very unpopular with many people in Britain before the war, yet he became an immensely effective wartime leader. Why? Do his speeches offer any clues to his success?

5. How does Churchill's style of oratory differ from that common among politicians today?

---

136.   **ADOLF EICHMANN**

TESTIMONY

(1961)

Adolf Eichmann (1906–62) was born in Germany, though his family soon moved to Linz, Austria, where he grew up. In 1932 he joined the then-illegal Austrian Nazi party, and soon became a member of the elite S.S. He left Austria for Germany, where he worked to overthrow the Austrian government, and was transferred to Berlin, where he attracted the notice of Heinrich Himmler and moved steadily up the hierarchy of the Security Service (S.D.). The function of the S.D. was to hunt down and persecute the enemies of Nazism, and Eichmann became a "specialist" in Jewish affairs. Following the unification of Austria and Germany in 1938, he returned home to begin the regime's work against Jews there. Eichmann was ultimately charged with implementing the deportation of Jews throughout Europe. His plans sent millions to the death camps. After the war, Eichmann was captured by American forces, but he managed to escape and flee Europe. After several years of wandering through the Middle East, he eventually settled in Argentina in 1958. He lived under an assumed name near Buenos Aires until he was kidnapped in 1961 by Israeli agents and put on trial in Jerusalem. He was hanged in May 1962.

This selection is taken from Lord Russell of Liverpool's account of the trial. A British jurist and historian, Lord Russell (1895–1981) used the transcripts of the trial to illustrate what Hannah Arendt has described as "the banality of evil."

Eichmann began his evidence by declaring that the statement made by him in Buenos Aires to the effect that he was going to Israel of his own free will to stand trial for his crimes was not a voluntary statement. Having regard to the circumstances of his capture no one really believed that it was.

His Counsel then asked him why he joined the Nazi Party which had for its ideology the persecution of the Jews.

Eichmann said that the real object of the Party was to fight the Treaty of Versailles. The slogan "War against Versailles" appeared on the banners of the National Socialist German Workers' Party. Versailles was a turning point in the history of Germany, and Versailles was responsible for all the tragedy of the German people, including some seven million unemployed.

When he joined the Party in 1932, he said, "The struggle against the Jews was a secondary problem because through it the Nazis could not possibly have gained power." The Party was, at that time, anti-Weimar rather than anti-Semitic.

In the early days after Hitler had become the undisputed Head of the State, after Hindenburg's death, the Party was supported by many of Germany's industrial leaders and backed by the leading bankers. Later, "after the early victories of the war *which was thrust upon Germany,* the helm of Government was passed on to others and it was only then that unbridled and senseless measures were taken which I was unable to anticipate because of my junior rank and humble status. . . ."

Eichmann was at great pains to establish the fact, early in his testimony, that he was never anything more than an emigration expert. . . . Nor was this all. As chief railway transport officer in charge of Jewish deportation from the occupied territories, for that is how he liked to regard himself, he eased the sufferings of the deportees.

"When Himmler issued his first directives about the deportation of the Jews," Eichmann said, "there was complete chaos particularly in the field of transport. . . ." He, Eichmann, was only a glorified railway official "concerned strictly with time-tables and technical transport problems. . . ."

EICHMANN: All I can say is, I never killed anyone. I have never ill-treated or beaten anyone. . . .

Eichmann also categorically denied that he visited Auschwitz camp in June 1941, after Himmler had decided to make it "Gas Chamber No. 1," or that he had discussed with the commandant of Auschwitz, Rudolf Höss, the best method of carrying out the executions.

On the contrary, he said, he accepted his orders very unwillingly and on many occasions had asked to be relieved of his appointment and given another more congenial one.

It was sad, he told the Court, that all this should happen to him, for he had always been in favour of the plan for the emigration of Jews to Madagascar, and he had never given a thought to "a blood-soaked solution" of the Jewish problem.

After visiting Kulm, in the Warthe area, where he had witnessed horrible things happening, he saw [Gestapo chief] Müller and asked to be given "some other kind of work" because he was "not suited for that particular kind of activity." Then he had actually seen an infant shot in his mother's arms, and this was as early as the autumn of 1941.

On another occasion he saw at Lemberg the "so-called fountain of blood." A short time before his arrival a number of Jews had been gassed there, and as a result of the gas used in the gas-chamber, and the hurried burial of the victims, "blood was spouting up through the earth and it looked like a ghoulish fountain." All these things he had seen during his first four visits to the extermination camps. He went reluctantly, but *he had to obey orders.* . . .

DR. SERVATIUS: You said during the police interrogation that you carried a burden of guilt. Could you tell the Court how you now regard this question of guilt?

EICHMANN: Some sixteen to twenty-four years have elapsed since all these events took place: what existed then exists no longer. It is difficult to say what constitutes guilt, and I must make the distinction between guilt from the legal point of view and from the human aspect. The facts in respect of which I am answerable to this Court concern the role which I played in connection with the deportations. When they took place they were in pursuance of an order given by the Head of the State and the guilt must be borne by those who were responsible for political decisions: when there is no responsibility there can be no guilt or blame. The responsibility must be examined from the legal point of view, and as long as human beings go on living together in society, no global solution can be found except the Government of a State based on law and order and abiding by these orders.... In order to safeguard the security of a State, it must find means to bind the individual, and this was done in Germany by making him take the oath. The question of conscience is a matter for the Head of State. One must trust and be loyal to the sovereign power. He who is led by a good Head of State is lucky. I had no luck. The Head of State ordered the deportations, and the part I played in them emanated from the master at the top, the Chief of the SS and the police. He was the man who passed on the orders to the Chief of the SIPO and SD, and he, in his turn, passed them on to Müller, my immediate superior, who passed them on to my department.... In the criminal code of the SS, it was laid down that the punishment for disobedience or insubordination would be death. I did all I could by legal means to obtain a transfer to other duties, but I did not succeed, and when in the autumn of 1939 I was transferred to the SIPO and SD this was done against my will and by order from above. I had to obey. I was in uniform at the time and there was a war on. When I went abroad in 1950 it was not because I was afraid of being brought to justice, but for political and family reasons.

My position was similar to that of millions who had to obey. The difference lies only in that my assignment was the most difficult and I had

to carry it. All those who say here that it was easy and did not require an effort to disobey orders give no reasons, and do not say what they would themselves have done. It is said that one could have feigned illness. This may have been a way for generals, but not for their subordinates. If it had transpired that the illness was simulated the result would have been extremely serious, and the binding chains of one's oath should be borne in mind.

Himmler said in his famous speech at Poznan that SS generals could ask to be transferred, but that applied only to generals. The small man could not have followed that course, especially when he was the recipient of secret orders. He could have shot himself, but he could not protest. Ethically I condemn myself and try to argue with myself. I wish to say, in conclusion, that I have regret and condemnation for the extermination of the Jewish people which was ordered by the German rulers, but I myself could not have done anything to prevent it. I was a tool in the hands of the strong and the powerful and in the hands of fate itself. That is what I have to say in answer to your question....

When, for the first time, I saw dead Jews I was utterly shattered, and the ghastly sight has never faded and has left an ineffaceable impression on my mind. But I was in the iron grip of orders to continue carrying out my duties despite what I had seen. Many times did I ask the Head of Amt IV to release me from these duties so that I should no longer have to continue to do this work. I have never spoken my mind so clearly before now, because I feared that it might be thought that I was trying to find an easy excuse for my behaviour and endeavouring to influence the final verdict by prevarication. That is not my intention. That is not my aim. My aim is to tell the whole truth whatever my sentence may be. May I say in conclusion that I regarded this violent solution of the Jewish problem as something hideous and heinous but, unfortunately, I was compelled to do what I did because of my oath of loyalty and allegiance.

JUDGE HALÉVI: But my question was, did you regard it as a crime?

EICHMANN: As the Head of the State had ordered it, and as my lawful superiors had passed on the orders to me, I felt that that was like a protective cloak. I would not go so far as to say that I shifted the responsibility on to them, but in my own mind I transferred the thought to them and, in so doing, I found some peace of mind. I felt that I bore no personal guilt, and was relieved by the knowledge that I played no direct part in the physical extermination of the Jews. The part that I did play was quite enough.

QUESTIONS

1. Why, according to Eichmann, did he join the Nazis?

2. How does Eichmann defend himself from the charges against him?

3. Hannah Arendt, in her book about the Eichmann trial, talks about "the banality of evil." What do you suppose she means?

4. How might a prosecutor respond to Eichmann's defense?

5. In capturing Eichmann, the Israeli government broke the law—he was kidnapped. Do you think the Israeli action was justifiable? Why or why not?

The Twentieth-Century Imagination

137.   VIRGINIA WOOLF

A ROOM OF ONE'S OWN
(1929)

Virginia Woolf (1882–1941) was born into a literary family and became one of the most important English writers of the early twentieth century. Her father was Sir Leslie Stephen, a distinguished critic and journalist, who educated Virginia at home rather than at school so that she grew up surrounded by the leading intellectuals of the day. She lived in central London and became a member of the Bloomsbury group, which included Vanessa and Clive Bell, E.M. Forster, John Maynard Keynes, and also Leonard Woolf, whom she married in 1912 and with whom she established a publishing firm. Virginia worked as a publisher while beginning her own career as a novelist. Her work was characterized by experimentation in form and character. Her most creative period was in the 1920s, when she published three novels and more than a dozen short stories as well as the autobiographical *A Room of One's Own*. Despite her successes, Virginia Woolf suffered from severe depression. In 1941 she took her own life.

A Room of One's Own is an extended version of two lectures she gave to English university students. It is a brilliant example of her method of drawing meaning from everyday events as well as an evocative, provocative account of the difficulties faced by women writers throughout the centuries.

All I could do was to offer you an opinion upon one minor point—a woman must have money and a room of her own if she is to write fiction; and that, as you will see, leaves the great problem of the true nature of woman and the true nature of fiction unsolved. I have shirked the duty of coming to a conclusion upon these two questions—women and fiction remain, so far as I am concerned, unsolved problems. But in order to make some amends I am going to do what I can to show you how I arrived at this opinion about the room and the money. I am going to develop in your presence as fully and freely as I can the train of thought which led me to think this. Perhaps if I lay bare the ideas, the prejudices, that lie behind this statement you will find that they have some bearing upon women and some upon fiction. At any rate, when a subject is highly controversial—and any question about sex is that—one cannot hope to tell the truth. One can only show how one came to hold whatever opinion one does hold. One can only give one's audience the chance of drawing their own conclusions as they observe the limitations, the prejudices, the idiosyncrasies of the speaker. Fiction here is likely to contain more truth than fact.

My aunt, Mary Beton, I must tell you, died by a fall from her horse when she was riding out to take the air in Bombay. The news of my legacy reached me one night about the same time that the act was passed that gave votes to women. A solicitor's letter fell into the post-box and when I opened it I found that she had left me five hundred pounds a year for ever. Of the two—the vote and the money—the money, I own, seemed infinitely the more important. Before that I had made my living cadging odd jobs from newspapers, by reporting a donkey show here or a wedding there; I had earned a few pounds by addressing envelopes, reading to old ladies, making artificial flowers, teaching the alphabet to small children in a kindergarten. Such were the chief occupations that were open to women before 1918. I need not, I am afraid, describe in any detail the hardness of the work, for you know perhaps women who have done it; nor the difficulty of living on the money when it was earned, for you may have tried. But what still remains with me as a worse infliction than either was the poison of fear and bitterness which those days bred in me. To begin with, always to be doing work that one did not wish to do, and to do it like a slave, flattering and fawning, not always necessarily perhaps, but it seemed necessary and the stakes were too great to run risks; and then the thought of that one gift which it was death to hide—a small one but dear to the possessor—perishing and with it myself, my soul—all this became like a rust eating away the bloom of the spring, destroying the tree at its heart. However, as I say, my aunt died; and whenever I change a ten shilling note a little of that rust and corrosion is rubbed off; fear and bitterness go. Indeed, I thought, slipping the silver into my purse, it is remarkable, remembering the bitterness of those days, what a change of temper a fixed income will bring about. No force in the world can take from me my five hundred pounds. Food, house and clothing are mine for ever. Therefore not merely do effort and labour cease, but also hatred and bitterness.

I need not hate any man; he cannot hurt me. I need not flatter any man; he has nothing to give me. So imperceptibly I found myself adopting a new attitude towards the other half of the human race.

What I find deplorable, I continued, looking about the bookshelves again, is that nothing is known about women before the eighteenth century. I have no model in my mind to turn about this way and that. Here am I asking why women did not write poetry in the Elizabethan age, and I am not sure how they were educated; whether they were taught to write; whether they had sitting-rooms to themselves; how many women had children before they were twenty-one; what, in short, they did from eight in the morning till eight at night. They had no money evidently; they were married whether they liked it or not before they were out of the nursery, at fifteen or sixteen very likely. It would have been extremely odd, even upon this showing, had one of them suddenly written the plays of Shakespeare, I concluded, and I thought of that old gentlemen, who is dead now, but was a bishop, I think, who declared that it was impossible for any woman, past, present, or to come, to have the genius of Shakespeare. He wrote to the papers about it. He also told a lady who applied to him for information that cats do not as a matter of fact go to heaven, though they have, he added, souls of a sort. How much thinking those old gentlemen used to save one! How the borders of ignorance shrank back at their approach! Cats do not go to heaven. Women cannot write the plays of Shakespeare.

Be that as it may, I could not help thinking, as I looked at the works of Shakespeare on the shelf, that the bishop was right at least in this; it would have been impossible, completely and entirely, for any woman to have written the plays of Shakespeare in the age of Shakespeare. Let me imagine, since facts are so hard to come by, what would have happened had Shakespeare had a wonderfully gifted sister, called Judith, let us say. Shakespeare himself went, very probably—his mother was an heiress—to the grammar school, where he may have learnt Latin—Ovid, Virgil and Horace—and the elements of grammar and logic. He was, it is well known, a wild boy who poached rabbits, perhaps shot a deer, and had, rather sooner than he should have done, to marry a woman in the neighbourhood, who bore him a child rather quicker than was right. That escapade sent him to seek his fortune in London. He had, it seemed, a taste for the theatre; he began by holding horses at the stage door. Very soon he got work in the theatre, became a successful actor, and lived at the hub of the universe, meeting everybody, knowing everybody, practising his art on the boards, exercising his wits in the streets, and even getting access to the palace of the queen. Meanwhile his extraordinarily gifted sister, let us suppose, remained at home. She was as adventurous, as imaginative, as agog to see the world as he was. But she was not sent to school. She had no chance of learning grammar and logic, let alone of reading Horace and Virgil. She picked up a book now and then, one of her brother's perhaps, and read a few pages. But then her parents came in and told her to mend the stocking or mind the stew and not moon about with books and papers. They would have spoken sharply but kindly, for they were substantial people who knew the conditions of life for a woman and loved their daughter—indeed, more likely than not she was the apple of her father's eye. Perhaps she scribbled some pages up in an apple loft on the sly, but was careful to hide them or set fire to them. Soon, however, before she was out of her teens, she was to be betrothed to the son of a neighbouring wool-stapler. She cried out that marriage was hateful to her, and for that she was severely beaten by her father. Then he ceased to scold her. He begged her instead not to hurt him, not to shame him in this matter of her marriage. He would give her a chain of beads or a fine petticoat, he said; and there were tears in his eyes. How could she disobey him? How could she

break his heart? The force of her own gift alone drove her to it. She made up a small parcel of her belongings, let herself down by a rope one summer's night and took the road to London. She was not seventeen. The birds that sang in the hedge were not more musical than she was. She had the quickest fancy, a gift like her brother's, for the tune of words. Like him, she had a taste for the theatre. She stood at the stage door; she wanted to act, she said. Men laughed in her face. The manager—a fat, loose-lipped man—guffawed. He bellowed something about poodles dancing and women acting—no woman, he said, could possibly be an actress. He hinted—you can imagine what. She could get no training in her craft. Could she even seek her dinner in a tavern or roam the streets at midnight? Yet her genius was for fiction and lusted to feed abundantly upon the lives of men and women and the study of their ways. At last—for she was very young, oddly like Shakespeare the poet in her face, with the same grey eyes and rounded brows—at last Nick Greene the actor-manager took pity on her; she found herself with child by that gentleman and so—who shall measure the heat and violence of the poet's heart when caught and tangled in a woman's body?—killed herself one winter's night and lies buried at some cross-roads where the omnibuses now stop outside the Elephant and Castle.

This may be true or it may be false—who can say?—but what is true in it, so it seemed to me, reviewing the story of Shakespeare's sister as I had made it, is that any woman born with a great gift in the sixteenth century would certainly have gone crazed, shot herself, or ended her days in some lonely cottage outside the village, half witch, half wizard, feared and mocked at. For it needs little skill in psychology to be sure that a highly gifted girl who had tried to use her gift for poetry would have been so thwarted and hindered by other people, so tortured and pulled asunder by her own contrary instincts, that she must have lost her health and sanity to a certainty. No girl could have walked to London and stood at a stage door and forced her way into the presence of actor-managers without doing herself a violence and suffering an anguish which may have been irrational—for chastity may be a fetish invented by certain societies for unknown reasons—but were none the less inevitable. Chastity had then, it has even now, a religious importance in a woman's life, and has so wrapped itself round with nerves and instincts that to cut it free and bring it to the light of day demands courage of the rarest.

Even so, the very first sentence that I would write here, I said, crossing over to the writing-table and taking up the page headed Women and Fiction, is that it is fatal for any one who writes to think of their sex. It is fatal to be a man or woman pure and simple; one must be woman-manly or man-womanly. It is fatal for a woman to lay the least stress on any grievance; to plead even with justice any cause; in any way to speak consciously as a woman. And fatal is no figure of speech; for anything written with that conscious bias is doomed to death. It ceases to be fertilised. Brilliant and effective, powerful and masterly, as it may appear for a day or two, it must wither at nightfall; it cannot grow in the minds of others. Some collaboration has to take place in the mind between the woman and the man before the act of creation can be accomplished. Some marriage of opposites has to be consummated. The whole of the mind must lie wide open if we are to get the sense that the writer is communicating his experience with perfect fullness. There must be freedom and there must be peace. Not a wheel must grate, not a light glimmer. The curtains must be close drawn. The writer, I thought, once his experience is over, must lie back and let his mind celebrate its nuptials in darkness. He must not look or question what is being done. Rather, he must pluck the petals from a rose or watch the swans float calmly down the river. . . .

How can I further encourage you to go about the business of life? Young women, I would say, and please attend, for the peroration is beginning, you are, in my opinion, disgracefully ignorant. You have never made a discovery of any sort of importance. You have never shaken an empire or led an army into battle. The plays of Shakespeare are not by you, and you have never introduced a barbarous race to the blessings of civilisation. What is your excuse? It is all very well for you to say, pointing to the streets and squares and forests of the globe swarming with black and white and coffee-coloured inhabitants, all busily engaged in traffic and enterprise and love-making, we have had other work on our hands. Without our doing, those seas would be unsailed and those fertile lands a desert. We have borne and bred and washed and taught, perhaps to the age of six or seven years, the one thousand six hundred and twenty-three million human beings who are, according to statistics, at present in existence, and that, allowing that some had help, takes time.

There is truth in what you say—I will not deny it. But at the same time may I remind you that there have been at least two colleges for women in existence in England since the year 1866; that after the year 1880 a married woman was allowed by law to possess her own property; and that in 1919—which is a whole nine years ago—she was given a vote? May I also remind you that the most of the professions have been open to you for close on ten years now? When you reflect upon these immense privileges and the length of time during which they have been enjoyed, and the fact that there must be at this moment some two thousand women capable of earning over five hundred a year in one way or another, you will agree that the excuse of lack of opportunity, training, encouragement, leisure and money no longer holds good. Moreover, the economists are telling us that Mrs. Seton has had too many children. You must, of course, go on bearing children, but, so they say, in twos and threes, not in tens and twelves.

Thus, with some time on your hands and with some book learning in your brains—you have had enough of the other kind, and are sent to college partly, I suspect, to be uneducated—surely you should embark upon another stage of your very long, very laborious and highly obscure career. A thousand pens are ready to suggest what you should do and what effect you will have. My own suggestion is a little fantastic, I admit; I prefer, therefore, to put it in the form of fiction.

I told you in the course of this paper that Shakespeare had a sister; but do not look for her in Sir Sidney Lee's life of the poet. She died young—alas, she never wrote a word. She lies buried where the omnibuses now stop, opposite the Elephant and Castle. Now my belief is that this poet who never wrote a word and was buried at the crossroads still lives. She lives in you and in me, and in many other women who are not here tonight, for they are washing up the dishes and putting the children to bed. But she lives; for great poets do not die; they are continuing presences; they need only the opportunity to walk among us in the flesh. This opportunity, as I think, it is now coming within your power to give her. For my belief is that if we live another century or so—I am talking of the common life which is the real life and not of the little separate lives which we live as individuals—and have five hundred a year each of us and rooms of our own; if we have the habit of freedom and the courage to write exactly what we think; if we escape a little from the common sitting-room and see human beings not always in their relation to each other but in relation to reality; and the sky, too, and the trees or whatever it may be in themselves; if we look past Milton's bogey, for no human being should shut out the view; if we face the fact, for it is a fact, that there is no arm to cling to, but that we go alone and that our relation is to the world of reality and not only to the world of men and women, then the opportunity will come and the dead poet who was Shakespeare's sister will put on the body which she has so often laid down. Drawing her life from the lives of the unknown who were her forerunners, as her brother did before her, she will be born. As for her coming without that preparation, without that effort on our part, without that determination that when she is born again she shall find it possible to live and write her poetry, that we cannot expect, for that would be impossible. But I maintain that she would come if we worked for her, and that so to work, even in poverty and obscurity, is worth while.

QUESTIONS

1. What does a woman need to be able to write fiction?

2. What was Woolf's life as an independent middle-class woman like before she received her legacy? What options were available to women of her class at the time?

3. How have ideas of women's abilities changed from the days of Woolf's imaginary Judith Shakespeare to the late 1920s?

4. How should a writer approach the question of gender, according to Woolf? Would she say that men could write about women?

5. Is Woolf satisfied with the progress of women in the literary world?

138.   **ALEXANDER SOLZHENITSYN**

ONE DAY IN THE LIFE OF IVAN DENISOVICH

(1962)

Alexander Solzhenitsyn (born 1918) is one of the most celebrated victims of Stalin's regime. A member of a family of intellectuals, Solzhenitsyn took a degree in mathematics just before the outbreak of the Second World War. He served in the Red Army and rose to the rank of captain of artillery. In 1945, however, he criticized Stalin and was sentenced to life imprisonment in Siberia, where he spent eleven years before being released on Stalin's death. Solzhenitsyn then began the teaching career that he had planned as a student and started to write. *One Day in the Life of Ivan Denisovich* was published at a time of liberalization in the Soviet Union and was an immediate international success. But, when Soviet policy changed, Solzhenitsyn was barred from any further publication. A number of his novels were smuggled to the West, where they were published to critical acclaim. In 1970 Solzhenitsyn was awarded the Nobel Prize in literature. In 1973 he was accused of treason and exiled.

One Day in the Life of Ivan Denisovich is a realistic depiction of life in the Siberian labor camps, a theme that dominates many of Solzhenitsyn's major works. He is interested in the ways in which his characters are able to maintain their dignity and humanity when faced with nearly unendurable conditions of deprivation.

Outside the moon shone brighter than ever. The lamps seemed to be paler now. The barracks cast deep shadows. The door to the mess hall lay beyond a broad porch with four steps. Now the porch too lay in shadow. But above it a small lamp was swaying, and creaking dismally in the cold. The light it cast was rainbowhued, from the frost maybe, or the dirt on the glass.

The camp commandant had issued yet another strict order: the squads were to enter the mess hall in double file. To this he added: on reaching the steps they were to stay there and not climb onto the porch; they were to form up in fives and remain standing until the mess orderly gave them the go-ahead.

The post of mess orderly was firmly held by "the Limper." Because of his lameness he'd managed to get classed as disabled, but he was a hefty son-of-a-bitch. He'd got himself a birch club, and standing on the porch would hit anyone who came up the steps without his say-so. No, not anyone. He was smart, and could tell, even in the dark, when it was better to let a man alone—anyone who might give him as good as he got. He hit the down-and-outs. Once he hit Shukhov.

He was called an orderly. But, looking closer into it, he was a real prince—he palled around with the cooks.

Today all the squads may have turned up together or there may have been delay in getting things in order, but there was quite a crowd on the porch. Among them was the Limper, with his assistant. The mess chief himself was there too. They were handling the crowd without guards—the bruisers.

The mess chief was a fat pig with a head like a pumpkin and a broad pair of shoulders. He was bursting with energy and when he walked he seemed nothing but a lot of jerks, with springs for arms and legs. He wore a white lambskin hat without a number on it, finer than any civilian's. And his waistcoat was lambskin to match, with a number on it, true, but hardly bigger than a postage stamp. He bore no number at all on his back. He respected no one and all the zeks were afraid of him. He held the lives of thousands in his hands. Once they'd tried to beat him up but all the cooks—a prize bunch of thugs they were—had leaped to his defense.

Shukhov would be in hot water if the 104th had already gone in. The Limper knew everyone by sight and, with his chief present, wouldn't think of letting a man in with the wrong squad; he'd make a point of putting the finger on him.

Prisoners had been known to slip in behind the Limper's back by climbing over the porch railings. Shukhov had done it too. But tonight, under the chief's very nose, that was out of the question—he'd bust you so bad that you'd only just manage to drag yourself off to the doctor.

Get along to the porch and see whether, among all those identical black coats, the 104th was still there.

He got there just as the men began shoving (what could they do? it would soon be time to turn in) as though they were storming a stronghold—the first step, the second, the third, the fourth. Got there! They poured onto the porch.

"Stop, you fuckers," the Limper shouted and raised his stick at the men in front. "Get back or I'll bash your heads in."

"Form fives, blockheads," he shouted. "How many times have I told you I'll let you in when I'm ready?"

"Twenty-seventh," the Limper called, "go ahead."

The 27th bounded up and made a dash for the door, and the rest surged after them. Shukhov, among them, was shoving with all his might. The porch quivered, and the lamp overhead protested shrilly.

"What again, you shits?" the Limper shouted in rage. Down came his stick, on a shoulder, on a back, pushing the men off, toppling one after another.

Again he cleared the steps.

From below Shukhov saw Pavlo at the Limper's side. It was he who led the squad to the mess hall—Tiurin wouldn't lower himself by joining in the hullabaloo.

"Form fives, hundred and fourth," Pavlo called from the porch. "Make way for them, friends."

Friends—just see them making way, fuck 'em.

"Let me through, you in front. That's my squad," Shukhov grunted, shoving against a back.

The man would gladly have done so but others were squeezing him from every side.

The crowd heaved, pushing away so that no one could breathe. To get its stew. Its lawful stew.

Shukhov tried something else. He grasped the porch rail on his left, got his arms around a pillar, and heaved himself up. He kicked someone's knee and caught a blow in the ribs; a few curses, but he was through. He planted a foot on the edge of the porch floor, close to the top step, and waited. Some of his pals who were already there gave him a hand.

The mess chief walked to the door and looked back.

"Come on, Limper, send in two more squads."

"One hundred and fourth," shouted the Limper. "Where d'you think *you're* crawling, shit?"

He slammed a man from another squad on the back of the neck with his stick.

"One hundred and fourth," shouted Pavlo, leading in his men.

"Whew!" gasped Shukhov in the mess hall. And, without waiting for Pavlo's instructions, he started looking for free trays.

The mess hall seemed as usual, with clouds of steam curling in through the door and the men sitting shoulder to shoulder—like seeds in a sunflower. Others pushed their way through the tables, and others were carrying loaded trays. Shukhov had grown used to it all over the years and his sharp eyes had noticed that S 208 had only five bowls on the tray he was carrying. This meant that it was the last tray-load for his squad. Otherwise the tray would have been full.

He went up to the man and whispered in his ear: "After you with that tray."

"Someone's waiting for it at the counter. I promised. . . ."

"Let him wait, the lazy bastard."

They came to an understanding.

S 208 carried his tray to the table and unloaded the bowls. Shukhov immediately grabbed it. At that moment the man it had been promised to ran up and tried to grab it. But he was punier than Shukhov. Shukhov shoved him off with the tray—what the hell are you pulling for?—and threw him against a post. Then putting the tray under his arm, he trotted off to the serving window.

Pavlo was standing in the line there, worried because there was no empty tray. He was delighted to see Shukhov. He pushed the man ahead of him out of the way: "Why are you standing here? Can't you see I've got a tray?"

Look, there was Gopchik—with another tray.

"They were arguing," he said with a laugh, "and I grabbed it."

Gopchik will do well. Give him another three years—he has still to grow up—and he'll

become nothing less than a breadcutter. He's fated for it.

Pavlo told him to hand over the second of the trays to Yermolayev, a hefty Siberian who was serving a ten-year stretch, like Shukhov, for being caught by the Germans; then sent him to keep an eye on any table where the men might be finishing. Shukhov put his tray down and waited.

"One hundred and fourth," announced Pavlo at the counter.

In all there were five of these counters: three for serving regular food, one for zeks on special diets (ulcer victims, and bookkeeping personnel, as a favor), and one for the return of dirty dishes (that's where the dish-lickers gathered, sparring with one another). The counters were low—about waist level. The cooks themselves were out of sight; only their hands, and the ladles, could be seen.

The cook's hands were white and well cared for, but huge and hairy: a boxer's hands, not a cook's. He took a pencil and made a note on the wall—he kept his list there.

The cook took an enormous ladle and stirred, stirred, stirred. The soup kettle had just been refilled, almost up to the brim, and steam poured from it. Replacing the huge ladle with a smaller one he began serving the stew in twenty-ounce portions. He didn't go deep.

"One, two, three, four. . . "

Some of the bowls had been filled while the stuff from the bottom of the kettle hadn't yet settled after the stirring, and some were duds—nothing but soup. Shukhov made a mental note of which was which. He put ten bowls on his tray and carried them off. Gopchik waved from the second row of posts.

"Over here, Ivan Denisovich, over here."

No horsing around with bowls of stew. Shukhov was careful not to stumble. He kept his throat busy too.

"Hey you, H 920. Gently, uncle. Out of the way, my boy."

It was hard enough, in a crowd like this, to carry a single bowl without slopping it. He was carrying ten. Just the same, he put the tray down safely, on the end of the table that Gopchik had cleared. No splashes. He managed, too, to maneuver the tray so that the two bowls with the thickest stew were just opposite the place he was about to sit down in.

Yermolayev brought another ten bowls. Gopchik ran off and came back with Pavlo, the last four in their hands.

Kilgas brought the bread tray. Tonight they were being fed in accordance with the work they had done. Some got six ounces, some nine, and Shukhov twelve. He took a piece with a crust for himself, and six ounces from the middle of the loaf for Tsezar.

Now from all over the mess hall Shukhov's squad began streaming up, to collect their supper and eat it where they could. As he handed out the bowls, there were two things he had to take care of: he had to remember whom he'd served, and he had to watch out for the tray—and for his own corner of it. (He put his spoon into a bowl—one of the "thick" ones. Reserved, that meant.) Fetiukov was among the first to arrive. But he soon walked off, figuring there was nothing to be scrounged that particular evening; better to wander around the mess, hunting for leftovers (if someone doesn't finish his stew and pushes his bowl back, there are always people hustling to pounce on it, like vultures).

The empty trays were handed in. Pavlo sat there with his double helping, Shukhov with his two bowls. And now they had nothing more to say to one another—the sacred moments had come.

Shukhov took off his hat and laid it on his knees. He tasted one bowl, he tasted the other. Not bad—there was some fish in it. Generally, the evening stew was much thinner than at breakfast: if they're to work, prisoners must be fed in the morning; in the evening they'll go to sleep anyway.

He dug in. First he only drank the broth, drank and drank. As it went down, filling his whole body with warmth, all his guts began to flutter inside him at their meeting with the stew.

Goo-ood! There it comes, that brief moment for which a zek lives.

And now Shukhov complained about nothing: neither about the length of his stretch, nor about the length of the day, nor about their swiping another Sunday. This was all he thought about now: we'll survive. We'll stick it out, God willing, till it's over.

He drained the hot soup from both bowls, and then tipped what was left in the second into the first, scraping it clean with his spoon. That set his mind at ease. Now he didn't have to think about the second and keep an eye or a hand on it.

Now that he could look freely he glanced at his neighbors' bowls. The one on his left was little more than water. The dirty snakes. The tricks they play! And on their fellow zeks.

He began to eat the cabbage with what was left of the soup. A potato had found its way into one of the bowls. A medium-sized spud, frost-bitten, hard and sweetish. There wasn't much fish, just a few stray bits of bare backbone. But you must chew every bone, every fin, to suck the juice out of them, for the juice is healthy. It takes time, of course, but he was in no hurry to go anywhere. Today was a red-letter day for him; two helpings for dinner, two helpings for supper. Everything else could wait.

Except, maybe, that visit to the Lett for tobacco. None might be left in the morning.

He ate his supper without bread. A double helping *and* bread—that was going too far. The bread would do for tomorrow. The belly is a demon. It doesn't remember how well you treated it yesterday; it'll cry out for more tomorrow.

He ate up his stew without taking much interest in what was happening around him. No need for that: he wasn't on the lookout for extras, he was eating his own lawful portions. All the same, he noticed that when the fellow opposite got up a tall old man—U 81—sat down in his place.

He'd been told that this old man had spent years without number in camps and prisons, and that he hadn't benefited from a single amnesty. Whenever one ten-year stretch had run out they shoved another onto him right away.

Now Shukhov looked closely at the man. He held himself straight—the other zeks sat all hunched up—and looked as if he'd put something extra on the bench to sit on. There was nothing left to crop on his head: his hair had dropped out long since—the result of high living, no doubt. His eyes didn't dart after everything going on in the mess hall. He kept them fixed in an unseeing gaze at some spot over Shukhov's head. His worn wooden spoon dipped rhythmically into the thin stew, but instead of lowering his head to the bowl like everybody else, he raised the spoon high to his lips. He'd lost all his teeth and chewed his bread with iron gums. All life had drained out of his face but it had been left, not sickly or feeble, but hard and dark like carved stone. And by his hands, big and cracked and blackened, you could see that he'd had little opportunity of doing soft jobs. But he wasn't going to give in, oh no! *He* wasn't going to put his nine ounces on the dirty, bespattered table—he put it on a well-washed bit of rag.

Shukhov came out with a full belly. He felt pleased with himself and decided that, although it was close to curfew, he'd run over to the Lett all the same. Instead of taking the bread to his barracks, he strode to Barracks 7.

The moon was high—clean and white, as if chiseled out of the sky. It was clear up there and there were some stars out—the brightest of them. But he had even less time for stargazing than for watching people in the mess hall. One thing he realized—the frost was no milder. One of the civilians had said, and this had been passed on, that it was likely to drop to - 25° in the night, and as low as - 40° toward morning.

QUESTIONS

1. Why do the cooks in the labor camp have such an enviable position? What is their standing among the other prisoners?

2. What are some of the strategies prisoners employ in the mess hall? What purpose do they serve?

3. Ivan considered his day a great success. Why?

4. How do the prisoners get along? How do they try to maintain their dignity?

5. What vision of Soviet society is shown in *One Day in the Life?*

139.   **JEAN-PAUL SARTRE**

EXISTENTIALISM

(1946)

Jean-Paul Sartre (1905–80) was born in Paris and grew up in the home of his grandfather, a professor at the Sorbonne. Sartre followed a traditional educational path, attending distinguished schools and finally studying at the Sorbonne. He worked as a high school teacher while beginning to develop the concept of existentialism. In 1938, he published his first novel, *Nausea,* a story of the extreme alienation of mankind. Even in his fiction, Sartre's philosophical inclinations were apparent, and he soon turned to writing directly theoretical works. *Being and Nothingness* (1943) was the most important statement of his views. During World War II he was interned in a German prison camp but continued to write, turning to drama as his medium—*The Flies* (1943) and *No Exit* (1944) were composed there. In 1964 he was awarded the Nobel Prize for Literature, which, characteristically, he refused to accept.

Existentialism was an attempt to explain and defend his philosophical views. Written in the intellectual and social chaos immediately following the Second World War, Sartre rejected what he believed were the delusory bromides of both bourgeois capitalism and Marxist communism (although in fact he later became a Marxist). He wrote in a very straightforward and simple manner, unlike his usual philosophical style, and explained the core of his doctrine. It is different from the concept of existentialism that has become diluted and absorbed into the cultural mainstream, shorn of both its atheism and its radicalism.

I should like on this occasion to defend existentialism against some charges which have been brought against it.

First, it has been charged with inviting people to remain in a kind of desperate quietism because, since no solutions are possible, we should have to consider action in this world as quite impossible. We should then end up in a philosophy of contemplation; and since contemplation is a luxury, we come in the end to a bourgeois philosophy. The communists in particular have made these charges.

On the other hand, we have been charged with dwelling on human degradation, with pointing up everywhere the sordid, shady, and slimy, and neglecting the gracious and beautiful, the bright side of human nature; for example, according to Mlle. Mercier, a Catholic critic, with forgetting the smile of the child. Both sides charge us with having ignored human solidarity, with considering man as an isolated being. The communists say that the main reason for this is that we take pure subjectivity, the *Cartesian I think,* as our starting point; in other words, the moment in which man becomes fully aware of what it means to him to be an isolated being; as a result, we are unable to return to a state of solidarity with the men who are not ourselves, a state which we can never reach in the *cogito*.

From the Christian standpoint, we are charged with denying the reality and seriousness of human undertakings, since, if we reject God's commandments and the eternal verities, there no longer remains anything but pure caprice, with everyone permitted to do as he pleases and incapable, from his own point of view, of condemning the points of view and acts of others.

Actually, it is the least scandalous, the most austere of doctrines. It is intended strictly for specialists and philosophers. Yet it can be defined easily. What complicates matters is that there are two kinds of existentialist; first, those who are Christian, among whom I would include Jaspers and Gabriel Marcel, both Catholic; and on the other hand the atheistic existentialists, among whom I class Heidegger, and then the French existentialists and myself. What they have in common is that they think that existence precedes essence, or, if you prefer, that subjectivity must be the starting point.

Atheistic existentialism states that if God does not exist, there is at least one being in whom existence precedes essence, a being who exists before he can be defined by any concept, and that this being is man, or, as Heidegger says, human reality. What is meant here by saying that existence precedes essence? It means that, first of all, man exists, turns up, appears on the scene, and, only afterwards, defines himself. If man, as the existentialist conceives him, is indefinable, it is because at first he is nothing. Only afterward will he be something, and he himself will have made what he will be. Thus, there is no human nature, since there is no God to conceive it. Not only is man what he conceives himself to be, but he is also only what he wills himself to be after this thrust toward existence.

Man is nothing else but what he makes of himself. Such is the first principle of existentialism. It is also what is called subjectivity, the name we are labeled with when charges are brought against us. But what do we mean by this, if not

that man has a greater dignity than a stone or table? For we mean that man first exists, that is, that man first of all is the being who hurls himself toward a future and who is conscious of imagining himself as being in the future. Man is at the start a plan which is aware of itself, rather than a patch of moss, a piece of garbage, or a cauliflower; nothing exists prior to this plan; there is nothing in heaven; man will be what he will have planned to be. Not what he will want to be. Because by the word "will" we generally mean a conscious decision, which is subsequent to what we have already made of ourselves. I may want to belong to a political party, write a book, get married; but all that is only a manifestation of an earlier, more spontaneous choice that is called "will." But if existence really does precede essence, man is responsible for what he is. Thus, existentialism's first move is to make every man aware of what he is and to make the full responsibility of his existence rest on him. And when we say that a man is responsible for himself, we do not only mean that he is responsible for his own individuality, but that he is responsible for all men.

If existence precedes essence, and if we grant that we exist and fashion our image at one and the same time, the image is valid for everybody and for our whole age. Thus, our responsibility is much greater than we might have supposed, because it involves all mankind. To take an individual matter, if I want to marry, to have children; even if this marriage depends solely on my own circumstances or passion or wish, I am involving all humanity in monogamy and not merely myself. Therefore, I am responsible for myself and for everyone else. I am creating a certain image of man of my own choosing. In choosing myself, I choose man.

This helps us understand what the actual content is of such rather grandiloquent words as anguish, forlornness, despair. As you will see, it's all quite simple.

First, what is meant by anguish? The existentialists say at once that man is anguish. What that means is this: The man who involves himself and who realizes that he is not only the person he chooses to be, but also a lawmaker who is, at the same time, choosing all mankind as well as himself, cannot help escape the feeling of his total and deep responsibility. Of course, there are many people who are not anxious; but we claim that they are hiding their anxiety; that they are fleeing from it. Certainly, many people believe that when they do something, they themselves are the only ones involved, and when someone says to them, "What if everyone acted that way?" they shrug their shoulders and answer, "Everyone doesn't act that way." But really, one should always ask himself, "What would happen if everybody looked at things that way?" There is no escaping this disturbing thought except by a kind of double-dealing. A man who lies and makes excuses for himself by saying "not everybody does that," is someone with an uneasy conscience, because the act of lying implies that a universal value is conferred upon the lie.

When we speak of forlornness, a term Heidegger was fond of, we mean only that God does not exist and that we have to face all the consequences of this.

The existentialist thinks it very distressing that God does not exist, because all possibility of finding values in a heaven of ideas disappears along with Him; there can no longer be an *a priori* Good, since there is no infinite and perfect consciousness to think it. Nowhere is it written that the Good exists, that we must be honest, that we must not lie; because the fact is we are on a plane where there are only men. Dostoievsky said, "If God didn't exist, everything would be possible." That is the very starting point of existentialism. Indeed, everything is permissible if God does not exist, and as a result man is forlorn, because neither within him nor without does he find anything to cling to. He can't start making excuses for himself.

If existence really does precede essence, there is no explaining things away by reference to a fixed and given human nature. In other words, there is no determinism, man is free,

man is freedom. On the other hand, if God does not exist, we find no values or commands to turn to which legitimize our conduct. So, in the bright realm of values, we have no excuse behind us, nor justification before us. We are alone, with no excuses.

That is the idea I shall try to convey when I say that man is condemned to be free. Condemned, because he did not create himself, yet, in other respects is free; because, once thrown into the world, he is responsible for everything he does. The existentialist does not believe in the power of passion. He will never agree that a sweeping passion is a ravaging torrent which fatally leads a man to certain acts and is therefore an excuse. He thinks that man is responsible for his passion.

The existentialist does not think that man is going to help himself by finding in the world some omen by which to orient himself. Because he thinks that man will interpret the omen to suit himself. Therefore, he thinks that man, with no support and no aid, is condemned every moment to invent man. Ponge, in a very fine article, has said "Man is the future of man." That's exactly it.

From these few reflections it is evident that nothing is more unjust than the objections that have been raised against us. Existentialism is nothing else than an attempt to draw all the consequences of a coherent atheistic position. It isn't trying to plunge man into despair at all. But if one calls every attitude of unbelief despair, like the Christians, then the word is not being used in its original sense. Existentialism isn't so atheistic that it wears itself out showing that God doesn't exist. Rather, it declares that even if God did exist, that would change nothing. There you've got our point of view. Not that we believe that God exists, but we think that the problem of His existence is not the issue. In this sense existentialism is optimistic, a doctrine of action, and it is plain dishonesty for Christians to make no distinction between their own despair and ours and then to call us despairing.

QUESTIONS

1. Sartre's philosophy was attacked from both the left and the right. What did his critics say about his work?

2. What does Sartre mean when he says that existence precedes essence?

3. Sartre believes that there is no God. How does this affect his worldview?

4. What is Sartre's view of individual responsibility?

5. Sartre's philosophy has been characterized as extremely pessimistic. Would you agree? How might his personal experiences have affected his views?

140.   SIMONE DE BEAUVOIR

THE SECOND SEX
(1949)

Simone de Beauvoir (1908–86) grew up in Paris and was educated in private Catholic schools. She took a degree in philosophy from the Sorbonne and taught philosophy at a number of evening colleges during the early part of her career. At this time she met Jean-Paul Sartre; they began a lifelong association, though both rejected marriage as a bourgeois institution. In the 1930s de Beauvoir took up writing as a full-time occupation, alternating between existential novels and academic treatises. She was particularly adept at portraying the complexities of personal relationships in a world without fixed values and beliefs. She also edited the magazine *Modern Times*, an influential intellectual journal.

The Second Sex examines the condition of modern women through a study of the subjugation of women throughout history. It is a bitter and incisive account and quickly became a seminal work in the developing women's liberation movement. It was widely translated; the first American edition appeared in 1953.

In a sense her whole existence is waiting, since she is confined in the limbo of immanence and contingence, and since her justification is always in the hands of others. She awaits the homage, the approval of men, she awaits love, she awaits the gratitude and praise of her husband or her lover. She awaits her support, which comes from man; whether she keeps the checkbook or merely gets a weekly or monthly allowance from her husband, it is necessary for him to have drawn his pay or obtained that raise if she is to be able to pay the grocer or buy a new dress. She waits for man to put in an appearance, since her economic dependence places her at his disposal; she is only one element in masculine life while man is her whole existence. The husband has his occupations outside the home, and the wife has to put up with his absence all day long; the lover—passionate as he may be—is the one who decides on their meetings and separations in accordance with his obligations. In bed, she awaits the male's desire, she awaits—sometimes anxiously—her own pleasure.

All she can do is arrive later at the rendezvous her lover has set, not be ready at the time designated by her husband; in that way she asserts the importance of her own occupations, she insists on her independence; and for the moment she becomes the essential subject to whose will the other passively submits. But these are timid attempts at revenge; however persistent she may be in keeping men waiting, she will never compensate for the interminable hours she has spent in watching and hoping, in awaiting the good pleasure of the male.

Woman is bound in a general way to contest foot by foot the rule of man, though recognizing his over-all supremacy and worshipping his idols. Hence that famous "contrariness" for which she has often been reproached. Having no independent domain, she cannot oppose positive truths and values of her own to those asserted and upheld by males; she can only deny them. Her negation is more or less thoroughgoing, according to the way respect and resentment are proportioned in her nature. But in fact she knows all the faults in the masculine system, and she has no hesitation in exposing them. . . .

It is understandable, in this perspective, that woman takes exception to masculine logic. Not only is it inapplicable to her experience, but in his hands, as she knows, masculine reasoning becomes an underhand form of force; men's undebatable pronouncements are intended to confuse her. The intention is to put her in a dilemma: either you agree or you do not. Out of respect for the whole system of accepted principles she should agree; if she refuses, she rejects the entire system. But she cannot venture to go so far; she lacks the means to reconstruct society in different form. Still, she does not accept it as it is. Halfway between revolt and slavery, she resigns herself reluctantly to masculine authority. On each occasion he has to force her to accept the consequences of her halfhearted yielding. Man pursues that chimera, a companion half slave, half free: in yielding to him, he would have her yield to the convincingness of an argument, but she knows that he has himself chosen the premises on which his rigorous deductions depend. As long as she avoids questioning them, he will easily reduce her to silence; nevertheless he will not convince her, for she senses his arbitrariness. And so, annoyed, he will accuse her of being obstinate and illogical; but she refuses to play the game because she knows the dice are loaded.

Woman does not entertain the positive belief that the truth is something *other* than men claim; she recognizes, rather, that there *is not* any fixed truth. It is not only the changing nature of life that makes her suspicious of the principle of constant identity, nor is it the magic phenomena with which she is surrounded that destroy the notion of causality. It is at the heart of the masculine world itself, it is in herself as belonging to this world that she comes upon the ambiguity of all principle, of all value, of everything that exists. She knows that masculine morality, as it concerns her, is a vast hoax. Man pompously thunders forth his code of virtue and honor; but in secret he invites her to disobey it, and he even counts on this disobedience; without it, all that splendid façade behind which he takes cover would collapse. . . .

Woman has the same faults because she is a victim of the same paternalistic oppression; she has the same cynicism because she sees man from top to toe, as a valet sees his master. But it is clear that none of woman's traits manifest an originally perverted essence or will: they reflect a situation. "There is dissimulation everywhere under a coercive regime," says Fourier. "Prohibition and contraband are inseparable in love as in trade." And men know that woman's faults indicate her situation so well that, anxious to maintain the hierarchy of sexes, they encourage in their companions the very traits that merit their contempt. No doubt the husband or lover is irritated by the faults of the particular woman he lives with, and yet when they extoll the charms of femininity in general, they believe it to be inseparable from its defects. If woman is not faithless, futile, cowardly, indolent, she loses her seductiveness. . . .

Not accepting logical principles and moral imperatives, skeptical about the laws of nature, woman lacks the sense of the universal; to her the world seems a confused conglomeration of special cases. This explains why she believes more readily in the tittle-tattle of a neighbor than in a scientific explanation. No doubt she respects the printed book, but she respectfully skims the pages of type without getting at the meaning; on the contrary, the anecdote told by some unknown in a waiting line or drawing-room at once takes on an overwhelming authority. Within her sphere all is magic; outside, all is mystery. She is unfamiliar with the criterion of plausibility; only immediate experience carries conviction—her own experience, or that of others if stated emphatically enough. As for her own self, she feels she is a special case because she is isolated in her home and hence does not come into active contact with other women; she is always expecting that destiny and men will make an exception in her favor. She believes in her intuitions much more firmly than in universally valid reasoning; she readily admits that they come from God or from some vague world-spirit; regarding some misfortune or accident she calmly thinks: "That will not happen to me."

French novelist and feminist Simone de Beauvoir (1908–86) participated in demonstrations for women's issues such as family planning. Her armband advocates the free use of abortion and contraception for birth control.

Regarding benefits, on the other hand, she imagines that "an exception will be made in my case": she rather expects special favors. The storekeeper will give her a discount, the policeman will let her through without a pass; she has been taught to overestimate the value of her smile, and no one has told her that all women smile. It is not that she thinks herself more extraordinary than her neighbor: she does not make the comparison. And for the same reason experience rarely shows her how wrong she is:

she meets with one failure after another, but she does not sum them up in a valid conclusion.

This shows why women do not succeed in building up a solid counter-universe whence they can challenge the males; now and then they rail at men in general, they tell what happens in the bedroom or at childbirth, they exchange horoscopes and beauty secrets. But they lack the conviction necessary to build this grievance-world their resentment calls for; their attitude toward man is too ambivalent. Doubtless he is a child, a necessitous and vulnerable body, he is a simpleton, a bothersome drone, a mean tyrant, a vain egotist; but he is also the liberating hero, the divinity who bestows values. His desire is gross appetite, his embrace a degrading duty; yet his fire and virile force seem like demiurgic power. When a woman says ecstatically: "He is a man!" she evokes at once the sexual vigor and the social effectiveness of the man she admires. In both he displays the same creative superiority; she does not conceive of his being a great artist, a great man of business, a general, a leader, without being a potent lover, and thus his social successes always have a sexual attractiveness; inversely, she is quick to see genius in the man who satisfies her desires. . . .

The ambiguity of woman's feelings toward man is found again in her general attitude toward herself and the world. The domain in which she is confined is surrounded by the masculine universe, but it is haunted by obscure forces of which men are themselves the playthings; if she allies herself with these magical forces, she will come to power in her turn. Society enslaves Nature; but Nature dominates it. The Spirit flames out beyond Life; but it ceases to burn when life no longer supports it. Woman is justified by this equivocation in finding more verity in a garden than in a city, in a malady than in an idea, in a birth than in a revolution; she endeavors to reestablish that reign of the earth, of the Mother, in order to become again the essential in face of the inessential. But as she, also, is an existent having transcendence, she can give value to that domain where she is confined only by transfiguring it: she lends it a transcendent dimension. Man lives in a consistent universe that is a reality conceivable in thought. Woman is at grips with a magical reality that defies thought, and she escapes from it through thoughts without real content. Instead of taking up her existence, she contemplates in the clouds the pure Idea of her destiny; instead of acting, she sets up her own image in the realm of imagination: that is, instead of reasoning, she dreams. Hence the fact that while being "physical," she is also artificial, and while being earthy, she makes herself etherial. Her life is passed in washing pots and pans, and it is a glittering novel; man's vassal, she thinks she is his idol; carnally humiliated, she is all for Love. Because she is condemned to know only the factual contingence of life, she makes herself priestess of the Ideal.

This ambivalence is evident in the way woman regards her body. It is a burden: worn away in service to the species, bleeding each month, proliferating passively, it is not for her a pure instrument for getting a grip on the world but an opaque physical presence; it is no certain source of pleasure and it creates lacerating pains; it contains menaces: woman feels endangered by her "insides." It is a "hysteric" body, on account of the close connection of the endocrine secretions with the nervous and sympathetic systems that control the muscles and the viscera. Her body displays reactions for which the woman denies responsibility; in sobs, vomiting, convulsions, it escapes her control, it betrays her; it is her most intimate verity, but it is a shameful verity that she keeps hidden. And yet it is also her glorious double; she is dazzled in beholding it in the mirror; it is promised happiness, work of art, living statue; she shapes it, adorns it, puts it on show. When she smiles at herself in the glass, she forgets her carnal contingence; in the embrace of love, in maternity, her image is destroyed. But often, as she muses on herself, she is astonished to be at one and the same time that heroine and that flesh.

Nature similarly presents a double face to her, supplying the soup kettle and stimulating mystical effusions. When she became a housekeeper and a mother, woman renounced her free roaming of field and wood, she preferred the quiet cultivation of her kitchen garden, she tamed the flowers and put them in vases; yet she is still entranced with moonlight and sunset. In the terrestrial fauna and flora she sees food and ornament before all; but in them a sap circulates which is nobility and magic. Life is not merely immanence and repetition: it has also a dazzling face of light; in flowery meadows it is revealed as Beauty. Attuned to nature by the fertility of her womb, woman is also swept by its animating breeze, which is spirit. And to the extent that she remains unsatisfied and, like the young girl, feels unfulfilled and unlimited, her soul, too, will be lost to sight down roads stretching endlessly on, toward unbounded horizons. Enslaved as she is to her husband, her children, her home, it is ecstasy to find herself alone, sovereign on the hillsides; she is no longer mother, wife, housekeeper, but a human being; she contemplates the passive world, and she remembers that she is wholly a conscious being, an irreducible free individual. Before the mystery of water and the leap of summits, the male's supremacy fades away. Walking through the heather, dipping her hand in the stream, she is living not for others, but for herself. Any woman who has preserved her independence through all her servitudes will ardently love her own freedom in Nature. Others will find there only pretexts for refined raptures; and they will hesitate at twilight between the danger of catching cold and an ecstasy of the soul.

QUESTIONS

1. How do women traditionally struggle against male domination? What are their tactics?

2. Why are women "illogical" or "obstinate"?

3. De Beauvoir implies that men and women think differently. How? Do you think she is correct, or is she only reinforcing an old stereotype?

4. Women have ambiguous feelings toward men, de Beauvoir says. Is this a positive or a negative thing, in her view?

5. Judging from de Beauvoir's work, has the status of women changed much from the days of Mrs. Beeton?

The Transformation of Eastern Europe

141.   **WINSTON CHURCHILL**

"THE IRON CURTAIN"

(1946)

Winston Churchill (1874–1965) was an artist, writer, historian, journalist, and twice prime minister of England (1940–45, 1951–55). He was a vigorous wartime leader, both in his aggressive military policies and in his inspirational speeches and public appearances. His ever-present cigar held between two raised fingers became a universal symbol of "V" for victory. Churchill led a coalition government; as an Allied victory in the Second World War grew near, the elements of his coalition came apart. He contested the 1945 general election as a Conservative, but the nation returned the Labor Party. For the next six years Churchill was leader of the opposition.

Churchill had long been an outspoken critic of Soviet communism but had quickly embraced the Soviets as allies against Nazi Germany. Nevertheless, he was wary of the peace settlement that gave the Soviets control of Eastern Europe. Early in 1946 Churchill accepted an invitation to tour the United States. At Westminster College in Fulton, Missouri, he and President Harry Truman were both given honorary degrees and Churchill gave the speech that is said to have initiated the Cold War between East and West. Churchill maintained that it was the duty of Britain and America to unite against the threat of Soviet communism.

I am glad to come to Westminster College this afternoon, and am complimented that you should give me a degree. The name "Westminster" is somehow familiar to me. I seem to have heard of it before. Indeed, it was at Westminster that I received a very large part of my education in politics, dialectic, rhetoric, and one or two other things. In fact we have both been educated at the same, or similar, or, at any rate, kindred establishments.

The United States stands at this time at the pinnacle of world power. It is a solemn moment for the American Democracy. For with primacy in power is also joined an awe-inspiring accountability to the future. If you look around you, you must feel not only the sense of duty done but also you must feel anxiety lest you fall below the level of achievement. Opportunity is here now, clear and shining for both our countries. To reject it or ignore it or fritter if away will bring upon us all the long reproaches of the after-time. It is necessary that constancy of mind, persistency of purpose, and the grand simplicity of decision shall guide and rule the conduct of the English-speaking peoples in peace as they did in war. We must, and I believe we shall, prove ourselves equal to this severe requirement.

I have a definite and practical proposal to make for action. Courts and magistrates may be set up but they cannot function without sheriffs and constables. The United Nations Organization must immediately begin to be equipped with an international armed force. In such a matter we can only go step by step, but we must begin now. I propose that each of the Powers and States should be invited to delegate a certain number of air squadrons to the service of the world organization. These squadrons would be trained and prepared in their own countries, but would move around in rotation from one country to another. They would wear the uniform of their own countries but with different badges. They would not be required to act against their own nation, but in other respects they would be directed by the world organization. This might be started on a modest scale and would grow as confidence grew. I wished to see this done after the first world war, and I devoutly trust it may be done forthwith.

It would nevertheless be wrong and imprudent to entrust the secret knowledge or experience of the atomic bomb, which the United States, Great Britain, and Canada now share, to the world organization, while it is still in its infancy. It would be criminal madness to cast it adrift in this still agitated and un-united world. No one in any country has slept less well in their beds because this knowledge and the method and the raw materials to apply it, are at present largely retained in American hands. I do not believe we should all have slept so soundly had the positions been reversed and if some Communist or neo-Fascist State monopolized for the time being these dread agencies. The fear of them alone might easily have been used to enforce totalitarian systems upon the free democratic world, with consequences appalling to human imagination. God has willed that this shall not be and we have at least a breathing space to set our house in order before this peril has to be encountered: and even then, if no

effort is spared, we should still possess so formidable a superiority as to impose effective deterrents upon its employment, or threat of employment, by others. Ultimately, when the essential brotherhood of man is truly embodied and expressed in a world organization with all the necessary practical safeguards to make it effective, these powers would naturally be confided to that world organization.

Now I come to the second danger of these two marauders which threatens the cottage, the home, and the ordinary people—namely, tyranny. We cannot be blind to the fact that the liberties enjoyed by individual citizens throughout the British Empire are not valid in a considerable number of countries, some of which are very powerful. In these States control is enforced upon the common people by various kinds of all-embracing police governments. The power of the State is exercised without restraint, either by dictators or by compact oligarchies operating through a privileged party and a political police. It is not our duty at this time when difficulties are so numerous to interfere forcibly in the internal affairs of countries which we have not conquered in war. But we must never cease to proclaim in fearless tones the great principles of freedom and the rights of man which are the joint inheritance of the English-speaking world and which through Magna Carta, the Bill of Rights, the Habeas Corpus, trial by jury, and the English common law find their most famous expression in the American Declaration of Independence.

All this means that the people of any country have the right, and should have the power by constitutional action, by free unfettered elections, with secret ballot, to choose or change the character or form of government under which they dwell; that freedom of speech and thought should reign; that courts of justice, independent of the executive, unbiased by any party, should administer laws which have received the broad assent of large majorities or are consecrated by time and custom. Here are the title deeds of freedom which should lie in every cottage home. Here is the message of the British and American peoples to mankind. Let us preach what we practice—let us practice what we preach. Neither the sure prevention of war, nor the continuous rise of world organization will be gained without what I have called the fraternal association of the English-speaking peoples. This means a special relationship between the British Commonwealth and Empire and the United States. Fraternal association requires not only the growing friendship and mutual understanding between our two vast but kindred systems of society, but the continuance of the intimate relationship between our military advisers, leading to common study of potential dangers, the similarity of weapons and manuals of instructions, and to the interchange of officers and cadets at technical colleges. It should carry with it the continuance of the present facilities for mutual security by the joint use of all Naval and Air Force bases in the possession of either country all over the world.

A shadow has fallen upon the scenes so lately lighted by the Allied victory. Nobody knows what Soviet Russia and its Communist international organization intends to do in the immediate future, or what are the limits, if any, to their expansive and proselytizing tendencies. I have a strong admiration and regard for the valiant Russian people and for my wartime comrade, Marshal Stalin. There is deep sympathy and goodwill in Britain—and I doubt not here also—towards the peoples of all the Russias and a resolve to persevere through many differences and rebuffs in establishing lasting friendships. We understand the Russian need to be secure on her western frontiers by the removal of all possibility of German aggression. We welcome Russia to her rightful place among the leading nations of the world. We welcome her flag upon the seas. Above all, we welcome constant, frequent and growing contacts between the Russian people and our own people on both sides of the Atlantic. It is my duty however, for I am sure you would wish me to state the facts as I see them to you, to place before you certain facts about the present position in Europe.

From Stettin in the Baltic to Trieste in the Adriatic, an iron curtain has descended across the Continent. Behind that line lie all the capitals of the ancient states of Central and Eastern Europe. Warsaw, Berlin, Prague, Vienna, Budapest, Belgrade, Bucharest and Sofia, all these famous cities and the populations around them lie in what I must call the Soviet sphere, and all are subject in one form or another, not only to Soviet influence but to a very high and, in many cases, increasing measure of control from Moscow. Athens alone—Greece with its immortal glories—is free to decide its future at an election under British, American and French observation. The Russian-dominated Polish Government has been encouraged to make enormous and wrongful inroads upon Germany, and mass expulsions of millions of Germans on a scale grievous and undreamed-of are now taking place. The Communist parties, which were very small in all these Eastern States of Europe, have been raised to preeminence and power far beyond their numbers and are seeking everywhere to obtain totalitarian control. Police governments are prevailing in nearly every case, and so far, except in Czechoslovakia, there is no true democracy.

The safety of the world requires a new unity in Europe, from which no nation should be permanently outcast. It is from the quarrels of the strong parent races in Europe that the world wars we have witnessed, or which occurred in former times, have sprung. Twice in our own lifetime we have seen the United States, against their wishes and their traditions, against arguments, the force of which it is impossible not to comprehend, drawn by irresistible forces, into these wars in time to secure the victory of the good cause, but only after frightful slaughter and devastation had occurred. Twice the United States has had to send several millions of its young men across the Atlantic to find the war;

but now war can find any nation, wherever it may dwell between dusk and dawn. Surely we should work with conscious purpose for a grand pacification of Europe, within the structure of the United Nations and in accordance with its Charter. That I feel is an open cause of policy of very great importance.

In front of the iron curtain which lies across Europe are other causes for anxiety. In Italy the Communist Party is seriously hampered by having to support the Communist-trained Marshal Tito's claims to former Italian territory at the head of the Adriatic. Nevertheless the future of Italy hangs in the balance. Again one cannot imagine a regenerated Europe without a strong France. All my public life I have worked for a strong France and I never lost faith in her destiny, even in the darkest hours. I will not lose faith now. However, in a great number of countries, far from the Russian frontiers and throughout the world, Communist fifth columns are established and work in complete unity and absolute obedience to the directions they receive from the Communist center. Except in the British Commonwealth and in the United States where Communism is in its infancy, the Communist parties or fifth columns constitute a growing challenge and peril to Christian civilization. These are somber facts for anyone to have to recite on the morrow of a victory gained by so much splendid comradeship in arms and in the cause of freedom and democracy; but we should be most unwise not to face them squarely while time remains.

I have felt bound to portray the shadow which, alike in the west and in the east, falls upon the world. I was a high minister at the time of the Versailles Treaty and a close friend of Mr. Lloyd-George, who was the head of the British delegation at Versailles. I did not myself agree with many things that were done, but I have a very strong impression in my mind of that situation, and I find it painful to contrast it with that which prevails now. In those days there were high hopes and unbounded confidence that the wars were over, and that the League of Nations

would become all-powerful. I do not see or feel that same confidence or even the same hopes in the haggard world at the present time.

On the other hand I repulse the idea that a new war is inevitable; still more that it is imminent. It is because I am sure that our fortunes are still in our own hands and that we hold the power to save the future, that I feel the duty to speak out now that I have the occasion and the opportunity to do so. I do not believe that Soviet Russia desires war. What they desire is the fruits of war and the indefinite expansion of their power and doctrines. But what we have to consider here today while time remains, is the permanent prevention of war and the establishment of conditions of freedom and democracy as rapidly as possible in all countries. Our difficulties and dangers will not be removed by closing our eyes to them. They will not be removed by mere waiting to see what happens; nor will they be removed by a policy of appeasement. What is needed is a settlement, and the longer this is delayed, the more difficult it will be and the greater our dangers will become.

From what I have seen of our Russian friends and Allies during the war, I am convinced that there is nothing they admire so much as strength, and there is nothing for which they have less respect than for weakness, especially military weakness. For that reason the old doctrine of a balance of power is unsound. We cannot afford, if we can help it, to work on narrow margins, offering temptations to a trial of strength. If the Western Democracies stand together in strict adherence to the principles of the United Nations Charter, their influence for furthering those principles will be immense and no one is likely to molest them. If however they become divided or falter in their duty and if these all-important years are allowed to slip away then indeed catastrophe may overwhelm us all.

Last time I saw it all coming and cried aloud to my own fellow-countrymen and to the world, but no one paid any attention. Up till the year 1933 or even 1935, Germany might have been saved from the awful fate which has overtaken her and we might all have been spared the miseries Hitler let loose upon mankind. There never was a war in all history easier to prevent by timely action than the one which has just desolated such great areas of the globe. It could have been prevented in my belief without the firing of a single shot, and Germany might be powerful, prosperous and honoured today; but no one would listen and one by one we were all sucked into the awful whirlpool. We surely must not let that happen again. This can only be achieved by reaching now, in 1946, a good understanding on all points with Russia under the general authority of the United Nations Organization and by the maintenance of that good understanding through many peaceful years, by the world instrument, supported by the whole strength of the English-speaking world and all its connections. There is the solution which I respectfully offer to you in this Address to which I have given the title "The Sinews of Peace?"

QUESTIONS

1. Britain emerged from the Second World War much weaker than it had been before 1939. Does Churchill's speech acknowledge the new role his country was prepared to play?

2. What will the postwar relationship between the United States and Britain be like? How does Churchill envisage Anglo-American relations?

3. What is the principal threat to the postwar peace?

4. How does Churchill propose that Soviet aggression be met?

5. What, in Churchill's view, was the role of the newly founded United Nations?

142.   NIKITA KHRUSHCHEV

REPORT TO THE COMMUNIST PARTY CONGRESS

(1961)

Nikita Khrushchev (1894–1971) came from a modest Russian background but rose rapidly in the ranks of the Communist Party, which he joined in 1918. He fought in the civil war against the so-called Whites and in 1925 became a full-time party official. Khrushchev was a loyal Stalinist and survived the worst of the party's purges in the 1930s. He emerged from the Second World War as a lieutenant general of the Red Army and a full member of the Politburo, the inner circle of the party. Khrushchev's great postwar achievement was rebuilding the Ukraine, one of the richest areas of the Soviet Union that had been devastated by the war. After Stalin's death, Khrushchev headed the Communist party in Moscow and then, after a bitter factional fight, was chosen first secretary of the Party to succeed Stalin. In 1956 Khrushchev began a policy of de-Stalinization, criticizing the excesses of that regime. This was only partly successful, and when a number of foreign policy blunders became apparent, the old-line party leaders acted to depose Khrushchev. He died in obscurity in 1971.

Khrushchev will always be remembered in the West for his dramatic action in the United Nations when, in disagreement with a statement from the U.S. ambassador, Khrushchev removed his shoe and banged it on the table. Khrushchev's report to the Party Congress of 1961 is a sample of his personal style—long-winded and bombastic but shrewdly to the point. In this report he concentrates on the international competition between capitalism and communism and his own goals for the Soviet people.

Comrades! Some six years have passed since the 20th Congress of the Communist Party of the Soviet Union. For our party, for the Soviet people, for all mankind these years have been of extraordinary, one might say world-historic, significance.

The Soviet motherland has entered the period of full-scale construction of communism along a wide front of great projects. The economy and culture of the Soviet Union are advancing sharply. The seven-year plan, a plan of mighty development of the productive forces of our motherland, is being successfully fulfilled. The creative forces of the masses of people are pouring forth as from thousands of springs throughout the whole country. The triumphant flights of Soviet men into outer space, the first in human history, are like a crown of splendid victories, a banner of communist construction raised high.

The activity of our party and state has been conducted in a complex international situation. More than once the imperialists have tried to bring the world to the brink of war, to test the strength of the Soviet Union and the courage of its peoples. Many bourgeois politicians have comforted themselves with illusions that our plans would fail and that the socialist camp would disintegrate. They undertook many provocations and acts of subversion against us. The Party, the entire Soviet people, exposed the intrigues of enemies and emerged with honor from all trials. Today the Soviet Union is stronger and more powerful than ever! *[Prolonged applause.]*

The Present World Situation and the International Position of the Soviet Union

Comrades! The competition of the two world social systems, the socialist and the capitalist, has been the chief content of the period since the 20th Party Congress. It has become the pivot, the foundation of world development at the present historical stage. Two lines, two historical trends, have manifested themselves more and more clearly in social development. One is the line of social progress, peace and constructive activity. The other is the line of reaction, oppression and war.

In the course of the peaceful competition of the two systems capitalism has suffered a profound moral defeat in the eyes of all peoples. The common people are daily convinced that capitalism is incapable of solving a single one of the urgent problems confronting mankind. It becomes more and more obvious that only on the paths to socialism can a solution to these problems be found. Faith in the capitalist system and the capitalist path of development is dwindling. Monopoly capital, losing its influence, resorts more and more to intimidating and suppressing the masses of the people, to methods of open dictatorship in carrying out its domestic policy and to aggressive acts against other countries. But the masses of the people offer increasing resistance to reaction's acts.

It is no secret to anyone that the methods of intimidation and threat are not a sign of strength but evidence of the weakening of capitalism, the deepening of its general crisis. As the saying goes, if you can't hang on by the mane, you won't hang on by the tail! *[Laughter in the hall.]* Reaction is still capable of dissolving parliaments in some countries in violation of their constitutions, of casting the best representatives of the people into prison, of sending cruisers and marines to subdue the "unruly." All this can put off for a time the approach of the fatal hour for the rule of capitalism. But such repressive measures still further expose the brigand nature of imperialism. The imperialists are sawing away at the branch on which they sit. There is no force in the world capable of stopping man's advance along the road of progress. *[Stormy applause.]*

The ruling circles of some imperialist powers have elevated subversive activities against the socialist countries to the level of state policy. With cynical frankness, the United States of America is spending hundreds of millions of dollars on espionage and subversion against the socialist countries and organizing so-called "guerrilla units," assembling in them criminal elements and cut-throats prepared to undertake the vilest crimes for money. For several successive years the United States has been holding provocational "captive nations weeks." The hired agents of the monopolies call "captive" all those peoples who have liberated themselves from imperialist bondage and taken the path of free development. Truly, imperialist demagogy and hypocrisy know no bounds! The monopolists' howl about "captive peoples" is like the cry of the pickpocket who shouts "Stop, thief!" *[Stir in the hall. Applause.]*

The imperialists' intrigues must never be forgotten. Our tremendous success in building a new life should not lead to complacency, to relaxation of vigilance. Of course, the greater the successes of socialism and the higher the living standard in each socialist country, the more the people rally around the Communist and Workers' Parties. This is one aspect of the matter, and a very gratifying aspect. But one must bear in mind another aspect also. As the solidarity of the peoples in all the socialist countries grows, the imperialists' hopes for the restoration of capitalist ways and for the degeneration of the socialist countries fade. World reaction therefore becomes more and more oriented toward striking a blow at the socialist states from outside in order through war to achieve the rule of capitalism throughout the world, or at least to check the development of the countries of socialism.

Our society is open to those people who come to us from abroad with open hearts. It is open to honest trade, to scientific, technical and cultural exchanges, to the exchange of truthful information. If it's an iron curtain we're talking about, where it really exists is in the world of capitalism, which, though dubbing itself the "free world," every now and then fearfully slams its gates shut to Soviet people, one moment to our cooks, the next to our chess players. There was a case where one state, which calls itself the "most open," was afraid to let in Soviet dancers. Can they really have feared that Russian folk dancing might shake the foundations of the capitalist world? *[Stir in the hall.]*

We have long proposed to the capitalist world that we compete not in an arms race but in improving the working people's lives. We are confident that capitalism cannot stand up under that kind of competition! We are confident that in the end all peoples will make the correct choice, will give their preference to the truly free world of communism and turn their backs on the so-called "free world" of capitalism. [*Applause.*]

Comrades! When the Party mapped the major measures for expanding our country's economy, bourgeois politicians and economists had quite a good deal to say about how the Communists were sacrificing the people's vital interests to heavy industry, about how production in the Soviet Union exists only for production's sake. What a vicious libel on socialism! Production not for the sake of production but for the sake of man is the sacred principle governing the activities of the Party and the Soviet state. Now everyone, even the most incorrigible skeptic and doubter, can once more see for himself that our party always honors its pledges to the people. [*Applause.*]

In the area of domestic policy, our party is setting Communists and the Soviet people the following tasks for the next few years:

The entire effort of the people must be directed toward fulfillment and overfulfillment of the seven-year plan—an important stage in the creation of the material and technical base for communism. We must continue to raise the level of material production and to keep the country's defenses up to the mark. As we seize new heights in the economic development of the Soviet homeland, we should bear in mind that only steady progress will assure us complete superiority and bring closer the day of our victory in the peaceful economic competition with capitalism.

We must strive to accelerate technical progress in all branches of socialist industry without exception. We must move forward particularly in power engineering, chemistry, machine building, metallurgy and the fuel industry. We must specialize enterprises on a broader scale, see to the integrated mechanization and automation of production processes and apply the achievements of modern science and technology and the experience of innovators more rapidly in production. Steady growth of labor productivity and reduction of production costs and an improvement in the quality of output must become law for all Soviet enterprises.

We must strive for a level of industrial and agricultural development that will enable us to meet the public's demand for manufactured goods and foodstuffs ever more fully. Funds that accumulate as a result of overfulfillment of industrial output plans should be channeled primarily into agriculture, light industry, the food industry and other consumer goods industries.

We must advance along the entire front of cultural and social development. There must be continuous progress in Soviet science, public education, literature and art. We must raise the working people's living standards, complete the adjustment of wages and the planned measures for shortening the working day and week, maintain a rapid pace in housing construction, and improve the pension system, trade, public catering, and medical and everyday services for the working people.

Our country is experiencing a great upsurge of creative effort. All the many nationalities of the Soviet Union look upon the building of communism as a cause near and dear to them and are working hand in hand and making invaluable contributions toward our common victory. Conscious of the grandeur of the tasks we pursue is multiplying the efforts of Soviet people tenfold, causing them to be more exacting of themselves and more intolerant of shortcomings, stagnation and inertia. We must take maximum advantage of the enormous motive forces inherent in the socialist system. [*Prolonged applause.*]

QUESTIONS

1. How does Khrushchev depict the state of the Soviet Union?

2. What is the Soviet view of the international situation?

3. Why does Khrushchev focus upon the iniquity of the Soviet Union's foreign enemies? How might such a focus be useful to him domestically?

4. What are the Party's plans for the future at home and abroad?

5. Khrushchev mentions Churchill's Iron Curtain in his address, a tribute to the power of the metaphor. Compare the two oratorical styles of the two statesmen.

143.   MIKHAIL GORBACHEV

PERESTROIKA
(1987)

Mikhail Gorbachev (1931–), the last leader of the USSR before its dissolution in 1991, was born to peasants from southwestern Russia. Starting his career as the driver of a combine harvester in 1946, he joined the Young Communist League and was soon marked out for advancement. Admitted to the prestigious Moscow State University Law School, he became a party member in 1953, and returned to his home region as a party official. By 1978 he was the party secretary for agriculture, and in 1979 he joined the Politburo, the center of Communist power. Gorbachev became general secretary of the party—the effective head of the Soviet state—in 1985. As general secretary, and later, president of the Soviet Union, he launched a series of radical reforms of government and society in the face of economic crisis. Overwhelmed by the rapid collapse of the Soviet Union from 1990 to 1992, Gorbachev found himself pushed to the sidelines by events.

Perestroika offers Gorbachev's analysis of what went wrong with Soviet society, and his prescriptions for its reform. Key to his plan is the continuation of Communist party dominance in the state, and the survival of socialism.

Perestroika—An Urgent Necessity

I think one thing should be borne in mind when studying the origins and essence of perestroika in the USSR. Perestroika is no whim on the part of some ambitious individuals or a group of leaders. If it were, no exhortations, plenary meetings or even a party congress could have rallied the people to the work which we are now doing and which involves more and more Soviet people each day.

Perestroika is an urgent necessity arising from the profound processes of development in our socialist society. This society is ripe for change. It has long been yearning for it. Any delay in beginning perestroika could have led to an exacerbated internal situation in the near future, which, to put it bluntly, would have been fraught with serious social, economic and political crises. . . .

Russia, where a great Revolution took place seventy years ago, is an ancient country with a unique history filled with searchings, accomplishments and tragic events. It has given the world many discoveries and outstanding personalities.

However, the Soviet Union is a young state without analogues in history or in the modern world. Over the past seven decades—a short span in the history of human civilization—our country has traveled a path equal to centuries. One of the mightiest powers in the world rose up to replace the backward semi-colonial and semi-feudal Russian Empire. Huge productive forces, a powerful intellectual potential, a highly advanced culture, a unique community of over one hundred nations and nationalities, and firm social protection for 280 million people on a territory forming one-sixth of the Earth—such are our great and indisputable achievements and Soviet people are justly proud of them.

I am not saying this to make my land appear better than it was or is. I do not want to sound like an apologist for whom "mine" means best and unquestionably superior. What I have just said is actual reality, authentic fact, the visible product of the work of several generations of our people. And it is equally clear that my country's progress became possible only thanks to the Revolution. It is the product of the Revolution. It is the fruit of socialism, the new social system, and the result of the historical choice made by our people. Behind them are the fears of our fathers and grandfathers and millions of working people—workers, farmers and intellectuals—who seventy years ago assumed direct responsibility for the future of their country. . . .

At some stage—this became particularly clear in the latter half of the seventies—something happened that was at first sight inexplicable. The country began to lose momentum. Economic failures became more frequent. Difficulties began to accumulate and deteriorate, and unresolved problems to multiply. Elements of what we call stagnation and other phenomena alien to socialism began to appear in the life of society. A kind of "braking mechanism" affecting social and economic development formed. And all this happened at a time when scientific and technological revolution opened up new prospects for economic and social progress. . . .

Declining rates of growth and economic stagnation were bound to affect other aspects of the life of Soviet society. Negative trends seriously affected the social sphere. This led to the appearance of the so-called "residual principle" in accordance with which social and cultural programs received what remained in the budget after allocations to production. A "deaf ear" sometimes seemed to be turned to social problems. The social sphere began to lag behind other spheres in terms of technological development, personnel, know-how and, most importantly, quality of work.

Here we have more paradoxes. Our society has ensured full employment and provided fundamental social guarantees. At the same time, we failed to use to the full the potential of socialism to meet the growing requirements in housing, in quality and sometimes quantity of foodstuffs, in the proper organization of the work of

Mikhail Gorbachev, leader of the former Soviet Union, in Lithuania following the declaration of independence by the local Communist party, 1989.

transport, in health services, in education and in tackling other problems which, naturally, arose in the course of society's development.

An absurd situation was developing. The Soviet Union, the world's biggest producer of steel, raw materials, fuel and energy, has shortfalls in them due to wasteful or inefficient use. One of the biggest producers of grain for food, it nevertheless has to buy millions of tons of grain a year for fodder. We have the largest number of doctors and hospital beds per thousand of the population and, at the same time, there are glaring shortcomings in our health services.

Our rockets can find Halley's comet and fly to Venus with amazing accuracy, but side by side with these scientific and technological triumphs is an obvious lack of efficiency in using scientific achievements for economic needs, and many Soviet household appliances are of poor quality.

This, unfortunately, is not all. A gradual erosion of the ideological and moral values of our people began. . . .

On the ideological plane as well, the braking mechanism brought about ever greater resistance to the attempts to constructively scrutinize the problems that were emerging and to the new ideas. Propaganda of success—real or imagined—was gaining the upper hand. Eulogizing and servility were encouraged; the needs and opinions of ordinary working people, of the public at large, were ignored. In the social sciences scholastic theorization was encouraged and developed, but creative thinking was driven out from the social sciences, and superfluous and voluntarist assessments and judgments were declared indisputable truths. Scientific, theoretical and other discussions, which are indispensable for the development of thought and for creative endeavor, were emasculated. Similar negative tendencies also affected culture, the arts and journalism, as well as the teaching process and medicine, where mediocrity, formalism and loud eulogizing surfaced, too.

The presentation of a "problem-free" reality backfired: a breach had formed between word and deed, which bred public passivity and disbelief in the slogans being proclaimed. It was only natural that this situation resulted in a credibility gap: everything that was proclaimed from the rostrums and printed in newspapers and textbooks was put in question. Decay began in public morals; the great feeling of solidarity with each other that was forged during the heroic times of the Revolution, the first five-year plans, the Great Patriotic War and postwar rehabilitation was weakening; alcoholism, drug addiction and crime were growing; and the penetration of the stereotypes of mass culture alien to us, which bred vulgarity and low tastes and brought about ideological barrenness increased. . . .

By saying all this I want to make the reader understand that the energy for revolutionary change has been accumulating amid our people and in the Party for some time. And the ideas of perestroika have been prompted not just by pragmatic interests and considerations but also by our troubled conscience, by the indomitable commitment to ideals which we inherited from the Revolution and as a result of a theoretical quest which gave us a better knowledge of society and reinforced our determination to go ahead. . . .

Perestroika means overcoming the stagnation process, breaking down the braking mechanism, creating a dependable and effective mechanism for the acceleration of social and economic progress and giving it greater dynamism.

Perestroika means mass initiative. It is the comprehensive development of democracy, socialist self-government, encouragement of initiative and creative endeavor, improved order and discipline, more glasnost, criticism and self-criticism in all spheres of our society. It is utmost respect for the individual and consideration for personal dignity.

Perestroika is the all-round intensification of the Soviet economy, the revival and development of the principles of democratic centralism in running the national economy, the universal introduction of economic methods, the renunciation of management by injunction and by administrative methods, and the overall encouragement of innovation and socialist enterprise.

Perestroika means a resolute shift to scientific methods, an ability to provide a solid scientific basis for every new initiative. It means the combination of the achievements of the scientific and technological revolution with a planned economy.

Perestroika means priority development of the social sphere aimed at ever better satisfaction of the Soviet people's requirements for good living and working conditions, for good rest and recreation, education and health care. It means unceasing concern for cultural and spiritual wealth, for the culture of every individual and society as a whole.

Perestroika means the elimination from society of the distortions of socialist ethics, the consistent implementation of the principles of social justice. It means the unity of words and deeds, rights and duties. It is the elevation of honest, highly-qualified labor, the overcoming of leveling tendencies in pay and consumerism. . . .

I stress once again: perestroika is not some kind of illumination or revelation. To restructure our life means to understand the objective necessity for renovation and acceleration. And that necessity emerged in the heart of our society. The essence of perestroika lies in the fact that *it unites socialism with democracy* and revives the Leninist concept of socialist construction both in theory and in practice. Such is the essence of perestroika, which accounts for its genuine revolutionary spirit and its all-embracing scope.

The goal is worth the effort. And we are sure that our effort will be a worthy contribution to humanity's social progress.

More Socialism and More Democracy

Perestroika is closely connected with socialism as a system. That side of the matter is being widely discussed, especially abroad, and our talk about perestroika won't be entirely clear if we don't touch upon that aspect.

Does perestroika mean that we are giving up socialism or at least some of its foundations? Some ask this question with hope, others with misgiving.

There are people in the West who would like to tell us that socialism is in a deep crisis and has brought our society to a dead end. That's how they interpret our critical analysis of the situation at the end of the seventies and beginning of the eighties. We have only one way out, they say: to adopt capitalist methods of economic management and social patterns, to drift toward capitalism.

They tell us that nothing will come of perestroika within the framework of our system. They say we should change this system and borrow from the experience of another socio-political system. To this they add that, if the Soviet Union takes this path and gives up its socialist choice, close links with the West will supposedly become possible. They go so far as to claim that the October 1917 Revolution was a mistake which almost completely cut off our country from world social progress.

To put an end to all the rumors and speculations that abound in the West about this, I would like to point out once again that we are conducting all our reforms in accordance with the socialist choice. We are looking within socialism, rather than outside it, for the answers to all the questions that arise. We assess our successes and errors alike by socialist standards. Those who hope that we shall move away from the socialist path will be greatly disappointed. Every part of our program of perestroika—and the program as a whole, for that matter—is fully based on the principle of more socialism and more democracy.

More socialism means a more dynamic pace and creative endeavor, more organization, law and order, more scientific methods and initiative in economic management, efficiency in administration, and a better and materially richer life for the people.

More socialism means more democracy, openness and collectivism in everyday life, more culture and humanism in production, social and personal relations among people, more dignity and self-respect for the individual.

More socialism means more patriotism and aspiration to noble ideals, more active civic concern about the country's internal affairs and about their positive influence on international affairs.

In other words, more of all those things which are inherent in socialism and in the theoretical precepts which characterize it as a distinct socio-economic formation.

We will proceed toward better socialism rather than away from it. We are saying this honestly, without trying to fool our own people or the world. Any hopes that we will begin to build a different, nonsocialist society and go over to the other camp are unrealistic and futile. Those in the West who expect us to give up socialism will be disappointed. It is high time they understood this, and, even more importantly, proceeded from that understanding in practical relations with the Soviet Union.

Speaking so, I would like to be clearly understood that though we, the Soviet people, are for socialism (I have explained above why), we are not imposing our views on anyone. Let everyone make his own choice; history will put everything in its place. Today, as I told a group of American public figures (Cyrus Vance, Henry Kissinger and others), we feel clearly as never before that, due to the socialist system and the planned economy, changes in our structural policy come much easier for us than they would in conditions of private enterprise, although we do have difficulties of our own, too.

We want more socialism and, therefore, more democracy.

As we understand it, the difficulties and problems of the seventies and eighties did not signify some kind of crisis for socialism as a social and political system, but rather were the result of insufficient consistency in applying the principles of socialism, of departures from them and even distortions of them, and of continued adherence to the methods and forms of social management that arose under specific historical conditions in the early stages of socialist development.

QUESTIONS

1. What, according to Gorbachev, has gone wrong with the Soviet Union? What is the nature of the crisis the USSR faces?

2. What, exactly, is "perestroika"? What does it mean?

3. What does Gorbachev think of the Russian Revolution? Was it successful or not?

4. What is the role of socialism and the Communist party in Gorbachev's plan?

5. Gorbachev claimed that perestroika was "new thinking." How is it new? Compare Gorbachev's work with General Secretary Khruschev's 1961 speech.

144.   **FRANCIS FUKUYAMA**

THE END OF HISTORY?

(1989)

Francis Fukuyama, an analyst for the United States Department of State, worked in Washington during the final days of the collapse of communism in Europe. His work involved planning U.S. government policy in an age when many of the verities of the post-World War II era seemed irrelevant. Diplomats and policy makers struggled in the late 1980s and early 1990s to come to terms with a world in the throes of dramatic, and wholly unforeseen, change. The reforms of Mikhail Gorbachev in the Soviet Union, the rise of Solidarity in Poland, and the retreat of leftist politics throughout the western world threw a whole generation raised upon the inevitability of the Cold War into ideological confusion.

Fukuyama, whose job was to make sense of these worldwide historical changes for policy makers, published this article in an attempt to explain what had happened. Using his understanding of the nineteenth-century German philosopher G. W. F. Hegel as a starting point, Fukuyama described the evolution of political society in the modern world. Political forms evolved through a complex interaction of forces in society—sometimes violent, and sometimes evolutionary—and this interaction resolved "contradictions," or conflicts: capital versus labor, slave against free, religious toleration against religious uniformity. Fukuyama argues that liberal democracy is the "final form of human government," because, unlike Communism, for example, it resolves the most fundamental contradictions inherent in modern society. "History," when understood as describing the process of political evolution whereby contradictions are resolved, was over. Liberal democracy—the "universal homogenous state"—had emerged triumphant.

In watching the flow of events over the past decade or so, it is hard to avoid the feeling that something very fundamental has happened in world history. The past year has seen a flood of articles commemorating the end of the Cold War, and the fact that "peace" seems to be breaking out in many regions of the world. Most of these analyses lack any larger conceptual framework for distinguishing between what is essential and what is contingent or accidental in world history, and are predictably superficial. If Mr.

Gorbachev were ousted from the Kremlin or a new Ayatollah proclaimed the millennium from a desolate Middle Eastern capital, these same commentators would scramble to announce the rebirth of a new era of conflict.

And yet, all of these people sense dimly that there is some larger process at work, a process that gives coherence and order to the daily headlines. The twentieth century saw the developed world descend into a paroxysm of ideological violence, as liberalism contended first with the remnants of absolutism, then bolshevism and fascism, and finally an updated Marxism that threatened to lead to the ultimate apocalypse of nuclear war. But the century that began full of self-confidence in the ultimate triumph of Western liberal democracy seems at its close to be returning full circle to where it started: not to an "end of ideology" or a convergence between capitalism and socialism, as earlier predicted, but to an unabashed victory of economic and political liberalism.

The triumph of the West, of the Western *idea*, is evident first of all in the total exhaustion of viable systematic alternatives to Western liberalism. In the past decade, there have been unmistakable changes in the intellectual climate of the world's two largest communist countries, and the beginnings of significant reform movements in both. But this phenomenon extends beyond high politics and it can be seen also in the ineluctable spread of consumerist Western culture in such diverse contexts as the peasants' markets and color television sets now omnipresent throughout China, the cooperative restaurants and clothing stores opened in the past year in Moscow, the Beethoven piped into Japanese department stores, and the rock music enjoyed alike in Prague, Rangoon, and Tehran.

What we may be witnessing is not just the end of the Cold War, or the passing of a particular period of postwar history, but the end of history as such: that is, the end point of mankind's ideological evolution and the universalization of Western liberal democracy as the final form of human government. This is not to say that there will no longer be events to fill the pages of *Foreign Affairs*'s yearly summaries of international relations, for the victory of liberalism has occurred primarily in the realm of ideas or consciousness and is as yet incomplete in the real or material world. But there are powerful reasons for believing that it is the ideal that will govern the material world *in the long run*. To understand how this is so, we must first consider some theoretical issues concerning the nature of historical change.

The notion of the end of history is not an original one. Its best known propagator was Karl Marx, who believed that the direction of historical development was a purposeful one determined by the interplay of material forces, and would come to an end only with the achievement of a communist utopia that would finally resolve all prior contradictions. But the concept of history as a dialectical process with a beginning, a middle, and an end was borrowed by Marx from his great German predecessor, Georg Wilhelm Friedrich Hegel.

For better or worse, much of Hegel's historicism has become part of our contemporary intellectual baggage. The notion that mankind has progressed through a series of primitive stages of consciousness on his path to the present, and that these stages corresponded to concrete forms of social organization, such as tribal, slave-owning, theocratic, and finally democratic-egalitarian societies, has become inseparable from the modern understanding of man. Hegel was the first philosopher to speak the language of modern social science, insofar as man for him was the product of his concrete historical and social environment and not, as earlier natural right theorists would have it, a collection of more or less fixed "natural" attributes. The mastery and transformation of man's natural environment through the application of science and technology was originally not a Marxist concept, but a Hegelian one. Unlike later historicists whose historical relativism degenerated into relativism *tout court*, however, Hegel believed that history culminated in an absolute moment—a moment in which a final, rational form of society and state became victorious.

The state that emerges at the end of history is liberal insofar as it recognizes and protects through a system of law man's universal right to freedom, and democratic insofar as it exists only with the consent of the governed.

Have we in fact reached the end of history? Are there, in other words, any fundamental "contradictions" in human life that cannot be resolved in the context of modern liberalism, that would be resolvable by an alternative political-economic structure? If we accept the idealist premises laid out above, we must seek an answer to this question in the realm of ideology and consciousness. Our task is not to answer exhaustively the challenges to liberalism promoted by every crackpot messiah around the world, but only those that are embodied in important social or political forces and movements, and which are therefore part of world history. For our purposes, it matters very little what strange thoughts occur to people in Albania or Burkina Faso, for we are interested in what one could in some sense call the common ideological heritage of mankind.

In the past century, there have been two major challenges to liberalism, those of fascism and of communism. The former saw the political weakness, materialism, anomie, and lack of community of the West as fundamental contradictions in liberal societies that could only be resolved by a strong state that forged a new "people" on the basis of national exclusiveness. Fascism was destroyed as a living ideology by World War II. This was a defeat, of course, on a very material level, but it amounted to a defeat of the idea as well. What destroyed fascism as an idea was not universal moral revulsion against it, since plenty of people were willing to endorse the idea as long as it seemed the wave of the future, but its lack of success. After the war, it seemed to most people that German fascism as well as its other European and Asian variants were bound to self-destruct. There was no material reason why new fascist movements could not have sprung up again after the war in other locales, but for the fact that expansionist ultranationalism, with its promise of unending conflict leading to disastrous military defeat, had completely lost its appeal. The ruins of the Reich chancellory as well as the atomic bombs dropped on Hiroshima and Nagasaki killed this ideology on the level of consciousness as well as materially, and all of the

proto-fascist movements spawned by the German and Japanese examples like the Peronist movement in Argentina or Subhas Chandra Bose's Indian National Army withered after the war.

The ideological challenge mounted by the other great alternative to liberalism, communism, was far more serious. Marx, speaking Hegel's language, asserted that liberal society contained a fundamental contradiction that could not be resolved within its context, that between capital and labor, and this contradiction has constituted the chief accusation against liberalism ever since. But surely, the class issue has actually been successfully resolved in the West. . . . [T]he egalitarianism of modern America represents the essential achievement of the classless society envisioned by Marx. This is not to say that there are not rich people and poor people in the United States, or that the gap between them has not grown in recent years. But the root causes of economic inequality do not have to do with the underlying legal and social structure of our society, which remains fundamentally egalitarian and moderately redistributionist, so much as with the cultural and social characteristics of the groups that make it up, which are in turn the historical legacy of premodern conditions. Thus black poverty in the United States is not the inherent product of liberalism, but is rather the "legacy of slavery and racism" which persisted long after the formal abolition of slavery.

As a result of the receding of the class issue, the appeal of communism in the developed Western world, it is safe to say, is lower today than any time since the end of the First World War. This can be measured in any number of ways: in the declining membership and electoral pull of the major European communist parties, and their overtly revisionist programs; in the corresponding electoral success of conservative parties from Britain and Germany to the United States and Japan, which are unabashedly promarket and antistatist; and in an intellectual climate whose most "advanced" members no longer believe that bourgeois society is something that ultimately needs to be overcome. This is not to say that the opinions of progressive intellectuals in Western countries are not deeply pathological in any number of ways. But those who believe that the future must inevitably be socialist tend to be very old, or very marginal to the real political discourse of their societies. . . .

[D]evelopments in the Soviet Union—the original "homeland of the world proletariat" . . . have put the final nail in the coffin of the Marxist-Leninist alternative to liberal democracy. It should be clear that in terms of formal institutions, not much has changed in the four years since Gorbachev has come to power: free markets and the cooperative movement represent only a small part of the Soviet economy, which remains centrally planned; the political system is still dominated by the Communist party, which has only begun to democratize internally and to share power with other groups; the regime continues to assert that it is seeking only to modernize socialism and that its ideological basis remains Marxism-Leninism; and, finally, Gorbachev faces a potentially powerful conservative opposition that could undo many of the changes that have taken place to date. Moreover, it is hard to be too sanguine about the chances for success of Gorbachev's proposed reforms, either in the sphere of economics or politics. But my purpose here is not to analyze events in the short-term, or to make predictions for policy purposes, but to look at underlying trends in the sphere of ideology and consciousness. And in that respect, it is clear that an astounding transformation has occurred.

Emigres from the Soviet Union have been reporting for at least the last generation now that virtually nobody in that country truly believed in Marxism-Leninism any longer, and that this was nowhere more true than in the Soviet elite, which continued to mouth Marxist slogans out of sheer cynicism. The corruption and decadence of the late Brezhnev-era Soviet state seemed to matter little, however, for as long as the state itself refused to throw into question any of the fundamental principles underlying Soviet society, the system was capable of functioning adequately out of sheer inertia and could even muster some dynamism in the realm of foreign and defense policy. Marxism-Leninism was like a magical incantation which, however absurd and devoid of meaning, was the only common basis on which the elite could agree to rule Soviet society.

What has happened in the four years since Gorbachev's coming to power is a revolutionary assault on the most fundamental institutions and principles of Stalinism, and their replacement by other principles which do not amount to liberalism *per se* but whose only connecting thread is liberalism. This is most evident in the economic sphere, where the reform economists around Gorbachev have become steadily more radical in their support for free markets. . . .

In the political sphere, the proposed changes to the Soviet constitution, legal system, and party rules amount to much less than the establishment of a liberal state. Gorbachev has spoken of democratization primarily in the sphere of internal party affairs, and has shown little intention of ending the Communist party's monopoly of power; indeed, the political reform seeks to legitimize and therefore strengthen the CPSU's rule. Nonetheless, the general principles underlying many of the reforms—that the "people" should be truly responsible for their own affairs, that higher political bodies should be answerable to lower ones, and not vice versa, that the rule of law should prevail over arbitrary police actions, with separation of powers and an independent judiciary, that there should be legal protection for property rights, the need for open discussion of public issues and the right of public dissent, the empowering of the Soviets as a forum in which the whole Soviet people can participate, and of a political culture that is more tolerant and pluralistic—come from a source fundamentally alien to the USSR's Marxist-Leninist tradition, even if they are incompletely articulated and poorly implemented in practice.

The Soviet Union could in no way be described as a liberal or democratic country now, nor do I think that it is terribly likely that *perestroika* will succeed such that the label will be thinkable any time in the near future. But at the end of history it is not necessary that all societies become successful liberal societies, merely that they end their ideological pretensions of representing different and higher forms of human society. And in this respect I believe that something very important has happened in the Soviet Union in the past few years: the criticisms of the Soviet system sanctioned by Gorbachev have been so thorough and devastating that there is very little chance of going back to either Stalinism or Brezhnevism in any simple way. Gorbachev has finally permitted people to say what they had privately understood for many years, namely, that the magical incantations of Marxism-Leninism were nonsense, that Soviet socialism was not superior to the West in any respect but was in fact a monumental failure. The conservative opposition in the USSR, consisting both of simple workers afraid of unemployment and inflation and of party officials fearful of losing their jobs and privileges, is outspoken and may be strong enough to force Gorbachev's ouster in the next few years. But what both groups desire is tradition, order, and authority; they manifest no deep commitment to Marxism-Leninism, except insofar as they have invested much of their own lives in it. For authority to be restored in the Soviet Union after Gorbachev's demolition work, it must be on the basis of some new and vigorous ideology which has not yet appeared on the horizon.

If we admit for the moment that the fascist and communist challenges to liberalism are dead, are there any other ideological competitors left? Or put another way, are there contradictions in liberal society beyond that of class that are not resolvable? Two possibilities suggest themselves, those of religion and nationalism.

The rise of religious fundamentalism in recent years within the Christian, Jewish, and Muslim traditions has been widely noted. One is inclined to say that the revival of religion in some way attests to a broad unhappiness with the impersonality and spiritual vacuity of liberal consumerist societies. Yet while the emptiness at the core of liberalism is most certainly a defect in the ideology—indeed, a flaw that one does not need the perspective of religion to recognize—it is not at all clear that it is remediable through politics. Modern liberalism itself was historically a consequence of the weakness of religiously-based societies which, failing to agree on the nature of the good life, could not provide even the minimal preconditions of peace and stability. In the contemporary world only Islam has offered a theocratic state as a political alternative to both liberalism and communism. But the doctrine has little appeal for non-Muslims, and it is hard to believe that the movement will take on any universal significance. Other less organized religious impulses have been successfully satisfied within the sphere of personal life that is permitted in liberal societies.

The other major "contradiction" potentially unresolvable by liberalism is the one posed by nationalism and other forms of racial and ethnic consciousness. It is certainly true that a very large degree of conflict since the Battle of Jena (1806) has had its roots in nationalism. Two cataclysmic world wars in this century have been spawned by the nationalism of the developed world in various guises, and if those passions have been muted to a certain extent in postwar Europe, they are still extremely powerful in the Third World. Nationalism has been a threat to liberalism historically in Germany, and continues to be one in isolated parts of "post-historical" Europe like Northern Ireland.

But it is not clear that nationalism represents an irreconcilable contradiction in the heart of liberalism. In the first place, nationalism is not one single phenomenon but several, ranging from mild cultural nostalgia to the highly organized and elaborately articulated doctrine of National Socialism. Only systematic nationalisms of the latter sort can qualify as a formal ideology on the level of liberalism or communism. The vast majority of the world's nationalist movements do not have a political program beyond the negative desire of independence *from* some other group or people, and do not offer anything like a comprehensive agenda for socio-economic organization. As such, they are compatible with doctrines and ideologies that do offer such agendas. While they may constitute a source of conflict for liberal societies, this conflict does not arise from liberalism itself so much as from the fact that the liberalism in question is incomplete. Certainly a great deal of the world's ethnic and nationalist tension can be explained in terms of peoples who are forced to live in unrepresentative political systems that they have not chosen.

While it is impossible to rule out the sudden appearance of new ideologies or previously unrecognized contradictions in liberal societies, then, the present world seems to confirm that the fundamental principles of socio-political organization have not advanced terribly far since 1806. Many of the wars and revolutions fought since that time have been undertaken in the name of ideologies which claimed to be more advanced than liberalism, but whose pretensions were ultimately unmasked by history. In the meantime, they have helped to spread the universal homogenous state to the point where it could have a significant effect on the overall character of international relations.

The passing of Marxism-Leninism first from China and then from the Soviet Union will mean its death as a living ideology of world historical significance. For while there may be some isolated true believers left in places like Managua, Pyongyang, or Cambridge, Massachusetts, the fact that there is not a single large state in which it is a going concern undermines completely its pretensions to being in the vanguard of human history. And the death of this ideology means the growing "Common Marketization" of international relations, and the diminution of the likelihood of large-scale conflict between states.

This does not by any means imply the end of international conflict *per se*. For the world at that point would be divided between a part that was historical and a part that was post-historical. Conflict between states still in history, and between those states and those at the end of history, would still be possible. There would still be a high and perhaps rising level of ethnic and nationalist violence, since those are impulses incompletely played out, even in parts of the post-historical world. Palestinians and Kurds, Sikhs and Tamils, Irish Catholics and Walloons, Armenians and Azeris, will continue to have their unresolved grievances. This implies that terrorism and wars of national liberation will continue to be an important item on the international agenda. But large-scale conflict must involve large states still caught in the grip of history, and they are what appear to be passing from the scene.

The end of history will be a very sad time. The struggle for recognition, the willingness to risk one's life for a purely abstract goal, the worldwide ideological struggle that called forth daring, courage, imagination, and idealism, will be replaced by economic calculation, the endless solving of technical problems, environmental concerns, and the satisfaction of sophisticated consumer demands. In the post-historical period there will be neither art nor philosophy, just the perpetual caretaking of the museum of human history. I can feel in myself, and see in others around me, a powerful nostalgia for the time when history existed. Such nostalgia, in fact, will continue to fuel competition and conflict even in the post-historical world for some time to come. Even though I recognize its inevitability, I have the most ambivalent feelings for the civilization that has been created in Europe since 1945, with its north Atlantic and Asian offshoots. Perhaps this very prospect of centuries of boredom at the end of history will serve to get history started once again.

QUESTIONS

1. Fukuyama's argument as excerpted here is principally centered upon the West. Could you argue that it applies to other parts of the world as well? Why or why not?

2. Why did liberal democracy succeed while other political systems did not?

3. Fukuyama did not predict the swift collapse of the Soviet Union after 1990 in his work—do you think those events support or discredit his argument?

4. The author excludes from his consideration of challenges to liberal democracy those he describes as "crackpot messiahs." What, from his point of view, are the real challenges to democracy? Do you think this view is adequate? Why or why not?

5. How important do you think this kind of analysis is for policy makers? How might a maker of foreign policy use this essay?

Toward a New World

145.

CHARTER OF THE UNITED NATIONS
(1946)

Drawn closer together in their struggle to defeat fascism at the cost of millions of lives, the leaders of the Allied nations were determined to find an effective means to maintain international stability after the Second World War. The prewar League of Nations had been a failure, partly because the United States had refused to join and partly because the League had proven incapable of enforcing its decrees. The victorious Allies envisioned something more powerful and universal. In 1946 representatives from around the world met in San Francisco to hammer out a plan to produce a workable international organization. The result was the United Nations. Divided between a General Assembly and a Security Council, the United Nations was to have the responsibility of mediating disputes between nations and, in the last resort, to send its own peace-keeping forces into troubled areas. The Charter of the United Nations was considered the first step in the direction of world government and toward the end of war.

WE THE PEOPLES OF THE UNITED NATIONS DETERMINED

to save succeeding generations from the scourge of war, which twice in our lifetime has brought untold sorrow to mankind, and

to reaffirm faith in fundamental human rights, in the dignity and worth of the human person, in the equal rights of men and women and of nations large and small, and

to establish conditions under which justice and respect for the obligations arising from treaties and other sources of international law can be maintained, and

to promote social progress and better standards of life in larger freedom,

AND FOR THESE ENDS

to practice tolerance and live together in peace with one another as good neighbors, and

to unite our strength to maintain international peace and security, and

to ensure, by the acceptance of principles and the institution of methods, that armed force shall not be used, save in the common interest, and to employ international machinery for the promotion of the economic and social advancement of all peoples,

HAVE RESOLVED TO COMBINE OUR EFFORTS TO ACCOMPLISH THESE AIMS.

Accordingly, our respective Governments, through representatives assembled in the city of San Francisco, who have exhibited their full powers found to be in good and due form, have agreed to the present Charter of the United Nations and do hereby establish an international organization to be known as the United Nations.

Chapter I: Purposes and Principles

Article I

The Purposes of the United Nations are:

1. To maintain international peace and security, and to that end; to take effective collective measures for the prevention and removal of threats to the peace, and for the suppression of acts of aggression or other breaches of the peace, and to bring about by peaceful means, and in conformity with the principles of justice and international law, adjustment or settlement of international disputes or situations which might lead to a breach of the peace;

2. To develop friendly relations among nations based on respect for the principle of equal rights and self-determination of peoples, and to take other appropriate measures to strengthen universal peace;

3. To achieve international cooperation in solving international problems of an economic, social, cultural, or humanitarian character, and in promoting and encouraging respect for human rights and for fundamental freedoms for all without distinction as to race, sex, language, or religion; and

4. To be a center for harmonizing the actions of nations in the attainment of these common ends.

Article 2

The Organization and its Members, in pursuit of the Purposes stated in Article 1, shall act in accordance with the following Principles.

1. The Organization is based on the principle of the sovereign equality of all its Members.

2. All Members, in order to ensure to all of them the rights and benefits resulting from membership, shall fulfill in good faith the obligations assumed by them in accordance with the present Charter.

3. All Members shall settle their international disputes by peaceful means in such a manner that international peace and security, and justice, are not endangered.

4. All Members shall refrain in their international relations from the threat of use of force against the territorial integrity or political independence of any state, or in any other manner inconsistent with the Purposes of the United Nations.

5. All Members shall give the United Nations every assistance in any action it takes in accordance with the present Charter, and shall refrain from giving assistance to any state against which the United Nations is taking preventive or enforcement action.

6. The Organization shall ensure that states which are not Members of the United Nations act in accordance with these Principles so far as may be necessary for the maintenance of international peace and security.

7. Nothing contained in the present Charter shall authorize the United Nations to intervene in matters which are essentially within the domestic jurisdiction of any state or shall require the Members to submit such matters to settlement under the present Charter; but this principle shall not prejudice the application of enforcement measures under Chapter VII.

Chapter II: Membership

Article 3

The original Members of the United Nations shall be the states which, having participated in the United Nations Conference on International Organization at San Francisco, or having previously signed the Declaration by United Nations of January 1, 1942, sign the present Charter and ratify it in accordance with Article 110.

Article 4

Membership in the United Nations is open to all other peace-loving states which accept the obligations contained in the present Charter and, in the judgment of the Organization, are able and willing to carry out these obligations.

Article 5

A Member of the United Nations against which preventive or enforcement action has been taken by the Security Council may be suspended from the exercise of the rights and privileges of membership by the General Assembly upon the recommendation of the Security Council. The exercise of these rights and privileges may be restored by the Security Council.

Article 6

A Member of the United Nations which has persistently violated the Principles contained in the present Charter may be expelled from the Organization by the General Assembly upon the recommendation of the Security Council.

Chapter III: Organs

Article 7

There are established as the principal organs of the United Nations: a General Assembly, a Security Council, an Economic and Social Council, a Trusteeship Council, an International Court of Justice, and a Secretariat.

Article 8

The United Nations shall place no restrictions on the eligibility of men and women to participate in any capacity and under conditions of equality in its principle and subsidiary organs.

Chapter VI: Pacific Settlements of Disputes

Article 33

1. The parties to any dispute, the continuance of which is likely to endanger the maintenance of international peace and security, shall, first of all, seek a solution by negotiation, enquiry, mediation, conciliation, arbitration, judicial settlement, resort to regional agencies or arrangements, or other peaceful means of their own choice.

2. The Security Council shall, when it deems necessary, call upon the parties to settle their dispute by such means.

Article 34

The Security Council may investigate any dispute, or any situation which might lead to international friction or give rise to a dispute, in order to determine whether the continuance of the dispute or situation is likely to endanger the maintenance of international peace and security.

Chapter VII: Action with Respect to Threats to the Peace, Breaches of the Peace, and Acts of Aggression

Article 39

The Security Council shall determine the existence of any threat to the peace, breach of the peace, or act of aggression and shall make recommendations, or decide what measures shall be taken in accordance with Articles 41 and 42, to maintain or restore international peace and security.

Article 41

The Security Council may decide what measures not involving the use of armed force are to be employed to give effect to its decisions, and it may call upon Members of the United Nations to apply such measures. These may include complete or partial interruption of economic relations and of rail, sea, air, postal, telegraphic, radio, and other means of communication, and the severance of diplomatic relations.

Article 42

Should the Security Council consider that measures provided for in article 41 would be inadequate or have proved to be inadequate, it may take such action by air, sea, or land forces as may be necessary to maintain or restore international peace and security. Such action may include demonstrations, blockade, and other operations by air, sea, or land forces of the Members of the United Nations.

Chapter XI: Declaration Regarding Non-Self-Governing Territories

Members of the United Nations which have or assume responsibilities for the administration of territories whose peoples have not yet attained a full measure of self-government recognize the principle that the interests of the inhabitants of these territories are paramount, and accept as a sacred trust the obligation to promote to the utmost, within the system of international peace and security established by the present Charter, the well-being of the inhabitants of these territories, and, to this end:

a. to ensure, with due respect for the culture of the peoples concerned, their political, economic, social, and educational advancement, their just treatment, and their protection against abuses;

b. to develop self-government, to take due account of the political aspirations of the peoples, and to assist them in the progressive development of their free political institutions, according to the particular circumstances of each territory and its peoples and their varying stages of advancement;

c. to further international peace and security;

d. to promote constructive measures of development, to encourage research, and to cooperate with one another and, when and where appropriate, with specialized international bodies with a view to the practical achievement of the social, economic, and scientific purposes set forth in this Article.

QUESTIONS

1. What is the mission of the United Nations?

2. How are members of the United Nations supposed to behave toward one another? What are their relative rights within the organization?

3. How are disputes between members to be resolved?

4. Under what circumstances may force be used in international affairs?

5. How does the Charter take into account the realities of postwar international relations?

146.

THE CHARTER OF ECONOMIC RIGHTS AND DUTIES OF STATES

(1974)

Beginning in the 1970s the leaders of underdeveloped states in the so-called Third World began to voice concerns about the relationship between foreign and domestic ownership of natural resources and about the obligations that industrialized nations owed to developing ones. These issues were becoming particularly troublesome in light of the energy crisis and the skyrocketing international indebtedness of Third-World nations. Third-World leaders called increasingly for programs that would guarantee world economic justice.

The Charter of Economic Rights and Duties of States was among the most visionary of the programs proposed. It was adopted by the General Assembly of the United Nations by a vote of 120 to 6 with 10 abstentions. Voting against the Charter were the United States, Great Britain, West Germany, Belgium, Denmark, and Luxembourg. The most serious issues relating to the Charter concerned the renationalization of resources and the obligation of underdeveloped states to pay compensation for reclaiming their own property.

Preamble

The General Assembly,

Reaffirming the fundamental purposes of the United Nations, in particular the maintenance of international peace and security, the development of friendly relations among nations and the achievement of international co-operation in solving international problems in the economic and social fields,

Affirming the need for strengthening international co-operation in these fields,

Reaffirming further the need for strengthening international co-operation for development,

Declaring that it is a fundamental purpose of the present Charter to promote the establishment of the new international economic order, based on equity, sovereign equality, interdependence, common interest and co-operation among all States, irrespective of their economic and social systems,

Desirous of contributing to the creation of conditions for:

- (*a*) The attainment of wider prosperity among all countries and of higher standards of living for all peoples,
- (*b*) The promotion by the entire international community of the economic and social progress of all countries, especially developing countries,
- (*c*) The encouragement of co-operation, on the basis of mutual advantage and equitable benefits for all peace-loving States which are willing to carry out the provisions of the present Charter, in the economic, trade, scientific and technical fields, regardless of political, economic or social systems,

(d) The overcoming of main obstacles in the way of the economic development of the developing countries,

(e) The acceleration of the economic growth of developing countries with a view to bridging the economic gap between developing and developed countries,

(f) The protection, preservation and enhancement of the environment,

Mindful of the need to establish and maintain a just and equitable economic and social order through:

(a) The achievement of more rational and equitable international economic relations and the encouragement of structural changes in the world economy,

(b) The creation of conditions which permit the further expansion of trade and intensification of economic co-operation among all nations,

(c) The strengthening of the economic independence of developing countries,

(d) The establishment and promotion of international economic relations, taking into account the agreed differences in development of the developing countries and their specific needs,

Determined to promote collective economic security for development, in particular of the developing countries, with strict respect for the sovereign equality of each State and through the co-operation of the entire international community,

Considering that genuine co-operation among States, based on joint consideration of and concerted action regarding international economic problems, is essential for fulfilling the international community's common desire to achieve a just and rational development of all parts of the world,

Stressing the importance of ensuring appropriate conditions for the conduct of normal economic relations among all States, irrespective of differences in social and economic systems, and for the full respect of the rights of all peoples, as well as strengthening instruments of international economic co-operation as means for the consolidation of peace for the benefit of all,

Convinced of the need to develop a system of international economic relations on the basis of sovereign equality, mutual and equitable benefit and the close interrelationship of the interests of all States,

Reiterating that the responsibility for the development of every country rests primarily upon itself but that concomitant and effective international co-operation is an essential factor for the full achievement of its own development goals,

Firmly convinced of the urgent need to evolve a substantially improved system of international economic relations,

Solemnly adopts the present Charter of Economic Rights and Duties of States.

Chapter I. Fundamentals of International Economic Relations

Economic as well as political and other relations among States shall be governed, *inter alia,* by the following principles:

(a) Sovereignty, territorial integrity and political independence of States;

(b) Sovereign equality of all States;

(c) Non-aggression;

(d) Non-intervention;

(e) Mutual and equitable benefit;

(f) Peaceful coexistence;

(g) Equal rights and self-determination of peoples;

(h) Peaceful settlement of disputes;

(i) Remedying of injustices which have been brought about by force and which deprive a nation of the natural means necessary for its normal development;

(*j*) Fulfillment in good faith of international obligations;

(*k*) Respect for human rights and fundamental freedoms;

(*l*) No attempt to seek hegemony and spheres of influence;

(*m*) Promotion of international social justice;

(*n*) International co-operation for development;

(*o*) Free access to and from the sea by landlocked countries within the framework of the above principles.

Chapter II. Economic Rights and Duties of States

Article 1

Every State has the sovereign and inalienable right to choose its economic system as well as its political, social and cultural systems in accordance with the will of its people, without outside interference, coercion or threat in any form whatsoever.

Article 2

1. Every State has and shall freely exercise full permanent sovereignty, including possession, use and disposal, over all its wealth, natural resources and economic activities.

2. Each State has the right:

(*a*) To regulate and exercise authority over foreign investment within its national jurisdiction in accordance with its laws and regulations and in conformity with its national objectives and priorities. No State shall be compelled to grant preferential treatment to foreign investment;

(*b*) To regulate and supervise the activities of transnational corporations within its national jurisdiction and take measures to ensure that such activities comply with its laws, rules and regulations and conform with its economic and social policies. Transnational corporations shall not intervene in the internal affairs of a host State. Every State should, with full regard for its sovereign rights, co-operate with other States in the exercise of the right set forth in this subparagraph;

(*c*) To nationalize, expropriate or transfer ownership of foreign property, in which case appropriate compensation should be paid by the State adopting such measures, taking into account its relevant laws and regulations and all circumstances that the State considers pertinent. In any case where the question of compensation gives rise to a controversy, it shall be settled under the domestic law of the nationalizing State and by its tribunals, unless it is freely and mutually agreed by all States concerned that other peaceful means be sought on the basis of the sovereign equality of States and in accordance with the principle of free choice of means. . . .

Article 4

Every State has the right to engage in international trade and other forms of economic cooperation irrespective of any differences in political, economic and social systems. No State shall be subjected to discrimination of any kind based solely on such differences. In the pursuit of international trade and other forms of economic co-operation, every State is free to choose the forms of organization of its foreign economic relations and to enter into bilateral and multilateral arrangements consistent with its international obligations and with the needs of international economic co-operation.

*The delegation of Senegal headed by Assane Seck, Minister for Foreign Affairs, at the
United Nations, New York, 1974.*

Article 5

All States have the right to associate in organizations of primary commodity producers in order to develop their national economies, to achieve stable financing for their development and, in pursuance of their aims, to assist in the promotion of sustained growth of the world economy, in particular accelerating the development of developing countries. Correspondingly all States have the duty to respect that right by refraining from applying economic and political measures that would limit it. . . .

Article 7

Every State has the primary responsibility to promote the economic, social and cultural development of its people. To this end, each State has the right and the responsibility to choose its means and goals of development, fully to mobilize and use its resources, to implement progressive economic and social reforms and to ensure the full participation of its people in the process and benefits of development. All States have the duty, individually and collectively, to co-operate in order to eliminate obstacles that hinder such mobilization and use.

Article 8

States should co-operate in facilitating more rational and equitable international economic relations and in encouraging structural changes in the context of a balanced world economy in harmony with the needs and interests of all countries, especially developing countries, and should take appropriate measures to this end. . . .

Article 10

All States are juridically equal and, as equal members of the international community, have the right to participate fully and effectively in the international decision-making process in the solution of world economic, financial and monetary problems, *inter alia*, through the appropriate international organizations in accordance with their existing and evolving rules, and to share equitably in the benefits resulting therefrom. . . .

Article 13

1. Every State has the right to benefit from the advances and developments in science and technology for the acceleration of its economic and social development.

2. All States should promote international scientific and technological co-operation and the transfer of technology, with proper regard for all legitimate interests including, *inter alia*, the rights and duties of holders, suppliers and recipients of technology. In particular, all States should facilitate the access of developing countries to the achievements of modern science and technology, the transfer of technology and the creation of indigenous technology for the benefit of the developing countries in forms and in accordance with procedures which are suited to their economies and their needs.

3. Accordingly, developed countries should co-operate with the developing countries in the establishment, strengthening and development of their scientific and technological infrastructures and their scientific research and technological activities so as to help to expand and transform the economies of developing countries.

4. All States should co-operate in research with a view to evolving further internationally accepted guidelines or regulations for the transfer of technology, taking fully into account the interests of developing countries. . . .

Article 15

All States have the duty to promote the achievement of general and complete disarmament under effective international control and to utilize the resources released by effective disarmament measures for the economic and social development of countries, allocating a substantial portion of such resources as additional means for the development needs of developing countries.

Article 16

1. It is the right and duty of all States, individually and collectively, to eliminate colonialism, *apartheid,* racial discrimination, neocolonialism and all forms of foreign aggression, occupation and domination, and the economic and social consequences thereof, as a prerequisite for development. States which practice such coercive policies are economically responsible to the countries, territories and peoples affected for the restitution and full compensation for the exploitation and depletion of, and damages to, the natural and all other resources of those countries, territories and peoples. It is the duty of all States to extend assistance to them.

2. No State has the right to promote or encourage investments that may constitute an obstacle to the liberation of a territory occupied by force. . . .

Article 19

With a view to accelerating the economic growth of developing countries and bridging the economic gap between developed and developing countries, developed countries should grant generalized preferential, non-reciprocal and non-discriminatory treatment to developing countries in those fields of international economic cooperation where it may be feasible.

Article 20

Developing countries should, in their efforts to increase their over-all trade, give due attention to the possibility of expanding their trade with socialist countries, by granting to these countries conditions for trade not inferior to those granted normally to the developed market economy countries. . . .

Chapter III. Common Responsibilities Towards the International Community

Article 29

The sea-bed and ocean floor and the subsoil thereof, beyond the limits of national jurisdiction, as well as the resources of the area, are the common heritage of mankind.

Article 30

The protection, preservation and enhancement of the environment for the present and future generations is the responsibility of all States. All States shall endeavor to establish their own environmental and developmental policies in conformity with such responsibility. The environmental policies of all States should enhance and not adversely affect the present and future development potential of developing countries. All States have the responsibility to ensure that activities within their jurisdiction or control do not cause damage to the environment of other States or of areas beyond the limits of national jurisdiction. All States should co-operate in evolving international norms and regulations in the field of the environment.

QUESTIONS

1. What is the new international economic order?

2. What seem to be the most important principles behind the creation of the new economic order?

3. Why do you think the Western powers opposed the adoption of the Charter?

4. What is the responsibility of the developed countries toward the undeveloped countries?

5. How would the full implementation of the Charter change the world economy?

147. KOFI ANNAN

REPORT ON THE FALL OF SREBRENICA

(1999)

Kofi Annan (1938–) was born in Ghana, West Africa. In 1996 he was elect-ed General Secretary of the United Nations. Educated in the United States and Switzerland, he spent thirty years rising through the ranks of the U.N., serving in a variety of positions from Africa to Europe to U.N. headquarters in New York. Annan played a role in the events described in this report as Special Representative of the Secretary General to the Former Yugoslavia, and, later, as Under-Secretary-General for Peace-Keeping Operations.

Annan's report is a candid assessment of U.N. involvement in the war in Bosnia-Herzegovina (1991–96). The collapse of the multi-ethnic state of Yugoslavia resulted in the outbreak of war between Bosnian Muslims deter-mined to secure their independence, and Bosnian Serbs, who, supported by the leadership of the Republic of Serbia, sought a "greater Serbia." This "greater Serbia" would include territory seized from Bosnia-Herzegovina, whose Muslim population was to be driven out of their homes to be replaced by Serbs. The report focuses upon the capture by Serbian forces of the town of Srebrenica, which the U.N. had declared a "safe area" for Muslim refugees. United Nations peacekeepers were unable to prevent a tragic massacre of civilians there.

X. Peacekeeping and the Peace Agreement

467. The tragedy that took place following the fall of Srebrenica is shocking for two reasons. It is shocking, first and foremost, for the magnitude of the crimes committed. Not since the horrors of World War II had Europe witnessed massacres on this scale. The mortal remains of close to 2,500 men and boys have been found on the surface, in mass grave sites and in secondary burial sites. Several thousand more men are still missing, and there is every reason to believe that additional burial sites, many of which have been probed but not exhumed, will reveal the bodies of thousands more men and boys. The great majority of those who were killed were not killed in combat: the exhumed bodies of the victims show large numbers had their hands bound, or were blindfold-ed, or were shot in the back or the back of the head. Numerous eyewitness accounts, now well corroborated by forensic evidence, attest to scenes of mass slaughter of unarmed victims.

468. The fall of Srebrenica is also shocking because the enclave's inhabitants believed that the authority of the United Nations Security Council, the presence of UNPROFOR peace-keepers, and the might of NATO air power, would ensure their safety. Instead, the Serb forces ignored the Security Council, pushed aside the UNPROFOR troops, and assessed correctly that air power would not be used to

stop them. They overran the safe area of Srebrenica with ease, and then proceeded to depopulate the territory within 48 hours. Their leaders then engaged in high-level negotiations with representatives of the international community while their forces on the ground executed and buried thousands of men and boys within a matter of days.

469. Questions must be answered, and foremost among these are the following: how can this have been allowed to happen? And how will the United Nations ensure that no future peacekeeping operation witnesses such a calamity on its watch? In this assessment, factors ranging from the most proximate to the more over-arching will be discussed, in order to provide the most comprehensive analysis possible of the preceding narrative.

A. The role of UNPROFOR forces in Srebrenica

470. In the effort to assign responsibility for the appalling events that took place in Srebrenica, many observers have been quick to point to the soldiers of the UNPROFOR Dutch battalion as the most immediate culprits. They blame them for not attempting to stop the Serb attack, and they blame them for not protecting the thousands of people who sought refuge in their compound.

471. As concerns the first criticism, the commander of the Dutch battalion believed that the Bosniacs could not defend Srebrenica by themselves and that his own forces could not be effective without substantial air support. Air support was, in his view, the most effective resource at his disposal to respond to the Serb attack. Accordingly, he requested air support on a number of occasions, even after many of his own troops had been taken hostage and faced potential Serb reprisal. These requests were unheeded by his superiors at various levels, and some of them may not have been received at all, illustrating the command-and-control problems from which UNPROFOR suffered throughout its history. However, having been told that the risk of confrontation with the Serbs was to be avoided, and that the execution of the mandate was secondary to the security of his personnel, the Dutch battalion withdrew from Observation Posts under direct attack.

472. It is true that the Dutch UNPROFOR troops in Srebrenica never fired at the attacking Serbs. They fired warning shots over the Serbs' heads and their mortars fired flares, but they never directly fired on any Serb units. Had they engaged the attacking Serbs directly it is possible that events would have unfolded differently. At the same time, it must be recognized that the 150 fighting men of the Dutch battalion were lightly armed and in indefensible positions, and were faced with 2,000 Serbs advancing with the support of armour and artillery.

473. As concerns the second criticism, it is easy to say with the benefit of hindsight and the knowledge of what followed that the Dutch battalion did not do enough to protect those who sought refuge in their compound. Perhaps they should have allowed everyone into the compound and then offered themselves as human shields to protect them. This may have slowed down the Serbs and bought time for higher level negotiations to take effect. At the same time, it is also possible that the Serb forces would then have shelled the compound, killing thousands in the process, as they had threatened to do. Ultimately, it is not possible to say with any certainty that stronger actions by the Dutch would have saved lives, and it is even possible that such efforts could have done more harm than good. Faced with this prospect and unaware that the Serbs would proceed to execute thousands of men and boys, the Dutch avoided armed confrontation and appealed in the process for support at the highest levels.

474. It is harder to explain why the Dutch battalion did not report more fully the scenes that were unfolding around them following the enclave's fall. Although they did not witness

mass killing, they were aware of some sinister indications. It is possible that if the members of the Dutch battalion had immediately reported in detail those sinister indications to the United Nations chain of command, the international community may have been compelled to respond more robustly and more quickly, and that some lives might have been saved. This failure of intelligence-sharing was also not limited to the fall of Srebrenica, but an endemic weakness throughout the conflict, both within the peacekeeping mission, and between the mission and Member States.

B. The role of Bosniac forces on the ground

475. Criticisms have also been leveled at the Bosniacs in Srebrenica: among them that they did not fully demilitarize and that they did not do enough to defend the enclave. To a degree, these criticisms appear to be contradictory. Concerning the first criticism, it is right to note that the Bosnian Government had entered into demilitarization agreements with the Serbs. They did this with the encouragement of the United Nations. And while it is true that the Bosniac fighters in Srebrenica did not fully demilitarize, they demilitarized enough for UNPROFOR to issue a press release, on 21 April 1993, saying that the process had been a success. Specific instructions from United Nations Headquarters in New York stated that UNPROFOR should not be too zealous in searching for Bosniac weapons and, later, that the Serbs should withdraw their heavy weapons before the Bosniacs gave up their weapons. The Serbs never did withdraw their heavy weapons.

476. Concerning the accusation that the Bosniacs did not do enough to defend Srebrenica, military experts consulted in connection with this report were largely in agreement that the Bosniacs could not have defended Srebrenica for long in the face of a concerted attack supported by armour and artillery. The defenders were an undisciplined, untrained,

poorly armed, totally isolated force, lying prone in the crowded valley of Srebrenica. They were ill-equipped even to train themselves in the use of the few heavier weapons that had been smuggled to them by their authorities. After over three years of siege, the population was demoralized, afraid and often hungry. The only leader of stature was absent when the attack occurred. Surrounding them, controlling all the high ground, handsomely equipped with the heavy weapons and logistical train of the Yugoslav army, were the Bosnian Serbs. There was no contest.

477. Despite the odds against them, the Bosniacs requested UNPROFOR to return to them the weapons they had surrendered under the demilitarization agreements of 1993. They requested those weapons at the beginning of the Serb offensive, but the request was rejected by UNPROFOR because, as one commander explained, "It was our responsibility to defend the enclave, not theirs." Given the limited number and poor quality of the Bosniac weapons held by UNPROFOR, it seems unlikely that releasing those weapons to the Bosniacs would have made a significant difference to the outcome of the battle; but the Bosniacs were under attack at that point, they wanted to resist with whatever means they could muster, and UNPROFOR denied them access to some of their own weapons. With the benefit of hindsight, this decision seems to have been particularly ill-advised, given UNPROFOR's own unwillingness consistently to advocate force as a means of deterring attacks on the enclave.

478. Many have accused the Bosniac forces of withdrawing from the enclave as the Serb forces advanced on the day of its fall. However, it must be remembered that on the eve of the final Serb assault the Dutch Commander urged the Bosniacs to withdraw from defensive positions south of Srebrenica town—the direction from which the Serbs were advancing. He did so because he believed that NATO aircraft would soon be launching widespread air strikes against the advancing Serbs.

479. There is also a third accusation leveled at the Bosniac defenders of Srebrenica, that they provoked the Serb offensive by attacking out of that safe area. Even though this accusation is often repeated by international sources, there is no credible evidence to support it. Dutchbat personnel on the ground at the time assessed that the few "raids" the Bosniacs mounted out of Srebrenica were of little or no military significance. These raids were often organized in order to gather food, as the Serbs had refused access for humanitarian convoys into the enclave. Even Serb sources approached in the context of this report acknowledged that the Bosniac forces in Srebrenica posed no significant military threat to them. The biggest attack the Bosniacs launched out of Srebrenica during the over two years during which it was designated as a safe area appears to have been the raid on the village of Višnjica, on 26 June 1995, in which several houses were burned, up to four Serbs were killed and approximately 100 sheep were stolen. In contrast, the Serbs overran the enclave two weeks later, driving tens of thousands from their homes, and summarily executing thousands of men and boys. The Serbs repeatedly exaggerated the extent of the "raids" out of Srebrenica as a pretext for the prosecution of a central war aim: to create a geographically contiguous and ethnically pure territory along the Drina, while freeing up their troops to fight in other parts of the country. The extent to which this pretext was accepted at face value by international actors and observers reflected the prism of "moral equivalency" through which the conflict in Bosnia was viewed by too many for too long.

C. The role of air power

480. The next question that must be asked is this: Why was NATO air power not brought to bear upon the Serbs before they entered the town of Srebrenica? Even in the most restrictive interpretation of the mandate the use of close air support against attacking Serb targets was clearly warranted. The Serbs were firing directly at Dutch Observation Posts with tank rounds as early as 5 days before the enclave fell.

481. Some have alleged that NATO air power was not authorized earlier, despite repeated requests from the Dutchbat Commander, because the Force Commander or someone else had renounced its use against the Serbs in return for the release of United Nations personnel taken hostage in May-June 1995. Nothing found in the course of the preparation of this report supports such a view.

482. What is clear is that my predecessor, his senior advisers (amongst whom I was included as Under-Secretary-General for Peacekeeping Operations), the SRSG (Special Representative of the Secretary General) and the Force Commander were all deeply reluctant to use air power against the Serbs for four main reasons. We believed that by using air power against the Serbs we should be perceived as having entered the war against them, something not authorized by the Security Council and potentially fatal for a peace keeping operation. Second, we risked losing control over the process—once the "key" was turned "on" we did not know if we would be able to turn it "off," with grave consequences for the safety of the troops entrusted to us by Member States. Third, we believed that the use of air power would disrupt the primary mission of UNPROFOR as we then saw it: the creation of an environment in which the humanitarian aid could be delivered to the civilian population of the country. And fourth, we feared Serb reprisal against our peacekeepers. Member States had placed thousands of their troops under United Nations command. We, and many of the troop contributing nations, considered the security of these troops to be of fundamental importance in the implementation of the mandate. That there was merit in our concerns was evidenced by the hostage crisis of May-June 1995.

483. At the same time, we were fully aware that the threat of NATO air power was all we had

at our disposal to respond to an attack on the safe areas. The lightly armed forces in the enclaves would be no match for (and were not intended to resist) a Serb attack supported by infantry and armour. It was thus incumbent upon us, our concerns notwithstanding, to make full use of the air power deterrent, as we had done with some effect in response to Serb attacks upon Sarajevo and Gorazde in February and April 1994, respectively. For the reasons mentioned above, we did not use with full effectiveness this one instrument at our disposal to make the safe areas at least a little bit safer. We were, with hindsight, wrong to declare repeatedly and publicly that we did not want to use air power against the Serbs except as a last resort, and to accept the shelling of the safe areas as a daily occurrence. We believed there was no choice under the Security Council resolutions but to deploy more and more peacekeepers into harm's way. The Serbs knew this, and they timed their attack on Srebrenica well. The UNPRO-FOR Commander in Sarajevo at the time noted that the reluctance of his superiors and of key troop contributors to "escalate the use of force" in the wake of the hostage crisis would create the conditions in which we would then always be "stared down by the Serbs."

E. The Role of the Security Council and Member States

488. With the benefit of hindsight, one can see that many of the errors the United Nations made flowed from a single and no-doubt well-intentioned effort: we tried to keep the peace and apply the rules of peacekeeping when there was no peace to keep. Knowing that any other course of action would jeopardize the lives of the troops, we tried to create (or imagine) an environment in which the tenets of peacekeeping (agreement between the parties, deployment by consent, and impartiality) could be upheld. We tried to stabilize the situation on the ground through cease-fire agreements, which

brought us into conflict with the defenders of the safe areas, whose safety depended on our use of force.

489. In spite of the untenability of its position, UNPROFOR was able to assist in the humanitarian process, and to mitigate some—but, as Srebrenica tragically underscored, by no means all—suffering inflicted by the war. There are people alive in Bosnia today who would not be alive had UNPROFOR not been deployed. To this extent, it can be said that the 117 young men who lost their lives in the service of UNPROFOR's mission in Bosnia and Herzegovina did not die in vain. Their sacrifice and the good work of many others, however, cannot fully redeem a policy that was, at best, a half-measure.

490. The community of nations decided to respond to the war in Bosnia and Herzegovina with an arms embargo, with humanitarian aid and with the deployment of a peacekeeping force. It must be clearly stated that these measures were poor substitutes for more decisive and forceful action to prevent the unfolding horror. The arms embargo did little more than freeze in place the military balance within the former Yugoslavia. It left the Serbs in a position of overwhelming military dominance and effectively deprived the Republic of Bosnia and Herzegovina of its right, under the Charter of the United Nations, to self-defense. It was not necessarily a mistake to impose an arms embargo, which after all had been done when Bosnia-Herzegovina was not yet a Member State of the United Nations. But having done so, there must surely have been some attendant duty to protect Bosnia and Herzegovina, after it became a Member State, from the tragedy that then befell it. Even as the Serb attacks on and strangulation of the "safe areas" continued in 1993 and 1994, all widely covered by the media and, presumably, by diplomatic and intelligence reports to their respective governments, the approach of the Members of the Security Council remained largely constant. The international community

still could not find the political will to confront the menace defying it.

491. Nor was the provision of humanitarian aid a sufficient response to "ethnic cleansing" and to an attempted genocide. The provision of food and shelter to people who have neither is wholly admirable, and we must all recognize the extraordinary work done by UNHCR* and its partners in circumstances of extreme adversity. But the provision of humanitarian assistance could never have been a solution to the problem in that country. The problem, which cried out for a political/military solution, was that a Member State of the United Nations, left largely defenseless as a result of an arms embargo imposed upon it by the United Nations, was being dismembered by forces committed to its destruction. This was not a problem with a humanitarian solution.

492. Nor was the deployment of a peacekeeping force a coherent response to this problem. My predecessor openly told the Security Council that a United Nations peacekeeping force could not bring peace to Bosnia and Herzegovina. He said it often and he said it loudly, fearing that peacekeeping techniques inevitably would fail in a situation of war. None of the conditions for the deployment of peacekeepers had been met: there was no peace agreement (not even a functioning cease-fire) there was no clear will to peace and there was no clear consent by the belligerents. Nevertheless, *faute de mieux,* the Security Council decided that a United Nations peacekeeping force would be deployed. Lightly armed, highly visible in their white vehicles, scattered across the country in numerous indefensible observation posts, they were able to confirm the obvious: there was no peace to keep.

493. In so doing, the Council obviously expected that the "warring parties" on the ground would respect the authority of the United Nations and would not obstruct or attack its humanitarian operations. It soon became

U.N. High Commission for Refugees

apparent that, with the end of the Cold War and the ascendancy of irregular forces—controlled or uncontrolled—the old rules of the game no longer held. Nor was it sufficiently appreciated that a systematic and ruthless campaign such as the one conducted by the Serbs would view a United Nations humanitarian operation, not as an obstacle, but as an instrument of its aims. In such an event, it is clear that the ability to adapt mandates to the reality on the ground is of critical importance to ensuring that the appropriate force under the appropriate structure is deployed. None of that flexibility was present in the management of UNPROFOR.

F. The failure to fully comprehend the Serb war aims

494. Even before the attack on Srebrenica began, it was clear to the Secretariat and Member States alike that the safe areas were not truly "safe." There was neither the will to use decisive air power against Serb attacks on the safe areas, nor the means on the ground to repulse them. In report after report the Secretariat accordingly and rightly pointed out these conceptual flaws in the safe area policy. We proposed changes: delineating the safe areas either by agreement between the parties or with a mandate from the Security Council; demilitarizing the safe areas; negotiating full freedom of movement. We also stressed the need to protect people rather than territory. In fact, however, these proposals were themselves inadequate. Two of the safe areas—Srebrenica and Zepa— were delineated from the beginning, and they were cited in our reports as relatively more successful examples of how the safe area concept could work. The same two safe areas were also demilitarized to a far greater extent than any of the others, though their demilitarization was by no means complete. In the end, however, the partial demilitarization of the enclaves did not enhance their security. To the contrary, it only made them easier targets for the Serbs.

495. Nonetheless, the key issue—politically, strategically and morally—underlying the security of the "safe areas" was the essential nature of "ethnic cleansing." As part of the larger ambition for a "Greater Serbia," the Serbs set out to occupy the territory of the enclaves; they wanted the territory for themselves. The civilian inhabitants of the enclaves were not the incidental victims of the attackers; their death or removal was the very purpose of the attacks upon them. The tactic of employing savage terror, primarily mass killings, rapes and brutalization of civilians, to expel populations was used to the greatest extent in Bosnia and Herzegovina, where it acquired the now-infamous euphemism of "ethnic cleansing." The Bosnian Muslim civilian population thus became the principal victim of brutally aggressive military and para-military Serb operations to depopulate coveted territories in order to allow them to be repopulated by Serbs.

496. The failure to fully comprehend the extent of the Serb war aims may explain in part why the Secretariat and the Peacekeeping Mission did not react more quickly and decisively when the Serbs initiated their attack on Srebrenica. In fact, rather than attempting to mobilize the international community to support the enclave's defense, we gave the Security Council the impression that the situation was under control, and many of us believed that to be the case. The day before Srebrenica fell we reported that the Serbs were not attacking when they were. We reported that the Bosniacs had fired on an UNPROFOR blocking position when it was the Serbs. We failed to mention urgent requests for air power. In some instances in which incomplete and inaccurate information was given to the Council, this can be attributed to problems with reporting from the field. In other instances, however, the reporting may have been illustrative of a more general tendency to assume that the parties were equally responsible for the transgressions that occurred. It is not clear in any event, that the provision of more fully accurate information to the Council

(many of whose Members had independent sources of information on the ongoing events) would have led to appreciably different results.

497. In the end, these Bosnian Serb war aims were ultimately repulsed on the battlefield, and not at the negotiating table. Yet, the Secretariat had convinced itself early on that the broader use of force by the international community was beyond our mandate and anyway undesirable. A report of the Secretary-General to the Security Council spoke against a "culture of death," arguing that peace should be pursued only through non-military methods. And when, in June 1995, the international community provided UNPROFOR with heavily armed Rapid Reaction Force, we argued against using it robustly to implement our mandate. When decisive action was finally taken by UNPROFOR in August and September 1995, it helped to bring the war to a conclusion.

G. Lessons for the Future

498. The fall of Srebrenica is replete with lessons for this Organization and its Member States—lessons that must be learned if we are to expect the peoples of the world to place their faith in the United Nations. There are occasions when Member States cannot achieve consensus on a particular response to active military conflicts, or do not have the will to pursue what many might consider to be an appropriate course of action. The first of the general lessons is that when peacekeeping operations are used as a substitute for such political consensus they will likely fail. There is a role for peacekeeping (a proud role in a world still riven by conflict) and there is even a role for protected zones and safe havens in certain situations. But peacekeeping and war fighting are distinct activities which should not be mixed. Peacekeepers must never again be deployed into an environment in which there is no ceasefire or peace agreement. Peacekeepers must never again be told that they must use their peacekeeping tools (lightly

armed soldiers in scattered positions) to impose the ill-defined wishes of the international community on one or another of the belligerents by military means. If the necessary resources are not provided (and the necessary political, military and moral judgments are not made) the job simply cannot be done.

499. Protected zones and safe areas can have a role in protecting civilians in armed conflict. But it is clear that they either must be demilitarized and established by the agreement of the belligerents, as with the "protected zones" and "safe havens" recognized by international humanitarian law, or they must be truly "safe areas," fully defended by a credible military deterrent. The two concepts are absolutely distinct and must not be confused. It is tempting for critics to blame the UNPROFOR units in Srebrenica for its fall, or to blame the United Nations hierarchy above those units. Certainly, errors of judgment were made (errors rooted in a philosophy of impartiality and non-violence wholly unsuited to the conflict in Bosnia) but this must not divert us from the more fundamental mistakes. The safe areas were established by the Security Council without the consent of the parties and without providing any credible military deterrent. They were neither protected areas nor "safe havens" in the sense of international humanitarian law, nor safe areas in any militarily meaningful sense. Several representatives on the Council, as well as the Secretariat, noted this problem at the time, warning that, in failing to provide a credible military deterrent, the safe area policy would be gravely damaging to the Council's reputation and, indeed to the United Nations as a whole.

500. The approach by the United Nations Secretariat, the Security Council, the Contact Group and other involved Governments to the war in Bosnia and Herzegovina had certain consequences at both the political and the military level. At the political level, it entailed continuing negotiations with the architects of the Serb policies, principally, Mr. Miloševic and Dr. Karadžic.

At the military level, it resulted in a process of negotiation with and reliance upon General Mladic, whose implacable commitment to clear Eastern Bosnia—Sarajevo if possible—of Bosniacs was plainly obvious and led inexorably to Srebrenica. At various points during the war, these negotiations amounted to appeasement.

501. The international community as a whole must accept its share of responsibility for allowing this tragic course of events by its prolonged refusal to use force in the early stages of the war. This responsibility is shared by the Security Council, the Contact Group and other Governments which contributed to the delay in the use of force, as well as by the United Nations Secretariat and the Mission in the field. But clearly the primary and most direct responsibility lies with the architects and implementers of the attempted genocide in Bosnia. Radovan Karadžic and Ratko Mladic, along with their major collaborators, have been indicted by the International Criminal Tribunal for the Former Yugoslavia. To this day, they remain free men. They must be made to answer for the barbaric crimes with which they have been charged.

502. The cardinal lesson of Srebrenica is that a deliberate and systematic attempt to terrorize, expel or murder an entire people must be met decisively with all necessary means, and with the political will to carry the policy through to its logical conclusion. In the Balkans, in this decade, this lesson has had to be learned not once, but twice. In both instances, in Bosnia and in Kosovo, the international community tried to reach a negotiated settlement with an unscrupulous and murderous regime. In both instances it required the use of force to bring a halt to the planned and systematic killing and expulsion of civilians.

503. The United Nations experience in Bosnia was one of the most difficult and painful in our history. It is with the deepest regret and remorse that we have reviewed our own actions and decisions in the face of the assault on Srebrenica. Through error, misjudgment and an

inability to recognize the scope of the evil confronting us, we failed to do our part to help save the people of Srebrenica from the Serb campaign of mass murder. No one regrets more than we the opportunities for achieving peace and justice that were missed. No one laments more than we the failure of the international community to take decisive action to halt the suffering and end a war that had produced so many victims. Srebrenica crystallized a truth understood only too late by the United Nations and the world at large: that Bosnia was as much a moral cause as a military conflict. The tragedy of Srebrenica will haunt our history forever.

504. In the end, the only meaningful and lasting amends we can make to the citizens of Bosnia and Herzegovina who put their faith in the international community is to do our utmost not to allow such horrors to recur. When the international community makes a solemn promise to safeguard and protect innocent civilians from massacre, then it must be willing to back its promise with the necessary means. Otherwise, it is surely better not to raise hopes and expectations in the first place, and not to impede whatever capability they may be able to muster in their own defense.

505. To ensure that we have fully learned the lessons of the tragic history detailed in this report, I wish to encourage Member States to engage in a process of reflection and analysis, focused on the key challenges the narrative uncovers. The aim of this process would be to clarify and to improve the capacity of the United Nations to respond to various forms of conflict. I have in mind addressing such issues as the gulf between mandate and means; the inadequacy of symbolic deterrence in the face of a systematic campaign of violence; the pervasive ambivalence within the United Nations regarding the role of force in the pursuit of peace; an institutional ideology of impartiality even when confronted with attempted genocide; and a range of doctrinal and institutional issues that go to the heart of the United Nations' ability to keep the peace and help protect civilian populations from armed conflict. The Secretariat is ready to join in such a process.

506. The body of this report sets out in meticulous, systematic, exhaustive and ultimately harrowing detail the descent of Srebrenica into a horror without parallel in the history of Europe since the Second World War. I urge all concerned to study this report carefully, and to let the facts speak for themselves. The men who have been charged with this crime against humanity reminded the world, and, in particular, the United Nations, that evil exists in the world. They taught us also that the United Nations' global commitment to ending conflict does not preclude moral judgments, but makes them necessary. It is in this spirit that I submit my report of the fall of Srebrenica to the General Assembly, and to the world.

QUESTIONS

1. What was the United Nations trying to accomplish in Srebrenica?

2. Why did the peace-keeping mission fail?

3. Did the U.N. achieve any of its objectives in Srebrenica?

4. How might similar failures be avoided in the future?

5. What does the fall of Srebrenica tell us about the "new world order"?

148.

REPORT OF THE 9/11 COMMISSION
(2004)

On September 11, 2001, the United States endured the worst terrorist attack in its history, the destruction of the World Trade Center in New York City and part of the Pentagon in Washington, D.C. Suicide attackers hijacked commercial airliners and piloted them into their targets. Another hijacked plane was prevented from reaching its target by the actions of its passengers, who died while foiling the attack. "9/11" became a turning point in American history, linking the North American continent to ongoing struggles in the Middle East, South Asia, and Africa. President George W. Bush declared a war on terrorism and subsequently published a list of nations that his administration claimed supported terrorism and were thus defined as "outlaw states." Among these was Iraq, on which the United States subsequently declared war. Several thousand people died in the attacks of 9/11, all of them civilians or police and emergency personnel. A series of state and national investigations began to discover the identity of the perpetrators, locate the networks that had aided them, and bring malefactors to justice. Other investigations targeted the shortcomings in U.S. security systems and defense networks.

In late 2002, Congress and the president created the National Commission on Terrorist Attacks Upon the United States (also known as the 9/11 Commission), an independent, bipartisan commission, to prepare a complete account of the circumstances surrounding the attacks. The commission was also mandated with providing recommendations designed to guard against future attacks. In July 2004, it issued its findings and recommendations, which are summarized in this selection.

EXECUTIVE SUMMARY

We present the narrative of this report and the recommendations that flow from it to the President of the United States, the United States Congress, and the American people for their consideration. Ten Commissioners—five Republicans and five Democrats chosen by elected leaders from our nation's capital at a time of great partisan division—have come together to present this report without dissent.

We have come together with a unity of purpose because our nation demands it. September 11, 2001, was a day of unprecedented shock and suffering in the history of the United States. The nation was unprepared.

A Nation Transformed

At 8:46 on the morning of September 11, 2001, the United States became a nation transformed.

An airliner traveling at hundreds of miles per hour and carrying some 10,000 gallons of jet fuel plowed into the North Tower of the World Trade Center in Lower Manhattan. At 9:03, a second airliner hit the South Tower. Fire and smoke billowed upward. Steel, glass, ash, and bodies fell below. The Twin Towers, where up to 50,000 people worked each day, both collapsed less than 90 minutes later.

At 9:37 that same morning, a third airliner slammed into the western face of the Pentagon. At 10:03, a fourth airliner crashed in a field in southern Pennsylvania. It had been aimed at the United States Capitol or the White House, and was forced down by heroic passengers armed with the knowledge that America was under attack.

More than 2,600 people died at the World Trade Center; 125 died at the Pentagon; 256 died on the four planes. The death toll surpassed that at Pearl Harbor in December 1941.

This immeasurable pain was inflicted by 19 young Arabs acting at the behest of Islamist extremists headquartered in distant Afghanistan. Some had been in the United States for more than a year, mixing with the rest of the population. Though four had training as pilots, most were not well-educated. Most spoke English poorly, some hardly at all. In groups of four or five, carrying with them only small knives, box cutters, and cans of Mace or pepper spray, they had hijacked the four planes and turned them into deadly guided missiles.

Why did they do this? How was the attack planned and conceived? How did the U.S. government fail to anticipate and prevent it? What can we do in the future to prevent similar acts of terrorism?

A Shock, Not a Surprise

The 9/11 attacks were a shock, but they should not have come as a surprise. Islamist extremists had given plenty of warning that they meant to kill Americans indiscriminately and in large numbers. Although Usama Bin Ladin himself would not emerge as a signal threat until the late 1990s, the threat of Islamist terrorism grew over the decade.

In February 1993, a group led by Ramzi Yousef tried to bring down the World Trade Center with a truck bomb. They killed six and wounded a thousand. Plans by Omar Abdel Rahman and others to blow up the Holland and Lincoln tunnels and other New York City landmarks were frustrated when the plotters were arrested. In October 1993, Somali tribesmen shot down U.S. helicopters, killing 18 and wounding 73 in an incident that came to be known as "Black Hawk down." Years later it would be learned that those Somali tribesmen had received help from al Qaeda.

In early 1995, police in Manila uncovered a plot by Ramzi Yousef to blow up a dozen U.S. airliners while they were flying over the Pacific. In November 1995, a car bomb exploded outside the office of the U.S. program manager for the Saudi National Guard in Riyadh, killing five Americans and two others. In June 1996, a truck bomb demolished the Khobar Towers apartment complex in Dhahran, Saudi Arabia, killing 19 U.S. servicemen and wounding hundreds. The attack was carried out primarily by Saudi Hezbollah, an organization that had received help from the government of Iran.

Until 1997, the U.S. intelligence community viewed Bin Ladin as a financier of terrorism, not as a terrorist leader. In February 1998, Usama Bin Ladin and four others issued a self-styled fatwa, publicly declaring that it was God's decree that every Muslim should try his utmost to kill any American, military or civilian, anywhere in the world, because of American "occupation" of Islam's holy places and aggression against Muslims.

In August 1998, Bin Ladin's group, al Qaeda, carried out near-simultaneous truck bomb attacks on the U.S. embassies in Nairobi, Kenya, and Dar es Salaam, Tanzania. The attacks killed 224 people, including 12 Americans, and wounded thousands more.

In December 1999, Jordanian police foiled a plot to bomb hotels and other sites frequented by American tourists, and a U.S. Customs agent arrested Ahmed Ressam at the U.S. Canadian border as he was smuggling in explosives intended for an attack on Los Angeles International Airport.

In October 2000, an al Qaeda team in Aden, Yemen, used a motorboat filled with explosives to blow a hole in the side of a destroyer, the USS *Cole*, almost sinking the vessel and killing 17 American soldiers.

The 9/11 attacks on the World Trade Center and the Pentagon were far more elaborate, precise, and destructive than any of these earlier assaults. But by September 2001, the executive branch of the U.S. government, the Congress, the news media, and the American public had received clear warning that Islamist terrorists meant to kill Americans in high numbers.

Who Is the Enemy?

Who is this enemy that created an organization capable of inflicting such horrific damage on the United States? We now know that these attacks were carried out by various groups of Islamist extremists. The 9/11 attack was driven by Usama Bin Ladin.

In the 1980s, young Muslims from around the world went to Afghanistan to join as volunteers in a jihad (or holy struggle) against the Soviet Union. A wealthy Saudi, Usama Bin Ladin, was one of them. Following the defeat of the Soviets in the late 1980s, Bin Ladin and others formed al Qaeda to mobilize jihads elsewhere.

The history, culture, and body of beliefs from which Bin Ladin shapes and spreads his message are largely unknown to many Americans. Seizing on symbols of Islam's past greatness, he promises to restore pride to people who consider themselves the victims of successive foreign masters. He uses cultural and religious allusions to the holy Qur'an and some of its interpreters. He appeals to people disoriented by cyclonic change as they confront modernity and globalization. His rhetoric selectively draws from multiple sources—Islam, history, and the region's political and economic malaise.

Bin Ladin also stresses grievances against the United States widely shared in the Muslim world. He inveighed against the presence of U.S. troops in Saudi Arabia, which is the home of Islam's holiest sites, and against other U.S. policies in the Middle East.

Specific Findings

Unsuccessful Diplomacy

Beginning in February 1997, and through September 11, 2001, the U.S. government tried to use diplomatic pressure to persuade the Taliban regime in Afghanistan to stop being a sanctuary for al Qaeda, and to expel Bin Ladin to a country where he could face justice. These efforts included warnings and sanctions, but they all failed.

The U.S. government also pressed two successive Pakistani governments to demand that the Taliban cease providing a sanctuary for Bin Ladin and his organization and, failing that, to cut off their support for the Taliban. Before 9/11, the United States could not find a mix of incentives and pressure that would persuade Pakistan to reconsider its fundamental relationship with the Taliban.

From 1999 through early 2001, the United States pressed the United Arab Emirates, one of the Taliban's only travel and financial outlets to the outside world, to break off ties and enforce sanctions, especially those related to air travel to Afghanistan. These efforts achieved little before 9/11.

Saudi Arabia has been a problematic ally in combating Islamic extremism. Before 9/11, the Saudi and U.S. governments did not fully share intelligence information or develop an adequate joint effort to track and disrupt the finances of the al Qaeda organization. On the other hand, government officials of Saudi Arabia at the highest levels worked closely with top U.S. officials in major initiatives to solve the Bin Ladin problem with diplomacy.

Lack of Military Options

In response to the request of policymakers, the military prepared an array of limited strike options for attacking Bin Ladin and his organization from May 1998 onward. When they briefed policymakers, the military presented both the pros and cons of those strike options and the associated risks. Policymakers expressed frustration with the range of options presented.

Following the August 20, 1998, missile strikes on al Qaeda targets in Afghanistan and Sudan, both senior military officials and policymakers placed great emphasis on actionable intelligence as the key factor in recommending or deciding to launch military action against Bin Ladin and his organization. They did not want to risk significant collateral damage, and they did not want to miss Bin Ladin and thus make the United States look weak while making Bin Ladin look strong. On three specific occasions in 1998–1999, intelligence was deemed credible enough to warrant planning for possible strikes to kill Bin Ladin. But in each case the strikes did not go forward, because senior policymakers did not regard the intelligence as sufficiently actionable to offset their assessment of the risks.

The Director of Central Intelligence, policymakers, and military officials expressed frustration with the lack of actionable intelligence. Some officials inside the Pentagon, including those in the special forces and the counterterrorism policy office, also expressed frustration with the lack of military action. The Bush administration began to develop new policies toward al Qaeda in 2001, but military plans did not change until after 9/11.

Problems Within the Intelligence Community

The intelligence community struggled throughout the 1990s and up to 9/11 to collect intelligence on and analyze the phenomenon of transnational terrorism. The combination of an overwhelming number of priorities, flat budgets, an outmoded structure, and bureaucratic rivalries resulted in an insufficient response to this new challenge.

Many dedicated officers worked day and night for years to piece together the growing body of evidence on al Qaeda and to understand the threats. Yet, while there were many reports on Bin Laden and his growing al Qaeda organization, there was no comprehensive review of what the intelligence community knew and what it did not know, and what that meant. There was no National Intelligence Estimate on terrorism between 1995 and 9/11.

Before 9/11, no agency did more to attack al Qaeda than the CIA. But there were limits to what the CIA was able to achieve by disrupting terrorist activities abroad and by using proxies to try to capture Bin Ladin and his lieutenants in Afghanistan. CIA officers were aware of those limitations.

To put it simply, covert action was not a silver bullet. It was important to engage proxies in Afghanistan and to build various capabilities so that if an opportunity presented itself, the CIA could act on it. But for more than three years, through both the late Clinton and early Bush administration, the CIA relied on proxy forces, and there was growing frustration within the CIA's Counterterrorist Center and in the National Security Council staff with the lack of results. The development of the Predator and the push to aid the Northern Alliance were products of this frustration.

Recommendations

Three years after 9/11, the national debate continues about how to protect our nation in this new era. We divide our recommendations into two basic parts: What to do, and how to do it.

What to Do? A Global Strategy

The enemy is not just "terrorism." It is the threat posed specifically by Islamist terrorism, by Bin

Ladin and others who draw on a long tradition of extreme intolerance within a minority strain of Islam that does not distinguish politics from religion, and distorts both.

The enemy is not Islam, the great world faith, but a perversion of Islam. The enemy goes beyond al Qaeda to include the radical ideological movement, inspired in part by al Qaeda, that has spawned other terrorist groups and violence. Thus our strategy must match our means to two ends: dismantling the al Qaeda network and, in the long term, prevailing over the ideology that contributes to Islamist terrorism.

The first phase of our post–9/11 efforts rightly included military action to topple the Taliban and pursue al Qaeda. This work continues. But long-term success demands the use of all elements of national power: diplomacy, intelligence, covert action, law enforcement, economic policy, foreign aid, public diplomacy, and homeland defense. If we favor one tool while neglecting others, we leave ourselves vulnerable and weaken our national effort.

What should Americans expect from their government? The goal seems unlimited: Defeat terrorism anywhere in the world. But Americans have also been told to expect the worst: An attack is probably coming; it may be more devastating still.

Vague goals match an amorphous picture of the enemy. Al Qaeda and other groups are popularly described as being all over the world, adaptable, resilient, needing little higher-level organization, and capable of anything. It is an image of an omnipotent hydra of destruction. That image lowers expectations of government effectiveness.

It lowers them too far. Our report shows a determined and capable group of plotters. Yet the group was fragile and occasionally left vulnerable by the marginal unstable people often attracted to such causes. The enemy made mistakes. The U.S. government was not able to capitalize on them.

No president can promise that a catastrophic attack like that of 9/11 will not happen again. But the American people are entitled to expect that officials will have realistic objectives, clear guidance, and effective organization. They are entitled to see standards for performance so they can judge, with the help of their elected representatives, whether the objectives are being met.

We propose a strategy with three dimensions: (1) attack terrorists and their organizations, (2) prevent the continued growth of Islamist terrorism; and (3) protect against and prepare for terrorist attacks.

QUESTIONS

1. How does the commission identify the terrorist threat to the United States?

2. How are terrorists recruited and motivated?

3. What was the role of diplomacy leading up to 9/11?

4. What is the commission's recommendation for the future?

ACKNOWLEDGMENTS

72. Henry IV, *The Edict of Nantes*. From *Readings in European History, Vol. II: From the Opening of the Protestant Revolt to the Present Day,* edited by James Harvey Robinson (Boston: Ginn & Company, 1906), pp. 183-185.

73. Cardinal Richelieu, *The Political Testament*. From *The Political Testament of Cardinal Richelieu,* translated by Henry Bertram Hill. Copyright © 1961 by the Regents of the University of Wisconsin. Reprinted by permission of the University of Wisconsin Press.

74. Hans von Grimmelshausen, *Simplicissimus*. From *Simplicius Simplicissimus* by Jans Jacob Christoffel von Grimmelshausen, translated from the original German edition of 1669 by Helmuth Weissenborn and Lesley Macdonald. Copyright © 1984 by the translators. Reprinted by permission of John Calder Publishers Ltd.

75. James I, *True Law of a Free Monarchy*. From *The Political Works of James I* edited by Charles Howard McIlwain. Copyright 1916 by the President and Fellows of Harvard College. Reprinted by permission of Harvard University Press.

76. Philippe Duplessis-Mornay, *A Defense of Liberty Against Tyrants*. Excerpts from *Readings in Western Civilization*, Vol. 6, ed. by Cochrane (3500 words). Reprinted by permission of the University of Chicago Press.

77. Sir William Clarke, *The Putney Debates*. William Clarke, *The Clarke Papers,* Vol. I, edited by C. H. Firth (London: Royal Historical Society, 1891), pp. 299-307, 311-312, 315-317, 325-327.

78. Thomas Hobbes, *Leviathan*. From Thomas Hobbes, *Leviathan,* edited by A. R. Waller (Cambridge: University Press, 1904).

79. John Locke, *Second Treatise of Government*.

80. Moliere, *The Would-Be Gentleman*. From Moliere, *Volume I: The Misanthrope (Le Bourgeois Gentilhomme)*, translated by Katharine Prescott Wormeley (Boston: Roberts Brothers, 1894), pp. 177–190

81. Duc de Saint-Simon, *Memoirs*. Duc de Saint-Simon, *Memoirs,* translated by Bayle St. John (London: Swan Sonnonschein & Co., 1900), pp. 357–365.

82. Galileo Galilei, *Letter to the Grand Duchess Christina*. From *Discoveries and Opinions of Galileo* by Galileo Galilei, translated by Stillman Drake. Copyright © 1957 by Stillman Drake. Used by permission of Doubleday, a division of Random House, Inc.

83. René Descartes, *Discourse on Method*. From *Descartes, Philosophical Writings*. Selected and translated by Norman Kemp Smith. Reprinted by permission of Macmillan, London and Basingstoke.

84. Thomas Mun, *England's Treasure by Foreign Trade*. In *Early English Tracts on Commerce,* edited by J. R. McCulloch (Cambridge: Cambridge University Press, 1954), pp. 121–126, 134–141.

85. Adam Smith, *The Wealth of Nations*. Adam Smith, *An Inquiry into the Nature and Class of the Wealth of Nations,* 2d edition, Vol. I, edited by James E. Thorold Rogers (Oxford: Clarendon Press, 1880), pp. 59–65.

86. Catherine the Great, *Memoirs*. From *The Memoirs of Catherine the Great*, edited by Dominique Maroger, with an introduction by G. P. Gooch. Translated from the French by Moura Budberg. Reprinted by permission of Hachette.

87. Maria Theresa, *Testament*. "Maria Theresa's Political Testament" from *The Habsburg and Hohenzollern Dynasties in the 17th and 18th Centuries* by C. A. Macartney. Copyright © 1970 by C. A. Macartney. Reprinted by permission of HarperCollins Publishers, Inc.

88. Viscount Bolingbroke, *The Idea of a Patriot King*. Viscount Bolingbroke, *Letters on the Spirit of Patriotism: The Idea of a Patriot King* (London: T. Davies, 1775), pp. 76–81, 83–85, 111–114.

89. Voltaire, *Candide*. From *Candide, Zadig, and Selected Stories by Voltaire* by Francoise Voltaire, translated by Donald M. Frame, copyright © 1961 by Donald M. Frame. Used by permission of Viking Penguin, a division of Penguin Putnam Inc.

90. Jean-Jacques Rousseau, *The Social Contract*. Jean-Jacques Rousseau, *The Social Contract*, translated by Rose M. Harrington (New York: G. P. Putnam's Sons, 1906), pp. 19–22, 130–131, 158–162.

91. Montesquieu, *Spirit of the Laws*. From Montesquieu, *Spirit of the Laws: A Compendium of the First English Edition*, translated and edited by David Carrithers. Copyright © 1977 by the Regents of the University of California. Reprinted by permission of the University of California Press.

92. Captain James Cook, *Journals*. From *The Journals of Captain Cook*, prepared from the original manuscripts by J.C. Beaglehole for the Hakluyt Society, 1955–67, selected and edited by Philip Edwards (London: Penguin Books Ltd., 1999), pp. 39–43, 45–47.

93. Joseph Crassons de Medeuil, *Notes on the French Slave Trade*. Joseph Crassons de Medeuil, "Notes on the French Slave Trade" from *The East African Coast* by G. S. P. Freeman-Grenville Press, 1962. Reprinted by permission of G. S. P. Freeman-Grenville.

94. Thomas Jefferson, *The Declaration of Independence*. In *Documents Illustrative of American History, 1606–1863*, edited by Howard W. Preston (New York: G. P. Putnam's Sons, 1893), pp. 210–215.

95. Cesare Beccaria, *On Crimes and Punishments*. From *On Crimes and Punishments* by Beccaria, translated by H. Paolucci, © 1963. Reprinted by permission of Prentice-Hall, Inc., Upper Saddle River, NJ.

96. Marquis de Condorcet, *The Progress of the Human Mind*. From *Sketch for a Historical Picture of the Progress of the Human Mind* by Marie-Jean de Condorcet, translated by June Barraclough. Reprinted by permission of The Orion Publishing Group Ltd.

97. Abbé de Sieyès, *What Is the Third Estate?* From *Documentary Survey of the French Revolution* by Stewart, John Hall, © 1951. Reprinted by permission of Prentice-Hall, Inc., Upper Saddle River, NJ.

98. Olympe de Gouges, *The Declaration of the Rights of Woman*. From *Women in Revolutionary Paris, 1789–1795*. Reprinted by permission of the University of Illinois Press.

99. Edmund Burke, *Reflections on the Revolution in France*. From Edmund Burke, *Reflections on the Revolution in France* (London: J. Dodsley, 1790), pp. 50–67, 70, 76–77, 95.

100. Arthur Young, *Political Arithmetic*. Arthur Young, *Political Arithmetic* (London: W. Nicoll, 1774), pp. 4–6, 287–296.

101. Samuel Smiles, *Self-Help*. Samuel Smiles, *Self-Help* (New York: A. L. Burt, n.d.), pp. 84–89.

102. Sir Edwin Chadwick, *Inquiry into the Condition of the Poor*. Edwin Chadwick, *An Inquiry into the Sanitary Condition of the Labouring Population of Great Britain* (London: W. Clowes and Sons, 1842), pp. 98–101, 111–112, 279.

103. Friedrich Engels, *The Condition of the Working Class in England*. Friedrich Engels, *The Condition of the Working-Class in England in 1844*, translated by Florence Kelley Wischnewetsky (London: George Allen and Unwin Ltd., 1892).

104. Jane Austen, *Pride and Prejudice*. Jane Austen, *Pride and Prejudice* (New York: Brentanos, 1915), pp. 3–7, 12–19.

105. Henrietta-Lucy, Madame de la Tour du Pin, *Memoirs*. *Memoirs of Madame de la Tour du Pin*, edited and translated by Felice Harcourt (New York: McCall Publishing Company, 1971).

106. Alexis Soyer, *Modern Housewife*. Alexis Soyer, *The Modern Housewife* (New York: D. Appleton & Co., 1850), pp. 336–338.

Mrs. Beeton's Book of Household Management. Mrs. Beeton, Household Management (n.p., 1909), pp. 9–12.

107. *Documents of the Irish Potato Famine.* Excerpts of Peel's letters from Sir Robert Peel from his *Private Papers,* edited by Charles Stuart Parker (London, 1889). *Report of the Mansion House Committee on the Potato Disease from Parliamentary Papers* (London, 1846), Volume XXXVII. Other excerpts from *Report of the British Relief Association for the Relief of the Extreme Distress in Ireland and Scotland* (London, 1849); *First Report of Belfast Ladies' Association* (Belfast, 6 March 1847); *A Voice for Ireland: The Famine in the Land* by Isaac Butt (Dublin University Magazine, April 1847); and *A Visit to Connaught in the Autumn of 1847* by James Hack Tuke (London, 1847).

108. J. S. Mill, *On Liberty.* John Stuart Mill, *On Liberty* (London: The Walter Scott Publishing Co., n.d.), pp. 17–18, 22–23, 225–226, 103, 106, 140–143.

109. Pierre Proudhon, *What Is Property?* P. J. Proudhon, *What Is Property?* in The Works of P. J. Proudhon, Vol. I (Princeton, MA: Benjamin R. Tucker, 1876), pp. 269–272, 276–279, 286–288.

110. *The Great Charter.* The Great Charter, in *Hansard's Parliamentary Debates,* Vol. LXII, Third Series (London: Thomas Hansard, 1842), pp. 1373–1381.

111. William II, *Letter to the Shogun.* From *Meiji Japan Through Contemporary Sources,* Volume 2, 1844–1882. Copyright © 1970, 1990 by The Centre for East Asian Cultural Studies for Unesco. Reprinted by permission. Bakufu, *Reply to the Government of Holland.* From *Meiji Japan Through Contemporary Sources,* Volume 2, 1844–1882. Copyright © 1970, 1990 by The Centre for East Asian Cultural Studies for Unesco. Reprinted by permission.

112. Karl Marx and Friedrich Engels, *The Communist Manifesto.* From *Manifesto of the Communist Party* by Karl Marx and Friedrich Engels. Authorized English translation edited and annotated by Friedrich Engels. All Rights Reserved, 1932. Reprinted by permission of International Publishers Co.

113. Alexander II and Prince Kropotkin, *The Emancipation of the Serfs.* From *A Sourcebook of Russian History,* George Verdansky. Reprinted by permission of Yale University Press.

114. Otto von Bismarck, *Reflections and Reminiscences* and *Speech to the Reichstag.* Otto Prince von Bismarck, *Bismarck: The Man and Statesman,* translated by A. J. Butler (London: Smith, Elder & Co., 1898).

115. Leo XIII, *Rerum Novarum (The Condition of Labor).* Leo XIII on the Condition of Labor, pp. 1–30 from *Five Great Encyclicals,* Paulist Press.

116. Charles Darwin, *The Descent of Man.* Charles Darwin, *The Descent of Man and Selection in Relation to Sex* (New York: D. Appleton and Co., 1913).

117. Friedrich Nietzsche, *Beyond Good and Evil.* From *Beyond Good and Evil* by Friedrich Nietzsche. Copyright © 1966 by Random House, Inc. Reprinted by permission of Random House, Inc.

118. Sigmund Freud, *The Interpretation of Dreams.* From *The Basic Writings of Sigmund Freud,* translated, edited, and with an introduction by Dr. A. A. Brill. Copyright 1939, renewed 1965, by Gioia B. Bernheim and Edmund Brill. Reprinted with permission.

119. E. Sylvia Pankhurst, *History of the Suffrage Movement.* E. Sylvia Pankhurst, *The Suffragette* (New York: Sturgis & Walton, 1912), pp. 1, 138–142, 324–328.

120. Beatrice Webb, *Women and the Factory Acts.* Beatrice Webb, *Women and the Factory Acts.* Fabian Tract No. 67 (London: The Fabian Society, 1896), pp. 1, 4, 9, 10–15.

121. J. A. Hobson, *Imperialism.* J. A. Hobson, *Imperialism* (New York: James Pott & Company, 1902), pp. 377–379, 381–383, 389–390.

122. Cecil Rhodes, *Confession of Faith.* From *Cecil Rhodes* by John Flint, Copyright © by John Flint. By permission of Little, Brown and Company.

123. Carl Veltin, *Social Life of the Swahilis.* Carl Veltin, "Social Life of the Swahilis" from *Swahili Prose Texts,* edited and translated by Lyndon Harries. Reprinted by permission of University of Wisconsin.

124. Rudyard Kipling, *"The White Man's Burden."* Rudyard Kipling, "The White Man's Burden," in *Rudyard Kipling's Verse, 1885–1918* (Garden City, NY: Doubleday, 1920), pp. 371–372.

125. George Orwell, "Shooting an Elephant." "Shooting an Elephant" from *Shooting an Elephant and Other Essays* by George Orwell, copyright © 1950 by Sonia Brownell Orwell and renewed 1978 by Sonia Pitt-Rivers, reprinted by permission of Harcourt, Inc.

126. *Voices from the Battle of the Somme*. From *Somme* by Lyn Macdonald, pp. 66–67, 218–219, 225–227, 72–73, 174, 208–209, 113–114. Used by permission of Penguin Books (UK).

127. Ernst Jünger, *Storm of Steel*. From *Storm of Steel* by Ernst Jünger, translated by Basil Creighton. Copyright 1929 by Doubleday, Doran & Company, Inc. Reprinted by permission of Chatto & Windus.

128. Woodrow Wilson, *The Fourteen Points*.

129. V. I. Lenin, *What Is to Be Done?* (Peking: Foreign Language Press, 1975).

130. J. M. Keynes, *The Economic Consequences of the Peace*. From *The Economic Consequences of the Peace* by John Maynard Keynes. Copyright 1920 by Harcourt Brace Jovanovich, Inc., and renewed 1948 by Lydia Lopokoka Keynes. Reprinted by permission of the publisher and Cambridge University Press.

131. Winifred Holtby, *Women and a Changing Civilization*. Permission to quote from *Women and a Changing Civilization* is granted by the estate of Winifred Holtby.

132. Benito Mussolini, *Fascist Doctrine*. From *Mussolini and Italian Fascism* by S. William Halperin. Copyright © 1964 by S. William Halperin. Reprinted by permission of Elaine P. Halperin.

133. Adolf Hitler, *Mein Kampf*. Excerpts from *Mein Kampf* by Adolf Hitler, translated by Ralph Manheim. Copyright © 1943 renewed 1971 by Houghton Mifflin Company. Reprinted by permission of Houghton Mifflin Company. All rights reserved.

134. *Memories of the Holocaust*. From *Witness to Holocaust* by Rhoda G. Lewin, Twayne Publishers, © 1990, Twayne Publishers. Reprinted by permission of the Gale Group.

135. Winston Churchill, *Speeches*. "The Sinews of Peace" and "Blood, Toil, Tears and Sweat" from *Winston S. Churchill: His Complete Speeches, 1897–1963, Volume VI, 1935–1942*, edited by Robert Rhodes James. Reprinted by permission of Chelsea House Publishers, LLC.

136. Adolf Eichmann, *Testimony*. From *The Record: The Trial of Adolf Eichmann* by Lord Russell of Liverpool. Copyright © 1962 by Lord Russell of Liverpool. Reprinted by permission of The Official Receiver of the Insolvency Services.

137. Virginia Woolf, *A Room of One's Own*. Excerpts from *A Room of One's Own* by Virginia Woolf, copyright 1929 by Harcourt, Inc. and renewed 1957 by Leonard Woolf, reprinted by permission of the publisher.

138. Alexander Solzhenitsyn, *A Day in the Life of Ivan Denisovich*. From *One Day in the Life of Ivan Denisovich* by Alexander Solzhenitsyn, translated by Ralph Parker, copyright © 1963 by E. P. Dutton and Victor Gollancz, Ltd. Copyright renewed © 1991 by Penguin USA and Victor Gollancz, Ltd. Used by permission of Viking Penguin Putnam Inc.

139. Jean-Paul Sartre, *Existentialism*. From *Existentialism and Human Emotions* by Jean-Paul Sartre. Copyright © 1957 by Philosophical Library. Reprinted by permission.

140. Simone de Beauvoir, *The Second Sex*. From *The Second Sex* by Simone de Beauvoir, translated by H. M. Parshley. Copyright 1952 and renewed 1980 by Alfred A. Knopf, a division of Random House, Inc. Used by permission of Alfred A. Knopf, a division of Random House, Inc.

141. Winston Churchill, *"The Iron Curtain."* "The Iron Curtain" by Winston Churchill in *Winston S. Churchill: His Complete Speeches, 1897–1963,* Volume VII, 1943–1949, edited by Robert Rhodes James. Copyright © 1983 by Chelsea House Publishers. Reprinted by permission.

142. Nikita Khrushchev, *Report to the Communist Party Congress*. From *Current Soviet Policies IV*, edited by Charlotte Saikowski and Leo Gruliow, from the translations of the Current Digest of the Soviet Press. Copyright © 1962 by the Joint Committee on Slavic Studies. Reprinted by permission of the Social Science Research Council.

143. Mikhail Gorbachev, *Perestroika*. Excerpts from *Perestroika* by Mikhail Gorbachev. Copyright © 1987 by Mikhail Gorbachev. Reprinted by permission of HarperCollins Publishers, Inc.

144. Francis Fukuyama, *The End of History?* From *The End of History?* by Francis Fukuyama. Copyright © 1989 by Francis Fukuyama. Reprinted by permission of International Creative Management, Inc.

145. *Charter of the United Nations* (1946).

146. *The Charter of Economic Rights and Duties of States* (1974).

147. http://www.un.org/News/ossg/srebrenica.org

148. *Report of the 9/11 Commission*. Excerpts from the *Executive Summary of the 9/11 Commission Report*, issued by the National Commission on Terrorist Attacks Upon the United States (9/11 Commission), July 24, 2004.

PHOTO CREDITS